Alexander Stewart

Nether Lochaber

The Natural History, Legends, and Folk-lore of the West Highland

Alexander Stewart

Nether Lochaber
The Natural History, Legends, and Folk-lore of the West Highland

ISBN/EAN: 9783744772907

Printed in Europe, USA, Canada, Australia, Japan

Cover: Foto ©Thomas Meinert / pixelio.de

More available books at **www.hansebooks.com**

WEASEL KILLING A HARE.—(Page 63.)

THE

NATURAL HISTORY, LEGENDS, AND FOLK-LORE
OF THE WEST HIGHLANDS.

BY

The Rev. ALEXANDER STEWART, F.S.A. Scot.;

MINISTER OF THE PARISH OF BALLACHULISH AND ARDGOUR.

EDINBURGH:

WILLIAM PATERSON.

MDCCCLXXXIII.

EDINBURGH: BURNESS AND COMPANY, PRINTERS TO HER MAJESTY.

TO

DONALD CAMPBELL, Esq., M.D.,

OF

CRAIGRANNOCH, BALLACHULISH,

IN PLEASANT RECOLLECTION OF HAPPY HOURS AT ONICH AND CRAIGRANNOCH,

AND

OF MANY A DELIGHTFUL MIDSUMMER RAMBLE,

THIS VOLUME IS INSCRIBED

WITH MUCH AFFECTIONATE REGARD BY HIS FRIEND

THE AUTHOR.

PREFATORY NOTE.

————◆————

THE contents of this volume made their first appearance in the shape of a series of papers from "Nether Lochaber" in the *Inverness Courier*, a well-known Northern Journal, long and ably conducted by the late Dr. ROBERT CARRUTHERS. They are now presented to the public in book form, in the hope that they may meet with a friendly welcome from a still larger constituency than gave them kindly greeting in their original shape, as from fortnight to fortnight they appeared.

At one time it was the Author's intention to rewrite and rearrange all, or almost all, these papers, adding, altering, or expunging as might be considered best. On second thoughts, however—second thoughts, besides, approved of by many literary and scientific friends, in whose judgment and good taste the Author has the utmost confidence—it was resolved to let them retain very much the form in which they first attracted attention, in the belief that any good that could result from a rewriting and reconstructing of them would be dearly purchased if it interfered, as it was almost certain to interfere, with their *prima cura* directness of phrase and freshness of local colouring.

In a volume dealing so largely with the Folk-Lore of the West Highlands and Hebrides, there are necessarily many Gaelic rhymes and phrases which at the first blink may tend to startle and repel the southern reader. These Gaelic quotations, however, the Author has taken care to translate into fairly equivalent English, so that even in this regard it is to be hoped the volume may prove equally acceptable to the Saxon, who is ignorant of the language of the mountains, as to the Celt, who knows and loves it as his mother tongue.

NETHER LOCHABER,
June 1883.

NETHER LOCHABER.

CHAPTER I.

THE weather [March 1868] with us here still continues wonderfully
genial and mild : taken all in all, the season may be noted as in this
respect perhaps without precedent in our meteorological annals. The
sun, with nearly eight degrees of southern declination, is not yet half-
way through *Pisces;* we are still three weeks from the vernal equinox,
and yet on our table before us, as we write these lines, there is as
pretty a posy of wild-flowers as you could wish to see, consisting of
daisies, primroses, and other modest beauties, the "firstlings of the
year," culled from bank and brae at a date when in ordinary
seasons the country, snow-covered or ice-bound, is but a bleak and
barren waste. Older and wiser people than ourselves confidently
predict "a winter in mid-spring" as yet in store for us ; but
meliora speramus, we had rather believe that to one of the mildest
winters on record will succeed a genial spring, a splendid summer,
and an abundant harvest. In any case, as somebody said of
Scaliger and Clavius, *Mallem cum Scaligero errare quam cum
Clavio rectè sapere :* I had rather, that is, be a partaker in the

A

errors of Scaliger, than a sharer in all the wisdom of Clavius. Even so, we had rather err with the optimists than be ranked with the pessimists, even when their predictions turn out the truest. In our forenoon ramble on Friday last did we not find a merle's nest in the close and well-guarded embrace of an old thorn root, with its pretty treasure of four brown-spotted, greyish-green eggs? and with our wild-flower bouquet before us, are we not better employed in crooning one of Burns' sweetest lyrics than in predicting evil, even if we were certain that our prediction should become true?—said lyric being that entitled *The Posie*, which, dear reader, if you do not know it already, you should incontinently get by heart. Here is a verse or two :—

> " Oh, luve will venture in where it daurna weel be seen ;
>   Oh, luve will venture in, where wisdom ance has been ;
>   But I will down yon river rove, amang the wood sae green—
>   And a' to pu' a posie to my ain dear May.

> " The primrose I will pu', the firstling o' the year,
>   And I will pu' the pink, the emblem o' my dear ;
>   For she's the pink o' womankind, and blooms without a peer—
>   And a' to be a posie to my ain dear May.

> " The lily it is pure, and the lily it is fair,
>   And in her lovely bosom I'll place the lily there ;
>   The daisy's for simplicity and unaffected air—
>   And a' to be a posie to my ain dear May.

> " The hawthorn I will pu', wi' its locks o' siller grey,
>   Where, like an aged man, it stands at break o' day ;
>   *But the songster's nest within the bush I winna tak away—*
>   And a' to be a posie to my ain dear May."

Mark that line in italics, and ponder its exquisite tenderness. How it must have irradiated, like a sudden flood of sunshine over a mountain landscape, the poet's heart as he penned it ! Here you have the germ of the doctrine afterwards more broadly taught by Coleridge in the well-known lines of the *Ancient Mariner :—*

" Farewell, farewell, but this I tell
  To thee, thou Wedding Guest,
He prayeth well, who loveth well
  Both man, and bird, and beast.
He prayeth best, who loveth best
  All things, both great and small ;
For the dear God who loveth us,
  He made and loveth all."

We love *The Posie* of Burns for its own sake, but we love it all the more, perhaps, because our attention was first directed to its sweet simplicity and tender beauty by one of our earliest and kindest friends, himself a poet of no mean order, the late Professor William Tennant, author of *Anster Fair*, in all its fantastical gaiety and homely mirth the most original poem, perhaps, to be found in the literature of our country.

A gentleman who resides at present in Cheltenham, a cadet of one of the oldest and most respectable families on the West Coast, and himself the head of a house not unknown in Highland story, has been so good as to send us a short Gaelic poem in manuscript, with a request that we should give an English version of it. With this request we very readily comply, such a task being to us a labour of love ; the poem itself, besides, being very beautiful, and the history of its composition extremely interesting, as throwing some light on the manners and customs of the olden times. The following prefatory note from the MS. itself sufficiently explains the origin of this quaint and curious Hebridean *Epithalamium :*—" It was the custom in the West Highlands of Scotland in the olden time to meet the bride coming forth from her chamber with her maidens on the morning after her marriage, and to salute her with a poetical blessing called *Beannachadh Bàird*. On the occasion of the marriage of the Rev. Donald Macleod of Durinish, in the Isle of Skye, this practice having then got very much into desuetude, and none being found prepared to salute *his* bride

agreeably to it, he himself came forward and received her with
the following beautiful address." We present our readers with the
original lines *verbatim et literatim*, precisely as they stand in the
MS., only omitting two lines that are partly illegible from their
falling into the sharp foldings of the sheet. The sense and tenor
of these lines, however, we have ventured to guess at and to
incorporate with our English version :—

BEANNACHADH BÀIRD.

Mìle fàilte dhuit le 'd bhrèid,
Fad' a rè gu'n robh thu slàn,
Moran laithean dhuit as sìth,
Le d' mhaitheas as le d' nì 'bhith fàs.
A chulaidh cheiteas a chaidh suas.
'S tric a thairin buaidh air mnaoi—
Bithse gu suilceach, ceiteach,
O thionnseain thu fhein 'san treubh.
An tùs do choiruith 's tu òg,
An tùs gach lò iarr Righ nan Dùl ;
Cha'n' eagal nach dean e gu ceart
Gach dearbh-bheachd a bhios 'nad rùn,
Bithsa fialuidh—ach bith glic.
Bith misneachail—ach bith stolt.
Na bith brith'nach, 's na bith balbh,
Na bith mear na marbh 's tu òg ;
Bith gleidhteach air do dhea ainm,
Ach na bith duinte 's na bith fuar ;
Na labhair fòs air neach gu olc,
'S ged labhras ort, na taisbean fuath.
Na bith gearannach fo chrois,
Falbh socair le cupan làn ;
Chaoidh dh' an olc na tabhair spèis—
As le 'd bhrèid ort, mìle fàilt !

Whether with the sense of the above we have succeeded in
catching anything of its quaint beauty and tenderness in the
following lines, is for the reader to judge :—

A Bard's Blessing.

Comely and *kerchief'd*, blooming, fresh and fair,
  All hail and welcome ! joy and peace be thine ;
Of happiness and health a bounteous share
  Be shower'd upon thee from the hand divine.
Wearing the matron's coif, thou seem'st to be
Even lovelier now than erst, when fancy-free,
Thou in thy beauty's strength did'st steal my heart from me.

Though young in years thou 'rt now a wedded wife ;
  O seek His guidance who can guide aright.
With aid from Him, the rugged path of life
  May still be trod with pleasure and delight ;
For He who made us bids us not forego
A single, sinless pleasure in this world of woe.

Be open-hearted, but be *eident* too,
  Be strong and full of courage, but be staid ;
Aught like unseemly folly still eschew—
  Be faultless wife as thou wast faultless maid !
Guard against hasty speech and temper violent,
And knowing when to speak, know also to be silent.

Guard thy good name and mine from smallest stain ;
  In manner still be kindly, frank, and free ;
If thou 'rt reviled, revile not thou again ;
  In hour of trial calm and patient be ;
And when thy cup is full, walk humbly still,
A careless, proud, rash step the blissful cup may spill !

With this bard's blessing on thy wedded morn,
  All at thy bridal chamber-door we greet thee ;
May every joy of truth and goodness born
  Through all thy life-long journey crowd to meet thee ;
And may the God of Peace now richly shed
  A blessing on thy kerchief-cinctured head !

The word *breid* in the original, which we have rendered *kerchief* and *coif*, was in the olden times the peculiar head-dress of married females, while virgins wore their braided locks uncovered, a simple ribbon to bind the hair, and occasionally a sprig of heather or modest flower by way of ornament, being the only head-dress that could with propriety be worn by a maiden in the good old anti-chignon days of our grandmothers. The Highland maiden's narrow ribbon for binding the hair was in the south of Scotland called a *snood*, probably from the old English *snod*—"neat, handsome"—a word still in use in the English border counties. In the south, even more pointedly than in the north, the emblematical character of the maiden ribbon or snood was recognised. It was only when a maiden became an honest, lawful wife that the coif—also called *curch* and *toy*—could be worn with propriety. If a damsel was so unfortunate as to lose pretentions to the name of maiden, without acquiring a right to that of matron, she was neither permitted to wear that emblem of virgin purity, the snood, nor advanced to the graver dignity of the coif or curch. In old Scottish songs there occur many sly allusions to such misfortunes, as in the original words of the popular tune of "Ower the muir amang the heather"—

> " Down amang the broom, the broom,
> Down among the broom, my dearie,
> The lassie lost her silken snood,
> That gart her greet till she was wearie."

And in a verse of a curious old ballad that we took down some years ago from the recitation of a grey-headed Paisley weaver—

> " And did ye say ye lo'ed me weel?
> Then, kind sir, ye maun marrie me;
> For that I maunna wear my snood
> Aft brings the saut tear to my ee."

The reverend author of the above lines was probably born about the year 1700, or perhaps ten or twenty years earlier, for we find that he died a man well advanced in years in 1760. In the *Scots Magazine* of that year there is the following notice of Mr Macleod's death :— " *Jan. 12th.*—At Durinish, in the Isle of Skye, the Rev. Donald Macleod, minister of that parish, a gentleman, says our correspondent, who adorned his profession, not so much by a literary merit, of which he possessed a considerable share, as by a consistent practice of the most useful and excellent virtues. To do good was the ruling passion of his heart; in composing differences, in diffusing the spirit of peace and friendship, in relieving the distressed, in promoting the happiness of the widow and orphan, his zeal was almost unexampled, his activity unmeasured, his success remarkable. It is almost unnecessary to add that he lived with a most amiable character, and died universally regretted."

A somewhat curious circumstance is the following :—One of the Rev. Mr. Macleod's daughters was married to Macleod of Berneray, she being that gentleman's *third* wife. Berneray was at the date of this third marriage seventy-five years of age, notwithstanding which he became by this lady the father of *nine children.* He lived a hale and hearty old man till he was upwards of ninety. He was reckoned in his day a splendid specimen of the stalwart, sterling, straight-forward, and chivalrous Highland gentleman, "all of the olden time."

CHAPTER II.

WITH occasional gales of wind and blustering showers [October 1868], that, from their chilliness and *snellness*, you suspect to be sleet, although you don't like as yet exactly to say so—meteorological phenomena, however, in no way strange or unusual on the back of the autumnal equinox—the weather with us here continues delightfully bright and breezy, and the country looks beautiful. Field and upland are still as freshly green as at midsummer, while the deep, rich russet hues and golden tints of the declining year, gleaming in the fitful sunlight, and intermingling their glories with the still beautifully fresh and unspotted foliage of our hardier trees and shrubs; with the ripe, ruddy bloom of the heather empurpling the moorland and the hill, and a perfect sea of "brackens brown" mantling the mountain side, and fringing, in loving companionship with the birch, the alder, and the hazel, the torrent's brink, as it leaps in foam from rock to rock and dashes downwards with its wild music to the sea,—all this, with a thousand indescribable accessories, scarcely perceptible indeed in the general effect, but all bearing their fitting part in the delightful whole, presents at this season, and never more markedly than this year, a scene that you never tire of gazing at, and declaring again and again, and with all your heart, to be "beautiful exceedingly." As you gaze on such a scene as this, you feel that no painter could paint it; that there is a something in it all too subtile and spiritual to be transferred to canvas by any art whatever. An imitation, indeed, of all that is palpable and tangible about it you may get, and it may be very beautiful perhaps, and a triumph of art in a way; but, even as you gaze in admiration, ready to grant the artist all the praise that is his due, are you not apt, remembering the scene as nature has it, to

" Start, for *soul* is wanting there ? "

But we must not be misunderstood. Painters and painting we love, and have always loved, and should be sorry, indeed, to be considered as in any way dead or indifferent to the power and beauty of the art. Painting, after all, however, and especially landscape painting, is but an *imitative* art, and the longer we live, and the more we are brought face to face with nature, the more shall we feel that there is a charm, an attractiveness, and a loveliness about her all her own—a *something* that you feel but cannot describe, that the artist as he gazes feels too, and strives to grasp and instil into his picture, but cannot charm into interminglement with his colours, " charm he never so wisely." Viewed æsthetically, nature in sooth consists not of matter only, but of matter and *spirit*, and therein is the secret of her surpassing power over us. You may subtly imitate and reproduce exact representations of her more prominent features and general outlines, and the painter, according as he is more or less gifted with the poetic *mens divina*, may infuse a moral *meaning* into his work, and a subtile beauty entirely independent of the mere manipulation of his subject—be it landscape, seascape, or cloudscape—and his work may impart instruction as well as pleasure and delight; but, granting all this, there shall still be something awanting even in the finest pictures, that something which we have ventured to call spirit—the spirit that pervades and permeates nature in all her works, that is her life, that may be " spiritually discerned " *in her*, but cannot be transferred to canvas.

In the collection of Jewish traditions known as the *Talmud* there is a very pretty story of Solomon and the Queen of Sheba, that will serve to illustrate our meaning better than the longest dissertation could be. It is to the following effect :—Attracted by his wealth, and wisdom, and power—the fame whereof had gone forth into all lands—the Queen of Sheba, the Beautiful, paid a visit to Solomon, the Wise, at his own court, that she might there admire the splendour of his throne and be instructed of his wisdom. Charmed with the courtesy and gallantry of the accomplished King, delighted with the magnificence and splendour of his court, and amazed at his surpassing wisdom, which, indeed, exceeded all that she had heard reported of it, the Queen still thought that Solomon could be outwitted, and she resolved to have the glory of puzzling and outwitting one so wise. To this end she one day presented herself before the King, bearing in one of her hands a wreath of natural flowers, the most beautiful she could gather, and in the other a similar wreath of artificial flowers, the most beautiful and like unto natural flowers that the cunning of herself and her handmaidens could fashion. Of the two wreaths the hues were of the brightest, and the flowers of the one wreath were as if they had been pulled off the same stalks that bore the flowers of the other. "Tell me now, O King," said the Queen as she stood at some distance from the throne whereon the monarch sate, "Tell me now, O King, which of these wreaths I hold in my hands is fashioned of artificial flowers, for one of them is so fashioned ; and which of them of natural flowers, that grew from out the earth, and imbibed their beauty and their brightness from the sun, for of such of a truth is one of them formed ?" And, lo, the King was perplexed and sorely troubled, for he wist not what answer to make, seeing that the two wreaths were as like one to another as twin sisters at their mother's breast, or twin lilies on the same stalk. And the courtiers of the King, and his princes, and his servants, were sorely grieved that the sagacity of the King should be at fault, and his superhuman wisdom at last fail. But, lo, the spirit of wisdom came upon the King in his perplexity. Observing some bees clustering outside, he ordered the window to be opened, and soon the bees came swarming into the court, and after hovering for a moment about the one wreath, they straightway left it and settled upon the other, which observing, "*That*," said the King, "*that*, and not the other, is the wreath of the flowers that grew from out the earth and in the sun, and were not fashioned with hands." And the Queen was mightily surprised at the exceeding wisdom of the King, and did obeisance unto Solomon, laying the wreaths of flowers upon the steps of the ivory throne that was overlaid with gold, and of which there was not the like made in any kingdom. And the courtiers, and the princes, and the servants of the King clapped their hands and cried, "O King! live for ever." If we are wise and judge aright, we shall always, like the bees of Solomon, be attracted by nature rather than by art, however beautiful. Our doctrine was never, perhaps, so briefly and pithily enforced as by the Macedonian conqueror on a certain occasion. A courtier one day asked him to listen to him how well he could, whistling, imitate the notes of the nightingale. Alexander declined the proffered musical entertainment with the contemptuous remark, "*I have heard the nightingale herself.*" No wonder that the would-be melodist slunk away abashed ; and such be the fate of all mere echoers and imitators when at any time they claim more than is their due, or would have us appraise their pinchbeck at the value of sterling gold. There is an amount of truth, and a hidden meaning and beauty, in Byron's lines, that he was himself perhaps unconscious of in the ribald mood of the moment, when, alluding to the statuary's art, he exclaimed—

> " I've seen much finer women, ripe and real,
> Than all the nonsense of their stone ideal."

It is astonishing how difficult of thorough eradication are certain superstitions, if once established amongst a people. Once let the popular mind become inoculated with error in this shape, and although times may change and the manners of the people may alter, though a new tongue even shall have succeeded the language in which the error was imbibed, and knowledge have spread and civilisation have steadily progressed, yet there the superstition still lurks, frightened it may be at the outward light, and, owl-like, ashamed to appear in the brightness of the blessed sunshine of unclouded truth, but ever ready, nevertheless, under favourable circumstances, to manifest itself, and assert its sway over its votaries, like certain fabled mediæval philters and potions that when administered are said to have lurked for years and years in the human system, till, under certain conditions, their subtle properties were called into active operation, and the desired effect was produced. A short time ago we spent an evening in the company of a gentleman from the south of Scotland, a distinguished antiquary and archæologist, and of wonderful skill in everything connected with the *folk-lore* of Scotland, whether of the past or present. In the course of conversation, "over the walnuts and the wine," our friend surprised us not a little by informing us that even at this day, in certain parts of the south-western districts of Scotland, the *Sortes Sacræ* are frequently resorted to by the people when they are in doubt or perplexity about anything of sufficient importance in their opinion to warrant their having recourse to this ancient mode of divination. The *Sortes Sacræ* are founded upon the more ancient *Sortes Virgilianæ*—Virgilian Lots, a method of divination which had at least the merit of being extremely simple, and not necessarily occupying much of the votary's time. What may be called the literary oracle, as distinguished from vocal oracles, was consulted in this wise: The operator having before him a copy of Virgil—the *sortes* were generally confined to the

Æneid—opened the volume *ad aperturam libri,* anywhere, at random, when the first passage that accidentally struck the eye was carefully read and pondered with as little reference as possible to its immediate context, and a meaning extracted from it which was supposed to indicate the issue of the event in hand, and which was to be considered inevitable and irrevocable as the fates had so decreed. A man with the knowledge thus obtained could not by any precaution or change of conduct avert the impending doom, good or evil; he could only put his house in order, and so arrange matters the best way he could; that if evil came it might be borne with dignity and patience; if good, that it might be enjoyed with moderation and devout gratitude to the gods. It is said that at the outbreak of the troubles that culminated in the Commonwealth, Charles I. and Lord Falkland found themselves on a certain day in the Bodleian Library at Oxford, when the latter jocularly proposed that they should inform themselves of their future fortunes by means of the *Sortes Virgilianæ;* and certainly, read by the light of after events, it must be confessed that the passages stumbled upon seem singularly ominous of the fate that overtook both. The passage read by the Martyr King was from the fourth book of the Æneid, and is as follows :—

> " At bello audacis populi vexatus et armis,
>   Finibus extorris, complexu avulsus Iuli,
>   Auxilium imploret, videatque, indigna suorum
>   Funera : nec, cum se sub leges pacis iniquæ
>   Tradiderit, regno aut optata luce fruatur,
>   Sed cadat ante diem, mediaque inhumatus arena."

Which Dryden, if with rather too much amplification, still very beautifully translates thus :—

> " Yet let a race untamed and haughty foes
>   His peaceful entrance with dire arms oppose,
>   Oppress'd with numbers in th' unequal field,
>   His men discouraged and himself expell'd :

> Let him for succour sue from place to place,
> Torn from his subjects and his son's embrace,
> First let him see his friends in battle slain,
> And their untimely fate lament in vain ;
> And when at length the cruel wars shall cease,
> On hard conditions may he buy his peace.
> Nor let him then enjoy supreme command,
> But fall untimely by some hostile hand,
> And lie unburied on the barren sand."

Lord Falkland's eye fell on the following lines in the eleventh book :—

> " Non hæc, O Palla, dederas promissa parenti.
> Cautius ut sævo velles te credere Marti !
> Haud ignarus eram, quantum nova gloria in armis,
> Et predulce decus primo certamine posset.
> Primitiæ juvenis miseræ ! bellique propinqui
> Dura rudimenta ! et nulli exaudita Deorum
> Vota, precesque meæ !"

—which the same translator has rendered as follows :—

> " O Pallas, thou hast failed thy plighted word,
> To fight with caution, not to tempt the sword ;
> I warn'd thee, but in vain, for well I knew
> What perils youthful ardour would pursue ;
> That boiling blood would carry thee too far,
> Young as thou wert to dangers, raw to war ;
> O curs'd essay of arms, disastrous doom,
> Prelude of bloody fields and fights to come,
> Hard elements of unauspicious war,
> Vain vows to heaven and unavailing care."

How the most pious man of his age, and one of the best kings that ever adorned a throne, suffered death at the hands of his rebellious subjects is well known. Poor Lord Falkland—a young nobleman of the most estimable character ; a poet and man of letters, so fond of books that he used to say that " he pitied unlearned gentlemen in a rainy day "—fell gallantly fighting for the royal cause in the battle of Newbury, before he had yet completed his thirty-fourth year. It is curious to find the eminent poet Abraham Cowley, a good man too—of whom at his death Charles II. was heard to say that "Mr. Cowley had not left a better man behind in England,"—it is curious, we say, to find him on a certain occasion seriously referring to the *Virgilian Lots*, and, what is more, avowing his firm belief in them! During the Commonwealth, Cowley was in Paris, where he acted as secretary to the Earl of St. Albans (then Lord Jermyn), and had a good deal to do with the negotiations that eventually led to the Restoration. In one of his letters, speaking of the Scotch treaty then in agitation, he says—seriously, observe, and in an official document—"The Scotch treaty is the only thing now in which we are vitally concerned. I am one of the last hopers, and yet cannot now abstain from believing that an agreement will be made; all people upon the place incline to that union. The Scotch will moderate something of the rigour of their demands; the mutual necessity of an accord is visible, the king is persuaded of it. *And, to tell you the truth (which I take to be an argument above all the rest), Virgil has told the same thing to that purpose.*" He had evidently consulted the *Virgilian Lots*, and a passage presenting itself that could somehow be twisted so as to point to a favourable issue to the Scotch business in hand, he accepts the oracle, and in all seriousness announces his belief in it! When we find a man of refinement and culture and high moral character like Cowley crediting such nonsense, can we much wonder at the lengths to which fanaticism and superstition carried people in those unhappy times? To understand why Virgil, of all the ancient poets, Roman or Greek, was selected as the oracle in this mode of divination, we must remember that the Mantuan bard had the credit amongst his countrymen of having been a sorcerer or necromancer and prophet as well as a poet, something like the British *Merlin*, or our own *Thomas the Rhymer* and *Michael Scott*, only more famous, perhaps. Would the reader suppose, for example, that the theory of volcanic action is all a myth, and that it is to the magic of Virgil, and to nothing else, that the south of Italy is indebted for all the earthquakes and subterranean convulsions that have afflicted it for centuries? Yet so it is, if we are to credit all the stories of " Virgilius the Magician " that were current during the Middle Ages. The celebrated Benedictine monk, *Bernard de Montfaucon*, author of *Antiquité Expliquée* one of the most learned and curious works in existence, repeats the story as it was told and credited in the Dark Ages. The following is from an old translation, quoted by Scott in his notes to the *Lay of the Last Minstrel*, in illustration of the magical spells attributed to the Ladye of Branksome Tower. Virgil it seems, among other things, was famous for his gallantries. On one occasion he fell in love with and carried away the daughter of a certain "Soldan," and the story proceeds :—"Than he thoughte in his mynde how he myghte marye hyr, and thoughte in his mynde to founde in the middes of the see a fayer towne, with great landes belongynge to it ; and so he did by his cunnynge, and called it Napells (Naples). And the foundacyon of it was of egges, and in that town of Napells he made a tower with iiii. corners, and in the toppe he set an apell upon an yron yarde, and no man culde pull away that apell without he brake it ; and thoroughe that yren set he a bolte, and in that bolte set he an egge, and he henge the apell by the stauke upon a cheyne, and so hangeth it still. And when the egge styrreth so should the town of Napells quake ; and when the egge brake, then shulde the town sinke. When he made an ende, he lette calls it Napells." Thomas of " Ercildoune," and he of " Balivearie," and the two *Merlins*,—for there were two of them, the Merlin of the Arthurian legends, and *Merdwynn Wylet*, or Merlin the Wild, who seems to have been a Scotchman, and whose grave is still pointed out beneath an aged thorn-tree at Drumelzier in Tweeddale,—these were accounted great magicians and " pretty fellows in their day ;" but what were they to Virgilius the earthquaker, who at least attained to such an enviable state of independence, that he is represented as frequently playing at pitch and toss with the "devyl," and cheating and outwitting that crafty potentate as if he were the veriest greenhorn ! The *Sortes Sacræ* were just the *Sortes Virgilianæ,* with this difference, that in the former case, instead of a copy of Virgil, the New Testament was used in the process of divination. The oracle is consulted in this case, according to our information, by the introduction at random of the wards end of a key (some allusion probably to the Apostolic keys) between the leaves of the closed volume, which is then opened at that place, and from the first verse that arrests the eye the desired knowledge is extracted. On inquiry, we find that this superstition was still occasionally practised in the Highlands of Scotland some fifty years ago, though we would fain hope and believe that it is now unknown. It is curious that it should still be frequently resorted to in the south-western districts. It seems to have been a very general as well as a very ancient mode of divination. Hoffman, in his *Lexicon Universale, &c.,* informs us that it was practised by the Jewish Rabbins with their sacred books, as well as by the Pagans from very early times, and was common amongst the Christians of the Middle Ages. We are informed by a gentleman, who spent many years in the East, that the Mahometans frequently resort to this method of divination, taking the Koran as their oracle.

CHAPTER III.

IN looking over some old papers the other day [October 1868] we
stumbled on some sheets of Gaelic MS. that had lain neglected for
years, and the very existence of which, indeed, we had well-nigh forgotten. One of these sheets contained the original of the following
lines. It is in many respects a curious composition, written in a sort
of rhythmical alliterative prose rather than in verse, somewhat in the
manner of the conversational parts of the Gaelic *Sgeulachdan* or
fireside tales of the olden time. Its tone throughout is gay and
lively, with an occasional admixture of humour and *double entendre*
that is very amusing, while its allusions to the manners and customs
and superstitious observances of a past age render it, to our thinking, extremely interesting. The sheet in our possession is only a
copy, the original, taken down from oral recitation, we believe,
being in a MS. collection of Gaelic poems and tales by Rev. Mr.
M'Donald, at one time minister of the parish of Fortingall, in
Perthshire. Having only internal evidence to judge from, it is
impossible with any confidence to assign even an approximate
date to such a production as this, but we are probably not far
wrong in placing it as early at least as the middle or close of the
last century. It bears no title in the original; we may call it—

THE BEWITCHED BACHELOR UNBEWITCHED.

The gudeman mumbled and grumbled full sore
  Over the butter-kits, all through the dairy :
Over cheese, over butter, and milk-pails, he swore
  " 'Tis the work, I'll be bound, of some foul witch or fairy.

How can I ever be happy or rich,
If robbed and tormented by fairy and witch,"
Quoth he ; and lo, with a sudden turn
He stumbled and spilt the cream-full churn !

He went to his mother (she dwelt in the cot
   Amid the hazels down by the linn :
Full well the wild birds loved that spot,
   And taught its echoes their merry din)—
He went to his mother, that Bachelor gruff :
   He was mild with her, though with others rough.

" Mother," quoth he, " I have not now
One-half the butter or cheese, I trow,
That loaded my dairy shelves when you
Had charge of my household and dairy too :
Tell me mother, what shall I do ?
I vow and declare that some fairy or witch
Is robbing me still—and doing me ill—I shall never be rich."

" My son," the mother mild replied,
   " See that you pay the fairies their due ;
A tribute due should ne'er be denied—
   Others don't grudge it, and why should you !
Nor thrive their flocks nor kine, I ween,
Who scorn or neglect the *shian* green."

" But, mother, the witch that lives down i' the glen ?"
" A widow, my son, with a fatherless oe,
Who has seen much sorrow and years of woe ;
Give her as heretofore, my son,
Of your curds and whey, and let her alone.
And oh, my son, if you would be rich,
And free from dread of fairy and witch.
And happy and well-to-do through life—
Go get thee, my son, a winsome wife !"

The bachelor hied him home full soon—
   He sent to the widow, far down in the glen,
A kebbuck of cheese as round as the moon,
   Of oaten cakes he sent her ten,
With a kindly message, " Come when you may
For curds and whey in the good old way."
He sent her withal, 'tis right you should know.
A braw new kilt for her fatherless oe.

And ever he saw that his maidens paid
　To the fairies their due on the *Fairy Knowe*,
Till the emerald sward was under the tread
　As velvet soft, and all aglow
With wild flowers, such as fairies cull,
Weaving their garlands and wreaths for the dance when the
　　moon is full !

And lo ! at last he took him a wife,
　A comely and winsome dame, I trow,
Who shed a sunshine over his life,
And silvered the wrinkles upon his brow.
　'Twas well with the kine, and well with the dairy,
Nor dreaded he ought from witch or fairy ;
(He had one of his own—she was hight *Wee Mary!*)
And often they went to the cot by the linn,
Where mavis and merle made merry din.

The English reader will probably require to be informed that
oe—the Gaelic *ogha*—signifies a grandchild, while *shian* (Gaelic
sithean) is a fairy knoll.　To show what a power fairies were at
one time in the land, and how wide-spread was the belief in them,
we have only to consider that there is perhaps not a hamlet or
township in the Highlands or Hebrides without its *shian* or green
fairy knoll so called.　Within half a mile of our own residence, for
example, there is a *Sithean Beag* and a *Sithean Mor*, a Greater and
Lesser Fairy Knoll ; there is, besides, a *Glacan-t' Shithein*, the Fairy
Knoll Glade, *Tobar-an-t' Shithein*, the Fairy Knoll Well ; and a
deep chasm, through which a mountain torrent plunges darkling,
called *Leum-an-t' Shithiche*, the Fairy's Leap, with which there is
probably connected some very wonderful story, although we have
been unsuccessful hitherto in meeting with any one able or willing
to repeat it.　The truth is, that a belief in fairies and fairyland, or
faery—faint, no doubt, and ill-defined now-a-days—still lingers ghost-
like, the shadow of its more substantial former living self, in our
straths and glens ; and, in accordance with the old superstition, it
is considered that the " good people " should only be spoken of on

rare and unavoidable occasions, and then only in serious and
respectable terms. Hence it is that you always find old people
reluctant to impart such fairy lore as may be known to them,
though garrulous enough on all other subjects; and hence, also,
it happens that in our old *Sgeuluchdan*—the *Arabian Nights
Entertainments* of our Celtic forefathers—although you find giants,
and dwarfs, and misbegotten beings of every imaginable shape and
size; animals, too, that can speak and reason and lend their superhuman aid to prince and peasant in extremity, as well as genii,
kelpies, and spirits of flood and fell, you rarely if ever meet with
one of the "good folks," or fairies proper, introduced upon the scene.
The people thoroughly *believed* in them, believed that they had a
veritable existence, and although invisible to mortal eye, that they
might be at your elbow at any moment; that they disliked being
spoken of at all as a rule, and that a disrespectful word about
them especially would inevitably be followed by some signal
punishment, or "mischance," as it was more cautiously termed in
the South—all this they believed, and therefore they held it wisest
to speak of fairies, good folks though they were, as seldom as
possible. The allusion to paying—

"The fairies their due on the fairy knowe,"

has reference to the custom, common enough on the western mainland and in some of the Hebrides some fifty years ago, and not
altogether unknown perhaps even at the present day, of each
maiden's pouring from her *cumanbleoghain*, or milking-pail, evening and morning, on the fairy knowe a little of the new-drawn
milk from the cow, by way of propitiating the favour of the good
people, and as a tribute the wisest, it was deemed, and most
acceptable that could be rendered, and sooner or later sure to be
repaid a thousand-fold. The consequence was that these fairy
knolls were clothed with a richer and more beautiful verdure than

any other spot, howe or knowe, in the country, and the lacteal riches imbibed by the soil through this custom is even now visible in the vivid emerald green of a *shian* or fairy knoll whenever it is pointed out to you. This custom of pouring lacteal libations to the fairies on a particular spot deemed sacred to them, was known and practised at some of the summer shielings in Lochaber within the memory of the people now living.

CHAPTER IV.

WE were early astir on the morning of the 5th November [1868]; with little thought, be sure, of Guy Fawkes or the Gunpowder Plot, intent only on witnessing, if we might be so fortunate, the transit of Mercury over the solar disc. The phenomenon in question we have seen referred to as an " eclipse " of Mercury, which it certainly was not. A celestial body is properly said to be eclipsed when, by the interposition of another and a nearer orb, it is temporarily hid from view. A star or planet so hidden by the body of the moon, for instance, is said to be " occulted." The sun is truly said to be eclipsed when the new moon at a particular conjunction steps in between us and him, and temporarily intercepts his beams. What again, for convenience sake, is called an eclipse of the moon, is really not an eclipse at all, so far at least as the terrestrial spectator is concerned ; it would be more strictly correct to call it simply a lunar obscuration. The temporary appearance of Venus and Mercury as circular and sharply defined black spots on the solar disc, has hitherto always, and very properly, been called in the language of astronomers a " transit " of the particular planet by name, such as the " transit of Venus," or the " transit of Mercury ; " and there is no reason to change the term, for it is expressive and true, which the word *eclipse,* applied to such a conjunction, certainly is not.

Be it called what it may, however—eclipse or transit—we were disappointed in not getting a glimpse of the phenomenon in question

on the present occasion. Although duly at our post from before
sunrise till the minute calculated for the last contact of the planet
with the solar disc, we were unable to obtain anything more than
the most momentary blink even of the larger orb, and, of course,
the detection of the black button-like disc of the planet itself, in
such circumstances, was altogether out of the question. The disappointment, however, was less annoying to us in this instance
from the fact that we had already been privileged to witness all the
phases of a similar conjunction from first to last on the 12th
November 1861. The next visible transit of Mercury does not
take place till the 6th of May 1878—ten years hence. There are
several other transits during the present century, invisible in our
country, however, and on the continent of Europe; but which will
probably afford much delight to many an eager watcher over the
length and breadth of the South American continent, and generally
over the islands of the Pacific Ocean.

Nor, with us here at least, was the night of the 13-14th instant
any way more favourable for observation than the dull beclouded
morning of the 5th itself. The night was calm and rainless, to be
sure, but a heavy impenetrable mass of dark grey clouds, so low as
to envelop all the mountain summits around, obscured the vault
from horizon to horizon, from sunset to sunrise, so that not a single
meteor could be seen by the keenest eye, even if above that pall of
cloud the display had been the most brilliant and splendid conceivable. From the fact, however, that in several places widely
distant from each other, from which we have had communications
on the subject, and where the sky was abundantly clear and
unclouded throughout, no unusual display of meteors was seen, the
probability is that we have on this occasion missed them in our
country, either because they came into contact with our atmosphere
in the daytime, when, of course, they would be invisible, or more
likely because our contact this year with the meteorolithic *annulus*

was of the slightest, and at a segment thereof where the meteoric bodies are least numerous, and thus we must patiently wait till we again dash through it at its densest before we can hope for such a magnificent meteor shower as astonished and delighted us all in 1866. Only at Oxford, as far as our country is concerned, was there anything like a meteor shower on the present occasion, and even there the display seems to have been too faint and uninteresting to have attracted much attention. Intelligence has reached our country from New York, however, that over that city, and over the States generally, the meteoric display of the morning of the 14th was very splendid indeed, though, owing to the morning being further advanced before it commenced, less of it was seen by the people at large than on some previous occasions. The weather with our Transatlantic cousins seems to have been all that could be desired, as it is stated that "astronomers and others were able to make very complete observations." The worst thing about our insular position with respect to matters astronomical is the extreme uncertainty with which anything like continuous observation can be conducted. The chances always are twenty to one that in Great Britain, at any given hour in any given place, the weather should be such as to render an observation of a celestial phenomenon impossible, or at the least partial and unsatisfactory. One thing, at least, is now pretty certain—that annually, and at a date that falls somewhere between sunset of the 13th and sunrise of the 14th November, we may confidently look for greater or less displays of these meteoric bodies, the only thing likely to interfere with the interesting pyrotechnic exhibition being an unfavourable state of the weather at a moment when we are most concerned that the sky shall be clear and cloudless.

Mr. Huggins, whose researches with the *spectroscope* have already made his name famous, has recently communicated a most interesting paper to the Royal Society, giving an account of the spectrum analyses of one of the smaller and commoner class of comets that was visible for a short time in the month of June last. Avoiding technical details, which might be uninteresting to some of our readers, we may simply mention that on testing the nucleus of this comet with the spectroscope, Mr. Huggins found that it was resolved into three broad "bands," precisely similar to the results obtained on examining with the same wonderful instrument such carbon as follows the transmission of electric sparks through olefiant gas. The conclusion arrived at by Mr. Huggins is, that the nucleus of the comet in question consisted solely of volatilised carbon. This paper of Mr. Huggins is altogether a most interesting one, and we may have something more to say about it on a future occasion.

The following is a translation—somewhat freely rendered—of an old Irst or St. Kilda song, the solitary island home of a score or two of hardy inhabitants, and by all accounts a happy and hospitable race too, who cling with an unquenchable love to their lonely rock, as if it were a perfect paradise, ocean-girt and storm-beaten though it be—

> " Placed far amid the melancholy main."

Except another specimen given in a small collection of Gaelic songs, edited by the late Rev. Mr. M'Callum of Arisaig, the original of the following is the only St. Kilda song that we have met with. Our copy was procured in this way : Some years ago we were dining on board H.M. Revenue cruiser "Harriet," Captain M'Allister. Going ashore on a fine moonlight night, one of the seamen who rowed our boat sang the song, which we had no hesitation in at once declaring to be of St. Kilda origin, which the man admitted was the case, he having picked it up many years before from an old woman who had spent some time on the island. Of the air, we can only remember that it was a wild, irregular sort of chant, very different from the soft low airs to which our main-land songs are for the most part sung, with the refrain or burden (represented by our *Alexandrines* in each stanza) given in a shrill falsetto that was somewhat disagreeable to the ear, although abundantly appropriate, probably, in the circumstances in which the song was composed, and when sung amid all the surroundings of the scene depicted.

THE ST. KILDA MAID'S SONG.

Over the rocks, steadily, steadily ;
Down to the clefts with a shout and a shove, O ;
  Warily tend the rope, shifting it readily,
Eagerly, actively, watch from above, O.
Brave, O brave, my lover true, he's worth a maiden's love :
(*And the sea below is still as deep as the sky is high above !*)

Sweet 'tis to sleep on a well feathered pillow,
Sweet from the embers the fulmar's red egg, O ;
  Bounteous our store from the rock and the billow ;
Fish and birds in good store, we need never to beg, O ;
Brave, O brave, my lover true, he's worth a maiden's love :
(*And the sea below is still as deep as the sky is high above !*)

Hark to the fulmar and guillemot screaming :
Hark to the kittiwake, puffin, and gull, O :
  See the white wings of solan goose gleaming ;
Steadily, men ! on the rope gently pull, O.
Brave, O brave, my lover true, he's worth a maiden's love :
(*And the sea below is still as deep as the sky is high above !*)

Deftly my love can hook ling and conger,
The grey-fish and hake, with the net and the creel, O ;
  Far from our island be plague and be hunger ;
And sweet our last sleep in the quiet of the Kiel, O.
Brave, O brave, my lover true, he's worth a maiden's love :
(*And the sea below is still as deep as the sky is high above !*)

Pull on the rope, men, pull it up steadily :
(*There's a storm on the deep, see the scart claps his wings, O*) ;
  Cunningly guide the rope, shifting it readily ;
Welcome my true love, and all that he brings, O !
Now God be praised, my lover's safe, he's worth a maiden's love :
(*And the sea below is still as deep as the sky is high above !*)

Our song needs but little elucidation. The reader who knows that the wealth of the St. Kildians mainly consists of the feathers and eggs of wild-fowl, to procure which they are obliged to hang suspended from ropes over the most dreadful precipices, in the clefts and along the otherwise inaccessible ledges of which the sea-fowl breed, will have no difficulty in understanding the general drift of the island maid's very spirited and very earnest song. It is, perhaps, unnecessary to say that as ling, conger, hake, and grey-fish are certain kinds of sea fish, so fulmar, guillemot, kittiwake, puffin, and scart are certain kinds of web-footed sea-fowl.

CHAPTER V.

CONSCIOUS at last that pouting and inordinate weeping became him not, and that, being constantly on the "rampage," like Mrs. Joe Gargery, was hardly consistent with his place in the calendar, April [1869] betimes resolved to "tak a thocht and mend," and now, like Richard, is himself again—all sunshine and smiles. The rain-gauge, to be sure, with stern impartiality, will still show an occasional "inch," or parts of an inch, if you are very particular in your inquiries, when examined of a morning, but its readings now at least are in no way appalling, for they represent the warm and genial rainfall of April showers, that, after all, are as necessary on the west coast at this moment, and as refreshing to the soil, as the orthodox cup of mulled port of an evening was believed to be to the weary traveller in the good old days of stage-coaches and post-chaises. The country, at all events, is looking very beautiful just now, everything so green and glad, so fresh and fair, and full of promise of a yet gladder, and gayer, and brighter day at hand, when the swallow, twittering, shall dart, a glossy meteor, in the sunlight, and the cuckoo shall challenge the truant school-boy to repeat its well-known notes, correctly if he can. Now is the time to hear our native song-birds at their best, warbling their sweetest strains, and to decide, once for all, if it be possible, which you like best; the loud, clear, silvery tinkle of the seed-shelling finch's rich and rapid song; the liquid and mellifluous warblings of the soft-billed tribes; or the soul-entrancing, round, rich, flute-like piping of the throstle, song-thrush, and merle. How it may fare with the reader who tries to decide the point we cannot say. For our own part, no decision that we could ever arrive at could keep its legs for two days together. No sooner did we decide that the sky-lark and its congeners had the best of it, than the goldfinch, with a score of lively cousins to aid and abet, challenged the verdict, and forced us to acknowledge *his* exquisite mastery in song—an admission made, however, only to be retracted again almost as soon as made, for in our walk on the evening of that self-same day did we not stand, and for the life of us couldn't help standing—breathless, and hushed, and still—to listen to the merle and song-thrush from the neighbouring copse pouring forth the indescribable riches of their God-taught vespers as the sun went down; and did we not, then and there, vow, in utter forgetfulness of finch and skylark, that no music of earth could for a moment compare, in execution and compass, in distinctness, and cheeriness, and purity of note, with these matchless twilight strains? The truth is that no music is equal to bird-music—wild-bird music, that is—in its season, and amid all its natural surroundings; and the probability is that we shall give the preference at any time to the melody of one bird over that of another, not on any well-defined principles of choice or selection in the matter, but simply in accordance with our own prevailing mood and temperament of the moment. Such, at least, has been our own experience; but the reader has every opportunity at this season of studying the question for himself and deciding. Except that of the nightingale, perhaps the music of no bird has attracted so much attention by its beauty and suggestiveness as the merry trill of the skylark's ascending song. The poets of every country in which it is to be found have vied with each other in their praises of the only bird that sings as he soars, and soars as he sings, scaling on quivering pinions the aerial terraces of heaven, until he can scarcely be discerned, a music-showering speck against

the back-ground of the blue profound ! The other day we fell in
with some curious verses by the French poet Du Bartas, in which
he strives, and not altogether unsuccessfully, to imitate the merry
trill and rhythm of the skylark's song :—

> " La gentille alouette, avec son *tire-lire,*
> *Tire-lire,* à *lire, et tire-liran tire ;*
> Vers la route du ciel, puis son vol vers ce lieu,
> *Vire et desire dire adieu Dieu, adieu Dieu !* "

The last line, if rapidly repeated with the proper beat and intonation,
will be found a really very successful imitation of the concluding
notes of the lark's well-known song. Many of our readers will
remember that the North Uist bard, Ian Mac Codrum, in his
Smeorach Chlann-Domhnuill, manages very happily to imitate
the *smeorach* or song-thrush's notes in the burden or chorus ; while
Alexander Macdonald—Mac Mhaighstir Alasdair—very naturally
falls, like the French poet, into an imitation of the wild-bird music
of the woods and groves in a stanza that may be quoted not
inappropriately at this season :—

> " Cha bhi crèutair fo chupan nan spèur
> 'N sin nach tiunndaidh ri'n speuràd 's ri'n dreach,
> 'S gun toir *Phoebus* le buadhan a bhlàis
> Anam-fas daibh a's caileachdan ceart,
> Ni iad ais-eiridh choitcheann on uaigh
> Far na mhiotaich am fuachd iad a steach,
> 'S their iad—*guileag-doro-hidola-hann*
> *Dh-fhalbh an geamhra's tha'n samhradh air teachd !* "

The lines of Du Bartas have little meaning in themselves, and are
untranslatable, being simply an attempt on the poet's part, in some
odd moment of hilarity and *abandon,* to embody the notes of
the skylark's song in something like articulate verse. The general
sense of Macdonald's lines describing the irrepressible inclination
of all living creatures to be jubilant and joyous at the return of
spring, cannot better be rendered than in the first part of Scott's
introductory stanza to the second canto of the *Lady of the*

Lake, only that the return of spring in the one case, instead of the return of morn in the other, prompts to the outburst of gladness and song :—

> " At morn the black-cock trims his jetty wing,
>   'Tis morning prompts the linnet's blithest lay,
> All Nature's children feel the matin spring
>   Of life reviving, with reviving day ;
> And while yon little bark glides down the bay,
>   Wafting the stranger on his way again,
> Morn's genial influence roused a minstrel grey,
>   And sweetly o'er the lake was heard thy strain,
> Mixed with the sounding harp, O white-hair'd Allan-bane ! "

CHAPTER VI.

THAT the people of Lochaber and the Western Isles should be rejoicing in the advent of heavy rains [August 1869], and seriously glad at the reappearance of clouds in the heavens and mists upon the mountain tops, may seem odd enough to those who know anything of our usual meteorological characteristics ; yet true it is, and of a verity that so it is, for here, as elsewhere, the heat was for many consecutive weeks intense, and the parching drought and fierce glare of a summer's sun from a constantly unclouded sky well nigh unbearable by man or beast, whether in the sheltered valley, where for days and days no breath of air shook the tiniest leaflet or ruffled the surface of the sullen tarn, or on the upland moor, where, if breath of air there was, it was hot and stifling as the breath of a furnace. Were it not for the occasional sea breezes, that sometimes of an evening swept over the almost pulseless deep, and copious falls of blessed night-dews, we should have been badly off indeed. But, as matters have turned out, we have much reason to be thankful, for if our crops are not quite so heavy as in average years, they are at least of excellent quality, and being ripe sooner than usual, we have a chance of getting them secured in a condition that will add immensely to their value. So thorough and persistent was the drought even with us, that springs failed that never before were known to refuse their waters to the thirsty ; and water-courses that heretofore, even in the driest years, still presented shady pools

c

connected by purling rivulets, were for weeks together arid and
waterless as the course of an ancient lava stream.   As you wandered
among the hills you could set your fusee alight on a stone in a
torrent bed over which in ordinary summers rolls a volume of
foaming waters.   The demand for beer wherever you went was in
these circumstances something wonderful ; and at times, on the
arrival of coach or steamer with its load of panting tourists, the
bawling from husky throats for a supply—an instant and copious
supply—of the delicious liquid was sufficiently amusing.   One of
the happiest illustrations of the proverbial close treading of the
ridiculous on the heels of the sublime, and the wafer-like thinness
of the partition that divides the sentimental from the absurd, was
Dr. Johnson's celebrated parody on the quasi-sentimental style of
poetry so much in vogue in his latter years—and sooth to say too
much in vogue in our day as well—a style as unlike the school of
Pope as you can well imagine, and the very antipodes of the sturdily
masculine and didactic strains which Johnson, an intellectual
giant—for there were giants in these days—alone accounted true
poetry :—

> " Hermit hoar, in solemn cell,
>   Wearing out life's evening grey,
> Smite thy bosom, sage, and tell
>   What is bliss ? and which the way ?
>
> " Thus I spoke ; and speaking sighed ;
>   Scarce repressed the starting tear ;
> When the smiling sage replied,—
>   ' *Come, my lad, and drink some beer !* ' "

And very well hit off, you will confess ; an arrow shot from an
Ulysses' bow at the puling whimperers of a namby-pamby sentimentalism that they miscalled poetry ; but if we dared for the
nonce to take these lines in a more serious and literal sense than
their author intended, we should say that in such hot and parching
weather as we have recently had, and are still having, there is more

"bliss" in a good draught of "Allsopp" or "Bass" than is dreamt of in the philosophy of the sentimentalists, and thousands upon thousands of this season's tourists are ready, we'll be bound, to homologate this statement.

It was Dr. Johnson, too, if we remember well, who spoke loudly and dogmatically, as was his wont, of the delightful feeling that one has in being rapidly whirled along a good road in a post-chaise; and remembering the unsteadiness of the "Rambler" on his pins, and his unwieldy corporation, one can readily understand that he found the means of locomotion referred to the easiest and most enjoyable possible. Our own experience of post-chaises has, sooth to say, been somewhat of the slightest, but in lieu thereof we would recommend a well-appointed public coach, with sound, well-cared-for horses, a steady and obliging driver and guard, good roads under foot, and a bright sky above all; and such a conveyance we on a recent occasion found the mail-coach between Fort-William and Kingussie to be; and such a driver and guard, the two in one, is the renowned "Davie Jack," who knows his work, and does it too, in a style that reminds one of the old "Defiance" in its palmiest days; while the weather, if anything, was too fine, too bright and cloudless—the best fault it could have, however, since it is impossible that the weather on any particular day should be faultless, any more than that any human being should be perfect. Nothing, indeed, can be finer than the drive through Lochaber and Badenoch to Kingussie, except perhaps the drive back again. With mountain scenery on all hands, unsurpassed even in the Highlands for wild, and savage, and solitary grandeur; with foaming torrents dashing down the steeps, torrents that at a distance and at this season look like so many threads of purest silver constantly being absorbed and inwefted with the river, that, with a voice more hushed, and a quieter, kindlier step, still gladdens and fertilises the valley as it seeks the sea; with loch and river scenery the most attractive and lovely ; and all, in short, that you can reasonably look for of the grand or beautiful from the sea coast to the central Highlands. With all this, and the redoubted "Davie" to handle the ribbons, as only "Davie" *can* handle them—said "Davie" the while as full of anecdote, and joke, and local tradition as an egg is full of meat—with all this we say, and much more that might be mentioned, the man who cannot enjoy such a journey at this season is little to be envied ; for, be his other qualities and qualifications what they may, his non-enjoyment of such a drive clearly proves one of two things,—either he is physically unwell, and out of sorts, and had better stay at home ; or, æsthetically, he has no eye for, and no appreciation of, some of the most splendid scenery in the Highlands, and in that case is less to be blamed than pitied. Even in winter we should say that this was the readiest, as well as the most pleasant, line of intercommunication between the north-western Highlands and the south. It were, finally, unpardonable in us, who enjoyed it so much, not to mention the very excellent break- fast on the up-journey, and the equally excellent and substantial "tea," or tea-dinner rather, on returning, to be had in the shep- herd's house at Moy. It may seem unromantic and prosaic to say so, but it is a fact nevertheless, that one's appreciation of the sublime and beautiful—let Mr. Edmund Burke say what he likes —is not a little enhanced by a due supply of creature comforts *pari passû*. If one cannot carry the comforts of home about with him, any more than honest Bailie Nicol Jarvie could carry about with *him* the comforts of the "Sautmarket," it is no small matter to meet with good cheer off a snow-white cloth, with the attentions of a smart, intelligent serving girl, in odd and out-of-the-way places, where you least expect it. Altogether, a trip by the Fort- William and Kingussie mail-coach during the present fine weather is very enjoyable indeed—superior, upon the whole, we should say, to the "Rambler's" post-chaise, not forgetting that the latter is a solitary and somewhat surly sort of business, whereas in the former you have the chance of pleasant and agreeable companionship, in addition to its other attractions.

For one to make a discovery, and to *think* that oneself has made a discovery, are two widely different things. We readily acknowledge the distinction. That we have made a discovery we shall not venture to affirm, but we think we have. Our discovery, if discovery it be, is this, that Sir Walter Scott is indebted for Dominie Sampson's "prodigious!" to Boswell's Life of Johnson. Who can think of the worthy, kind-hearted, most unsophisticated, and withal most learned, albeit life-long kirkless parson, without instantly recalling his favourite exclamation of *" Pro-di-gi-ous ?"* We stumbled on our discovery in this wise :—A few evenings ago we were reading the third volume of a very fine edition of Boswell's "Johnson," kindly placed at our disposal by Lady Riddell of Strontian—and a good edition of a good book is no small matter to one so far removed from libraries as we are—when we came to a page that described Johnson's meeting with a gentleman who had been his companion at Pembroke College, Oxford, some fifty years previously. Mr. Edwards, for that was the gentleman's name, and Boswell accompanied Johnson home, where, in course of conversation, Mr. Edwards said, addressing Johnson, " Sir, I remember you would not let us say *prodigious* at college. For even then, sir (turning to Boswell), he was delicate in language, and we all feared him." Now, can any one doubt that it was having his attention particularly called to the word in this passage that made Scott first ponder the absurdity of using a word of such volume and import on every trifling occasion, and caused him, possibly at a long subsequent date (for Scott's memory, as we know, was *prodigiously* retentive—there the word, you will observe, is pat and appropriate enough—prodigiously retentive, we say, of words, phrases, and odd turns of expression)—to put it so frequently as an exclamation of

unspeakable, indescribable import into the mouth of honest
Sampson, whom you can no more help laughing at, at times, than
you can loving him with all your heart *always?* The matter, after
all, may seem a trifle, and it *is* a trifle, but such trifles are dear to
the lovers of literature. Were Boswell in the flesh subsequent to
the publication of *Guy Mannering,* and had his attention drawn
to such a matter, slight as it seems, what a delightful chapter of
gossip he could write about it, with fresh reminiscences of his long
and intimate intercourse with his "illustrious friend," for whom
till his dying day he cherished so much veneration and awe, ever-
more mingled with most pardonable pride that he knew him as no
one else knew him, and loved him as no one else loved him, or
perhaps could love him.

We have just been reading our friend Professor Blackie's poem
on "Glencoe." The manner in which he "goes at" his subject, to
use a sporting phrase, the life, and vigour, and *swing,* and fervour
of the whole, is most refreshing in these days of poetical (save the
mark!) namby-pambyisms, and eminently characteristic of the
learned Professor when at his best. Here you have him, like a
knight of the Middle Ages, high in his stirrups, with lance in rest,
"*Dh'aindeoin co theireadh e!*" blazing on his shield, and who
shall dare to stop his fierce career against the perpetrators of the
foulest deed on record? Less polished and less artistic than
Aytoun's "Widow of Glencoe," it is, nevertheless, the better
poem, *on such a subject,* of the two. Its very ruggedness and stern
headlong force are its chief charm, they best befit the theme.
Blackie is terribly in earnest; with Aytoun you cannot help feeling
it was a mere matter of sentiment and no more.

CHAPTER VII.

DURING a week's pleasant and gentle thaw [February 1870], we had
hoped that the worst of winter was come and gone; but to our no
small disappointment the genial interregnum has been followed by
another heavy fall of snow, and a wonderfully keen and biting frost,
which, borne on the wings of a surly nor'easter, has again bound up
the earth as if with fetters of iron. Under such circumstances the
sea-coast, we take it, presents the most dreary and desolate-looking
winter picture imaginable; far more so, to our thinking, than either
moss, or moorland, or mountain range. There is a something inexpressibly dismal and *dowie* in the black crape-like belt of sea
beach which divides a landscape deeply clad with snow and frost-
bound, from the dull and leaden coloured deep beyond; the dashing
of the waves of said deep upon the shore, uttering the while a
sadly funereal and dirge-like moan. If our inland friends, in view
of the wintry waste around *them*, take up the cry of "O the dreary,
dreary moorland"—we, dwellers by the sea coast, have the best
possible right to finish the Tennysonian line by exclaiming "O the
barren, barren shore." It must, by the way, have been on some
fair *summer* eve that the Crown officials first thought of depriving
landowners of the sea-shore privileges hitherto enjoyed by them;
had it been in *winter*, the idea, it strikes us, would have withered
in the bud; they would have fled the very sight of the dark and
dreary "foreshore," and wisely confined themselves to the shelter
of their Woods and Forests!

It is worthy of record that the present severe snow-storm was ushered in by a very splendid and in many respects peculiar auroral display. Shortly after dark on Friday evening, a faint auroral film, over which an occasional streamer flashed impetuously, overspread the northern heavens. All this, however, soon died away, and the north assumed a cold, clear, frosty aspect. Between seven and eight o'clock many meteors, some of them of great brilliancy and beauty, were observed to cross and recross the zenith and its neighbourhood in all directions. Towards the latter hour, however, these ceased, and all of a sudden, in a very few seconds at most, the whole celestial hemisphere from E.N.E. to W.S.W.—from horizon to horizon—appeared completely spanned by a magnificent auroral arch, eight degrees in breadth ; like a glorious bridge of a single semi-circular span, with its edges or parapets of a deep blood-red colour, and its centre part or roadway of frosted silver ; the rest of the heavens, in all directions, being the while of an inky blue, and cold and cloudless, without the slightest appearance of anything like streamers to be seen anywhere. Some idea of the brilliancy of this auroral arch may be formed from the fact that such bright stars as Arcturus, Castor and Pollux, Aldebaran, Mars, and others, which lay along its path, became quite dim, and when located near the centre and brightest part of the stream, almost invisible. Even Venus, which once or twice was overlapped for a few minutes by the arch's margin only, lost all its lustre and sheen, and had a burdened anxious aspect, as if the forehead and " face divine " of a mighty intelligence laboured under the shade of deep and profound thought. For upwards of an hour did this splendid auroral arch continue to span the heavens from horizon to horizon, and undergoing little or no change, until its final disappearance, by what seemed a process of gradual contraction into itself and towards its terminus in the east-north-east, whence it started. Such was the very singular meteoric phenomena by which a severe snow-storm and an amount of cold almost unparalleled in its intensity was ushered in on the western sea-board of Scotland in February of the year of grace 1870.

And how fares it with our feathered favourites, the wild birds, in these hard times? Fertile as they are in resources, and indefatigable in providing for the wants of the passing hour, all their little shifts must frequently prove inadequate to the supply of their daily wants in such trying times as these. St. Valentine's day has come and gone, but neither in copse, nor hedgerow, nor ivy-mantled wall, find we as yet any traces of nidification, nor has the love-prompted warble, in past years so loud and incessant at this season, been yet heard around us. The robin only cheeps; the sparrow simply chirps; the linnet merely twitters; and even the "gay chaffinch" can only give us a disconsolate "fink, fink," in place of his well-known glad burst of choicest and cheeriest song. The mellow chaunt of the merle and song-thrush delights not yet the ear from copse or brake at early morn or evening-tide. The intense and piercing cold, which, on the wings of the northern blast, sweeps over the land as we write, and as it moans, and sighs, and wildly shrieks by starts in its progress over the deep, causes the lone sea-bird to utter its eeriest and wildest cry, has succeeded in freezing, not only the rivulet and the pool, but has actually bound up the voice of gladness and every source of joyful utterance in all our feathered friends as well. But "*nil desperandum,*" better times are coming. Fields will yet be green, trees will yet be leafy, rivers unbound from icy fetters will yet dance merrily in the sun, and laugh with all their ripples, as they hasten seawards; and then "again shall flowers appear on the earth; the time of the singing of birds shall have come, and the voice of the turtle be heard in our land."

Are glanders incurable? is a very ugly, but doubtless a very important question, which is being at present keenly discussed in the columns of several metropolitan journals. By *glanders* is meant, not the equine disease in the equine subject properly so called, and which comes so frequently under the treatment of the veterinary surgeon, but the same frightful disease when introduced either by accident or design into the *human system.*   Is *it* curable ? This is the question, and the general impression seems to be, that when it once fairly lays hold of the human system, it is, like hydrophobia, quite and utterly incurable.   We do not pretend to know anything of the subject, and we allude to it merely to say that we well recollect of hearing, on undoubted authority, of a patient who was actually cured of glanders, caught, if we remember rightly, from eating some beans found in a manger in which a horse having the disease had recently been feeding.   All the circumstances connected with the case and cure were related in our hearing by the late Dr. John Reid, Professor of Anatomy in the University of St. Andrews, one evening that we dined at his house during our attendance at the University.   It is now some eighteen or twenty years ago, and we were then too young and thoughtless to give that attention to the subject which it deserved. We recollect, however, that the case was said to have occurred in Edinburgh, and to have been treated in the infirmary of that city, and that the patient, on his recovery, having been found shrewd, intelligent, and steady, was afterwards appointed one of the janitors of that institution.   There must be some medical gentleman still in Edinburgh able to speak to a case of such importance ; and amongst others present on the occasion that we heard Professor Reid refer to it, were, if we rightly remember, Principal Sir David Brewster and Professor Martin, now of Aberdeen, and at that time Mathematical Master in the Madras College of St. Andrews.

The other evening a one pound note, which a lady friend of ours had just received by post, was handed to us, with a request that we should try and decipher some writing which was observed on the back of it. After some little trouble, we were a good deal amused to find that the writing in question really consisted of the following lines :—

> " I am a note of the British Linen ;
> I've long been kept by L. Mackinnon ;
> Where'er you go you'll find them willing
> To give for me just twenty shilling.—L. M'K."

We have no idea who this poetical L. Mackinnon is or was, but it is pretty evident, we think, that both he and the British Linen Company's Bank note had very excellent opinions of themselves. It was Lady Louisa Stewart, if we rightly recollect, who sent Sir Walter Scott a copy of the following lines, which she discovered on the back of a battered bank note which had come into her possession. It will be observed that they are in all respects immeasurably superior to Mr. L. Mackinnon's :—

> " Farewell, my note, and wheresoe'er ye wend,
> Shun gaudy scenes, and be the poor man's friend ;
> You've left a poor one ; go to one as poor,
> And drive despair and hunger from his door."

Let cynics growl and snarl as they list, some people HAVE hearts, and the author of the above lines, be sure, had a right warm and kindly one.

CHAPTER VIII.

ONE swallow doesn't make a summer, says the proverb, and unless one fine day (the 19th) makes a spring, we haven't for the last six weeks [February 1870] and more had a single hour of a character to be disassociated from one of the wettest and wildest winters on record. No sooner has one storm died away, less from any voluntary cessation on its part than from sheer exhaustion of its forces, than, after a slushy, sludgy interregnum of brief duration, it has been succeeded in every instance by another and another still of equal or greater violence and fury, so that of quiet or calm we have known little, and of sun or moon or stars we have seen hardly the briefest glimpse since Old New Year's Day. When Foote, the incomparable comedian (Johnson said of him that " the dog was irresistible "), after acquiring and dissipating several fortunes, was at last lucky enough to be able to set up his carriage in a more dashing style than ever, he selected as his motto, and emblematical of his career, the words *Iterum, Iterum, Iterumque !* (Again, and Again, and Again !) It has struck us that if the Meteorological Society were to apply to the Herald's College for a crest and armorial bearings to be displayed on the title-page of their volume of " Transactions " for the first quarter of the current year, we, should they do us the honour to consult us, would suggest a cloud-cumulus, rain-surcharged, proper on the shield, with Aquarius and the " watery " Hyades as supporters ; Eolus ordering " a fresh hand to the bellows " as a crest, and the *Iterum, Iterum, Iterumque* of Foote's chariot as a motto of singular appropriateness and meaning. How delighted, by the way, must our amphibious friend Mr. Symons be in the midst of all this rainfall! *His* crest again should be a man's head on a fish's body in an overflowed meadow, *natant*, and his supporters an *anemometer* and *rain-gauge* proper! It is needless to say that anything like spring work is with us not only in a very backward state, but has hardly been commenced. Before the end of February we had our own corn seed and potatoes in the ground last year. If we get them down this year any time during the next month, it will be earlier than the weather at the date of the present writing promises. Our ornithological studies extend over a greater number of years than we care at this moment very accurately to count; but never have we known our wild-birds so listless and loveless on Shrovetide Eve as they are this season. Except an occasional carol from the wren, who has a soul as big as that of his namesake Sir Christopher, who built the dome of St. Paul's (the wren also, by the way, is a dome-builder), and an irregular strophe at rare intervals from the redbreast, our woods are songless, and of nidification there is not a sign. *Meliora sperāre*, nevertheless, is sound philosophy. Let us hope for better things: He is faithful that promised that *while the earth remaineth, seed-time and harvest, and cold and heat, and summer and winter, and day and night, shall not cease*. Scott has few finer passages than the following, which we are fond of repeating in such a season as this. It occurs in his epistle to William Stewart Rose, introductory to the first canto of *Marmion*, and, though very beautiful, is seldom quoted :—

> " No longer Autumn's glowing red
> Upon our Forest hills is shed ;
> No more, beneath the evening beam,
> Fair Tweed reflects their purple gleam ;
> Away hath passed the heather bell
> That bloomed so rich on Needpath fell ;

Sallow his brow, and russet bare
Are now the sister-heights of Yair.
The sheep, before the pinching heaven,
To sheltered dale and down are driven,
Where yet some faded herbage pines
And yet a watery sunbeam shines :
In meek despondency they eye
The wither'd sward and wintry sky,
And far beneath their summer hill
Stray sadly by Glenkinnon's rill :
The shepherd shifts his mantle's fold,
And wraps him closer from the cold ;
His dogs no merry circles wheel,
But, shivering, follow at his heel ;
A cowering glance they often cast,
As deeper moans the gathering blast.
　" My imps, though hardy, bold, and wild,
As best befits the mountain child,
Feel the sad influence of the hour,
And wail the daisy's vanished flower ;
Their summer gambols tell, and mourn,
And anxious ask—Will spring return,
And birds and lambs again be gay,
And blossoms clothe the hawthorn spray ?
　" Yes, prattlers, yes. The daisy's flower
Again shall paint your summer bower ;
Again the hawthorn shall supply
The garlands you delight to tie ;
The lambs upon the lea shall bound,
The wild birds carol to the round ;
And while you frolic light as they,
Too short shall seem the summer day."

On her rich roll of worthies, Scotland has but few names of whom
she has more reason to be proud than that of Walter Scott. If we
had even said *not one*, an objector might perhaps find the assertion
more difficult to disprove than he wots of. Nor has the star of his
marvellous power and influence for good set or been extinguished ;
it has only been clouded for a season by the intervention of exhalations of the " earth, earthy "—exhalations that the growth of a
healthier and holier taste is already dissipating, and the Wizard's

star shall reappear in undiminished lustre, and young and old will clap their hands and rejoice in its purity and power. Some years ago arose a school of poetry that flared and flickered for a season, and found admirers on the same mysterious principle, we suppose, that Antoinetta Bourignon and Joanna Southcott found followers. It was happily styled the "spasmodic" school; and it died and disappeared—the best thing it could do. A new school has succeeded, that may be called the sensuous, and, we had almost said, the lascivious, and with a strong tendency to the reproduction in modern guise of all that was worst and best in the ancient Greek drama. Of this school, Mr. Swinburne is, *facile princeps*, the chief. It also will last but for a season, and will die and disappear ignominiously, as did its predecessor. There is yet another school, that has existed for some time longer—full of *missyism*, sentimentalism, and languid *goodyism*—"too good for banning, too bad for a blessing." *It* also is slowly dwindling, and dwining, and dying, and must soon expire, leaving people hardly any better or worse than it found them. And so with the novels of the day, with their "sensations," their seductions, murders, and unspeakable horrors, worse than were mingled in the bubbling cauldron of the witches in *Macbeth: their* day is doomed; for purer taste, banished but for a moment, must reappear—is already reappearing—and people, awakening as if from a dream, will once again consent to quench their thirst at healthier fountains, and to wander in less questionable bye-paths. The poetry and novels of Scott will then resume their attraction and reassert their influence and power; and whithersoever *he* leads, no parent need be ashamed to follow, or feel obliged in the interests of morality to forbid and forego the companionship of wife or children through scenes where there is everything to delight and nothing to offend. It is well that in the world of poetry and fiction, as in social and political affairs, the maxim holds true that—

" *Res nolunt diu male administrari.*"

Of Mr. Gladstone, the politician, there are many more enthusiastic admirers than ourselves, though we would not willingly be supposed to yield to any one in our ardent admiration of his ripe scholarship and unrivalled eloquence ; but we shall think better of him while we live, and have a kindlier and warmer interest in all he says and does, on account of his recent eulogium on the character and writings of Sir Walter Scott.

And who can speak of Scott, or think of Abbotsford and Melrose and the classic Tweed at the present moment, without also thinking of Allerly and Sir David Brewster, one of the greatest men of science that Scotland has ever produced ; and greater far, as sometimes happens in such cases, *out* of it than *in* it, for during full forty years, wherever, throughout the habitable parts of the earth, science had lit her lamp and could count her votaries, however humble, *there* the name of David Brewster was familiar as a household word, and his discoveries known and applauded. He was the first really distinguished man of letters and science we ever knew, and it was while writing one of the earlier chapters of this work, on a subject in which he felt the keenest interest, and in connection with which we had occasion to mention his name, that the grand old man, venerable in honours and in years, was breathing his last, with a Christian resignation to the Divine will, and a Christian's joyful faith in the Divine mercy and goodness. Passing through the valley of death, he feared no evil, for his Lord and Saviour sustained his steps. Through the first Lady Brewster (*née* Macpherson), to whom we had the honour of being known before we had yet seen her distinguished husband, we were fortunate enough to be admitted, at the very beginning of our curriculum at college, to a degree of familiarity with the Principal of our University, that our relative positions would not otherwise have warranted, and which we have the satisfaction to remember we had sense enough to value highly and to be proud of even at that early age. It was by his practised hand that the instrument was adjusted through which we had our first view of two of the most beautiful sights that the telescope reveals to us—Jupiter with his belts and retinue of attendant moons, and Saturn with his rings; and very patient and good-natured and kindly were his replies to our eager questionings with regard to the nature of the wonders then first opened to our gaze. Sir David, if forced into it, could fight, and never turned his back on an assailant. If you hit him, he hit again, and he always hit severely; but he was, notwithstanding, a man of kindest heart and most amiable disposition, and it would be difficult to meet with any one more cheerful or courteous or pleasant within the circle of his own family and in his daily intercourse with his acquaintances and friends. *Requiescat in pace:* he was in truth a great man. Not often does it happen that in the same country, and within so short a time of each other, two such stars so large and lustrous as Faraday and Brewster have disappeared from the firmament of science. A century may elapse ere the thrones they have left vacant shall again be adequately filled. There is something extremely beautiful and affecting in one of Sir David Brewster's last utterances upon earth. On the morning of his death, Sir James Simpson, standing by his bedside, remarked that it had been given to him to show forth much of God's great and marvellous works; and the dying philosopher solemnly and quietly replied, "Yes, I have found them to be great and marvellous, and I have found and felt them to be *His.*"

CHAPTER IX.

For several years past [March 1870] the spring fishing with "long lines" in our western lochs has been so unsuccessful as to be hardly worth the while engaging in it. At our very doors, where with the hand-line during the summer and autumn months, some ten or twelve years ago, we could almost always depend on a large basketful of the finest rock cod, gurnard, haddock, and flounder, as the result of a couple of hours fishing, more recently very few, and sometimes none at all, could be caught, with the cunningest exercise of all the patience and piscatorial skill at our command, while in winter and spring the long-line fishing of grey cod, skate, and ling, and eel has been equally disappointing. Why it should be so no one would venture to say ; the utmost you could get out of the oldest fisherman on the coast was an admission of the fact, with a shake of the head and a shrug of the shoulders, that if so disposed you could very readily interpret into the line, albeit unknown to him, that—

"'Twas true 'twas pity, pity 'twas 'twas true,"

a cautious reticence on the point that was altogether praiseworthy, for really and truly nobody did know or could say anything satisfactory in explanation of the mystery. Was it owing to the multiplication of the number of steamers, screw and paddle, constantly coming and going, and like Tennyson's "years" at their unamiable meeting, "roaring and blowing," keeping the waters in

perpetual turmoil, and scaring the fish from their usual haunts?
Such an hypothesis could be seriously entertained for a moment
only to be rejected. Could it be owing to any cyclical meteorological changes, or to anything anomalous in the order of the
seasons? Admitting that something of this kind has been going
on for some time, and is still going on, it was readily seen, nevertheless, that it was all too inappreciable and remote to have had
the result complained of—to cause that in the waters of "the
great deep" which it had failed to effect in any noticeable way on
the dry land. Or, was it that the fish themselves, by reason of
their numberless enemies, afloat and ashore, were actually diminish-
ing in numbers, and so necessarily becoming scarcer from year to
year? No one, however, knowing anything of the economy of the
fish in question, could for a moment entertain such an idea. The
fecundity of these fish is something incredible. We once had the
roe of a female cod, that weighed (the fish) six lbs., first boiled hard,
and then divided with tolerable exactness into so many ounces, and
counting the number of eggs in one ounce, and multiplying by the
number of ounces in the entire roe, we found, at a rough calcula-
tion, that in that single fish, of no great size, there were upwards
of *a million and a half* of eggs—each egg destined to become a
fish, and, barring accidents, to attain to the average age and size of
its kind. But however we may try to account for the scarcity of
these fish in our lochs for several years back, it is an agreeable
duty to have to record that during the past winter and spring there
has been a marked improvement alike in the quantity and quality
of the fish caught all along the western seaboard. Not only have
the common fish of our own coasts been taken in considerable
numbers, but several kinds of fish formerly known only as occasional
visitors to our shores have this season been plentiful in all our
lochs, and have well repaid the diligence of their captors. The
long-nosed skate, for example, formerly a rare fish with us, has this

season been common.   It is known to ichthyologists as the *Raia chagrinea*, and is not only excellent eating, but from its enormous liver supplies a large quantity of very fine oil, that burns with a clearer and steadier light than that of any other fish with which we are acquainted.   We are convinced, by the way, that, used medicinally, it would be found equally efficacious with cod liver oil in all cases where the latter is recommended, whilst its rather agreeable taste and flavour would render it a tolerably palatable dose in its purest and strongest state, which cod oil never becomes, manufacture, and decoct, and clarify it as you may.   A very fine specimen of the *Chagrinea* was caught here about ten days ago.   It was cut up and disembowelled before we saw it, but we should guess that its weight when taken off the hook could not have been less than 70 lbs.   All the skates are ugly brutes, and the long-nosed *Chagrinea* is at once perhaps the ugliest and the best of its tribe. Some people don't eat skate, nor can we say that we are partial to it ourselves, though we once heard a noted *gourmand* declare that the " wing of a skate was equal to a shoulder of a salmon."   We should, for our own part, rather have the salmon.   While in Oban about a month ago, an extremely fierce-looking and ugly fish, the name and character whereof not a little puzzled its captors, was brought for our inspection.   Luckily for our credit as a naturalist, we had previously seen more than one specimen of the same fish with the St. Andrews fishermen, it being by no means a rare visitor to the eastern and north-eastern shores of Scotland.   It was the wolf or cat-fish, closely related to the family of the Gobies (*Gobioidæ*), the *Anarrhicas lupus* of ichthyologists.   The head of this curious and most repulsive-looking fish has some peculiar markings, which, with the fierce glaring eyes and their position in the face, and the formidable array of long, sharp-pointed, recurved teeth, give it much of the expression of an enraged cat, and hence doubtless its common name.   For the same reasons, and on account probably of its character as a fierce, relentless tyrant among more amiable and less powerful fish, it is known among the Channel Islands and along the coasts of England as the *wolf*-fish. The only fish at all approaching it in ugliness and repulsiveness of features is the better-known angler or fishing-frog (*Lophius piscatorius*), which also, by the way, is not so common of late years on our western coasts as it used to be.

CHAPTER X.

Birds—Contest between a Heron and an Eel.

WITH the exception of a slight drizzle on Saturday the last ten days have been wonderfully fine for the season [February 1870]. Seldom, indeed, have we been so near realising the "ethereal mildness" of Thomson's "Spring" so early in the year. And, in sooth, it was high time that some such pleasant change in the weather should take place, for no living wight can remember anything so incessant and persistent as were the rain and the storm of the previous six weeks.

> " When frost and snow come both together,
> Then sit by the fire and save shoe leather,"

quoth Jonathan Swift, the honest Dean of St. Patrick's, being evidently no curler, and more given to satire than to snow-balling; but really for the six weeks above specified nothing less than the direst necessity could tempt one to any other pastime than the prudential and prosaic one recommended in the couplet. Grant him but license to grumble, however, and man can endure, and that scathlessly, much more than he wots of. And how easily is he after all restored to equanimity and even cheerfulness! Here we are already, placid and pleased, enjoying the fine weather; the cold and the wet and the boisterous gales of January and December altogether forgotten, or, if remembered, remembered only to give zest to the bright and sunshiny present. And never, we believe, were song-birds in such free and full song on St. Valentine's day. Morning and evening (the interval, you must know, dear reader, is as yet passed in tender dalliance and nest-building), from copse and woodland, ring out the richest strains of our native warblers, thrush, redbreast, blackbird, throstle, white-throat, wren (whom the Germans, on account of his indomitable pluck and pre-eminence as a songster, term the *kingbird*), and a score of other "musical celebrities," vie with each other in the richness and the melody of their incomparable song. Within a month, should the weather continue favourable as at present, most of our wild-birds will have finished their nests, and commenced the labours of incubation. We trust that our readers will do all they can this season to prevent children and *others* from what is called "birds'-nesting," one of the most cruel pastimes to which any one could turn himself. All good men, and most great ones, have been remarkable for their attachment to animals, both domesticated and wild, and particularly to song-birds. Listen to Virgil's passing allusion to the subject in his *Georgics*, a magnificent poem, of itself sufficient to immortalise the name of any one man :—

> " Qualis populea mœrens Philomela, sub umbra," &c.,

thus rendered into English :—

> " Lo, Philomela from the umbrageous wood,
>   In strains melodious mourns her tender brood,
>   Snatch'd from the nest by some rude ploughman's hand,
>   On some lone bough the warbler takes her stand ;
>   The live-long night she mourns the cruel wrong,
>   And hill and dale resound the plaintive song."

And hear our own matchless "ploughman bard," in one of his sweetest lyrics, *The Posie* :—

> " The hawthorn I will pu', wi' its locks o' siller grey,
>   Where, like an aged man, it stands at break o' day,
>   *But the songster's nest within the bush I winna tak away—*
>   And a' to be a posie to my ain dear May."

Verily, dear reader, he who wrote *that* verse, despite the pious murmurings of the rigidly righteous, and the cold shudderings of religious fanaticism at his shortcomings, must have been a man of largest heart and widest sympathies; and, properly understood, there is much truth, and no irreverence, in his own finding, that even

> " The light which led astray
> Was light from heaven."

We were much amused the other day at seeing a heron, a long-necked, long-legged bird, doubtless familiar to the reader, for once in a "fix." We say "for once," for it is a most sagacious bird and thoroughly master of its own particular *rôle*, which, it is needless to say, is principally fish-catching. We were amusing ourselves on the sea-shore during low-water, watching the habits of periwinkles, hermit-crabs, star-fish, &c., when we observed a heron at some hundred yards distance, leaping about, wriggling its body, and performing other strange and unheron-like antics, as if it had suddenly gone mad. Knowing the staid and sober habits of the bird in general, we at once came to the conclusion that something extraordinary "was up," and determined, if possible, to discover what it was. Making a slight *détour* to avoid alarming him—for it was a *he*, a very handsome, full-crested male—we easily managed to creep within fifty yards or so of him, and the cause of his excitement and unwonted posturings became at once apparent. He had caught an eel (a great dainty with the heron family) of about two feet in length, and of girth like a stout walking-stick, notwithstanding which, however, Mr. Heron would soon have satisfactorily dined upon it, had he not made a slight mistake in the mode of striking his prey. The eel was held in the heron's bill at a point only some three or four inches from the extremity of its tail, the greater part of its body and its head being thus left at liberty to twist, and wriggle, and wallop about *ad libitum*. To swallow the eel in this position the heron knew was impossible, and to let it go, even for an instant, for the purpose of getting a better "grip" of his slippery customer was altogether out of the question. The heron was standing on the very margin of the sea, into which the eel, if for a moment at liberty, would have shot like an arrow. It was too large to be tossed into the air and recaught in its descent, as herons frequently do with other fish ; and in short the heron was at his wit's end, and wist not what to say or do. To make matters worse, the eel was wriggling and twisting about its captor's legs, *breechless and exposed legs* be it observed, and might, for all we or the heron knew, take one of them at any time between its teeth, and sharp and cruel, as probably the heron knew, are an eel's teeth when any part of an enemy has the misfortune to get between them. Apprehensive, doubtless, of some such danger, the heron danced and shuffled about, lifting now one leg and now another, as if he had been practising a new and somewhat complicated hornpipe. He would at one time leap a foot or two to one side, and immediately after spring into the air as many inches, attempting the while to strike his prey against the stones, but always failing in doing this effectually, owing to want of sufficient "purchase" and the insecurity of his hold. Having watched this novel combat for some time, we made a rush to the scene of action, hoping to succeed in surprising, perhaps, both the spoiler and his prey. We were disappointed. The heron instantly took wing, carrying the eel for some instance in his sharp-edged and powerful bill, but finally dropping it into the sea, doubtless confessing to himself, as he indignantly winged his flight to another fishing ground, that once in his life at least he had caught a Tartar.

CHAPTER XI.

THOUGH by no means everything that we could wish it, the weather
of the last fortnight [July 1870] was a decided improvement on
that of the preceding, and people have managed to get their hay
secured in tolerably good condition after all. No appearance of
the much-dreaded potato blight as yet; pity that it should show its
unwished-for face this year at all, for a finer crop never lay ripening
in the ground. Something has been done in herring fishing, and
there is some prospect of our having enough for local consumption
at all events, and perhaps a little over, which is no small matter in
those dear times. Other kinds of fish are plentiful, and, with
sufficient leisure for the pastime, there is hardly anything of the
kind more enjoyable in fine weather than an afternoon's or early
morning's fishing with rod or hand-line. You never, besides, see
the country so well as on these occasions, or so thoroughly understand the full force of the poet's beautiful line, that in such scenes

" 'Tis distance lends enchantment to the view."

Any number of trout, too—few of them, however, of any size—may
be caught at present in our inland lochs and mountain streams, and
a dish of these speckled beauties, fresh from the basket, is a very
good thing indeed, though the grilse and salmon eater may turn up
his nose in contempt and derision of such "small deer." Let him;
we shall be always prepared to take over *his* share along with our
own! A curious request was made to us a short time ago by a

well-known book "deliverer," who frequently passes this way, one
of the keenest and most successful fishers on lake or river we ever
knew, and a very quiet decent man to boot.   " Will you allow me,
sir, to put down some worms in your place ?"   " To put down
what ?" we exclaimed in surprise.   " Worms, sir, brindled worms
for fishing with, when the rivers are swollen after heavy rains."
We begged to have a look at the worms, and they proved to be a
variety of the common earthworm that we had never seen before,
the difference consisting in their being rather smaller in size than
the common earthworm, and prettily speckled and streaked all over
their length, whence, doubtless, their name of *brindled* worms.   A
lot had been sent to him from Alyth, in Perthshire, very cunningly
done up in a bunch of damp moss ; and, having a few left over after
a week's most successful fishing, he wished to deposit them in this,
a central part of his peregrinations, that they might multiply and
be recoverable at any time he wanted them.   Holding one by the
middle, between index finger and thumb, in a manner that would
have delighted the heart of old Izaak Walton, the worm wriggling
and twisting the while with all the liveliness of an eel in similar
circumstances, " There, sir," he exclaimed, looking at the lively
" brindled " as if he loved it, " there, sir, is a bonny ane ! no trout
that ever swam could resist having a dash at *that* in a brown and
swollen stream."   In answer to our questions, he told us that the
brindled colour of the worm had, he thought, a good deal to do
with the trout's liking for it, but, in his opinion, the brisk and
lively motions of the worm upon the hook was the main attraction.
The thing was so manifestly *alive* and active, and likely to escape,
if not caught at once, that the trout made a rush at it, with his eyes
shut, so to speak, and only discovered how thoroughly he had been
done, when, hooked and landed, he lay flopping helplessly about on
the green grass by the burn side.   Getting piscator a spade, he
searched about for a suitable spot, and buried his worms beneath

the turf as tenderly as if he were laying babies asleep in their cradles. "There now, sir," he remarked, as he finished his colonising, "they will breed fast, and soon be plentiful enough hereabouts, and they will destroy the common earthworm till not one can be found." So that you see we had an interesting lesson on bait angling and the natural history of earthworms very unexpectedly from a very unexpected quarter. We still watch with interest if the assertion turns out to be true, that the brindled worm exterminates the common earthworm, notwithstanding their close relationship. Such a thing we know is quite possible, a notable case in point being the extermination of the old well-known black rat by the more modern coloniser, the brown.

The amount of *viva voce* information that one can pick up, not by going actually to look for it, but in the most casual and incidental manner, from all sorts of people with whom one may be brought in contact, is simply extraordinary. Some, to be sure, will have nothing to tell; they are as Dead Sea fruit, full of mere ashes, that never had sap or substance for good to themselves or anybody else. Others, again, may know much, but they are cautious and reserved, and never venture beyond the most superficial and commonplace *chit-chat;* but the great mass of people, if you approach them courteously and frankly, will be found communicative enough, and if you go deftly about it, you seldom work long in such mines without bringing some ore to the surface. A day or two ago, for instance, we were sitting on a rock by the roadside on the opposite shore of Appin, having rowed ashore from our fishing ground to have a smoke and a drink of sparkling water from one of the many rivulets that, like so many silver threads in some rich embroidery, twist and twine with a glad music of their own adown the green slopes of Benavere. An old man passing along the way, with a bundle of rushes under his arm, saluted us with the quiet and undemonstrative courtesy so characteristic of his class all over

the Highlands. We invited him to sit down beside us, and at once
he sat down and entered into conversation with us about the
weather, crops, fishing, and other such obvious matters as are
seldom overlooked during the first five minutes of a roadside crack
at this season. By-and-by we asked him about the bundle of
rushes. There were too few of them to be of any use as thatch,
and we observed that they were not of the kind generally used
in basket-making—a common amusement for the idle hours of
shepherds, herdboys, and others in the past generation, who made
very pretty rush baskets for carrying eggs, butter, and other such
light goods to the nearest shop, and bringing back the tea, sugar,
&c., usually taken in exchange. What were his rushes for then?
He gathered them, he told us, from time to time, always selecting
the largest and best, for the sake of their *pith*, which served as wick
for his lamp; and he showed us the process of extracting the pith
on the spot. He first split the rush longitudinally, by running his
thumb-nail along its length, and then pressing his thumb trans-
versely against the pith, he ran it along until the whole beautifully
soft and white substance was gathered into a bundle free of its skin,
the pith still remaining unbroken by the deftness of the process,
and easily extended at will to its original length. This pith is
inserted in the same manner as wick in the lamp, and answers its
purpose admirably. We recollect seeing the thing before, but it is
many years since, and we had thought that cotton had everywhere,
even in the remotest parts of the Highlands, long since superseded
the primitive rush pith as wick for lamps. "All the people about
me," said the old man, "now use paraffin lamps and cotton wicks,
but although perhaps I could afford these as well as they can, I
prefer the good old rush-light of my boyhood. I remember," he
continued, "when all the people in our hamlet gave a day's work
to the tenant of the adjoining farm for leave to gather rushes for
their lamps in the proper season. Fish oil of our own manufacture

was always used, and you will perhaps be surprised to hear, sir,
that the lamp was often a "*buckie shell.*"   "A buckie shell!" we
exclaimed, "how did you manage to fix it properly?   You probably
glued its keel to a piece of wood or something of that kind?"
"No, sir," was the response, "we did not fix it at all.   It was
suspended from a *cromag* or hook of wood or iron projecting from
the wall near the fire-place by a string, one end of which was
firmly tied round the hollow dividing the whorl at the smaller end
of the shell, and the other round the furrow at its larger circumference near the lip.   The loop of the string was then thrown over
the hook, and thus suspended, the shell was filled with oil and a
rush pith inserted as wick, and it made a very good lamp indeed, at
once economical and serviceable.   I recollect," said the old man
with a smile, "that my father, God rest him! who was a very
economical man, and hated everything like extravagance or waste,
allowed us just a shellful of oil for the winter's night.   When that
much was spent, we had to tell our tales, sing our songs, and go on
with the work we might have in hand by such light as was afforded
by the blazing peat-fire, or let it alone till the next evening, just as
we pleased."   Our friend concluded by declaring in very emphatic
phrase that "the people now are less industrious than they were
then; have more money in their hands, but use it less wisely; are
less truthful, less honest, less to be depended upon in every way
than were the people of his boyhood and their immediate pre-
decessors."   "*Laudator temporis acti,*" but there is some truth in
it.   You should have heard how grandly and with what an air of
dignity the old fellow spoke that concluding sentence in the most
beautiful and rhythmical Gaelic.   The *buckie* shell referred to above
is the *Buccinum undatum,* or common *whelk,* constantly to be met
with on almost every shore.   It is to be understood, we suppose,
that the larger specimens only would be used as lamps in the
manner described by our venerable friend.

Of British quadrupeds—perhaps of all existing quadrupeds—the pluckiest, and, according to its size and weight, by far the strongest, is the common weasel (*Mustela vulgaris*). The other day a man in our neighbourhood brought us a common brown hare, large and in excellent condition, that had been hunted and killed by a weasel in a very extraordinary manner. In the evening the man was going up a green glade on the wooded hill-side in search of his cows, when he heard what he took to be the screaming of a child on the other side of a small hazel copse which he was passing at the moment. Supposing it to be a child searching for cows like himself, that had fallen and hurt itself, or that had perhaps been attacked by some stirk or quey, angry at being disturbed in a favourite bit of grazing ground, he ran forward, and hearing the screaming repeated, was astonished to find that it proceeded from a hare that toilsomely and with staggering steps was struggling up the steep. On closer inspection, about which there was no difficulty, for by this time the poor hare was, in race-course phrase, about " pumped out," and could barely stagger along, he was more than astonished to observe that a weasel was extended *couchant* along the hare's back, with his muzzle deeply sunk into the vertebræ of his victim's neck, a position from which no exertion on the hare's part could possibly dislodge him. Picking up a stone, the man rushed forward and threw it with all his might, not so much at the hare as at its lithe and blood-thirsty rider. The hare, however, was hit, and fell, and with a gasp or two was dead ; less from the blow than from the terrible injuries inflicted by the weasel's teeth, from which, under any circumstances, it was impossible that the poor animal could have recovered. Before the man and a dog which accompanied him could get at the wary weasel, it had with proverbial agility made good its escape. On examining the hare, we found that it was in truth dreadfully wounded, the ruthless *Mustela* having manifestly gone to work in a very scientific manner, the little red-eyed wretch's motto being "Thorough!" Once fairly on the back of his victim, he anchored himself firmly by his teeth right in the centre of the nape of the neck, just where the head is articulated to the cervical vertebræ; and as no exertion of the hare could shake him off, he leisurely dug down, drinking the blood and eating as he dug, until the poor hare, faint and exhausted, could only stagger about in response to each cruel dig of the dental spurs of its terrible rider. That a creature so diminutive—weighing only about as many ounces as a hare weighs pounds—should be able thus to mount and master an animal so much bigger than itself, seems extraordinary, and is only to be accounted for by a lithe agility in the assailant, to be met with in no other creature perhaps, coupled with indomitable courage and instinctive blood-thirstiness. We recollect some years ago that an old man, a James Cameron, belonging to Achintore, near Fort-William, was savagely assaulted by a colony of weasels, and very severely wounded before he could get rid of his assailants. He was employed by a neighbour to remove a cairn of small stones from a grass field, in which it had long been an eyesore, from the centre of which cairn, when he had wheeled away several barrows-full, six or seven weasels rushed out and attacked him. So sudden and unexpected was the attack, that before he could do anything to defend himself, his hands and chin and cheeks—for they instinctively flew at his throat, which was luckily guarded by the thick folds of a homespun cravat—were severely bitten. One or two he killed by taking them in his hands, dashing them to the ground, and trampling them under his feet; but the others stuck to him with the pertinacity and viciousness of angry bees, and it was only by running into a house that was at hand, for aid and protection, that they ceased their attack and left him. Happening to be in Fort-William that day, we recollect examining the man's wounds, and getting the story of the weasel assault from his own lips. We remember remarking how astonishingly deep and formidable were the wounds, to be made by the comparatively small teeth, short though sharp, of the weasel ; and what was worse, they festered again and again, and gave the man much pain and trouble ere they fully healed up and disappeared. An old gamekeeper tells us that he once saw a fallow deer fawn, upwards of six weeks old, killed by a weasel in one of the Callart parks precisely as this hare was killed, and a fawn at that age will weigh three times as much as a brown hare in ordinary condition. In common with most people, we have rather a dislike to the weasel, though one cannot but view with respect the courage and pluck that carry him safely through such exploits as these.

CHAPTER XII.

WE have just had a week of the finest weather imaginable, dry, bright and breezy, and with uninterrupted sunshine. The greater part of our hay crop has, in consequence, been secured in splendid condition, without a drop of rain, in fact—a piece of rare good fortune in Lochaber. We do not know if the extraordinary aspect of the sun at its rising and setting on Monday, the 13th instant [June 1870], was noticed elsewhere by any of our readers. On the morning of the day in question it presented a strangely mottled, yellowish copper-coloured disc, so singularly unusual as to induce an old seaman, nearly eighty years of age, in our neighbourhood, to call our attention to the circumstance. In the evening a little before its setting, it assumed a lurid blood-red colour, which was very remarkable, and forcibly reminded us at the moment of Scott's lines in *Rokeby*—

> " No pale gradations quench his ray,
> No twilight dews his wrath allay ;
> With disc like battle-target red,
> He rushes to his burning bed,
> Dyes the wide wave with bloody light,
> Then sinks at once—and all is night."

We were unanimous in predicting an immediate and violent storm of wind and rain, but the next morning came in bright, breezy, and cloudless, and such it has continued ever since. Such phenomena, and the nature of the weather following them, are always worth recording. Virgil, in his first *Georgic* instructs the husbandman to confide in those indications of the weather afforded by the aspect of the sun, for the rather curious reason, however, that the obscuration of the solar orb gave faithful warning of the impending fate of Cæsar ! A very striking instance of a form of sophism, well known to the logician, in which an accidental circumstance is assumed as sufficient to establish efficient connection. On the morning of Wednesday last we had a smart touch of frost here in exposed situations—a strange and anomalous phenomenon in the dog-days truly ! But when we remember that Mr. Glaisher (who *for purely scientific purposes* has put his life into greater peril than any other living man), in his recent aerial ascent met with a regular snow-storm at the elevation of only about one mile above the earth's surface, we shall not wonder so much, perhaps, that a frost current should, under certain circumstances, occasionally penetrate earthwards even in the dog-days. We should have stated above that on the 13th we carefully examined the solar disc with an excellent four-feet telescope belonging to Ardgour, when it presented only two "spots" or *maculæ*, and neither of these of remarkable size or form, situated close together on the orb's south-western limb.

We are are glad to observe that the " Demoiselle " or Numidian crane recently shot at Deerness has been preserved, and is to fall into careful keeping. Its feeding on oats, however, is very extraordinary, and only to be accounted for by the supposition that its natural food was so scarce in a locality so unlike its own sunny clime, that it was fain to fill its crop with the readiest possible edible that presented itself. The *snowy owl*, a specimen of which is stated to have been recently shot in Sutherland, is by no means a rare visitor in Britain. A pair, male and female, in full plumage, were shot on the links of St. Andrews, by Captain Dempster, of the Indian Army, in the winter of 1847, and are now, we believe, to be seen in the University museum of that city. They have been known to breed in Shetland, but never, so far as we are aware, on the mainland, or anywhere, indeed, farther south than 59° or 60° of latitude. Is the specimen in Mr. M'Leay's possession male or female? What is the colour of its plumage—pure white, or slightly barred and mottled with brown? These are important questions, and every account of such rare visitors should be as minute in such particulars as possible. The snowy owl, like the Arctic fox, hare, ermine, &c., his supposed to cange its plumage with the season, the immaculate white of its winter dress being exchanged for a summer garb of mixed, spotted, and barred brown and white. It is highly important that such a point as this should be decided. The scientific name given it—*Surna nyctea*—is incorrect. It is probably a misprint for *Strix nyctea*, so styled by Linnæus, and after him continued as most appropriate by succeeding naturalists without exception. In Sweden, where it breeds and is very common, it is said to feed principally upon hares, hence Buffon calls it *La Chouette Harfang*, the latter word being the Swedish for the white or Alpine hare. It was the French naturalists, also, who first gave the name *Demoiselle* to the Numidian crane, its symmetry of form, tasteful disposition of plumage, and elegance of deportment, in their opinion, fully justifying the complimentary appellation. Its economy was first carefully studied, and a correct description of it given, about the beginning of the present century by the naturalists who accompanied the French expedition to Egypt under Napoleon, who, whatever his faults were, was at least neither indifferent to, nor neglectful of, the interests of the arts and sciences. Does the *fieldfare* breed in Scotland? We are afraid the reply must still be in the negative. We have little doubt that the bird seen by Mr. Fraser of Hamilton was the missel-thrush, and that the nest and egg in his possession belong to the same bird, that is, the *Turdus vixivorus*, and not to

its congener the *Turdus pilaris.* We are led to this opinion by
the fact that the female missel-thrush is very like the fieldfare in
plumage, and not very noticeably different in size. The nest
referred to by Mr. Fraser was, he says, situated in the fork of a
tree, about fourteen feet from the ground, *exactly about the height
the throstle generally fixes upon for its nest,* whereas, according to
our best authorities, the fieldfare builds at the top, or very near " the
top of the tallest pines." We give but little weight to the shape
and markings of the egg as described, for it frequently happens
that the eggs of different birds, even of the same species, differ in
a very remarkable manner. The hint, however, that the fieldfare
may sometimes breed in Scotland is worth attending to, and we
have marked it down for future inquiry and investigation. It was
for long a question of fierce debate whether or not the well-known
woodcock bred in this country. The matter has, however, been of
late years completely set at rest by the researches of naturalists,
clearly bringing out the fact that it not only breeds in Scotland,
but that such an event, instead of being rare, is, on the contrary,
of comparatively frequent occurrence. This very season, about the
middle of May, one of Ardgour's keepers brought us the wings of
a young woodcock, with the quill feathers still pulpy and soft,
which, of the original bird, was all he could secure from the clutches
of a hawk that was breakfasting on the dainty morsel in the woods
of Coirrechadrachan. We also understand that at least two woodcock's nests, with eggs in them, were known to some parties in
this neighbourhood at the beginning of the season. It is, therefore,
possible that the fieldfare may yet be proved to breed in Scotland,
but the evidence for the establishment of such a fact must be much
stronger than that brought forward by Mr. Fraser.

CHAPTER XIII.

IF of late we had to admit—somewhat reluctantly be it confessed—that it was " wet, *very* wet," even for Lochaber, we have
it in our power now at length [1st August 1870] to strike a
different key-note, and to say that it is dry, *very* dry; bright, *very*
bright; hot, *very* hot,—so dry, bright, and hot, in fact, that one
might as well be on the banks of the Nile or Niger as on the
shores of Loch Leven, were it not for a delightful sea breeze that
never fails to come to cheer and gladden us evening and morning;
and *then* you may fancy—that is, if you can swim, dear reader—
the unspeakable delight of a headlong plunge into the cool and
sparkling waters of the advancing tide ! The heat is in truth something extraordinary, and if it weren't that you felt yourself fast
retrograding into the same condition, it would be an amusing study
to watch a certain class of people, generally the most staid and stiff
and correct possible, who, as a rule, would rather die than violate
the least of the proprieties, now going about in a semi-nude state,
as if they had just escaped from a lunatic asylum, panting the while
as if they were in the last stage of asthma, and streaming with
perspiration as if they had resolutely made up their minds to melt
away and dissolve like untimely snowballs.

Crops everywhere are splendid, and, after all the rain of the
earlier part of the season, which gave them *growth*, this is just the
weather that suits them in their present stage, strengthening and
consolidating their tissues, and bringing them to a rapid and healthy

maturity. The meadow hay crop is unusually heavy everywhere. We saw a field belonging to Mr. Maclean of Argdour in the act of being cut the other day, and we never saw anything finer or heavier fall before a scythe. This is precisely the weather for securing such a heavy swathe in good order, although one cannot but feel for the poor scythesman, who, brown as an Indian and bathed in sweat, wields his glittering weapon under a burning, blazing sun, such as at a pinch might serve the turn of our cousins of Jamaica or Demerara. Some idea of the extraordinary heat and drought of the past week may be gathered from the fact that it was frequently found possible to stack or carry into the barn in one day the hay that had only been cut on the day previous—something hitherto unheard-of, we should say, in Lochaber, or, indeed, in any part of the Highlands.

We cannot recollect having ever before seen all kinds of fungi so plentiful as they are throughout Lochaber this season. You meet mushrooms of all sizes and of all shapes, both edible and poisonous ; while fairy rings are so common that you may encounter one or more of them in every bit of old pasture and in every greenwood glade. One of these rings we had the curiosity to measure a few days ago, and we found its diameter to be precisely fifteen feet, giving it a circumference of upwards of fifty feet, as nearly as possible a a perfect circle, the emerald outline, studded with its peculiar pretty white, button-like *Agaraci*, amid the lighter green of the surrounding herbage, as distinct and easily traceable, even at several hundred yards distance, as ever was halo round the moon. We noticed that a cow, happening to come the way while we were examining another of these fairy rings, ate them all with evident relish, browsing so steadily along and around, that when she completed the circle she had not left a single one. We hope that they agreed with her, though we should not like to have joined in the repast, for we have a salutary horror of the whole mushroom tribe. The so-called edible mushroom is said to be delicious when properly cooked : should it ever in any form be a dish on a table at which we are seated, we promise to give our share of it, *totus, teres atque rotundus,* whole and unimpaired, to the first that will accept it. To the present intense heat, coming so suddenly on the back of long-continued rains, is probably due the extraordinary abundance of all kinds of fungi.

The shoal of whales at present disporting themselves in Lochiel, intending probably, tourist fashion, to visit Inverness by-and-by, *via* the Caledonian Canal, if they can only arrange it with the authorities, did us the honour to visit Loch Leven, spending an entire day with us, evidently very much to their own satisfaction, if one might judge from their lively somersaultings and incessant gambollings. These whales —a shoal of some five or six hundred, we should say—were a very interesting sight as they gambolled about within a hundred yards of us, blowing loudly the while and lashing the sea with foam, until you might have heard the hurly-burly from the top of the highest mountain in the neighbourhood. They were of all sizes, from full growth, and old age perhaps, down to veriest babyhood. In the shoal, two kinds of whale were mingled together in apparent amity and good-fellowship : the common bottlenose (*Balænoptera acuto-rostrata* of La Cèpede—the highest authority on cetaceous animals), measuring some twenty or twenty-five feet in length, and the broad-nosed or rorqual whale (*Balæna musculus,* Linn. ; *B. rorqual,* La Cèpede), from fifty to sixty feet in length, and appearing beside a bottlenose, as they came to the surface to breathe, like a Clydesdale horse beside a Shetland pony. It will be strange if our friends at Fort-William do not manage to bag some of them ere they repass the narrows at Corran Ferry.

The heat is oppressive within doors ; but Loch Leven, we observe, is darkening under a rippling breeze from the south-east, and we are off for a sail in our tidy, little craft, that, with lugsail sheeted home, will go to windward of anything of equal size on the coast.

CHAPTER XIV.

Herrings—*Chimæra Monstrosa*—Cure for Ringworm—Cold Tea Leaves for inflamed and blood-shot Eyes—An old Incantation for the cure of Sore Eyes—A curious Dirk Sheath—A Tannery of Human Skins.

HOWEVER unproductive the herring fishing season may be *quoad* herrings, and this has so far been the worst of a series of bad seasons [September 1870], it rarely fails to provide more or less grist for our mill in the shape of some rarity in marine life worth chronicling. A very ugly and repulsive-looking fish, extremely rare too, was sent us recently for identification. It was caught in Sallachan Bay, in our neighbourhood, having become entangled in the corner of a drift net which the fishermen were hauling into their boat in the grey morning, after a long, wearisome, and profitless night's labours. We had seen the fish before, though not often, and had therefore no hesitation in recognising it as the *Chimæra monstrosa*—a scientific name, by the way in which its lack of beauty is plainly enough indicated—a cartilaginous fish, two feet in length, and of somewhat elongated and hake-like form. The general colour is a dull leaden white, mottled on the under parts with small spots of rusty brown. On examining the contents of the stomach, they were found to consist of some very small herring fry, along with partly digested fragments of the adult fish, whence it may be concluded that the *Chimæra's* favourite prey, when they can be had, is herring; a conclusion at which we might also easily arrive from the fact that it is seldom or never met with on our shores, except when herring are more or less plentiful. At one time the *Chimæra* must have been a less rare fish than it is now, for it has a Gaelic name, "*Buachaille-an-Sgadain*," the Herring Herd or Herdsman. It was probably comparatively common in the good old times, when even our more inland western lochs swarmed annually with herring shoals, and so large was the capture, that the salt to cure them, on which there was a considerable duty at the time, was frequently retailed over a vessel's side at a shilling the lippy. The late Colonel Maclean of Ardgour, who attained a great age, with intellect clear and unimpaired, and who was most particular and exact in all his statistics, has repeatedly assured us that, in his younger days, say a hundred years ago, *fifty thousand pounds* worth of herring used to be captured annually in Lochiel alone. We don't suppose that for many years past herring to the value of a tenth of that sum have been caught in all the lochs between the Mull of Cantyre and the Point of Ardnamurchan.

The reader probably knows what *ringworm* is—a fungoid eruption on the skin, not uncommon in the spring and early summer in children and young people of plethoric habits. There is a very wide-spread belief over the West Highlands and in the Hebrides that ringworm can be readily cured by rubbing it over and around once or twice with a gold-ring—a woman's marriage ring, if it can be had, being always preferred. In our younger days we recollect seeing the cure applied on more than one occasion, whether with the desired result, or ineffectually, we do not know—we probably little thought in those days of kilts, *cammanachd*, and barley bannocks, of inquiring. For many years we had neither seen nor heard anything either of the disease or of its popular cure, until, by the merest accident, it came under our notice a few days ago. Riding home one evening last week, we observed two little girls and a sturdy long-legged *haflin* lad sitting patiently in front of a cottage, the door of which was shut and locked. The youngsters, rather better dressed than usual, had come from a considerable distance, and we wondered what they could be doing there. On mentioning the matter next day, we had the story in full as follows :—The three were suffering from ringworm. The owner of the cottage has a marriage ring of wonderful efficacy in curing this epidermic distemper. They had come from one of the inland glens to be operated upon, but the possessor of the ring was away in Glasgow, and only returned home by steamer late that evening. When she did arrive, the young people were duly manipulated and ring-rubbed *secundum artem ;* and in four and twenty hours thereafter we were gravely assured they were quite healed. Any gold ring is usually employed, but the particular ring referred to in this case is much sought after on such occasions, because, as our informant said, it is of "guinea gold," by which we suppose very pure gold, with the least possible alloy, is meant ; and because it is the property of a widow who was married to one husband more than fifty years. A belief in the virtue of gold rings in cures of ringworm is, as we have said, very wide-spread and honestly held by many. Whether, in common phrase, there is "anything in it," or the whole affair is sheer nonsense, we shall not take it upon us to decide. We merely submit a common and curious article of popular belief for the consideration of our grave and learned dermatologists and the faculty at large. One thing is certain,—the owner of the marvellous ring makes no vulgar profit by her frequent use of it in such cases. She is in comfortable circumstances, and the whole affair, as far as she is concerned, is a mere labour of love.

Another popular cure, which for the first time came under our notice recently, and which in many cases is really efficacious, as we have heard averred by those who have been benefited by its use, is the application of a poultice of *cold tea leaves* to an inflamed or blood-shot eye. A handful of the leaves is taken from the pot, and placed between two folds of thin cotton or muslin, and applied to the eye at bed-time, kept in its place, of course, by a handkerchief or other band tied round the head. In cases of weak or inflamed eyes from any cause, this is reckoned, in this and the surrounding districts, "the sovereignest thing on earth." And one can quite understand how tea leaves, at once cooling and astringent, employed in this way, may benefit a hot and inflamed eye. It is a simple application at all events, and always at hand ; and when more pretentious remedies are not readily attainable, one would be unwisely prejudiced, if not actually foolish, to suffer long without giving it a fair trial.

A less simple and less readily available cure for sore eyes is the following in old Gaelic verse :—

Leigheas Sul.

Luidh Challum-Chille agus spèir,
Meannt agus tri-bhilead corr,
Bainne atharla nach do rug laodh ;
Bruich iad a's chirich air brèid,
S'cuir sid rid' shùil aig tra-nòin,
Air an Athair, am Mac agus Spiorad nan gràs,
'S air Ostal na seirce ; bi'dh do shùilean slàn
Mu'n eirich a gheallach 's mu'n till an làn.

In English, literally—

(Take of) St. Columba's wort and dandelion,
(Of) mint and a perfect plant of marsh trefoil,
(Take of) milk from the udder of a quey
(That is heavy with calf, but that has not actually calved),
Boil, and spread the mixture on a cloth ;
Put it to your eyes at noon-tide,
In the name of Father, Son, and the Spirit of Grace,
And in the name of (John) the Apostle of Love, and your eyes
shall be well
Before the next rising of the moon, before the turning of next
flood-tide.

We were recently shown a great curiosity—a dirk sheath said to be made of human skin. Its history, as related to us by the owner, is as follows :—In the summer of 1746, about two months after the battle of Culloden, a detachment of *Saighdearan Dearge*, red (coated) soldiers, or Government troops, was passing through Lochaber and Appin on its way to Inveraray, the men amusing themselves, and enlivening the tedium of the march, by burning and plundering as they had opportunity. When passing through the Strath of Appin, a young woman was observed in a field, busily engaged in the evening milking her cow. A sergeant or corporal of the band leaped over the wall into the field, and putting his musket to his shoulder, shot the cow dead upon the spot ; after which gallant exploit he began the most brutal ill-treatment of the woman. She, however, defended herself with great courage, and as she retreated towards the shore, she picked up a stone, which she hurled at her persecutor with such good aim that it struck him full on the forehead, stretching him for the moment senseless upon the grass. She then fled towards a boat that was afloat on the beach, and leaping in, rapidly rowed towards *Eilean-bhaile-na-gobhar*, an island at a considerable distance from the mainland, where she was safe from further annoyance. The tradition is so minute and precise that the heroine's name is given as *Silas-Nic-Cholla*, or Julia MacColl ; and our informant declared himself to be her great-grandson. The sergeant, stunned and bleeding, was picked up by his comrades, and carried to the place of halt for the night, near *Tigh-an Ribbi*, where, before morning, he died of his wound. His body was buried in the old churchyard of Airds, but was not allowed to rest there. On the disappearance of the soldiers from the district, the body was exhumed by the people, and cast into the sea ; not, however, before a brother of *Silas-Nic-Cholla* flayed the right arm from the shoulder to the elbow, and of the skin thus flayed was made a dirk sheath, and this sheath we saw and handled with no little curiosity a week or two ago. The sheath is of a dark brown colour, limp and soft, with no ornament except a small virle of brass at the point, and a thin edging of the same metal round the orifice, on which is inscribed the date "1747," and the initials "D. M. C." There is no reason, we suppose, to doubt the genuineness of the article, though we hardly expected to find human skin—if it be human skin—of such thickness. It may, however, be partly the result of the tanning process which it probably underwent, and of time. In connection with this strange relic of a past age may be stated the extraordinary fact—incredible, indeed, if it were not thoroughly authenticated—that during the horrors of the French Revolution there was a tannery of human skins for many months in operation at Meudon. The raw material, so to speak, of this strange manufacture, was the skins of the scores and hundreds that were daily guillotined. It is asserted that "it made excellent wash-leather." Montgaillard, a prominent character of the period, who had the curiosity to visit the works, and saw the tanning process in full operation, makes the following curious observation :—"The skin of the men was superior in toughness and quality to shamoy ; that of the women good for almost nothing, so soft in texture, and easily torn, like rotten linen !" We have had some rebellious revolutions, civil wars, and all the rest of it in Great Britain and Ireland, with their attendant iniquities, bad enough in all conscience, but the French may fairly boast of having beat us ; a tannery of human skins is a venture and enterprise that no one has been pushing and patriotic enough yet to undertake amongst us, even when axe and gallows wrought their hardest in days happily long since passed away.

CHAPTER XV.

THE weather [October 1870] with us here on the West Coast continues wonderfully mild and open for the latter end of October. Were it not, indeed, for an occasional sprinkling of snow along the mountain summits of an early morning, and finding as you wander about the pathways everywhere bestrewn with fallen leaves, we might find some difficulty in persuading ourselves, in weather so bright and summer-like, that the season was at all so far advanced as it really is, that 1870, with its immediate predecessor—the *anni mirabiles* of the century—had already so nearly run its allotted course. A striking proof of the exceptional mildness of the weather since mid-August is the fact that a young wood-pigeon or ring-dove (*Columba palumbus*), not yet nearly full fledged, was brought to us a few days ago from a nest in the woods of Coirrechadrachan. We have kept it with the view of rearing it as a pet, though the chances are all against us, the produce of such late incubations having always less robustness and vitality about them than birds hatched in spring or early summer. There is a little difficulty, as a rule, in rearing the ring-dove, and getting it to become even troublesomely tame, until it purrs and *kur-doo's* about your feet, and rubs himself against you with all the familiarity and *empressement* of a kitten begging for its morning allowance of milk. It is, however, exceedingly quarrelsome and pugnacious among other pets, and so jealous of any attention bestowed on any one but itself, that it will pout and sulk for half a day if it considers itself injured in this respect; and yet so little grateful is it for any amount of kindness you may show, it that when full-grown it will take the first opportunity that offers to escape into its native wild woods, never more to look near you. One that we reared from the nest several years ago had one very amusing habit. Every morning after being fed he would watch the nursery door, which opened off the kitchen, until he got it ajar, when he would leap upon the dressing-table and spend a couple of hours in admiring himself in the looking-glass, preening his feathers and strutting about and *kur-dooing* to his *alter ego* with the most beauish, self-satisfied air imaginable, the poor bird being evidently under the impression that his own reflection was a Mademoiselle Ring-dove of irresistible attractions, and whom he persuaded himself he was on these occasions busily courting in the manner most approved of amongst the most fashionable circles of ring-dovedom. His death was a singular one. A large Aylesbury duck, with whom he used to have constant quarrels, he being invariably in fault and always the aggressor, got a hold of him one day near her ducking pond, and in a scuffle, which the ring-dove himself had causelessly provoked, dragged him into the water, and beat him with her wings until he was, like Ophelia, " drown'd, drown'd."

We never see these very handsome wild birds, or hear their soft melodious cooing of summer eve from the neighbouring woods, but we think of Shenstone's beautiful lines—

> " I have found out a gift for my fair :
>   I have found where the wood-pigeons breed ;
>   But let me that plunder forbear,
>   She will say 'twas a barbarous deed :
>   *For he ne'er could be true, she averr'd,*
>   *Who could rob a poor bird of its young ;*
>   *And I lov'd her the more when I heard*
>   *Such tenderness fall from her tongue.*
>
> " I have heard her with sweetness unfold
>   How that pity was due to a dove ;
>   That it ever attended the bold,
>   And she called it the Sister of Love.

> But her words such a pleasure convey,
>   So much I her accents adore,
> Let her speak, and whatever she say,
>   Methinks I should love her the more."

In the same poem—the *Pastoral Ballad*—occurs this exquisite verse :—

> " When forced the fair nymph to forego,
>   What anguish I felt at my heart!
> Yet I thought—but it might not be so—
>   'Twas with pain she saw me depart.
> She gazed as I slowly withdrew ;
>   My path I could hardly discern :
> So sweetly she bade me adieu,
>   I thought that she bade me return."

But alas, and woe the while ! William Shenstone of the Leasowes, with his many tuneful contemporaries, are forgotten, or at least unread, by the present generation, and the poetasters of our day claim Parnassus, its Castalian spring and Temple of Apollo, for their own ! All we can is that *in ré poetica* the taste of an age tolerant of such an usurpation is little to be commended.

A gentleman in the opposite district of Appin sent us a message a few days ago begging us to go and have a look at what he termed a *rarissimus piscis*, a most rare fish that had been caught in a scringe net along with a lot of sethe and mackerel. In complying with such messages we can seldom be charged with dilatoriness, as most of our friends will bear witness. Nor was it otherwise in this case ; *Cha be'n ruith ach an leùm*, as the Highlanders say— it was not a run but a rush, with a leap and a bound—when they would emphatically characterise a person's conduct in going about anything with extraordinary alacrity. The fish in question we found to be an old acquaintance of ours, though so rare on the west coast that we never saw or heard of it before during a twenty years' residence in the country, and constantly, too, on the out-look for everything in the shape and semblance of a *rara avis*, whether

F

encased in fur, feather, or scales. It was the gar-fish of British zoologists, known in ichthyological nomenclature as the *Belone vulgaris* of the family *Scomberesocidæ*, having the body, which is covered with minute scales, elongated to a degree almost conger-like. It is frequently captured on the east coast, sometimes intermingling with mackerel and haddock shoals in considerable numbers. We have seen it in the Perth, Dundee, and Edinburgh fish markets; never, as we have said, on the west coast. It is said to be excellent eating when in proper season, although there is a prejudice against its use amongst the fishermen themselves; and it is a remarkable fact, by the way, that some of the finest fish in the sea—most in esteem, at all events, with the fish-eating public —are frequently rejected by their professional captors for their own eating in favour of what we should call the coarser and inferior kinds. For a long time we thought this was entirely a matter of economy, those that brought the largest price in the market being sold, and the inferior sorts kept for their own consumption. Subsequently we had abundant opportunities of finding out that it was far otherwise. An east coast fisherman will give the preference at any time, for his own eating that is, to a flounder, however flabby and flaccid, over a whiting or plaice; he will eat the hake rather than the finest cod or haddock, and considers the wing of a skate, dried in the smoke until it is of the colour of the darkest mahogany, with a *bouquet* the very opposite, be sure, of the ottar of roses, a tit-bit with which, in his estimation, neither sea-trout, mackerel, nor turbot can for a moment bear comparison. Fishermen, too, we have observed with some surprise, seldom eat their fish fresh; they prefer it salted—salted, moreover, as a rule to a degree that to other people would render it almost uneatable. For the prejudice against the gar-fish there is, however, some excuse. In popular superstition, " *lang-nebbed* " things have always been in bad odour; and the gar-fish's snout is greatly elongated, so much so that it bears no small resemblance to a curlew's bill, giving it a wicked, vicious look, that its structure otherwise, however, belies; for it is altogether incapable of hurting anything bigger than the very small fry and marine insects on which it feeds. The prejudice against the gar-fish is no doubt to be accounted for in part by the curious fact that its bones are of a dirty green colour, strange and perhaps disagreeable to an eye accustomed to the ivory-like whiteness of the osseous structure of most other fishes that are brought to table. We have seen specimens of the gar-fish captured by the St. Andrews fishermen that exceeded three feet in length: the fish more immediately referred to only measured nineteen inches. Our friend has since written us a note to say that on being shown to a gentleman, "professing to know something of ichthyology," he declared it to be a specimen of the pipe-fish, which is just about as correct as if a man said that a pelican was a parrot, or a pig was a giraffe.

In one particular, at least, we resemble Dr. Samuel Johnson. We have never during our whole lifetime once worn a nightcap. "I had the custom by chance," replied the "Rambler," with a growl at Boswell's inquisitiveness on the subject, "and perhaps no man, sir, shall ever know whether it is best to sleep with or without a nightcap." But if we don't wear a nightcap, some of our neighbours do, and to one of these useful articles of nocturnal *toilette* befell the following adventure a short time ago. One of our neighbours, a fine old Highlander, still straight as a pine tree, and strong and stalwart withal, though already past the grand climacteric, having had occasion to be in the south in the early summer, bought himself a speck and span new nightcap, which, neatly folded up along with some braws for the gudewife, formed a parcel of which, you may be sure, he was exceedingly careful on the return journey, constantly "keeping his eye on it" all the way from the Broomielaw to Ballachulish Pier, and watching over its safety as anxiously as if it contained the wealth of the Rothschilds in Bank of England notes, or the title-deeds of an earldom. When at last produced at home, and displayed before the admiring gaze of a select few in every imaginable angle of light, it was really a very fine nightcap, a sort of ribbed magenta-coloured " Kilmarnock," with a tassel at top, in which were intermingled all the hues of the rainbow, such a splendid tassel as was never before seen in Lochaber : Cardinal Antonelli might have been proud of it as a pendant to his hat. Having at last been sufficiently admired, the nightcap was duly put to its proper use, and was found to answer its purpose perfectly; but one night, while yet the gay Kilmarnock retained almost all its pristine bloom, lo! it was amissing at bedtime from its usual place of honour on the corner of its owner's pillow, greatly to his annoyance you may believe, and not a little to the surprise and consternation of his amiable bedfellow. Then, and for weeks afterwards, all search for the missing nightcap was but so much fruitless labour; nothing could be seen or heard of it, and it was finally agreed on all hands that it must have been stolen by some person whose honesty became weak as water in view of the Kilmarnock's rare magenta colour and gay pendulous tassel. And the nightcap in very truth *was* stolen, though the thief was probably actuated less by the brilliancy of its colours than the cozy feel of its soft and silken texture. Some time in mid-autumn the mystery was cleared up in this wise. The nightcap owner was one day engaged in redding up his barn preparatory to the ingathering of his crops, when a large rat bolted from between his feet, and, scuttling across the floor, disappeared, rat fashion, in a hole in the divot wall. A spade was instantly got, and the hole dug about until its innermost recess was reached, in which was found a gigantic dam rat with a litter of a dozen or more young ones. These were all of them of course straight-way despatched, and the cozy nest of moss, dried grass, and nibbled straw scattered about, when lo! as its foundation appeared the long missing *bonnet de nuit*, the incomparable Kilmarnock, without a rent or tear, and its colours as bright almost, and its tassel bobbing as coquettishly as when first displayed on the points of the shopman's distended fingers over the counter in the Cowcaddens. There was great rejoicing over the reappearance of the nightcap, which is now again prized as highly and watched over as carefully as if it were the nightcap of Fortunatus; and the owner, a wag and humorist in a quiet way, as are most of our old Highlanders, has composed a song on the subject (*Oran do m' Churrachd-oidhche*), which, after some coaxing, we got him to repeat to us some days ago. It pleased us immensely, and made us laugh until our sides were sore. For the benefit of our readers we may dash off a translation of it some evening or other when we are " i' the vein."

Going to call at Ardgour House one day last week, and taking a short cut through the woods, we came across the keeper just as he had shot a roebuck, the largest we think we ever saw, and with the finest head. The horns were something extraordinary, both as to size and shape, so much so, indeed, that although we have in our day met with many fine ones, we never saw anything for a moment to be compared with these. We have, for instance, a roebuck's head of our own, kindly given us some years ago by Lochiel, the horns on which are allowed to be uncommonly good ones; but we find that they are nearly two inches shorter in the beam, and less by nearly a whole inch in circumference of root of antler at its junction with the skull than those of the specimen shot in Ardgour on Tuesday.

CHAPTER XVI.

ONE of Dryden's best poems, and in many respects one of the most
curious poems in the language, is the *Annus Mirabilis*, an effusion
of historical panegyric, which, after the lapse of two centuries, no
one can read unmoved or undelighted, so beautifully is it written,
so masterly is the versification, and so vividly are its events por-
trayed. The year commemorated is 1666, and the "wonders"
that entitled it to such pre-eminence were the naval war with the
Dutch and Danes and the great fire in London. If 1666, however,
was an *annus mirabilis*, surely 1870 is an *annus mirabilior*, a more
wonderful year still, nay, an *annus mirabilissimus*, if you like, for
you shall go back in our annals very far indeed—much farther, if
you try it, than at the outset you might think at all necessary—
before you meet its match. Just consider, first of all, the great
Franco-Prussian war, with its countless hosts of slain; with its
sieges of Strasbourg, Metz, and Paris, not to mention strongholds
of less importance; its capitulation of Sedan and captive Emperor;
the Empire ruined, and a Republic in its place, with all that may
yet happen ere peace is proclaimed and the Germans have recrossed
the Rhine. Think, again, of the promulgation of the doctrine of
Papal Infallibility, so speedily, and let us say unexpectedly, followed
by the capture of Rome and the dethronement of this very infallible
Pope as a temporal Prince, by the *Catholic* (*proh pudor!*) King
of Italy. At home, a daughter of the Queen, with the royal
consent and concurrence, marries one of that Queen's subjects, for

we suppose we may regard the matter as a *fait accompli*, an event so unheard-of and unusual that we must go back for an exact parallel for more than two hundred years, when the Duke of York, afterwards James II., "a man of many woes," married the Lady Anne Hyde, daughter of Lord Chancellor Clarendon, whose history of the Rebellion is one of the most interesting, and, on account of its inimitable portraiture, one of the most valuable works of its kind in the English language. If to all this be added such events as the loss of the "Captain," built and armed on a principle, the ultimate adoption or rejection of which will so materially affect the navy of the future; the revision of the Authorised Version of the Scriptures; and many other matters, both at home and abroad, that will readily occur to the reader, this may be regarded as a very wonderful year indeed. Occupying the centre, as it were, of all these events, we are too near them at present to appraise either their magnitude or importance at their legitimate value. Not the man at the base of a lofty tower, but he who stands at some distance from it can take its proportions aright, and we may depend upon it that the reader of the history of our period a hundred years hence will turn to the page that records the events of 1870 as at once the most interesting and important in the annals of many centuries. Reverting for a moment to the *Annus Mirabilis* of Dryden, it is but fair to acknowledge that they seem to have had one wonder to boast of in 1666 that we cannot claim for 1870, to this date at least; the wonder in question being two blazing comets in the nocturnal sky. Describing the English fleet advancing to attack the enemy at night, the poet, with a boldness of hyperbole for which he is always remarkable, says—

> " To see that fleet upon the ocean move,
>   Angels drew down the curtains of the skies ;
> And Heaven, as if there wanted lights above,
>   For tapers, made two glaring comets rise ! "

But if we have no comets to boast of in 1870, let not the reader forget that the 14th November is nigh at hand, and that he who gets up betimes on the morning of that day, and watches till the daybreak, will assuredly witness a sight more startling, and grand and "glaring" than Dryden's comets, wonderful and startling as they doubtless were. We must be permitted one other extract from this extraordinary poem. It describes the state of the contending fleets and the feelings of their respective crews on their withdrawing for a time from an engagement that resulted in something like what at the present day we should call a drawn battle :—

> " The night comes on, we eager to pursue
>   The combat still, and they ashamed to leave
> Till the last streaks of dying day withdrew,
>   And doubtful moonlight did our rage deceive.
>
> " In th' English fleet each ship resounds with joy,
>   And loud applause of their great leader's fame ;
> In fiery dreams the Dutch they still destroy,
>   And, slumbering, smile at the imagin'd flame.
>
> " Not so the Holland fleet, who, tired and done,
>   Stretch'd on their decks, like weary oxen lie ;
> Faint sweats all down their mighty members run
>   (Vast hulks which little souls but ill supply).
>
> " In dreams they fearful precipices tread,
>   Or, shipwreck'd, labour to some distant shore ;
> Or in dark churches walk among the dead ;
>   They wake with horror, and dare sleep no more."

We do not know whether the reader will agree with us, but we look upon these verses as wonderfully fine, and upon the *Annus Mirabilis* as, of its class, amongst the finest, if not the very finest, poem in the language.

Even from a meteorological point of view, this year, in our part of the country at least, has had not a little of the *mirabilis* about it. Byron, we know, awoke one morning and found himself famous, and we awoke one morning last week and found ourselves in mid-winter, albeit the previous day had been mild, and calm, and sunny, and bright as if it were Whitsuntide, rather than the Eve of St. Luke the Evangelist. Since then we have had incessant storms, shifting about and sometimes blowing from every point of the compass within the four-and-twenty hours, with such deluges of rain as Lochaber alone can supply in season, or sometimes, *entre nous, out* of season as well. The mountain summits are, at the moment we write, covered with a lamb's-wool-like coating of virgin snow, and the air has become so chill and raw that we were fain some days ago to don our winter habiliments for the season. We have no right or reason to complain, however; a finer summer and autumn were never known in the Highlands, and since winter must come some time or other, it is better that it should come in season. The fourth week of October is not a bit too early for snow, and sleet, and storms, so that when we hear the winds howling over ferry and firth, and the waves breaking with sullen roar upon the vexed strand, and listen to the rattle and the dash of rain and sleet upon the window panes, we shall, first taking care that the shutters are properly closed and the curtains drawn, just draw our arm-chair a little nearer the fire, which our " lassie," you may be sure, has trimmed betimes, like Horace's boy, *large reponens* peats and coals thereon, and then, with the *Courier, Scotsman,* or *Standard* on our knee, or a stray copy of the *Saturday Review* or *Spectator*, which some distant friend has kindly sent us, or some fresh volume from Ardgour's library, the worst we, shall say will be in the words of poor old *Lear*, " Blow wind, and crack your cheeks! rage! blow!" blessing God the while that if our lot be a humbler one, it is also a happier one than the poor old king's.

A good deal has been written about the enormous numbers of killed and wounded in the present Franco-Prussian war, the fact being nevertheless, as we learn on competent authority, that notwithstanding the improvements made of late years in arms of precision, there were, considering the numbers engaged, quite as many men disabled as in the good old days of " Brown Bess " in the wars of the first Napoleon and in our battles in India. Mr. Hill Burton, in one of his recently published volumes of the *History of Scotland*, and an admirable and very impartial history it is, tells us that in the battle of Langside, an historical combat on the issue of which so much in the after history of England and Scotland depended, 10,000 men were engaged for three-quarters of an hour, with a loss to the Queen's party of 300 *hors de combat*, while the victors only lost *one man !* A very extraordinary fact certainly ; but a more wonderful fact still, and neither Mr. Burton nor his reviewers seem to be aware of it, is that of the battle of *Tippermuir*, fought in 1644, between the Covenanters and the famous Marquis of Montrose, in which Montrose was victorious without the loss of a single man on his own side, although of the Covenanters between four and five hundred were killed in the battle and pursuit. Another curious thing connected with the battle of Tippermuir was this : a body of Highlanders, keen enough for the fray, were without arms of any kind, when Montrose, pointing to the stones that thickly strewed the field, advised them to try these to begin with, and they did, appropriating the arms of their enemies as they fell, and using them with such effect that the battle proper was over in less than half an hour. The only other battle that we can recollect in which such primitive weapons as stones were employed by the combatants was that of *Cappel*, fought in 1531, between the Protestants of Zurich and the Catholics of the neighbouring cantons. It was in this battle that the celebrated reformer Zwingle, or Zwinglius, met his death. He was first of all knocked down by a stone that, fiercely hurled, struck him on the head, and then, with the exclamation, " Die, obstinate heretic," the sword of Fockinger of Unterwalden pierced his throat, and the reformer was no more.

The reader has, of course, seen in the papers how beleaguered Paris keeps up communication with Belgium and the provinces, by means of balloons and carrier pigeons. Of balloons and ballooning we have no practical experience ; of carrier pigeons we do know something, the bird being as well-known to us as is a robin redbreast to a gardener. We kept them for some time, but were obliged to get quit of them on account of their ineradicable propensity to purloin our neighbours' turnip seed from the drill immediately after being sown and before they got time to sprout. All pigeons have this habit, but the carrier worse and more persistently than any other. The speed and power of wing appertaining to the carrier pigeon is extraordinary, and if not well attested would be deemed incredible. We remember, for instance, that at the Christmas of 1845, when a student at the University of St. Andrews (*best* as well as *oldest* university in Scotland, gainsay it who may !) we spent our holidays at Kirkmichael, a pleasant little village in the Highlands of Perthshire. On leaving St. Andrews we took with us a carrier pigeon, a magnificent bird. On the 1st of January 1846, at the hour of noon precisely, we gave this bird, with a bit of narrow blue ribbon tied under his wing, his liberty on the bridge of Kirkmichael. When let out of his basket he instantly soared up in a sort of spiral flight, ascending and ascending cork-screw fashion until he seemed to the eye no bigger than a wren, then straight and swift as an arrow from a bow he urged his flight southwards, and became lost to view. On returning to St. Andrews, we found that our bird had reached his dovecot, eagerly watched and waited for by his owner, as the College bells were chiming one o'clock on the same day, so that it must have done the distance, about fifty-four miles as the crow flies, in about one hour, or very nearly at the rate of a mile a minute. Now, it must be remembered that this was the bird's ordinary flight. He doubtless sought his distant home in what one might call a brisk and business-like manner, nor swerved, we may be sure, an inch from his course, nor loitered by the way. He was going well—*very* well, if you like—throughout, but not going his best. The probability is that under extraordinary pressure, with a falcon in chase, for instance, the same bird could and would have gone twice as fast, or at a rate of something more than a hundred miles an hour. If the reader likes to experiment in this direction, he can easily try it with the common domestic pigeon, as we have done more than once. Years ago we recollect a brother of ours taking, at our suggestion, a common black and white pigeon from the dove-cot here to Oban, where, at a preconcerted hour on a day agreed upon, he set it at liberty. The bird took nearly two hours to do the distance, some twenty-three or twenty-four miles as the crow flies; but it probably lingered some time by the way to feed, as, instead of being well fed, which should always be strictly attended to, it received no food at all on the morning of its liberation at Oban. The house-pigeon, however, is useless except for comparatively short distances, and even then is never to be much depended upon. His extreme domesticity predisposes him to pay a visit to every dovecot on the route, and to fraternise with every flock of brother pigeons he may happen to fall in with. His peculiar mode of flight, besides, and his extreme timidity, mark him out as an easy and desirable prey for any keen-eyed hawk or falcon that may be at the moment *impransus*, as Johnson in his early days once signed a note in London—dinnerless. The common pigeon, too, wings his flight at a comparatively low altitude, and becomes an easy shot to any one with a gun ready to hand when it passes by. Not so the true carrier pigeon, which flies at a great height, far out of range of needle-gun or artillery—out of range of human sight, in fact ; so that it is never in danger of being brought to grief, as was poor Gambetta in his balloon when passing above the Prussian lines the other day. The velocity with which some birds fly is almost incredible. A hungry falcon, with his blood up and in eager pursuit of his quarry, will fly at the rate of 150 miles an hour, and keep it up too until his object is attained ; and the tremendous impetus of the bird at such a speed accounts for the dreadful wounds that a falcon inflicts when it strikes its prey, sometimes ripping up a grouse, or blackcock, or mallard, from vent to breastbone, as if it had been done by the keen edge of a butcher's cleaver. A goshawk (*Falco palumbarius*) belonging to Henry of Navarre—the Henri Quatre of after days—having its royal owner's name engraved on its golden *varvels*, made its escape from Fontainbleau in 1574, and was caught in Malta within four-and-twenty hours afterwards—a distance of 1400 miles, or at the rate of sixty miles an hour, supposing him to have been on the wing the whole time. But a hawk never flies by night, so that, on a fair computation, the bird's speed in winging the enormous distance must have been at the rate of at least 100 miles an hour. We have calculated that a snipe, thoroughly alarmed, and going its best, can fly at the rate of a mile a minute, and there are other well-known birds equally fleet of wing. Nor must it be supposed that the velocity of birds is a mere " flash-in-the-pan," so to speak—a " spurt," as it were—which could not be kept up. The long-sustained flights of migratory birds proves the contrary—that birds are not only inconceivably fleet, but, to use a racing term, that they can *stay* as well. Of our more familiar birds, we should say that the common wild duck of our meres flies with greater velocity than any other bird with which the reader is likely to be well acquainted.

CHAPTER XVII.

IT must have been in view of some such scene [November 1870] as
the early morning presents to the eye at present that Horace began
his celebrated ode to Augustus—

> " Jam satis terris nivis, atque diræ
> Grandinis misit Pater "—

Enough, enough of snow and direful hail! Or if you prefer the
wintry scene in the ninth Ode—

> " Vides, ut alta stet nive candidum
> Soracte, nec jam sustineant onus
> Sylvæ laborantes : gelûque
> Flumina constiterint acuto ? "

Which our countryman Theodore Martin thus renders—

> " Look out, my Thaliarchus, round !
> Soracte's crest is white with snow,
> The drooping branches sweep the ground,
> And, fast in icy fetters bound,
> The streams have ceased to flow."

The snow-clad Soracte itself could not wear a colder or wintrier
aspect than does our own Ben Nevis at this moment. We have, in
truth, had a great deal of sleet and snow and rattling hail showers
of late, with bitterly cold winds and frost enough to induce one to
don his warmest habiliments when venturing abroad, and thoroughly

to appreciate the comforts of a bright and blazing fire within doors.
Winter, in short, has fairly set in; and we must just battle with
its inclemencies as best we may until a more genial season has come
round. And an unusually inclement and severe winter is this
likely to prove. Our lochs and estuaries are swarming with Arctic
sea-fowl, that already venture quite close to the shore, and seek
their food in the most sheltered bays, a sure sign that much cold
weather, with heavy gales from the north and north-west, cannot
be far away. Among these web-footed visitors from the far north we
have observed two that are extremely rare on our part of the west
coast, even in the severest winters. One of these is the ratch or
auklet (*Alca alle*, Linn.), a very pretty little black and white
diver, the smallest bird of the genus with which we are
acquainted, a little more rotund in form and of a robuster frame
than the well-known *dipper* of our streams, but otherwise very
like it. Another is the gadwall (*Anas strepera*), a species of duck
very rare in our north-western waters—a very pretty little duck,
with a remarkably loud and harsh voice, so loud that on a calm
frosty day it reaches you over a sea surface distance of several miles.
We have only identified the latter at a distance by the aid of a
powerful binocular. It is not a difficult bird to recognise, however,
on account of its distinct markings, and we are as confident that
we have repeatedly seen it during the present month as if we had
it in our cabinet. And talking of birds, what does the reader think
the Prussians are up to now? Annoyed at the ballooning and
pigeon-carrying by means of which beleaguered Paris manages to
keep up communication with the outer world, the Germans are
training falcons to be employed in coursing and capturing such
carrier pigeons as may be observed passing over their outposts and
siege works. Such at least is one item in the last batch of news
notes from Versailles. If the Prussians really mean this, all we
can say is that it is "a fine idea, but impracticable," as Hannibal

said of Maharbal's suggestion to push on to the capture of the
Capitol after the battle of Cannæ. In the first place it is allowed
on all hands that a few months at most, probably a few weeks,
must decide the fate of Paris one way or other, while a hawk, to be
employed as proposed, requires years of carefullest training ere it
can be depended upon as an aerial cruiser in any way subject to
human control, nor, even if it were otherwise, could a sufficient
number of falcons for the purpose be procured in Europe or elsewhere. Such an attempt at an aerial blockade must prove a failure.
Even from a well-trained hawk, under the most favourable circumstances, a carrier pigeon ought to be able in nine cases out of ten to
make good its escape by reason of the velocity and altitude of its
flight. Depend upon it that in all time to come ballooning and
pigeon carrying will be employed by a besieged city, as Paris
employs them now ; and while gas can be had to inflate a balloon,
and a carrier-pigeon is available, there is nothing that a besieging
force can do to prevent the constant voyaging of such aerial
messengers. One result of this war will be that carrier pigeons
will be bred in larger numbers, and more highly valued than ever
—carrier pigeon dovecots in each city at the public expense—while
aerial navigation by means of balloons, having lost much of its
terrors, will more and more become a common and every-day mode
of locomotion. There is an "Aeronautical Society" in England,
which boasts the names of many distinguished men on its roll of
members, but which, nevertheless, couldn't in twenty years have
done so much for aerial navigation as the Franco-Prussian war has
done in little more than a month. Most people, by the way, have
been disgusted with the King of Prussia's repeated appeals for
Divine aid and pretended recognition of Divine guidance, while
wading at the head of his forces knee-deep in a *mare magnum* of
bloodshed and carnage from the Rhine to the Seine. One anecdote,
apropos of a king's pretended piety and close alliance with the

Divine powers in all his undertakings, we have not seen quoted. It is this : some person once calling on John Forster, took occasion to remark that the Emperor Alexander (of Russia) was a very pious man. "Very pious, indeed," observed Forster, with tremendous sarcasm, "Very pious, indeed; I am credibly informed that he said grace ere he swallowed Poland ! "

Preparations on a large scale are being made on the Continent and in America for observing the great solar eclipse of the 22d December, with a care and precision never known in the examination of a similar phenomenon. Never before, indeed, could a solar eclipse be observed and analysed in its every phase as this one will be. Aided by the spectroscope, polariscope, photometer, and photograph, with the most powerful telescopes, and meteorological and magnetic instruments of the utmost delicacy and exactness, it will be strange, indeed, if our knowledge of the chemistry and constitution of the great central orb is not very largely increased on this occasion. In our country the eclipse will be a partial one only. At the moment of maximum obscuration, supposing the sun to consist of twelve digits, about nine digits, or three-fourths of the disc, will be occulted. According to Edinburgh mean time the eclipse will begin at 10 h. 54 m. morning ; maximum observation, 0 h. 8 m. afternoon ; and of eclipse, 1 h. 22 m. afternoon. A glass of very moderate powers is sufficient for observing such partial eclipses. Partial though this eclipse is, however, no phenomenon of the kind of equal magnitude will be seen again in our country till August 1887, when the eclipse will be very nearly, though not quite, total.

Never, perhaps, has the solar disc been so constantly and so largely crowded with *maculæ*, or "spots," as during the present year. Some of these spots have recently been very large. On the 9th of the present month, for instance, there was an immense circular spot as nearly as possible on the centre of the solar disc, like a bull's-eye in a bright target of living light, which a little before sunset was plainly visible to the naked eye. It was the evening of the Fort-William market day, and we drew the attention of several people returning from the fair to the unusual phenomenon. One jolly old fellow, who had probably been largely patronising the " tents " on the market stance throughout the day, would insist upon it that he saw, not one big spot on the sun, but two or more —and perhaps he did. A few days previously a perfect stream of *maculæ* of all sizes might easily be observed along the solar equator, looking for all the world as if a flock of ravens were at the moment passing, in struggling order within the telescope's field of view, between us and the sun. At the moment we write these lines, there is a very large spot half-way between the solar centre and its western limb, that towards sunset, if the sky is clear, might, we think, be discerned by the unaided eye. Auroral displays, too, still continue to render our nights, though at present moonless, and frequently cloudy withal, bright and cheerful by their broad and mysterious effulgence.

The November meteors of the present year seem to have made little or no display anywhere. Here it was wet and cloudy, so that we could not have seen them even if the sky was ablaze with them.

CHAPTER XVIII.

WITH the exception of two, or at most three, tolerably fine days at the beginning of the month, December [1870] has been hardly less rainy and generally disagreeable than November itself, and this, although in November a fall of 18 inches—1500 tons of rain water to the imperial acre—was duly registered. A recent communication from Skye went to show that in the matter of rainfall that island is far ahead, not only of Lochaber, but of every other station in the kingdom—a pluvial pre-eminence which we had really thought belonged to ourselves, but which, claimed for Skye on the impartial authority of the rain-gauge, we give up ungrudgingly, simply exclaiming with Meliboeus in the Virgilian eclogue—

> " Non equidem invideo, miror magis."
> (In sooth I feel not envy, but surprise.)

With such a rainfall as is claimed for Skye, one only wonders how it is that the inhabitants of the island seem not to suffer a whit because of it. As a rule, they are a robust and remarkably long-lived people ; and, what is even more surprising, they are exceedingly good-humoured and cheerful—the pleasantest people in the world to meet with, whether at home or abroad. There is an old Gaelic apologue current in Lochaber, which may perhaps have some bearing on the point :—" It was long, long ago that, in the grey dawn of an intensely cold January morning, after a wild night of drift and snow, the heathcock of Ben Nevis clapped his wings, and, in a loud, prolonged, interrogative crow, addressed his first cousin by the father's side, the heathcock of Ben Cruachan—'How do you feel yourself this morning, dear heathcock of Cruachan?' 'So, so,' with a feeble attempt at wing-clapping, responded the heathcock of Cruachan; 'So, so; miserable enough, believe me, after such a night as last night was. And if I am thus miserable down here, it only puzzles me to understand how you can at all endure it, and live up there on Ben Nevis.' 'Thanks, my dear fellow,' with a second vigorous clapping of his wings, quoth the Ben Nevis bird; 'Thanks, my dear fellow, for your kind and cousinly solicitude for my welfare. Know this, however, that, bad as it doubtless is up here on Ben Nevis, *I am made to it.*'" We can only suppose that our friends in Skye bear this prodigious rainfall with such philosophic equanimity and impunity because, like the heathcock of Ben Nevis, they are "made to it." The first time we heard this apologue was many years ago, in the cabin of one of the Messrs. Hutcheson's steamers. A rubicund visaged drover—a fine-looking man, of burly frame and Atlantean shoulders—had just swallowed quite half-a-tumblerful of potent and unadulterated "Talisker" at a gulp rather than a draught, when his parish clergyman, who happened to be reclining on a sofa at the opposite side of the cabin, got up and expostulated with his parishioner for drinking ardent spirits in such a way as that; prophesying that unless he stopped it very quickly it would kill him, and only wondering that it had not killed him long ago. The drover, who was not aware until then that his minister was on board, and a witness to his potations, respectfully took off his broad bonnet, and, with a bow, begged to repeat the apologue, which he did, *ore rotundo,* in the most beautiful Gaelic; the application being so manifestly apt and pertinent to his particular case that we all burst out a laughing, the venerable clergyman—now, alas, no more!—enjoying it as much as any one that the tables had been so cleverly turned upon him. Fables apart, however, the fact of the matter seems to be simply this, that the humidity of the climate along our western sea-board, and amongst the Hebrides, is in nowise inimical to robust health or longevity. It is of course disagreeable enough at times, and frequently a sad drawback on our agricultural prosperity; but a minute examination of the vital statistics of the Western Highlands and Islands would probably go far to show that our superabundance of rain is rather favourable to health and long life than otherwise. *Ach bi'dh sin mar a chithear da,* a beautiful Gaelic phrase literally. · But be that particular matter *as it may seem to it,*—what would most please us at this moment would be a month or more of the good old-fashioned winters of our boyhood, when everything was blanketed for weeks together in soft and virgin snow, and the earth was at times so braced and bound with frost that under the rapid tread and multitudinous rush of all the village schoolboys at play, it rang again like a hollow globe of iron ! It is now, alas, dribble and drip, and splash, slop, and slush from year's end to year's end.

We are indebted to our excellent friend Mr. Snowie, of Inverness, for a very curious and valuable stag's head, admirably stuffed, which reached us the other day by steamer. It is a splendid trophy, a veritable *Cabar-Féidh,* which the Chief of the Mackenzies himself, when the clan was at its proudest, might be glad to have to adorn the entrance-hall of Brahan Castle. The antlers are of immense girth and spread; one, except for the brow tine, what is called a *cabar-slat ;* the other with two tines, each of them almost big enough for an antler of itself. We have seen many grand and curious heads in our day, both *cabar-slats* and multicornute; but this, which is properly neither the one nor the other, is, from its size and peculiar style of antlers, a trophy to be singled out and admired in a collection of the best heads of the kingdom. It faces

us as we write from the opposite wall of our study, and constantly
reminds us of Scott's magnificent description of the stag that led
Fitzjames and his attendants such a merry dance in the *Lady of
the Lake.* We must be pardoned for quoting a passage with which
every one is familiar :—

> " As Chief, who hears his warder call,
>   ' To arms ! the foemen storm the wall,'
>   The antler'd monarch of the waste
>   Sprang from his heathery couch in haste.
>   But, ere his fleet career he took,
>   *The dew-drops from his flanks he shook ;*
>   *Like crested leader proud and high,*
>   *Toss'd his beam'd frontlet to the sky ;*
>   A moment gazed adown the dale,
>   A moment snuff'd the tainted gale,
>   A moment listened to the cry,
>   That thicken'd as the chase drew nigh ;
>   Then, as the foremost foes appeared,
>   With one brave bound the copse he clear'd
>   And, stretching forward free and far,
>   Sought the wild heaths of Uam-Var."

And yet some stupid people will ask if Scott was a poet !
Even Landseer never painted anything finer or truer to the
life than that word-painting of Scott's.   Every one admits that
Homer was a poet : well, then, search the *Iliad*, point out anything
better, or anything, *entre nous*, quite as good, and when you have
found it, please let us know, and we promise to reperuse the
passage, with every attention and care, in the original of Homer
himself, as well as in the translations of Pope, Cowper, and Blackie ;
and if you are right and we are wrong, we shall not hesitate to
confess it, and humbly cry *peccavi.*   Meantime we shall continue
steadfast in our belief that Scott *is* a poet, and not only a poet, but
a poet of the highest order ; more " Homeric," too, than any other
poet you can name, either of the present or past century ; and that
Mr. Gladstone has had the good sense and penetration to discover

this, and the courage to avow it, is one, and not the least, of many things which make us have a liking for that distinguished statesman and scholar.

A lady, to whom we are indebted for numberless obligations of a like nature, has sent us a copy of an old Gaelic lullaby or baby-song, the composition of which must clearly be referred to the days when cattle-lifting forays and *spuilzies* of every description were in high fashion and favour with the gentlemen of the north—

> " When tooming faulds, or sweeping of a glen,
> Had still been held the deed of gallant men."

It is in many respects so curious that we venture on a translation of it. Attached to it is a very pretty air, low and soft and subdued as a lullaby air should be, though consisting but of a single part, as was always the case with such compositions, unlike ordinary songs, which generally had two parts, and admitted of endless variations, according to the taste and vocal capabilities of the singer. It is proper to state that our version is not intended to be sung to the original air, for which the measure we have selected is unsuitable. Our only object has been to convey to the English reader the general sense, with something of the spirit and manner, of the original.

A Lullaby.

> " Hush thee, my baby-boy, hush thee to sleep,
> Soft in my bosom laid, why should'st thou weep ;
> Hush thee, my pretty babe, why should'st thou fear,
> Well can thy father wield broadsword and spear.

> " Lullaby, lullaby, hush thee to rest,
> Snug in my arms as a bird in its nest ;
> Sweet be thy slumbers, boy, dreaming the while
> A dream that shall dimple thy cheek with a smile.

> " Helpless and weak as thou 'rt now on my knee,
> My eaglet shall yet spread his wings and be free—
> Free on the mountain side, free in the glen,
> Strong-handed, swift-footed, a man among men !

" Then shall my *dalt'* bring his *muim'* a good store
　Of game from the mountain and fish from the shore ;
　Cattle, and sheep, and goats--graze where they may—
　My *dalta* will find ere the dawn of the day.

" Thy father and uncles, with target and sword,
　Will back each bold venture by ferry and ford ;
　From thy hand I shall yet drain a beaker of wine,
　And the toast shall be—*Health and the lowing of kine!*

" Then rest thee, my foster-son, sleep and be still,
　The first star of night twinkles bright on the hill ;
　My brave boy is sleeping—kind angels watch o'er him,
　And safe to the light of the morning restore him.
　Lullaby, lullaby, what should he fear,
　Well can his father wield broadsword and spear !"

To the proper understanding of this curious composition, a few words of comment and elucidation may be necessary. The lullaby must be understood as sung by a foster-mother to her foster-son, the Gaelic words from which the exigencies of verse oblige us to retain in our paraphrase. In lulling her charge to sleep, the foster-mother fondly anticipates the time when the boy on her knee shall have become a full-grown and perfect man ; her *beau-ideal* of a perfect man, observe, being that, like the heroes of ancient song, he should be brawny limbed, strong of hand, and swift of foot, able and willing at all risks to seize and appropriate his neighbour's goods, especially his cattle, whenever necessity—an empty larder—or honour urged him to the adventure. The coolness with which the old lady commits her foster-son to the immediate care and guardianship of the heavenly powers, in the self-same breath in which she hopes and believes that he will, when he becomes a man, prove an active and expert thief—a stealer of beeves from the pastures of neighbouring tribes, in utter defiance of the decalogue—is ludicrous in the extreme. To understand it aright, we must recollect that in former times it was accounted not only lawful but honourable among hostile tribes to commit depredations on one another; and as hostility among the clans was the rule rather than the exception, every species of depredation was practised,— cattle-lifting raids, however, being accounted the most honourable of all, and in the conduct of which the best gentlemen of the clan might without a blush take an active part. The "lowing of kine," *geùmnaich bhà*, occurring in this lullaby, was an old toast of the cattle-lifting times, that the late Dr. Macfarlane of Arrochar told us, he himself had often heard when a young man at baptismal feasts and bridals on Loch Lomond side. The secret of it is this: The *geùmnaich*, or "lowing," implied that the cattle were strangers to the glen, whilst those that belonged to the glen itself, and were the *bona fide* property of the clan, if such there were, were quiet and staid and well-behaved, as decent cattle should be. The cattle "stolen or strayed," as the advertisements have it, "lowed," and were troublesome; while those born and bred in the glen were content to graze in peace, and to "low" only when they deemed it absolutely necessary. "The lowing of kine," therefore, was a toast that meant neither more nor less than success to the cattle-lifting trade! As ancient Pistol says—

" ' Convey,' the wise it call. ' Steal !' foh, a fico for the phrase."

CHAPTER XIX.

Snow continues to accumulate on the mountain summits [December 1870], which all around, from Ben Nevis to Ben Cruachan, and from the peaks of Glen-Arkaig to Benmore in Mull, now present so many *Sierra Nevadas*, while you are conscious at last, and to an extent that admits of no possible mistake on the subject, that the wind, which, whether it blows adown the glen or across the sea, has a chill and penetrating edge to it, is neither the breeze of autumn nor the zephyr of summer, but the breath of winter itself—the hoary-headed and icicle-bearded season, that, with all its drawbacks, has its uses in the general economy as well as its gentler *confrères* in the annual. With the exception of one or two pet days, the weather of the past fortnight has been stormy and wild, with heavy falls of rain on the lowlands, and sleet and snow among the mountains. In no one season since we first became a student of the heavens, now more than a quarter of a century ago, have we had so many splendid exhibitions of *aurora borealis* as the last three weeks have presented us with in a series of *tableaux vivants*, which, while they charmed and delighted the intelligent observer, made the vulgar gape in astonishment and alarm. In every instance these auroral displays have invariably been followed within twelve hours by heavy gales of wind and much rain, and so constantly have we noticed this sequence throughout the observations of many years, that there is perhaps no meteorological prediction on which we should be disposed to venture with so much confidence and boldness as that within twelve or fifteen hours of a bright auroral display there shall be a storm, and that that storm shall be of heavy rain or sleet, as well as of high wind. We speak principally of the West Highlands, but we have no doubt that observation would prove the phenomena to be the same throughout the kingdom. If we were in command of a ship at sea, we should consider ourselves quite as justified in making all necessary preparations for a coming storm on the back of a brilliant aurora, as we should on observing a sudden fall in the barometer, the only difference being that the " merry dancers " give you longer notice of the approaching gale than does the mercury. The latter exclaims, " Look out ! " and if you don't look out, and that instantly, calling all hands and making everything snug, you come to grief, while time enough generally elapses after the auroral warning, to enable you to prepare at leisure for the coming storm, and, if it catch you napping, the fault is all your own. The recent auroral displays seem to have been very general over the whole of Europe, and are said to have been unusually brilliant in Canada and the Northern States of America. A more than ordinarily severe and protracted winter may be expected after all these aerial perturbations, which, when a French *savant* remarked the other day to a compatriot, " *Tant pis,*" replied the chassepot-bearing *mobile*, with the invariable shoulder shrug and grin, " *Tant pis pour Messieurs les Prussiens !* "—thinking, no doubt, of the disastrous retreat from Moscow, and hoping to see it repeated in a different direction at no distant day. Except the wren and redbreast, whose pluck is indomitable, and who are never altogether out of voice, our singing birds are now songless and silent, or if they do utter a note, it is but a cheep and a chirp, not a song, another sign that our winter is to be regarded as having fairly set in. We notice, besides, that some of our winter visitors from

Arctic seas have made their appearance along our shores, while we observe that the rook and grey crow have already begun to frequent the beach at low water in search of what may be picked up in the way of a meal, a sure sign that they also look upon it as already come, and that their food in more inland parts has disappeared until a kindlier season has come round.

A very large raven (*Corvus corax*), the biggest specimen of this bird we have ever seen, was trapped at the head of Glencreran a few days ago by a bird-catcher that annually pays the West Highlands a visit at this season. It was a female, as fat and plump as a Michaelmas goose, and weighed within an ounce or two of four pounds. The plumage, as might be expected in a bird of such high condition, was perfect, with the exception of two of the upper alar feathers, which were perfectly white, an abnormality, however, that only rendered the specimen all the more interesting. The raven is the craftiest and shyest of birds, never venturing within shot of fowling-piece or rifle, and more difficult than any other bird, perhaps, to be outwitted or circumvented in any way. With all his craft and caution, however, the raven is, when occasion calls, one of the most courageous and boldest of birds. At the time of nidification, for instance, the male will fearlessly attack the largest falcon and drive him from what he considers his own proper territory, nor will he shun the combat, as we have often observed, even with the osprey or bald buzzard when they met in mid air on their predatory excursions, and a sufficient *casus belli* has been found or feigned by either belligerent. We remember seeing an encounter of this kind several years ago, which continued nearly an hour, and was a very pretty and interesting sight, the combatants performing the most beautiful aerial evolutions as they charged, and parried, and soared, and swooped in fierce and determined conflict. We noticed that the raven frequently uttered his hoarse and threatening croak, as if to intimidate his opponent, while the osprey fought in perfect silence. The combat finally resulted in a drawn battle, the belligerents separating as if by mutual consent, and slowly winging their flight in opposite directions. The probability is that the raven's pugnacity was excited on this occasion (March 1863) by the osprey's cruising about, however unwittingly, in the vicinity of the precipice in a cleft of which the female raven was at the time brooding on her nest. At such a time the raven will boldly attack the passing eagle, and harass and annoy it until the eagle, pestered and teased by the assault, rather than in any way alarmed, with great good nature evacuates the territory which the raven claims as its own. The raven has from the earliest ages been accounted a bird of evil omen, and an object of superstitious dread and awe, and allusions to the bird in this connection are to be met with in the literature of most countries, the raven being as cosmopolitan as man himself. Its croak, so disagreeable, and dismal, and hoarse, and startling; its colour, a funereal black; its habitat, the lonely and demon-haunted mountain peaks, giddy precipices, and dreary solitudes; its lamb-slaying and carrion-eating propensities; its shy and suspicious manner, as if he knew that he had done evil and was apprehensive of well-merited punishment—all combine to render him in the first instance a noticeable and remarkable bird, and one sure to be selected for frequent reference in the days of bird divination, a superstition of which traces may probably be found in the early history of every country, and thus it would readily be raised to the " bad eminence " of a bird of evilest omen—

> " The hateful messenger of heavy things,
> Of death and dolour telling."

The Moor of Venice says—

> " It comes o'er my memory,
> As doth the raven o'er the infected house,
> Boding to all."

And you remember *Macbeth*, and cannot fail to catch the allusion—

> " The raven himself is hoarse,
>   That croaks the fatal entrance of Duncan
>   Under my battlements."

During his tour in the Highlands with Dr. Johnson, Boswell writes a highly characterestic letter to David Garrick, and, describing their visit to *Macbeth's* Castle, says—" The situation of the old castle corresponds exactly to Shakspeare's description. While we were there to-day, it happened oddly that a raven perched upon one of the chimney tops and croaked. Then I, in my turn, repeated ' The raven himself,' &c." Now, if a raven in truth did so perch, all we can say is that it was a very curious place for a raven to be, or ravens, within a hundred years, must have very much changed their habits and nature. The explanation probably is that it was a *tame* raven, or a rook perhaps, or, likeliest of all, that it was a common jackdaw (*Corvus monedula*), a pert, impudent, and garrulous little gentleman in black—no bigger than a dovecot pigeon—that Mr. Boswell mistook (*proh pudor !*) for the grave, stately, and sagacious raven, who is as much bigger, and weightier, and wiser than his loquacious cousin the daw, as Samuel Johnson was bigger, and weightier, and wiser than his travelling companion, James Boswell. It is curious to meet with the following on the authority of no less renowned a personage than the valorous and puissant knight Don Quixote de la Mancha, the flower of chivalry. " Have you not read, sir," proceeds the knight, " the annals and histories of England, wherein are recorded the famous exploits of King Arthur, whom in our Castilian tongue we perpetually called King Artus, of whom there exists an ancient tradition, universally received over the whole kingdom of Great Britain, that he did not die, but that by magic art *he was transformed into a raven*, for which reason it cannot be proved that from that time to this any Englishman hath killed a raven."

We have just called the raven our "friend," nor are we at all ashamed so to designate a bird whom we have known long, and regarding whom, if other people speak nothing but evil, we at least can speak a great deal that is good.   There is a well-known proverb to the effect that a certain potentate of sable hue is not so black as he is painted, nor is the raven.   First of all, he is an apt scholar, and a bird generally of much sagacity, of long memory, and ready wit.   It is on record that on one occasion when the Emperor Augustus was returning victorious from a battlefield, a tame raven that had received his lesson, and remembered it to the letter, alighted on the conqueror's chariot, and saluted him in these words —*Ave Cæsar, Victor, Imperator !*   The Emperor was pleased, as he well might be, and ordered the raven a handsome pension for life. Bechstein, who probably knew more about the habits and economy of ravens, especially in their tame state, than any other ornithologist before his day or since, vouches for the facility with which they may be taught to speak, and for their sagacity and docility generally. He tells the following amusing story :—" A very clever raven was kept at a nobleman's residence in the district of Mannsfeldt. Among other things he could say, 'Well, who are you?' very strongly and distinctly.   One day, as he was walking about among the grass in the garden, he observed a setter dog which remained near him, and kept constantly walking after him.   Not liking to be thus watched and followed, the raven turned rapidly round and sternly exclaimed, 'Well, who are you?'   The dog was alarmed at this, hung his tail, and ran hastily away, and not until he had gained a considerable distance did he turn round and howl."   The raven, besides, is a thorough anti-Mormonite, and wouldn't live in Utah for the world.   If he visits the polygamist colony at all, it is always under protest against the institutions of that delectable land, and to be ready to pick the bones of the first many-wived "elder" he may catch *in articulo mortis.*   Rather should the raven

be elected to a seat upon the bench of bishops, for he is ever careful
to fulfil the apostolic injunction to be the husband but of one wife;
and until accident or old age deprives him of her, he is the model
and pattern of faithful and affectionate husbands, never violating
his conjugal vows, not even to the extent of the most innocent of
flirtations or the most Platonic of intimacies with a neighbouring
raveness, even though she should be younger, and sleeker, and
glossier than his own. The raven, in short, when he pairs, which
he does at the earliest moment permitted by the laws of ravendom,
pairs for life, and while his first choice is spared to him he will no
more think of paying court to another, be her charms what they
may, than he will of dying of hunger while there is a bone to pick,
a tender lamb, or braxied sheep within a circuit of a hundred miles
of his eyrie, in the most inaccessible cleft of yonder beetling precipice. We might now say something if we liked of the raven's
usefulness in the general economy as a hard-working and indefatigable inspector of nuisances, and how putrid animal matter of every
description disappears, as if by magic, wherever he is known and
appreciated; but this is a utilitarian age, and as we hate utilitarianism,
we are content merely to hint that the raven deserves special regard
as a sanitary reformer. We prefer insisting on the fact that the
raven is a gentleman of very ancient descent, being able, in the
clearest manner, to trace his pedigree in unbroken line up to
the days of "Captain" Noah himself, as Byron irreverently styles
the patriarch. When any one in our day becomes distinguished
and attracts our special regard, we instantly set to work to trace
his descent, and although he himself can hardly tell who was his
grandfather, we are never satisfied until we have, by hook and by
crook, traced his ancestry to the Ragman Roll or the Norman
Conquest, and, having.thus ennobled him to our own entire satisfaction, we cease not to pet and praise him until he is dead, and
then the newspapers swarm with obituary notices of the distinguished

man who has just departed, and a monument, erected by public subscription, concludes the farce. The raven's ancestor was un-questionably with Noah in the ark, and although he has incurred some odium in connection with the assuaging of the waters, we confess we cannot well tell why, for all that the ancient, and beautiful, and simple narrative says of him is this: "And he sent forth a raven, which went forth to and fro, until the waters were dried up from off the earth." On the point of ancestry, in short, there is no bird that has a better right to hold up his head than the raven. And just consider: wasn't Dickens' stuffed raven "Grip" sold the other day for a hundred and twenty guineas! although if his portrait in the *Graphic* is to be depended on, he never was a handsome specimen of the family, or if he was, then the man who stuffed and "set him up" should have received a flogging for his pains. Should the reader wish to know more about our friend *Corvus corax*, we can confidently recommend him to make the acquaintance, the intimate acquaintance if he can, of "The Raven" to be met with in the works of Edgar Allan Poe, the most weird and wonderful raven that has ever yet appeared in song or story.

CHAPTER XX.

NOVEMBER closed with a week of the most delightful weather one could wish for at this season [December 1870], cold, but crisp and clear; nor has December thus far shown any tendency to exceptional "rampaging" either, though come it must, if we are not much mistaken, and in a style we fear that will cause it to be remembered. Woodcocks, fieldfares, redwing thrushes, snow buntings, and starlings are at this moment more plentiful than we ever saw them before; while Arctic sea-fowl in great numbers crowd our creeks and bays, and immense flocks of *grallatores*, curlews, gedwits, purrs, dunlins, and oyster-catchers, may be seen all along our shores diligently attending the sea margin as the tide recedes, or with weird and wild scream urging their eccentric flights from an exhausted sandbank in indefatigable search of "fresh fields and pastures new." Creeping among the rocks on the back of Cuilchenna Point, a quiet, sequestered shore, seldom visited by anybody but ourselves at this season, one evening last week, watching a pair of web-feet that we finally decided to be *smews*, a species of *merganser*, we were unexpectedly treated to an exhibition of aquatic feats that we had never before seen equalled, and that we thought no animal, biped or quadruped, could accomplish in an element not properly its own. Squatted on the beach behind two huge boulders, a narrow opening between which enabled us to look seawards, and to see without being

seen, we were watching the elegant smews as they preened themselves, floating gracefully the while, without the movement of a
web, on the calm surface of the cold, clear sea, when right before
us, and within less than a dozen fathoms of the shore, a dark
object suddenly dashed to the surface with a flop and a splash,
and as suddenly disappeared. We took it to be a seal in pursuit
of some fish, as is his wont; but on its reappearance a minute or
so afterwards, we were delighted to see that it was not a seal, but a
large otter hard at work in chase of some favourite fish for supper;
and small blame to him for that same, for if one might judge from
his exertions in the pursuit, he was dreadfully hungry and
thoroughly in earnest, not yet having dined, perhaps, nor even
broken his fast since the preceding evening, for your otter (*Lutra
vulgaris*) is for the most part an evening and nocturnal feeder.
Nothing could exceed the elegance and ease with which the otter
performed the most extraordinary and complicated evolutions in
pursuit of his prey, his long, lithe body, pliant and supple as an
eel's, twisting and twining in every direction as the fish darted
hither and thither, or swept in rapid circles in its efforts to escape.
Its tail, we noticed, seemed to act not merely as a rudder in aid
of its owner's incessant perisaltations, but to be in constant motion
like a propeller, as if to assist the broad and muscular web feet in
every act of natation. For ten minutes or more, perhaps, did the
chase continue, the fish, that seemed to be either a haddock or sea-
trout of some three or four pounds weight, occasionally leaping
bodily out of the water in its efforts to escape from the unfriendly
attentions of its stern pursuer, the said pursuer, like a staunch hound,
doubling as the fish doubled, circling as it circled, and diving as it
dived, with a persistency and perseverance that it was impossible
to elude, until at last, fairly beaten in his own element, the fish
was captured in a pool of shallow water, whither it had darted in
its terror and bewilderment, the otter instantly pouncing upon it

and seizing it in his mouth, as you have seen a terrier deal with a rat. At this moment we rushed from our concealment with a shout, hoping to frighten the otter and get hold of the fish, but Monsieur Lutra was too quick for us. With the fish in his mouth he plunged into the sea, and in a second had disappeared among some boulders that would probably have afforded him a secure asylum, even if we had a pack of otter hounds to aid in our attempt at the dislodgment of a gentleman so cunning.

With the common otter of our inland rivers and lakes we have been more or less familiar since our school-boy days; but we cannot recollect having ever seen a marine otter until this occasion. Our naturalists seem to be very generally agreed that the sea otter and that of our rivers and fresh-water lakes are one and the same animal,—an opinion from which we are not at this moment prepared to dissent, though the animal referred to above seemed to us to be larger in size, blacker in colour, with more prominent ears, and a bigger, bushier tail than any specimen, living or dead, that had hitherto come under our notice. Certain peculiarities, however, of form and colouring in the individual are frequently attributable to accidental circumstances. We remember seeing a very fine dog otter many years ago, that its owner had succeeded in rendering comparatively tame, and of some use in the capture of fish for its master's table, as well as for its own sustenance. The animal belonged to the innkeeper at Bridge of Tilt, in Athole, and was usually kept chained in an empty stall in the stable. It was very good-natured and docile, and evinced its satisfaction on being stroked with the hand and patted by a curious purring, sort of half whine half bark, altogether unlike the utterance of any other animal with which we are acquainted. We saw it presented with a dish of milk, which it readily lapped up, using its tongue by way of spoon, as a dog does under similar circumstances. With a collar round its neck, to which a long rope

was attached, it was frequently taken to the river, where it never
failed to catch fish, first driving them, after the manner of a collie
with a flock of sheep, into the nearest pool in which there was a
considerable depth of water, when he pounced upon them with the
agility of a wild cat, and seldom failed to secure two or three of
the best and biggest fish in the shoal ere they could manage to
escape. We were assured, however, that the best place to see the
otter at work was not the river, but one of the moorland lochs, in
the depths of which he was perfectly at home. Here he exhibited
the most astonishing feats of agility in pursuit of his prey; his
activity and matchless swimming powers being backed by a pertinacity and cunning that left neither trout nor pike much chance
of escape. Having marked out and selected the fish to be captured,
it was observed that he stuck to it with the staunchness of a well-
trained hound through all its doublings and windings, as if for
the moment the loch contained none but it, until he had fairly run it
down; the capture generally taking place among the reeds that
bordered the margin of the mere, into which the fish always rushed
on becoming sensible that its adversary was not to be eluded in
open water. If left to himself, it was remarked that the otter was
somewhat dainty and fastidious of taste, rarely eating more of a
captured fish than a little at the back of the head and about the
pectoral fins, when, after a short rest, he was ready to start in
pursuit of another. If this be the habit of otters in their wild
state—as there is reason to believe it is—one can fancy how terribly
destructive to fish they must be, killing ten times more than they
actually eat, and these, too, the best and biggest fish they can meet
with in their depredations. Even a single pair of otters, with a
family to rear, must be a terrible scourge on any river they may
select to honour with their attentions for a season; nor is the
marine otter, we may be sure—such as we saw the other day—less
destructive when he takes up his residence in the vicinity of

salmon fishings.   Whatever the price of salmon in the market, depend upon it that the otter's larder is always well supplied.

The semi-domesticated otter above referred to, after leading a not unuseful life for a year or two under the careful and always kindly superintendence of its intelligent owner, managed at last somehow to break its chain and escape, and was never more seen or heard of.   The only other curious thing about this animal that we can recollect was his deadly aversion to every feathered creature that came near him.   Whether goose or duck, barn-door fowl or pigeon, he seemed to detest them all, and would readily, and with every sign of anger, kill such as he could get hold of, not to eat them, observe, for that he was never known to do, but just because he disliked them.   To all other animals he could be easily reconciled, and was on good and even friendly terms with all the dogs, cats, and pigs about the place, particularly manifesting his love for his stable companions, the horses, by whining in his strange fashion and straining on his chain to the utmost, as if he would fain welcome them with a caress, when after a day's work in the fields they returned to the stable of an evening.   We are not aware that, except milk, which it would readily lap and seemed to enjoy, this otter was ever known to touch anything in the shape of food except its natural fish diet.   In the old *Sgeulachdan*, or fireside tales of the ancient Highlanders, we frequently meet with the "*dun* otter" or *dobhran donn*, as one of the *dramatis personæ*.   He is generally introduced to us under an amiable character, rescuing neglected merit from obscurity, relieving distressed damsels, or succouring the widow and orphans with bountiful supplies of silvery fish from the tarn amongst the mountains, or the eddying pool beneath the cascade in the glen. The amiable and friendly otter sometimes turns out to be an enchanted prince, who, timeously released from the spell that has doomed him to amphibious habits and quadrupedal form, assumes his proper shape, and marries the always virtuous and beautiful, though frequently humble, heroine of the tale. In the Hebrides to this day the otter is looked upon with some degree of superstitious reverence, and a bit of otter skin worn by way of charm is regarded as an antidote against infection in fever and small-pox, a preservative from death by drowning, and of singular efficacy in bringing the labours of parturition to a happy issue. A mole on a person's skin, whatever its place or proportions, is in the Hebrides never reckoned a deformity. It is regarded rather as a " beauty spot" than otherwise, and believed to betoken a long life and good luck to the fortunate possessor. In the West Highlands and Hebrides such a mark on the skin is called a *ball-dobhrain*, an otter mark or otter spot, and is no more accounted a blemish or deformity than was the mole on the right lip of Dulcinea del Toboso by Don Quixote, though it looked " like a whisker, and had seven or eight red hairs in it above a span long ! " In some places a piece of otter skin placed on the head under a woman's coif, and worn inside a man's blue bonnet, is supposed to relieve the headache and prevent baldness, while gentle friction along the affected part with the furry side of a bit of otter skin is esteemed of sovereign efficacy in erysipelas or " rose." The following is a somewhat free rendering from the Gaelic of a fable occurring in an old *Sgeulachd*, with which many of our west coast readers at least must be acquainted. The moral is obvious.

THE OTTER AND FOX.

The otter had caught in the pool below
A silvery salmon so full of roe,
And clambering bore it over the rocks,
When who should he meet but his cousin the fox.
" Friend," quoth the wily fox, ' pray go
And bring me a fish from the pool below—
I 've not tasted fish for a year or mo'.

Leave here thy salmon ; go, haste thee back,
We 'll dine together and have our crack ;
Believe me, dear otter, that over one's food
The face of a friend is always good."

The otter tumbled into the stream
Where the floating foam was white as cream ;
He sought and searched in each cranny and hole,
But not a fish could he find in the pool.
" Well," quoth the otter, " I 'll hasten back
To my cousin the fox, and we 'll have our crack
Over the salmon I left above ;
One fish will go far that is eaten in love ;
'Tis large, and fat, and full of roe,
And, fairly divided, will serve for two."

Clambering over the rocks in haste
The otter returned to join his guest ;
But guess his surprise when he reached the spot ;
Where the fox had been—the fox was not,
And nought of the salmon that could be seen
But some silvery scales where the salmon had been !
The otter but said, " 'Tis my belief
My cousin the fox should be hanged for a thief ;
He'll never again make me his tool,
For myself alone I'll haunt the pool."

CHAPTER XXI.

Storms—An "inch" of Rain—*Atherina Presbyter—Lophius Piscatorius*—Mr. Mortimer
Collins' misquotation from the *Times*.

A FINER winter [January 1871] never was known all over the West
Highlands and Hebrides. Some tempestuousness is to be looked
for at this season, and some tempestuousness we have had, but
of actual winter rigour and cold we have hardly had a trace. Only
twice during the winter have we had any frost, and even then
it was but slight and of short duration. On several occasions,
however, we have had such terrible rainfalls as are only known
perhaps within sight of the mountain peaks of Jura and Mull and
Morven. On the 19th of January, and again on the 23d, the
rainfall within a given time was heavier than anything known even
with us for many years past. In about sixteen hours on the 19th,
4·19 inches fell, and quite as much, if not more, on the 23d.
Now, does the reader know what an inch of rain means? It means
a gallon of water spread evenly over a surface of something like
two square feet, or, to put it in a more striking and intelligible
form, it means a fall of a *hundred tons* upon an acre of land;
so that in sixteen hours on the 19th upwards of *four hundred*
tons of rain fell on every acre of land for miles and miles around
us. It will be confessed that thus the country was for once at
least well soaked and saturated. All our rivers and mountain
torrents were, of course, in full flood, and throughout the night,
when it had calmed down a little, the "noise of many waters,"
as you lay awake on your pillow and listened, made wild and
eerie music enough, to which the fitting bass was the boom of

the storm-driven rollers as they broke in sullen thunder along the shore. We had occasion to be across Corran Ferry on the wettest of these days, bad as it was, and, in spite of waterproofs and haps of most approved texture and form, we returned in the evening so soaked and drenched and *droukit,* to use an expressive Scotticism, that we might as well have been for half an hour up to our chin, over head and ears for that matter of it, in the deepest pool of the Rhi. When changing our clothes in our own room after getting home, we managed to raise a quiet laugh with ourselves over it all, by the recollection of the music and words of a favourite Scotch reel not altogether inapplicable to our then condition. The reel in question is a well-known one, though we forget at present its proper distinctive name. It is, we think, one of Neil Gow's. A gudewife, presumably of Amazonian heart, and also of Amazonian proportions, makes her husband wince and quail, and conduct himself with becoming amiability and decorum, as she sings—

> " Mur 'bi'dh agam ach trudair bodaich,
>   Bhogain anns an allt e ;
> Mur 'bi'dh agam ach trudair bodaich,
>   Bhogain anns an allt e ;
> Bhogain agus bhogain agus bhogain th'ar a cheann e,
> 'S mur 'bi'dh a glan 'nuair bhidh e tioram,
>   Bhogain 'rithisd ann e ! "

Not very easily turned into English, but this is something like it—

> " If my gudeman were cross and dour,
>   I'd dip him in the burn, O !
> If my gudeman were cross and sour,
>   I'd dip him in the burn, O ;
> I 'd dip the dear o'er head and ears until he'd grane and girn, O,
> And till he promised better things, he'd get the tother turn, O."

While stripping, it struck us that we were quite as wet on the occasion in question, as if for our sins we had undergone all the "dipping" threatened by the gudewife in the old reel; and the idea put us into good humour until tea and other fireside comforts made us forget all the pelting of the pitiless storm. How the remainder of winter and early spring may turn out meteorologically, it is impossible to forecast with any confidence, but meantime our old people, in their own opinion, at least, weatherwise and shrewd *quoad hoc*, are gravely shaking their heads over what they deem an unusual dearth of frost and snow in mid-winter.

Our West Coast storms, if in one sense sometimes disagreeable enough, rarely fail, however, to bring us a good thing in the shape of hundreds of tons of drift-ware, which, gathered and spread on the land, is found to be a valuable fertiliser. It is a labour, besides, which falls to be done in a season when there is little else to occupy the people's time, and saves an immense deal of trouble when the spring comes round, for the land is ready for the plough and the immediate reception of the seed, whatever the crop—thus saving at once the manure heap for purposes in which farmyard manure is indispensable, and all the trouble of long cartage afield. In collecting his share of a huge swathe of this drift-ware the other day, one of our neighbours found a dead fish, quite fresh and unmutilated, which being new to him, though a fisherman and sea-shore man all his life, he thought might be interesting to us. He accordingly brought it to us, and to us also it was new, and as such, of course, exceedingly interesting. We puzzled long over it ere we satisfied ourselves that we had determined its identity. It was a small fish, some six inches in length, and of smelt-like shape and form and colouring, but it was not a smelt. After some little trouble, we finally decided that it was a species of atherine (*Atherina*) belonging to the *Mugilidæ* or mullet family. Our particular specimen was the *Atherina presbyter*, a not uncommon visitor on some of the south of England shores, but so rare in our seas that, as we have already said, we never saw a specimen before. We are told that the atherine is very good eating, and we can quite believe it, for it is a pretty, delicate-looking little fish, that, nicely fried until properly crimp and brown, ought to taste well. A much commoner fish, but interesting in this instance for the great size of the specimen, was an angler, fishing-frog, or sea-devil (*Lophius piscatorius*), which was cast ashore near Corran Ferry last week. This was the largest individual of the species—the ugliest, perhaps, of all fishes—that we ever saw. It measured five feet seven inches from snout to tip of tail, and weighed fifty-three pounds. It was poor and fleshless, and had died seemingly of sheer inanition or atrophy; had it been in full condition, it would have weighed a third more. Its terrible mouth, with its formidable array of sharp recurved teeth, was enough to scare a friend that accompanied us to a distance, though we assured him that the brute was dead and harmless. On opening out its jaws to a fair extent—that is, as far as we thought the animal itself would open them easily if need were, we placed a large turnip from a pit that was conveniently at hand, a turnip nearly as large as a man's head, easily within the horrid cavern. We would willingly have taken this specimen home with us, for the purpose of preserving the skeleton, but we had no conveyance with us, and any idea of carrying it was out of the question. It had, besides, evidently lain some time on the beach, and its odour on moving it in the least was, the reader may believe, the very antipodes of Eau de Cologne or ottar of roses. We contented ourselves therefore with slitting open its stomach with our pocket-knife, and found it, as we expected, perfectly empty, containing nothing in the shape of food, except the tips of two claws and small bits of the carapace of a not uncommon species of crab, the velvet fiddler (*Portunas puber*). The Highlanders of the west coast and Hebrides call the angler *Mac Làmhaich*, properly *Mac Làthaich*—the son (that is, *inhabitant*) of the mud or ooze; a very expressive and appropriate name for it, for it is essentially a *mud* fish, in which, half buried and *perdu*, it hides and watches, tiger-like, for its prey. The naturalist meets with many things to puzzle him, and it has always puzzled us to account for the large size of this animal's head and mouth, altogether disproportioned to the size of the rest of the body. No matter how insatiable the cravings of the brute's maw—to use a Miltonic word—no matter how gluttonous soever of appetite, the head and mouth, and number and size of teeth, do seem unnecessarily formidable, monstrous indeed, for any conceivable work that they can be called upon to perform ; and yet there is unquestionably good reason for it all, if we could only find it out. It may interest some of our readers to know that the sea-devil belongs, ichthyologically, to the Acanthopterygious family of fishes. *Acanthopterygious !* what a staggerer to any one except a learned ichthyologist at a Spelling *Bee.*

Mr. Mortimer Collins and others are recently down, somewhat hypercritically we can't help thinking, on Mr. Tennyson's occasional natural history references throughout his poems. The fun is that in almost every instance in which fault is found with him, Mr. Tennyson is right and his critics wrong ! Here is one example of this hypercriticism in which Mr. Mortimer Collins is fairly hoist with his own petard. Mr. Tennyson writes—

"In spring a fuller crimson comes upon the robin's breast."

Upon which Mr. Collins comments—"As a fact, that fuller crimson comes in autumn, as all know who watch the half-shy, half-familiar bird—

"That ever in the haunch of winter sings."

Here Mr. Mortimer Collins is partly right and largely wrong, while Mr. Tennyson is altogether right. It is true that our native song-birds, moulting in autumn or early winter, assume at this season a thicker, warmer, fresher plumage after all the wear and tear consequent on the labours of nidification, incubation, and love-making throughout the spring and summer; but it is equally true that it is only in spring, as Mr. Tennyson correctly asserts, that our wild birds assume their gaudiest and gayest attire, every colour and shade of colour in the individual bird's feathering there and then only being at its best and brightest. And when we remember that spring is the season of love and incipient song, we should be very much surprised, and with good reason, if the fact were otherwise. So far as our recollection serves us, Mr. Mortimer Collins, or any one else, will find it rather difficult to catch Mr. Tennyson tripping in the direction indicated. We should say that the Poet Laureate was rather remarkable than otherwise for his fidelity to nature and truth in all his local colouring.

Some time ago, by the way, we had occasion to call attention to the exceeding frequency of misquotation in our current literature, and in quarters, too, where one would least expect it. Here is a curious and very unpardonable instance, all things considered. In a review of the *South Kensington Handbooks,* in the *Times* of the 18th January, a sentence opens thus—"It is well-known that *weary* lies the head that wears a crown?" Every one will see that the manifest intention here is to quote from the monologue of the poor harassed and sleepless King in Shakespeare's Henry IV. (part second), one of the finest things that even Shakespeare ever wrote, and we had thought too well-known by every one with any pretensions to literature to be misquoted. The concluding lines are these :—

> " Can'st thou, O partial sleep, give thy repose
> To the wet sea-boy in an hour so rude ;
> And in the calmest and most stillest night,
> With all appliances and means to boot,
> Deny it to a king ? Then, happy, low, lie down :
> *Uneasy* lies the head that wears a crown."

CHAPTER XXII.

A BRILLIANT display of aurora borealis on the early morning of the 8th [February 1871] led us to conclude that a change of weather was not far distant; and before sunset of that same day the wind had gone round from east by south to south-west, and a drizzling rain, with a very much milder temperature than we had known for three months, told us that, for the present at least, King Frost had agreed to suspension of hostilities. Since then it has been mostly wet, with occasional hailstone showers, and turbulent withal, if not actually stormy. The revictualling of Paris under the terms of the capitulation and armistice was not a more sensible relief to the starving inhabitants than was the recent thaw to our wild birds on sea and shore. The moment they became convinced that it was no sham, but a real, veritable thaw, they revived amazingly. Shaking off the torpidity in which cold and want had so pitilessly bound them, they took heart, and bustled about in search of such food as might now be procured by diligent seeking in copse and hedgerow, by pool and stream. An occasional strophe, sadly inconsecutive and discordant, may now again be heard when the sun shines out and the storm has lulled, from some of our hardier warblers, and we have observed that in some instances rooks have begun to pair; but our bird-world, upon the whole, is far from what it should be at this date; more taken up, like vanquished

France, with the thought of the mere necessities of life and the re-establishment of their exhausted energies, than with love or music, or the gaiety and *abandon* so characteristic in ordinary seasons of our feathered friends on the back of St. Valentine's Day. The meridian sun, however, is now steadily climbing zenithwards, and the day perceptibly lengthening apace, so that our wild birds, rapidly gathering strength, and daily improving in tone and tune, may, after all, arrive at their day of jollity and joyousness sooner than we anticipated. We captured a beautiful *Scarlet Emperor* butterfly a few days ago, as brisk and lively as possible, on a window pane in Ardvulin Cottage, Ardgour. How beautiful, by the way, and how suggestive of spring and vernal delights in a land of plenitude and peace, is the following from the Song of Solomon :—" For, lo, the winter is past, the rain is over and gone ; the flowers appear on the earth ; the time of the singing of birds is come, and the voice of the turtle is heard in our land ; the fig-tree putteth forth her green figs, and the vines with the tender grapes give a good smell."

Another animal besides the hedgehog has of recent years made its appearance in Lochaber, though previously unknown, so far as we are aware, anywhere in the West Highlands. The animal in question is the water-rat, water-vole, or British beaver. The last is, perhaps, its most appropriate name, for the animal is neither kith nor kin to the rat, while very much in its economy and habits, as well as in its corporeal structure, particularly its dentition, allies it not remotely to the beaver tribe. In size, the water-vole is more robust in body and larger in every way than the common rat, with a more silken pile, and a bigger and brighter eye. It frequents the banks of streams and ponds, feeding on the more delicate aquatic plants, and on the bark and tender shoots of the willow, alder, and such other shrubs as love to grow

" The quiet waters by."

That such an animal inhabited Lochaber was accidentally revealed
to us two years ago, and so unmistakeably that there was no room
for doubt or hesitation in the matter. We were returning from
Fort-William on a beautiful summer afternoon, walking by the hill
route through Lundavra, when having already accomplished more
than half the distance at our best pace, we sat down to rest and
solace ourselves with a pipe—not the Arcadian musical instrument,
observe, but the more prosaic article anathematised in the royal
Counterblast—by the side of a canal-like reach in the River Rhi,
as it slowly winds through Glenshelloch, when our attention was
drawn to a splash in the water at a short distance above us, to
which, however, we gave but little heed, taking it for the lively
flop of a half-pound trout engaged in fly-catching for supper.
Another and a louder splash, however, aroused our curiosity, and
induced us to creep cautiously in the direction whence the sound
proceeded, and there, sure enough, disporting themselves round a
gnarled alder stump that projected into the stream from the water-
line on the opposite bank, were a pair of water-voles, full-grown,
and brisk and lively as ever we had seen them in our younger
days in the upper reaches of the beautiful Eden in Fifeshire, a
favourite habitat. After watching their gambols for some time,
we threw a pebble into the pool, when they instantly dived and
disappeared, only to emerge in a few seconds near a large boulder
further up the stream, behind which, and cunningly concealed
beneath the overhanging bank, was their hole, into which they
popped as readily as does an alarmed mouse into a wall crevice.
As they dived and pursued their subaqueous flight in the direction
of their hole, the eye could follow their every movement, for the
water was as clear as crystal. Keeping very near the bottom, it
seemed as if they progressed partly by swimming and partly by
running along the gravel, at any rate with amazing celerity and
ease. We noticed that about their necks and shoulders their pile

appeared as if adorned with numberless tiny pearls—air bubbles, in
fact—that adhered to their fur, and that, frequently shifting the
position like quicksilver drops, as the animals moved, had a very
pretty effect.   Since that time the water-vole has been repeatedly
seen about the lower reaches of the same river, between the Inchree
Falls and the highway.   It has also been seen in some parts of the
Blackwater above Kinlochleven.   Ardent disciples of Izaak Walton
and others interested in the preservation of trout and salmon hold
the water-vole in great dislike, under the belief that it feeds largely
on fry and ova.   The accusation we believe to be unfounded, as
much so as the egg-eating charge against the hedgehog.   We shall
not attempt to prove a negative, the *onus probandi* of their aver-
ments logically resting with the accusers ; but we will say that we
have known the water-vole for many years, and at one time had
every opportunity of studying its habits, and we never had cause
to entertain the slightest suspicion that it was anything else than a
vegetable feeder.   We recollect once questioning old John Robertson of Perth, than whom a better fisher, whether on lake or stream,
never cast a fly or impaled a worm, about the water-vole's alleged
liking for fish-spawn and fry.   His reply was in these words, " I
dinna believe it, sir ; I have fished in maist feck o' the rivers, burns,
and lochs in Perth, Fife, and Kinross, and other counties forbye,
and the fish were just as plentiful where the splash o' the *gleb*
(a local name for the water-vole) was heard a'maist at every cast o'
the line, as where none could be seen for days together."   We
know, besides, that the late Professor John Reid of St. Andrews,
one of the most distinguished comparative anatomists of his day,
and who had dissected many of them, was of opinion that the
water-vole was a vegetable feeder and nothing else, he having
never been able to detect anything to lead him to the conclusion that it fed on fish or their spawn.   Suspicion of the
water-vole's being addicted to the malpractices in question was

first of all grounded on the fact that fish-bones were frequently
found along the banks of the streams he inhabited, and sometimes
about the entrance of, and even in, the hole which was his habitat
and home; and on this evidence alone the water-vole soon got
into very bad repute indeed. As to the finding occasionally of
fish bones along a water-vole inhabited stream, although the fact is
indisputable, it really goes for nothing, suspicious as it looks,
for similar relics of defunct trouts and troutlets may be seen any
day on the margin of streams where a water-vole was never yet
known to exist. The real culprits in such cases are the otter,
the common rat (a great fish-eater in shallow streams and almost
as expert a swimmer as the vole itself, only that it cannot dive so
well), the heron, king-fisher, and grey crow, all of whom are
fond of fish, either as an article of constant diet, or as an occasional
make-shift in default of more legitimate fare. As to the fish
bones to be sometimes met with in the water-vole's holes, the
dusky-coated and white-vested dipper and the beautiful plumaged
king-fisher are alone to blame. The castings, indeed, of a single
pair of king-fishers would of itself suffice to account for all the fish
bones one meets with by the banks of ponds and streams, for the
beautiful *Alcedo* is a voracious fish-devourer, and his hole going
backwards and upwards some three or four feet into the bank,
invariably a perfect charnel-house of bleached fish bones of
minnows and troutlets. The number of small fish that a pair
of king-fishers, with their young, dispose of in a single season must
amount to many thousands, and as the larger bones at least are
always cast or regurgitated, their presence may always be taken as
a sure indication that the spot has recently been the haunt of the
most beautifully coloured of British birds. When the bones of
larger fish, however, are met with, the blame, if blame there be,
must be shifted from the king-fisher to the shoulders of one or
other or all of the animals above mentioned. It is only fair that

the spirit of our laws, which accounts a man innocent until he
is proved guilty, should be extended to beasts and birds as
well.   In this view of the matter the water-vole has good reason
of complaint that it has been over hastily and unwarrantably
condemned on insufficient evidence, without even the form of
a fair and impartial trial.   Unlike Ritson, the antiquary and
balladist, who, although he was a strict vegetarian in diet, holding
all manner of animal food in utter abhorrence, and writing a volume
on the subject, was yet as cross-grained and as irascible as a
wasp, the water-vole, like a true vegetarian, is quiet and unobtrusive even to timidity, leading an inoffensive life, and in his play
hours, which—in proof of his good sense, let us remark—are very
numerous, as frolicsome and sportive as a kitten.   He will show
fight, it is true, if attacked in his hole or otherwise brought to bay,
and his bite, whether on the nose of an over-venturesome terrier, or
the hand that would rashly seize him, is very severe and difficult
to heal ; but it is only doing him the merest justice that those who
know him should bear witness that in general character and
disposition he is the most peaceable and harmless of animals.

CHAPTER XXIII.

March—The Story of a Spanish Dollar—The Spanish Armada—The "Florida"—*Faire-Chlaidh*, or Watching of the Graveyard—Molehill Earth for Flowers.

A FALL of snow on Monday, followed by keen frost during three consecutive nights, rendered the past week [March 1871], as to mere cold at least, the most wintry of the season; but with a bright sun circling at mid-March altitude, the frost had no time to penetrate the soil to any depth, and spring work has been steadily pushed on, with hardly any retardation. In the upland glens, however, the frost was for some days intense, and had it continued much longer, weakly sheep must have suffered severely. But *solvitur hiems*, the frost is gone; the weather is now again open, and mild and spring-like, and our wild birds—scores of them within a stone's cast of our window as we write—only seem all the more jubilant because of the past week's temporary dip of temperature to the freezing-point. "Speed the plough"—one of our very best Scotch reels, by the way—should now be the cry, at once earnest and cheery, of every one connected with arable land, for what says the old Gaelic proverb—

> " Am fear nach cuir 'sa Mhàrt,
> 'Sanmoch a bhuaineas e."

He that sows not in March shall have a late ingathering.

A coin was sent us for identification a few days ago, the history of which strikes us as interesting. We had no difficulty in determining it to be a silver Spanish dollar of the time of Philip II. It is much corroded and worn, but the following letters of the original inscription are distinctly legible :—Ph. II., D.G. Hisp: et Ind: Rex. 1585.   On the reverse disc is what seems to have been intended for the prow of a ship between two palm trees.   The owner of this coin tells us that it came into his possession in the following manner :—A brother of his, who owned and commanded a coasting schooner about fifty years ago, chancing to be becalmed while passing through the Sound of Mull, thought it best to come to anchor for the night.   Next morning, when getting under weigh, the anchor, as it came to the bows, was found to have brought up a large mass of tangle.   While clearing this away, the edge of the coin was observed sticking out from among a lot of sand and shingle attached to the tangle roots, and having been secured and handed to the Captain, he ever after kept it in his purse as a "luckpenny," on which he set a high value, and all the more so, perhaps, that it happened to be found on the morning of Easter Sunday, a fact that to him, as a good Catholic, had a significance and meaning that the rest of the crew took no account of.   Be this as it may, he was from that day an exceedingly prosperous and lucky man in all his undertakings, and till the day of his death he carried the coin about him wherever he went, as a "luck-penny" and talisman of extraordinary virtue.   The present owner, too, sets a very high value on this numismatic talisman, which, he declares, hardly anything would induce him to part with.   During the ten years that it has been in his possession, he assures us that he has been prosperous and successful as he never was before, with never a moment's illness ; and although too sensible and shrewd a man actually to assert that the coin has any-thing to do with it, it is a fact that he very seriously looks upon his Spanish dollar as a sort of "lee-penny," giving its possessor a fair chance of an amount of health and wealth, that without it he might struggle for in vain.   This nonsense apart, however, the question remains, What business had a Spanish dollar in the bottom of the Sound of Mull? How came it there? Our theory is that the coin originally belonged to some one connected with the great "Invincible Armada" of 1588. It is a well-known historical fact that, after the defeat of the Armada, the already shattered and discomfited fleet, in attempting to return to Spain by sailing round Scotland and Ireland, was overtaken by a dreadful storm, in which many of the ships were wrecked. One ship, named the "Florida," ran for shelter into the Sound of Mull, and while at anchor off Tobermory harbour, was captured and destroyed by a body of Mull and Morvern men, under the command of Maclean of Duart. This fact is sufficiently attested by a remission, under the Privy Seal, to that chief for his share in the somewhat questionable transaction, bearing date the 20th March 1589. The "Florida" was destroyed by being blown up, with all her armament and stores, and many of her crew—a treacherous and cruel act, for Scotland at least was then at peace with Spain—and it is probable that the Spanish dollar so recently examined by us reached the bottom of the Sound on that occasion, and there remained till fished up in the curious manner above related, upwards of two centuries afterwards. Some of the timbers of the submerged "Florida" have from time to time been brought to the surface, and a casket formed out of part of her windlass was presented by Sir Walter Scott to George IV., during his visit to Scotland in 1822.

An unsuccessful attempt, by means of divers, was made in 1740 to recover some of a large amount of treasure said to have been sunk in her; but some very beautiful brass guns were brought up, one of which is still to be seen at the Castle of Dunstaffnage, near Oban, and another, we believe, at Inveraray. These were last made to speak loud and lustily, not against a Queen of England, as was their original errand to our shores, but in honour of the marriage of the daughter of a Queen of Great

Britain with the son of a Scottish Duke, who now owns the lands which belonged to the Macleans, by whom the "Florida," carrying those very guns, was destroyed. Thus does "the whirligig of time bring about its revenges." Some years ago we were shown by a gentleman in Glasgow a large ebony-stocked pistol, beautifully carved and inlaid with mother-of-pearl and silver, which was said to have been secured from the wreck of the "Florida." We recollect that the corroded state of the barrel and lock abundantly satisfied us at the time that, whether it had belonged to the "Florida" or not, it had at all events long lain in water, and more probably, from the peculiar form of corrosion, in salt water than in fresh. As to the dollar, we have only further to state that its owner now thinks more of it than ever: our suggestion as to its very probable connection with the Spanish Armada having largely enhanced its value in his estimation. Its mere intrinsic value as a bit of silver would, we think, be fully and fairly appraised at something like twenty pence sterling.

We were the other day accidentally brought into contact with a curious superstition, which, although not peculiar to this district, but common, we believe, over all the Highlands, was yet quite new to us. We were sailing past the beautiful island of St. Mungo, in Loch Leven, the burial-place for many centuries of the people of Nether Lochaber and Glencoe, when the following conversation took place between ourselves and an old man who managed the sails while we steered. It was all in Gaelic, of course, but we give the substance in English :—" You were at the funeral on the island the other day, sir?" interrogatively observed our companion. " I was, indeed," we replied. "John ——," he continued, naming the deceased, "was a very decent man." " He was a fine old Highlander, shrewd and intelligent," we replied, "and, what is more, I believe a very good man." "Donald ——," naming a

person we both knew, "is very ill, and not likely to last long.'
"I saw him to-day," we observed, "and I fear that what you say
is true : he cannot last long." "Well, sir, it will be a good thing
for John —— (the person recently buried); his term of watching
will be a short one." "I do not understand what you mean," we
observed, with some curiosity. "The man is dead and buried ;
what watching should he have to do?" "Why, sir, don't you
know that the *spirit* of the last person buried in the island has to
keep watch and ward over the graves till the spirit of the next
person buried takes his place?" "I really did not know that," we
replied. "Is it a common opinion that such is the case, and do
you believe it yourself?" "Well, sir, it is generally believed by
the people ; and having always heard that it was so, I cannot well
help believing it too. The spirit whose watch it is, is present there
day and night. Some people have seen them : my mother, God
rest her ! once pointed out to me, when I was a little boy, an
appearance, as of a flame of light on the island, slowly moving
backwards and forwards, and she assured me it was the watching
spirit going his rounds." "What particular object has the spirit in
watching?" we asked. "Well, I don't exactly know," was the
answer. "He just takes a sort of general charge of the Island of
the Dead, until his successor arrives." We have since found that
a belief in this superstition is common among the old people. The
spirit or ghost is supposed to be to a certain extent unhappy, and
impatient of relief while in the discharge of this office, and thus, it
is considered, that the sooner after a funeral there is occasion again
for the opening of a grave, the better it is for the spirit of the last
person interred, who then, and not till then, passes finally and
fully to his rest.

We have to warn such of our readers as dwell by the sea,
and all "who go down to the sea in ships, and see His wonders
in the deep," that unusually high tides may be expected

in connection with the new moon of the 18th. The highest tide, however, is not likely to be exactly coincident with the change of the moon, but at the time of the second or third flood thereafter. Along our Scottish coasts the tidal wave will probably be highest on the morning of the 20th, so that this notice may yet be sufficiently timeous. Much, however, will depend on the state of wind and weather, as to the height the tide may attain at any particular place. In any case, it can do no harm to be prepared.

To such of our readers as may be engaged in the rearing and tending of flowers at this season we very willingly communicate a hint that may be found useful. And it is this. In filling flower-pots or window-sill boxes, there is frequently considerable difficulty in procuring soil that will be at once sufficiently rich, free of weed seeds, and finely pulverised. The despised and sadly persecuted mole provides the very thing wanted, and in little round heaps, waiting only to be gathered, commonly called molehills. For flowers, whether in pots or borders, there is nothing so good as molehill earth. The *rationale* of the thing is, as is well-known to every one in the least acquainted with the natural history of the interesting velvet-coated subterranean tunnelists, that they live on worms and insect larvæ. These are always found in the best soil, which is hurled to the surface in round heaps by the industrious little animal while in pursuit of his prey, and in so pulverised a state, and so free of weed seeds, as to be above all others the soil most suitable for all manner of ordinary floriculture. With such soil we have grown the purest dahlias and wallflowers we ever saw anywhere. The old Royalist toast, "To the little gentleman in the black velvet coat!" was in sly allusion to the death of a high personage from injuries received by his horse stumbling over an insignificant molehill, and whose name by the way is disagreeably connected with a dark deed done heretofore in Glencoe, whose wild gorge and frowning precipices are in view as we write. But if any of our readers will feel cause of gratitude to the mole on the hint above given, as they bend over a moss rose or dahlia which has grown in soil so procured, why, we shall be glad for all our sakes. For our reader's, in that he or she has been gratified in such a delightful and holy taste as flower culture ; for our own, that the secret was ours to divulge ; and for the mole's sake, poor persecuted fellow, for he sadly needs a friend.

CHAPTER XXIV.

IF somewhat over-showery for the comfort of tourists, whose season [June 1871] may now be said to have fairly commenced, the weather with us on the west coast is at least all that the agriculturist and sheepowner could wish it to be, for pasture everywhere is rich and abundant to a degree that has rarely been known even here, while crops of all kinds never perhaps presented a healthier or more luxuriant growth. The truth is that a certain amount of rainfall, and that amount a large one, is absolutely necessary for the wellbeing of our crops in the West Highlands, and the longer we live the more do we feel the truth and force of the saying of a shrewd old gentleman, at his own dinner table many years ago, to the effect that he had always observed that the season in which there was some difficulty in getting peats secured in good condition was invariably the best for Lochaber and the neighbouring districts from a pastoral and agricultural point of view. This is particularly observable this year, for while you cannot as yet see a stack of this season's peats anywhere, the country is clothed in richer, greener verdure, the woods are leafier, and crops of every description more luxuriant than we can recollect to have been the case for at least a dozen years past. If anybody wishes to see the West Highlands in all their magnificence and beauty, now is the season, for, go where you may, turn whithersoever you will, wander forth

at any hour and in any direction, you cannot fail to be charmed
with the infinite variety of pictures that present themselves for
your admiration, pictures which, while they only charm and
enchant the ordinary beholder, delight at once and distress the
artist—delight him by their marvellous beauties, but distress him
not the less, because he cannot with all his cunning transfer these
beauties in their entirety to canvas.   An American gentleman
whom we met the other day candidly confessed that, although he
had gone over most of his native land, and made the tour of Continental Europe and the East, he had not in all his travels seen
anything more beautiful than the shores of Loch Linnhe, Loch Leven,
and Lochiel at sunset on a fine evening in June.   The late Dr.
Aiton of Dolphinton told us on his return from Palestine that he
had seen nothing at all to equal Loch Linnhe on a summer's evening.
In all the breadth of his native Doric, which he always employed
in familiar conversation, he declared there was "naething in a' the
Archipelago till touch't," and we have heard Dr. Norman Macleod
on his return from India express himself very much to the same
effect.   The Queen says in her *Journal* that "the scenery in Loch
Linnhe is magnificent—such beautiful mountains."

A specimen of a very rare bird, shot by the keeper in Ardgour
Garden a few days ago, has been kindly sent to us by Mr. Maclean.
It turns out to be a male in beautiful plumage of the turtle-dove
(*Columba turtur*, Linn.; *La tourterelle* of Buffon), a bird rarely
seen anywhere in Scotland, and which, except in this instance, has
never, so far as we are aware, been met with in the West
Highlands.   We remember seeing a young bird, a female in imma-
ture plumage, that was said to have been shot somewhere near
Falkland Palace in the summer of 1847, from which it was
reasonably concluded that a pair of these beautiful birds had in
that year at least nidified and reared their young somewhere in the
Howe of Fife.   Except in the case of the specimen now before us,

we are not aware that it has ever been met with anywhere in the
north or north-western counties.   The turtle is, as we have said,
an exceedingly beautiful and handsome bird, the breast of a delicate
vinaceous tint, and a black patch on either side of the neck, each
feather of which is tipped with a crescent of pure white, giving it
a very elegant and striking appearance.   It is less bulky and less
rotund in form than the common dove, its shape more nearly
resembling that of the blue jay or throstle cock, which latter it also
about equals in size.   We have never seen this bird in confinement, but it is said to exhibit a remarkable degree of tenderness
and sagacity, whether as a cage or chamber bird.   On the Continent
it is kept not only for its tameness and beauty, but because it is a
common belief among the people that it attracts to itself bad
humours, and is to a family in the matter of diseases what a
lightning-rod is to a building in a thunderstorm.   Bechstein, a
shrewd and intelligent man, seems to think that the belief in
question, absurd as it may appear to us, is not so ill-founded after
all, for he says quietly, " Thus much at least is certain, that during
the illness of men it readily becomes sickly."   The explanation
probably is that, being a tender and delicate bird, the odour and
effluvia attendant on certain human ailments affects it as described.
Other birds are occasionally similarly affected; thus, when our
own children were laid up with a very bad kind of scarlatina, our
cage-birds, gold and green finches, were out of sorts for some time,
drooping and dejected and unable to sing as usual, though the
month was April, when they should have been in all respects at
their best and in full and free song.   You may be sure, by the
way, that we were not a little pleased with a paragraph which
appeared the other day about the male cockatoo that dropped the
egg, very much, no doubt, to the astonishment of his amiable
mistress.   When some years ago we ventured to assert that males
of various birds, notably the common domestic cock, sometimes

dropped an egg, the thing was scouted as ridiculous, and from Dan to Beersheba, from London to John O'Groat's, the cry was that it couldn't be, that it was impossible ; one writer going so far in his scepticism as plainly to declare that " he would as soon believe that a bull had given birth to a calf." Much was the chaffing that we had to endure in connection with the subject, and our most intimate friends could hardly believe that we were serious in it at all. And yet we were perfectly in earnest ; we had known the thing happen repeatedly, and since then a very fine cock goldfinch of our own, one of the best singers, too, we have ever heard, laid an egg in his cage which is still in our possession, and several of our correspondents having had their attention directed to the subject, have assured themselves that, not only is the thing possible, but in the case of the domestic cock at least, and of many cage-birds, of rather common occurrence. It is a very odd and curious thing, no doubt, and difficult of explanation, but there are thousands of undisputed facts in natural history in the same category, the existence of which is beyond all question, though the how, and why, and wherefore is a mystery.

From our window, as we write these lines, we can see quite a fleet of herring boats sailing up Loch Linnhe on their return from the fishing stations at Barra, Lochmaddy, and the Lewis—a very pretty sight—not less than two hundred or more boats under full sail, stretching in one long line from Corran Ferry to the Sound of Mull, looking at this distance for all the world like the notes in a line of complicated printed music.

CHAPTER XXV.

WITH an occasional fine day [August 1871], the past fortnight must, we fear, be characterised as having been upon the whole wet —*very* wet, a stranger would say—and not a little stormy withal. We had a tremendous thunderstorm early on Sunday morning, with the most magnificent display of forked lightning that we have ever seen, while the very earth seemed to quake and tremble under the crash of peal upon peal of thunder, so near and loud at times as to be absolutely terrible. It is no wonder that the soundest sleepers were awakened from their midnight slumbers by the hurly-burly. We ourselves got up for a time, and sat at our window, watching the lightning that darted incessantly among the mountain summits with startling vividness, revealing their serrated peaks at times through the very heart of the thunder-cloud as distinctly as if it were clearest noonday. Rain, too, fell the while in torrents, that instantly filled river and mountain stream to overflowing; and as the storm passed away, and we retired to rest in the grey, uncertain twilight of the early dawn, we were lulled into a sleep, that lasted well nigh until noon, by the weird and wild music of "the noise of many waters." We thought, as we sat alone in the midst of that magnificent storm, of him (was it John Foster?) who, on a similar occasion, turned round to his companion and remarked, in a tone of deep solemnity, "It is a fine night; *the Lord is abroad!*" Crops, though generally further from maturity than is usual at this date, continue to grow rapidly, and everywhere present a strong and healthy appearance,—"a guarantee," as newspaper editors say, "of their good faith" and honest intentions in the direction of a bounteous yield when cometh the season of ingathering. Potatoes are now in full flower; and a very pretty sight, if you deign to look at it with an unprejudiced eye, is a potato field in blossom at this season. If the incomparable esculent were not cultivated for its utility and value as an article of food, it would still deserve a place in our gardens for its elegance and beauty simply as a flower. Nothing but its commonness causes its beauty as a flowering plant to be so constantly overlooked. We are in the midst of our hay season, and we are only anxious about good weather for securing it in tolerable order. Eight consecutive days of dry, breezy weather would be of incalculable value to us at this moment. Anything will grow, and grow luxuriantly, on the West Coast: our difficulties only begin with the season of ripening and after preservation. If there be any truth in the old Scottish saying, that "a year of nuts will also be a year of corn," then may the grain-growers of the West Highlands at least already congratulate themselves, for we have seldom seen the hazel boughs so laden with nut clusters; and a prettier sight than a hazel wood so laden, either now or when decked in its autumnal robes, it would be difficult to conceive. It is, besides, a fragrant, cleanly wood, through which you can at any time dash fearlessly and at will, all the better of your contact with the leaves, branches, and nut clusters, when you have reached the open beyond. There is not a leaf in the woods so thoroughly clean, so fragrant when you have crushed it in your hand, so soft and pleasant to the touch in its every stage, as the leaf fresh plucked from the hazel bough. And *apropos* of hazel nuts, a gentlemen from the south of England, at present resident in our neighbourhood, told us something the other day that we did not know before. "In our part of England," observed our friend, "the hazel is common, and grows to a

K

larger size, has more pretentions to the name of tree, in fact, than here with you ; and our nuts, I should say, must be larger, juicier, and in all respects better than yours." (A " soft impeachment," at which, for the honour of Nether Lochaber, we took the liberty of gravely shaking our head in token of dissent). " We seldom, however," he went on, " can get a ripe hazel nut in autumn, the reason being that in many places they are gathered while yet in a half-formed and green state. You look surprised, but the reason is this : the husk of the green, unripe hazel nut is rich, as you must be aware, in a bitterly sharp and astringent acid, that must have often made your teeth water when you have essayed to crack a nut in a state of immaturity. This acid, then, you must know, is valuable as a *mordant* (a technical term) in the printing and dyeing of cotton and other fabrics, and it commands a high price in the market accordingly. It is a maxim in commerce that demand creates supply ; and the consequence is, that every year in the month of July, when the nuts are at their greenest, and the acid in their husks at its acridest, women and children plunder the woods of their hazel nut clusters, which are sold to the manufacturers, who, by a process of crushing by machinery, and washing and maceration, extract all the acid, to be employed, as I have already mentioned, in cotton printing and dye works." So far in substance, if not in *ipsissimis verbis,* our friend. All we could reply was that we should be sorry indeed to see our own bonny hazel woods similarly despoiled. Another thing told us by this friend somewhat surprised us. He observed our servant girl carrying a bundle of potato "shaws" into the byre, and asked us what they were for. On our replying that these were the shaws of the potatoes taken up for dinner, and that they were thrown before the cows, and devoured by them with avidity on their return from their hill pasture in the evening, he earnestly advised us never to do so again ; that in England it was never done, because it was found that potato shaws given to milch cows not only lessened the quantity of milk yielded, but actually vitiated the milk itself, giving it a disagreeable taste, and making it decidedly unwholesome. All we could answer was that we had known potato shaws given to milch cows all over the Highlands since ever we could remember, and that we had never known or heard any of the evils stated to result from the use of them. What says the reader? It is true, no doubt, that the potato belongs botanically to a family of plants many of whom are highly poisonous—such as the common *deadly nightshade* of our lanes and roadsides, for example—and it is averred that, although the tuber of the potato is healthy and nutritious when *cooked*, it is a poison in its raw state, and that its stem, leaves, flower, and "apple" are all more or less poisonous; and yet we have known boys, while the blight was yet unheard of, and when potatoes were more prolific of apples or plums than they have ever been since, eat the large, soft, full, ripe apples with relish, and they never suffered the slightest inconvenience in consequence that ever we heard of. As a boy we have often ate them ourselves, and very saccharine, juicy, and pleasant flavoured we recollect they were, not at all unlike the purple plum of our gardens in taste and flavour, and hardly inferior to it as a pleasant succulent *bonne bouche.* Cattle, as we know, will greedily eat the fresh shaws, as they will a decidedly poisonous plant, the hemlock (*Celticè, Iteotha*); and it is a well-known fact that in severe cases of scurvy on board ships that have to go long voyages a feast of *raw* potatoes is an immediate and certain cure; so that after all it would seem that if the potato is originally a poisonous plant, cultivation has eradicated all, or almost all, traces of the evil. As to the deleterious effects of the shaws on the milk of cattle we have our doubts, our amiable and learned friend above mentioned to the contrary notwithstanding. And while on such subjects let us record a piece of information received from an old woman in our neighbourhood a few days ago. We were cutting some green ferns on the hillside, when the old lady in question, who happened to pass the way at the time, stood to have a crack with us about the weather and crops and things in general, said crack concluding somewhat as follows :— "You are cutting ferns, sir," said the old lady, "what are you to make of them if you please, sir?" "They are for bedding," we replied, "bedding for the cows and pony." "Well, sir," she rejoined, "there is no harm in bedding the pony with them ; they will do *him* no evil ; but take an old woman's advice, and don't put them under your cows." "Why so," we asked in astonishment. "What can be cleaner, fresher, fragranter for bedding, whether for horse or cow, than these nice green ferns? Just look how beautiful and soft they are." "Still, sir," she persisted, "you must not place them under your cows, particularly your milch cows ; if you do, their udders will assuredly fester, and they will go wrong in their milk. I have known it happen often, and no sensible person in the country ever does such a thing now-a-days. Ferns cut in autumn when brown and ripe make excellent bedding for milch cows as for all other cattle, but July cut ferns, green, juicy, and unripe, should never be used for bedding milch cows. I do not pretend to tell you why they should produce the evils I have mentioned, but I do know that if I had fifty cows I had rather have them without bedding at all than put such green, fresh ferns as those under them." We stood for the moment aghast at this piece of information, which was perfectly new to us, and from the positive and decided tone of the old lady, a shrewd intelligent woman of her class, we felt that there must be something in it. On inquiry we have since found that the old lady's belief in the evil of ferns—green, unripe ferns, that is—as bedding for milch cows, is common among the people of this part of the West Highlands. Whether the whole affair is a mere superstition, the fern having always been accounted a sacred plant in the High-

lands, or whether there is really some foundation in fact for the belief
that a bedding of green ferns causes the udders of cows to swell and
fester as is alleged, we are not at this moment prepared to say; perhaps some of our readers may be able to throw light on the subject.
It is just possible that green-cut ferns, when pressed by the recumbent
animal, may exude an acrid juice that, coming in contact with the
tender udder, may be absorbed with the effects alleged. Meantime
we doubt it. One thing we know is this, that cattle are fond of
lying down among growing ferns in their every stage, and that
both roe and red deer frequently make their lair among growing
ferns at this season. Do you remember, by the way, Scott's
magnificent description in *Marmion* of a fern-couched deer
roused from his midnight lair by the awful tolling of the passing
bell over the living entombment of poor Constance in the monastery
of Lindisfarne ?—

> " Slow o'er the midnight wave it swung,
> Northumbrian rocks in answer rung ;
> To Warkworth cell the echoes roll'd,
> His beads the wakeful hermit told.
> The Bamborough peasant raised his head,
> But slept ere half a prayer he said ;
> So far was heard the mighty knell,
> The stag sprung up on Cheviot Fell,
> Spread his broad nostril to the wind,
> Listed before, aside, behind,
> Then couch'd him down beside the hind,
> *And quaked among the mountain fern,*
> *To hear that sound so dull and stern."*

Than the whole of the trial and doom of poor Constance, who
" loved not wisely but too well," in the second canto of *Marmion*,
even Scott never wrote anything more solemn or terrible.

CHAPTER XXVI.

Harvest—Scythe and Sickle *v.* Reaping Machines— Potatoes — Garibaldi and Potatoes at Caprera—Fishing —*Platessa Gemmatus,* or Diamond Plaice—Mushrooms—The Poetry of Fairy Rings—Harvest-Home.

WITH such fine weather as we enjoy at present, September [1871] is one of the pleasantest months of the year. Harvest operations are now in full swing, and the redbreast—having moulted, and proudly conscious of the splendour of his scarlet vest—has already begun his autumnal song—more delectable now and more appreciated, because now, with the exception of an occasional voluntary from the wren, he only sings, whereas his vernal strains are lost in their amalgamation with the full chorus of a thousand performers. It is pleasant now, as you saunter or ride along, to listen to the merry laughter of the reapers afield, and to their song, as, *moré majorum,* it floats in chorus on the gale : pleasant, too, to us at least, and far from unmusical, the frequent sound of the whetting of scythe and sickle in every direction—the bloodless weapons—as they are deftly handled in the process, glancing brightly in the sunlight ! Reaping " machines" and " steam " ploughs may be very good things in their way, but we are not ashamed to confess that we are glad that, as yet at least, we know nothing of them in the West Highlands. The utilitarian must be content if we admit all their value and importance from *his* point of view, while at the same time we yet assert that wherever they appear all the poetry of agriculture incontinently becomes plain prose—*Sic transit gloria Cereris.* Very excellent, at all events, are our crops this season, and very excellently are they being harvested. A good deal has already been secured in barn and stackyard, and in such condition, too, as is but rarely possible under the weeping skies of the west coast. The weather is still so favourable that our people are working with a will, and making every exertion to have their harvesting concluded while it lasts. Potatoes still continue sound and untainted, although an occasional *spottiness* of the leaf in some fields shows that our old enemy the "blight" has not yet forgot the time of his coming. The crop is now, however, about ripe, and may be considered very much out of danger for the season. In our last, we had a good deal to say about this invaluable root, and how it should be brought to table; and to show that such a subject-matter is not quite so *infra dig.* as some of our readers might suppose, listen to what the *Times* says of Garibaldi's doings at Caprera. After recounting the General's failures in connection with his orchard, the acclimation of the silk-worm, &c., the *Times* proceeds :—" Garibaldi, however, points with exultation to his potato fields. No species of the favourite root is neglected, and there is no treat he so heartily enjoys as a dish of his own potatoes, baked with his own hand under embers, in the open air—a treat which calls up reminiscences of his camp life on the Tonale or the Stelvis, or of his pioneer's experience in the backwoods of the Mississippi or the Plate." We wonder if this "hero in an unheroic age," who yet disdains not to exult in his potato fields, or to cook his delicious "earth apples," as the French so happily term them, in the embers with his own hand— we wonder if he eats his fish with his fingers? We could lay a wager that he does; that in eating his ember-roasted potatoes in the open air, with some broiled *tunny,* let us suppose, as a fitting accompaniment—(the *Thynnus vulgaris,* in highest esteem with the ancients as with the moderns, abundant about Caprera and all the shores of Provençe, Sardinia, and Sicily, and than which, indeed, there is hardly any better fish)—we could lay a wager, we say, that in eating his potatoes and fish *al fresco* he discards the use of knife and fork utterly, eating his fish with his fingers, and using the running brook beside him as a convenient finger-glass.

There is a lull at present in our herring fishing, rather because, however, of the paramount claims of harvest operations on the attention of our people just now, than from any dearth of the fish in our lochs. In a week or ten days, when all or most of the corn has been cut, the fishing will be resumed, and it is hoped with success. In an old Fingalian tale it is very beautifully said— " Rejoice, O my son, in the gifts of the sea; for they enrich you without making any one else the poorer." A rather rare fish in our western waters was caught a few days ago by our excellent neighbour, J. P. Grant, Esq., who occupies Cuilchenna House this season. Mr. Grant was good enough to send this odd fish for our inspection, and we determined it to be a species of *plaice* (*Platessa*) —and the handsomest of the family—the *Platessa gemmatus* of ichthyologists, commonly called the diamond or diamond-spotted plaice. This very handsome fish is quite as good on the table as it is beautiful when fresh from its native element. Another fish, rare on the west coast, was captured by ourselves with the rod while mackerel fishing last week. It was a specimen of the sapphirine gurnard (*Trigla hirundo*), one of the family of "hard-cheeked" fishes, of which the common red or cuckoo gurnard (*Trigla cuculus*) is a familiar example. A peculiarity in all the family is the abnormal development of the pectoral fins, so large in one species as to enable it to fly bird-like for short distances in the air. All our readers must have heard and read of the flying-fish (*Trigla volitans*), even if they have never seen it. It is of the gurnard family—a very near relation, indeed, of our common gurnard. All the "hard-cheeked" fishes, without exception, are excellent eating. Our sapphirine gurnard was delicious.

We do not know whether any of our readers has observed it

to be the case elsewhere, but in this and the neighbouring districts we have again and again remarked how very plentiful all kinds of mushrooms—the whole family of *Agarici*—are this season. Never have we seen so many beautiful " fairy rings," many of them almost mathematically perfect circles. Although they are always interesting and beautiful, you cannot help being a little startled, and feeling a shade of awe mingling with your curiosity and admiration, as you suddenly come upon one of these emerald rings in burnside meadow or upland glade, and contrast the vivid green and well-defined periphery of the charmed circle with the general every-day colour of the surrounding verdure. We are not surprised—on the contrary, we can perfectly understand—how in the good old times, ere yet the schoolmaster was abroad, or science had become a popular plaything, people— and, doubtless, very honest, decent people too—attributed those inexplicable emerald circles to supernatural agency; if, indeed, anything connected with the " good folks" or " men of peace" could properly be called *super*-natural in times when a belief in fairies, and every sort of fairy freak and frolic, was deemed the most correct and natural thing in the world. Didn't these circles, it was argued, appear in the course of a single night? In the sequestered woodland glade, nor herd nor milkmaid could see anything odd or unusual as the sun went down, and, lo ! next morning, as they drove their flocks afield, there was the mysterious circle, round as the halo about the wintry moon. Was not the colour, too, of these circles green, and not only green, but a deeper, richer, and more vivid green than natural verdure is ever seen to be? and whose work, therefore, could it be but that of the fairies, whose own favourite, peculiar colour was green, that no mere mortal durst wear but at his peril, and who, it was well known, delighted to dance hand-in-hand in merry circles round, footing it featly, as the owl flittered ghost-like by the scene, all by the silvery light of the moon, until the dawn of day. As Tom D'Urfey has it—

> " O how they skipped it,
>   Capered and tripped it,
>   Under the greenwood tree !"

The popular belief in the origin of these bright green circles, that
they were caused by fairy feet in many a midnight merry-go-round,
is frequently alluded to in the poetry alike of Celt and Saxon.
Thus a fairy song of the time of Charles the First begins—

> " We dance on hills above the wind,
>   And leave our footsteps there behind,
>   Which shall to after ages last,
>   When all our dancing days are past."

The reader will probably remember Queen Mab's very quaint and
beautiful song in Percy's *Reliques of English Poetry* :—

> " Come, follow, follow me,
>   You fairy elves that be :
>   Which circle on the green,
>   Come follow Mab your queen.
> Hand in hand let's dance around,
> For this place is fairy ground.
>
> " Upon a mushroom's head
>   Our table-cloth we spread ;
>   A grain of rye or wheat,
>   Is manchet which we eat :
> Pearly drops of dew we drink,
> In acorn cups fill'd to the brink.
>
> " The grasshopper, gnat, and fly,
>   Serve for our minstrelsy :
>   Grace said, we dance a while,
>   And so the time beguile ;
> And if the moon doth hide her head,
> The glow-worm lights us home to bed.
>
> " On tops of dewy grass
>   So nimbly do we pass,
>   The young and tender stalk
>   Ne'er bends when we do walk ;
> Yet in the morning may be seen
> Where we the night before have been."

Another poet says—

> " O'er the dewy green,
> By the glow-worm's light,
> Dance the elves of night,
> Unheard, unseen.
> Yet where their midnight pranks have been,
> The circled turf will betray to-morrow."

Nor was the superstition unknown to Shakspeare ; was there anything unknown to *him ?* Listen :—

> " And nightly meadow-fairies, look you sing,
> Like to the Garter's compass, in a ring ;
> The expressure that it bears, green let it be,
> More fertile-fresh than all the field to see ;
> And, *Honi soit qui mal y pensè*, write
> In emerald tufts, flowers, purple, blue, and white :
> Like sapphire, pearl, and rich embroidery,
> Buckled below fair knighthood's bending knee !
> Fairies use flowers for their charactery."

And if we know better now-a-days than to believe these green circles to be fairy rings, we also know better than to give the slightest credence to certain authors of our own day who have gravely asserted that they are caused by electricity. We prefer the fairy agency theory, as the more poetical and picturesque of the two, for, as to the truth of either, why, the one is every whit as true as the other. Fairy rings, as we continue for convenience sake to call them, are, in truth, caused by a species of mushroom (*Agaricus pratensis*), the sporule dust or seed of which, having fallen on a spot suitable for its growth, instantly germinates, and constantly propagating itself by sending out a net-work of innumerable filaments and threads, forms the rich green rings so common everywhere this season. On the outer edge of this ring, and sometimes also, though more rarely, on the inner edge, grows the perfect plant, the fruit, the mushroom proper itself ; and if some of our modern wiseacres had only had half an eye in their

heads and the least particle of gumption, they could easily have
gone to the fields and seen all this for themselves, instead of lazily
theorising on the origin of the apparent mystery in their dressing-
gowns and slippers by the fireside, and sagely ascribing the whole
to the agency of electricity! There was a time, you may remember,
when it was the fashion to ascribe everything that people didn't
readily understand to electricity—very convenient certainly, but if
you pushed these *savans* a little, and asked them what this electricity
itself was, they were incontinently dumb, or, if they talked, they
were bound to talk nonsense. We can forgive, and even admire,
the fairy dance theory, for it is full of poetry and beauty, and in
an age when people seldom troubled themselves to trace natural
phenomena to their source, it was, upon the whole, a rather happy
conjecture; if it was not the actual *vrai*, it had of *vraisemblance*
about it enough to recommend it to the acceptance of the multitude.
Grant but the existence of fairies, and the rest was easy of belief.
The "electricity" theory, on the contrary, was unpardonable: it
was not only false in fact, but it had nothing whatever about it to
recommend it either to one's faith or fancy. Hardly more excusable
than the electricity theorists themselves are those authors who tell
us that the West received the first hint of the existence of fairies
from the East at the time of the Crusades, and that almost all
our fairy lore is traceable to the same source; the fact being,
nevertheless, that Celt and Saxon, Scandinavian and Goth, Lap
and Fin, had their "duergar," their "elfen," without number, such
as *dun elfen, berg-elfen, munt-elfen, feld-elfen, wudu-elfen, sae-elfen,*
and *waeter-elfen*—elves, or spirits, of downs, hills, and mountains,
of the fields, of the woods, of the sea, and of the rivers, streams,
and solitary pools—fairies, in short, and a complete fairy mythology,
long centuries before Peter the Hermit was born, or Frank and
Moslem dreamt of making the Holy Sepulchre a *casus belli*. It is
a curious fact in connection with fairy lore, and we have not seen

it noticed elsewhere, that although these anomalous beings are always credited with much capriciousness, and are constantly described as sensitive in the extreme to anything like slight or insult, keenly vindictive in their dispositions and easily irritated, they are never represented as encompassing the *death* of human beings. They tease, terrify, and torment in a thousand ways where they take a dislike, but they never *kill*. Their power is described as great, but it is also limited—the issues of life and death are beyond their reach. In the fairy song (*temp.* Charles I.) first quoted, there are two amusing verses indicating such pranks as fairies *could* play on mortals, if mortals offended them. Thus concludes Queen Mab her song :—

> " Next turned to mites in cheese, forsooth,
> We get into some hollow tooth ;
> Wherein, as in a Christmas hall,
> We frisk and dance, the devil and all !

> " Then we change our wily features,
> Into yet far smaller creatures,
> And dance in joints of gouty toes,
> To painful tunes of groans and woes."—

A pathology of toothache and gout that we recommend to the attention of the faculty. The fairy ring agaric is one of the British species of mushroom that may be eaten with safety. For our own part we abominate the whole tribe. Our table may be scantier at times than we could wish, but it will be scantier far than a kind Providence has ever yet permitted it to be before we shall think of dining or supping on funguses. *Chacun à son goût*, however, and if anybody wants mushrooms in abundance, now is the time, and Nether Lochaber is the place for them.

The new moon that comes in this morning (the 6th) will be the harvest moon of the year. It is full on the 20th, and for a few evenings before and after will be very beautiful, and well worth attention. If you can command telescopic aid on the occasion, so much the better, but even without it, it were strange if we could not view with admiration and delight the silver orb that probably at some such conjunction as that of the 20th, when walking in her brightness and her beauty, tempted the patriarch of old to kiss his hand in acknowledgment of her excellency, and bow before her in adoration.

CHAPTER XXVII.

The disappearance of the glories of Autumn, and the advent of Winter—Innovations and Innovators—New Version of the Scriptures—The *Milkmaid and her Fairy Lover*, translated from the Gaelic.

ICHABOD ! the glory is departed [November 1871]. The gorgeous autumnal hues, which were so beautiful when we penned our last, have already passed away. In the first fierce breath of winter the trees have shed their golden glories, while the few remaining leaves that still cling trembling to branch and bough, shrivelled up and blackened at their edges, present only that pallid, corpse-like hue that betokens approaching dissolution, making you sad and thoughtful as you gaze, and reminding you that everywhere, on all hands, last while it may, the end of all life is death. It is a sad lesson for the moment, doubtless, but a useful one ; and even at its worst, when the thought bears heaviest upon us, the cloud presents its silver lining, and a gleam of gladness bursts upon the soul, in the recollection that as sure as all things are subject to decay and death, so sure are decay and death themselves but the vassals of a brighter life and more excellent glory. In one of our Scripture Paraphrases there is a very beautiful reference to the decay of nature at this season, and to the hope that gladdens us amidst all the desolation of the scene :—

> " All nature dies, and lives again :
>   The flow'r that paints the field,
>   The trees that crown the mountain's brow,
>   And boughs and blossoms yield,

" Resign the honours of their form
　　At Winter's stormy blast,
And leave the naked leafless plain
　　A desolated waste.

" Yet soon reviving plants and flow'rs
　　Anew shall deck the plain ;
The woods shall hear the voice of Spring,
　And flourish green again !"

We have no patience with your innovators, whether in matters
of Church or State.　We do not deny, indeed, that certain innovations may be sometimes permissible, even if not absolutely necessary,
that by their adoption things may be done more decently and in
order ; nor do we object even to a radical change in a given direction, when such a change has by common consent become
imperative.　We believe, in fact, in development and progress ;
only let that progress and development be slow and sure, that
they may be lasting ; gradual, that they may be graceful, and fall
easily into their place, without unnecessary jostling or disturbance
of the established order of things.　*Festina lente*—hasten slowly—
was the motto of the learned Erasmus, and *quoad hoc* it is ours
also ; and, if you care to know it, is our creed in affairs political
and ecclesiastical.　Some people, however, seem born to be innovators and nothing else, and the innovator, *pure et simple*, is
surely a pest.　He seems to have been born never to know peace
himself, and never, as much as in him lies, to permit others a
moment's rest or peace, or quiet either.　Your thoroughbred,
full-blooded innovator always reminds us of our first housekeeper
—a very good woman in her way, too, but who had a perfect
craze for shifting and reshifting, adjusting and readjusting, as well as
dusting and redusting every article of furniture throughout the house,
at all sorts of unseasonable hours, and when to ordinary mortals
such labour seemed utterly uncalled for.　When we were at
home she went " at it " in out-of-the-way closets and bedrooms as
much and as often as the immediate calls of the moment per-

mitted. But when she got us away from home for a day or two, how she did enjoy it! How she did luxuriate in the power to innovate "at her own sweet will"—the quotation, by the way, is rather inapt, for her temper was somewhat of the sourest. Sometimes when we came back after a day or two's absence, we could hardly believe it to be the same house, so great was the change in the place and position of everything. At last the thing became unbearable. One evening, on our return from a walk, we found our writing-table, at which we had been employed during the day, carefully placed in the darkest corner of the room, with its drawers, containing letters, paper, pens, &c., jammed up hard and fast against the wall, while books and manuscripts were most artistically arranged in pyramidal form, the ink-bottle representing the graceful entablature on the top of a book-case, where it must have cost her no small pains, and a great deal of stretching on tip-toe, even with the aid of a chair, to place them. The thing was too absurd for any one to be really angry ; but we pretended to be so, and at last peace was proclaimed, under a sort of compromise that she should arrange and readjust all the rest of the house at her pleasure, as often and as radically as she chose, but that *that* particular room, having been put to rights to our mutual satisfaction once for all, must in all time coming be let alone. This treaty being duly ratified, was upon the whole faithfully observed by the contracting parties. The mischief, however, with your thorough-bred innovator is that you can never completely satisfy him, his appetite for change is insatiable, he will make no compromise with you. Grant him all he asks to-day, and as sure as to-morrow comes, he is at it anew. If you gave him the whole world, and his own way everywhere and in everything, he would be in worse plight than the conqueror who wept because there were no more worlds to subdue, and fret himself to death that there were no more changes for him to effect. The probability is that, rather than be idle, he would, in hunting phrase, "hark back" upon his old track, and diligently undo all he had spent his life in doing, and without much regard to the consequences.

We have been led into these remarks by the recollection, when quoting the above verses of the Eighth Paraphrase, that there are at this moment some people busily bestirring themselves in the matter of a new translation of the Scriptures, to supersede the authorised version now in use. Now, we most solemnly protest against all this, as a most rash proposal, ill-advised, and utterly uncalled for. At present we object very much on the same principle that we should object to a painting by one of the old masters being cleansed and retouched by a modern R.A., however eminent in his own person, or on the same principle that we should feel tempted to kick the ladder from under the feet of a man we should detect white-washing a stately pile of the olden time, under the plea, forsooth, that in obliterating weather stains, and freely applying putty and paint, he was thereby improving, renovating, and beautifying the whole fabric. That there are verbal inaccuracies in our authorised version of the Scriptures is on all hands admitted ; let these be rectified, if people please, and let the corrections so made, under adequate authority, appear in the form of marginal notes opposite the passage amended, but let the body of The Book stand as it is—intact. The edifice, as it exists, is too grand, and stately, and beautiful, and hallowed, not to suffer under the proposed remodelling, even in the most competent hands.

But to turn to a different theme. The following is a translation from the Gaelic, as literal as we could make it, with anything like due regard to the spirit and manner of the original. It is a fairy song, if song it can be called, from the manuscript volume referred to in a former communication. Fairy tales, both in prose and verse, were common with our Celtic forefathers, and, if we only examine them with sufficient care, we shall find that, underlying all their quaintness, there is always to be found a substratum of

sound and healthy moral. It bears no title in the original, but we
may call it—

The Milkmaid and her Fairy Lover.

Gaily the milkmaid came tripping along ;
The echoes so loved her, they joined in her song ;
The hare and the wild-roe that browsed in the glade,
The bird on the bough swinging high over-head—
They saw and they heard, but they feared not—they KNEW the milkmaid.

Abundant her tresses, bright golden their hue ;
And soft as a dove's was her eye in its blue ;
Elastic her footstep, and lightsome and free
As a fawn's when in gladness it skips o'er the lea—
Of the old and the young the delight, and the pride of Glentallon was she.

In secret she met with the *Hunter in Green*,
Beside the lone fountain of Coirre-na-Sheen ;
A gallant more gay ne'er did maiden behold,
His manner so gentle, his bearing so bold ;
By his side freely dangled, and well could he wind it, a bugle of gold !

Full fondly he kissed her—she thought it no sin,
Though she knew not his name, nor his kith, nor his kin ;
They plighted their troth by the fount's bubbling stream,
Where oft, it is said, when frail mortals but dream,
The fairies hold revel, and trippingly dance in the moon's mellow beam.

On the Eve of St. Agnes the maiden confessed,
As was proper she should, all her sins to the priest ;
When she left him, the blush in her check mantled high ;
There was care in her step, and a tear in her eye.
Yet pure was the maiden and spotless, I ween, as a star in the blue of
   the sky.

Next day, by the fountain of Coirre-na-Sheen,
The milkmaid again met the *Hunter in Green*.
As he kissed her she quietly slipped under his vest
A relic she long had worn next to her breast—
'Twas a relic in sooth the most sacred—a *Cross* that the holy St. Colomb
   had blessed.

And lo ! in the place of the *Hunter in Green*
('Twas all by the fountain of Coirre-na-Sheen),
A brown, withered twig, so elf twisted and dry,
Was all—'twas amazing—the maid could espy !
While the *Cross*, with a bright burning light round its edges, beside it
   did lie.

And the maid grasped the *Cross*, which devoutly she kissed,
And hid it again in the snow of her breast ;
Homewards she turned her with pensive steps slowly,
But her heart was at peace—meek, submissive, and lowly,
As maid and as mother (the *Cross* at her breast) she passed a life holy.

Often still wake the echoes of Coirre-na-Sheen,
At the blast of thy bugle, O *Hunter in Green !*
Go get thee a mate from the green fairy knowe—
A cross-bearing maid dare not wed such as thou :
Let fairy wed fey, and let mortal wed mortal. Come, *Annabel*, stir up
the fire till it blaze in a lowe !

The moral of the fairy song is instantly apparent. A young lady—miss or milkmaid—is not to hold clandestine appointments with any young gentleman, however lovable and attractive, until at least she knows who and what he is, whence he cometh and whither he goeth. Having met and loved, however, she is instantly to consult those who are older and wiser than herself, and, under their friendly care and direction, she is to be sure that, on her own part and on that of her lover, all shall be pure and holy. The touch at the end is admirable. We must suppose a mother telling the story, herself and sons and daughters sitting round the fire, which, in the absorbing interest of the tale, has been for the time neglected. "Annabel," addressed at the close, we must fancy to be the eldest daughter, just entering upon womanhood. The whole moral of the story, flung obliquely at her head in the command to stir the fire and make it blaze, is exquisite, and we can fancy the gentle "Annabel" quietly smiling to herself the while—she also having a secret—as she cheerily obeys the maternal mandate.

CHAPTER XXVIII.

AFTER a month's cold, clear weather, with dry, parching, northerly winds—the finest heather-burning season that ever was seen— a considerable rainfall during the past week has been welcomed as a boon rather than otherwise, and the country around is all the greener and gladder because of it [April 1872.] During an after- noon's ramble on Saturday we found a redbreast's nest, a black- bird's, and a chaffinch's, all with their full complement of eggs in them; while the nests of several other species, some completed and some still abuilding, were to be found by diligent searching in almost every likely locality. For many years past there has been no such favourable season for wild birds. An amusing scene a day or two ago was the following :—One of our hens, disregarding the companionship of the rest, and desirous of more freedom of action, in a matter so important, than the hen-house could supply, took to laying her eggs in a hole she had scratched out under an old hazel root in a neighbouring copse. Complaints were by-and- by brought into the house that although this hen regularly dropped her quotidian egg in the spot selected, it was found that, unless immediately taken away from her, the egg was sure to be sucked by some sly thief who doubtless enjoyed such a delicacy at this season amazingly, and all the more so, we daresay, that his pilferings had hitherto passed undetected, despite the strictest vigilance on the part of those more immediately interested. It was very annoying, as you may believe, morning after morning to find the fresh and pearly shell at the nest's side, its contents abstracted through a gaping hole in its bulge, instead of the snowy treasure, *totus, teres atque rotundus*, as it should be. Appealed to for such assistance as we could render in detecting and punishing the culprit, whoever he might be, we began by setting a trap for ground vermin, properly baited, and as cunningly as possible placed, but without result. Determined, however, to discover the petty larcenist, if possible, we took advantage of an idle forenoon last week to sit and watch the nest from a distance, our object in the first instance being to find out who the depredator really was; we could afterwards and at our leisure take such steps as we might deem advisable for his capture. Selecting a convenient spot whence we could see without being seen, and provided with a powerful binocular, we watched and waited with the most exemplary diligence and patience, and were rewarded, after some time, by discovering the culprit to be neither rat, stoat, nor weasel, nor other quadrupedal marauder, but a common crow, or rook rather—*Corvus frugilegus*, Linnæus calls him, though *Corvus omnivorus* would be nearer the mark—a large old male bird, as he afterwards proved to be, who had doubtless in his day sucked many an egg and sacked many a homestead of its callow fledglings. We first observed him alighting on the branch of a large ash tree, whence he had a full view of the nest, and there he sat with much patience, preening his feathers, and uttering an occasional *craa*, as if to encourage the hen in her labours. No sooner did the latter, having deposited her egg, leave the nest with the usual cackle of self-congratulation, than Monsieur Corvus glided from his perch, and in a twinkling, by the dexterous use of head and bill, had the egg rolled out on the grass by the nest's side. Turning it round and round, and rolling it over and over, stepping back at times as if the better to contemplate its pearly whiteness and handsome proportions, and already in imagination rolling the sweet morsel under his tongue, he finally stepped forward, and with his pick-axe-like bill delivered a stroke at the egg's bigger end, which made a sufficiently large hole for him to suck away at comfortably. And how he did seem to enjoy it! Removing his bill now and again as if to draw breath, and looking up and around with an air of innocence and self-satisfaction that was exceedingly comical. Meanwhile, so intent was *Corvus* on his egg-flip, that we managed to creep quite close to the scene unperceived by him, resolved to give him a good fright at least, if we could do no more. We took advantage of a moment when he had his head buried in the egg up to the eyes to start to our feet, uttering at the instant a favourite shout of ours in such circumstances—a sort of war-whoop, a legacy, we suppose, from our Fingalian ancestors—and the happiness of *Corvus*, sucking his egg in such fancied security, vanished like a dream. With a prolonged *cra-a-a* he made a sudden dig into the egg in his fright, his bill passing clean through it, and spreading his wings he fluttered upwards, the egg sticking over his bill and eyes like a mask, and preventing him from seeing anything, and causing him to perform the most ridiculous evolutions ever exhibited perhaps by a bird on wing. Fluttering along obliquely, with many a dolorous *cra-a*, he came to the ground like a collapsed balloon in a neighbouring field, where we hoped to capture him, but just as we ran up to him he managed to shake the egg from his head, and in an instant was up and away and out of sight at a rate that must have brought him to Culloden Moor within the hour if he stopped not by the way. A bird rarely fails to profit by experience, least of all a crow, and we have no hesitation in saying that the particular rook in question will remember his egg-shell mask and our unearthly war-whoop till his dying hour.

And while on such subjects, let us ask the reader by the way if he has noticed that cocks don't crow now-a-days as they used to do? We refer of course to the common barndoor fowl—*Gallus domesticus*, the domestic cock. He, we assert, does not now-a-days crow with the same regularity and timeousness, nor with the clear, clarion notes with which he did

"Salutation to the morn,"

say a score of years ago. This may seem a startling assertion, but any one who deigns to turn his attention to the subject will find that it is true. The cock-crowing and wing-clapping of the House of Commons when in the humour is no doubt highly creditable to that august assembly. (It was Boswell, if we recollect well, who imitated the lowing of a cow to admiration, and was naturally very proud of so rare an accomplishment.) But the march of civilisation, and cross-breeding, which you may call "internationalism" if you like, have been the ruin of our cocks, so far as crowing is concerned. They may weigh more than they did a score of years ago, and present a plumper form on the table, but their crowing is gone : at the best it is but a harsh, spasmodic, unmusical half-scream half-wheeze, altogether unlike the loud and lusty, the clear, ringing notes of the cock-crowing of our boyhood days. Our cocks are no longer chanticleers, but chantiqueers. If you have occasion to sit up at night, or to start on a journey betwixt midnight and morning, the cock no longer lends you any countenance or aid in the matter— he sleeps on his perch in utter oblivion of the passing hours, and as heedless of the "watches of the night" as the brooding hen in the coop beneath him. The day may dawn, and the sun may flood the mountain peaks with light, glad and golden, without a note of welcome or recognition on the part of the bird that, from the earliest ages until recent years, was known as the herald of the dawn, and deservedly held in high honour and esteem as the vigilant sentinel of the homestead throughout the midnight and early morning hours. Any convivial " Willie " whom it so pleases may now brew his " peck o' maut," if the Inland Revenue will let him, and sit down to enjoy it with his boon companions into all the hours of the night and morning, unwarned of the flight of time by anything like a cock-crow. The moon may fill her silver horn, and shine bright as aforetime, " to wile them hame," and the day may " daw," but the cock's " *crawing* " will no longer convey its notes of warning and expostulation. If the bird crows at all, it is sometime throughout the day, generally, we have noticed, in the afternoon, when nobody thanks him for it, and then in notes so discordant as to make your teeth water, as if you had suddenly bitten deep into an unripe apple, with the chance of a headache for the rest of the evening. The last time we heard a cock crow in the good old fashion was in an out-of-the-way corner of Arisaig, some three years ago. Being a stranger in the place, and having to sleep on a " shake-down " on the floor of our room, our sleep was less sound than usual, but throughout the night we were cheered by the companionship of a cock that was roosting in an out-house not far from our window. Shortly after midnight he announced the first watch of the night as ended, and afterwards at intervals, of as nearly as possible two hours, his clear, clarion notes, repeated two or three times, startled the stillness of the glen, until at last the rising sun invited him to the labours of the day, and called us to boot and saddle. Nor is the degeneracy and demoralisation of the modern domestic cock less apparent in another direction. Surrounded by his harem, he used to be considered the *beau-ideal* by common consent of all that is gallant, and courteous, and brave. With proud step and stately bearing he led his dames about, finding for them the sunniest spots wherein to bask and dust themselves when the day was at its height. He diligently searched for, and rarely failed to find, the particular corner wherein food was most abundant, scratching with might and main that the ladies of his court might have as little unnecessary trouble as possible, rarely eating anything himself until they had first of all picked the best and biggest share; and if he came across any dainty tit-bit that his followers had overlooked, he took it up in his bill, and by certain peculiar notes reserved for such occasions, called them around him, dropping the toothsome morsel with strict impartiality at his feet, to be picked up by the first to respond to his summons. Now all this is changed. They may sun and dust themselves when and where they please, or not at all, for all he cares. Instead of being the active leader and gallant protector in feeding excursions, he is content to be no more than as any other of the band, exhibiting the utmost selfishness and greed in gobbling up the first grain-pickle or earthworm that comes in the way, nor is he, *proh pudor!* ashamed even to cuff and drive away his decidedly better halves, when the mean wretch has, by accident rather than by any diligence of his own, fallen on a good scratching-place. Neither do you find in the cock of the present day the pugnacity and pluck, the indomitable courage and love of warfare, once so characteristic of the genus, from the tiniest bantam to the lordliest gamecock, that would rather die than cry quarter or show the white feather to an opponent. We don't suppose that the reader, any more than ourselves, has seen a cock-fight for years; not from any elevation of morals, we submit, in Monsieur Gallus, or increase at all of amiability, but from sheer poltroonery and want of pluck. He will still bully about among his hens, and fight with them, and we have seen some of them turn upon him and give him a good drubbing, as he deserved; but a fair stand-up fight with another cock—oh no, we never mention it!—he has still the spurs, but no longer the heart for it. When afield at the head of his following, if the shadow of a suspicious bird on wing, as likely to be a crow as a gled or hawk, or other bird of prey, passes along, instead of the old warning note to his wives, with preparation on his own part to receive the enemy *à l'outrance*, be he who he may, he is the first himself, in Yankee phrase, to skedaddle and make tracks for a place of security and shelter, leaving his hens to their fate. Our bill of indictment *contra gallum*, the reader may say, is a heavy one, but it is in the main very true, as any one who chooses may satisfy himself when he has the opportunity. How, then, do we account for it? Well, it is very difficult satisfactorily to account for it in any way. We are inclined to the belief that the demoralisation of our domestic cock is to be traced to the introduction into our country of such splay-footed, loutish, awkward fowls as the "Cochin China," "Bramahpootra" *et hoc omne genus*, whose brains seem to have subsided into the feathers on their feet, and whose only good quality is their size, and even that is dearly purchased, we suspect, when the immense feeding they require is taken into account. These fowls have spread everywhere, so that, except in some out-of-the-way localities, a cock or hen of the old native breed, of blood pure and uncontaminated by foreign intermixture, is very rarely to be met with, while cross-breeds and mongrels of every shape and size are abundant in all directions. Whatever the good qualities of these latter in other respects, courage, gallantry, and pluck are not of the number. Just inquire into the subject for yourself, good reader, and you will find that, neither physically, intellectually, nor morally is the cock of the present day to be compared for a moment with the gallant, handsome, proud-stepping biped of your boyhood.

CHAPTER XXIX.

The Vernal Equinox—Beauty of Loch Leven—Astronomical Notes—How an old Woman supposed to possess the Evil Eye escaped a cruel death.

THE vernal equinox has come and gone, unaccompanied this year [April 1872], as it was unheralded and unannounced, by anything like the storms that from the earliest times have been observed to be attendant on the sun's crossing the equator. It is by no means certain, however, that these storms may not even now be a-brewing, to make themselves yet felt in all their fierceness, for we have noticed in recent years particularly that what are called the "equinoctial gales" quite as frequently follow, as accompany or precede, the exact equality of day and night. We have just had a fortnight of genuine March weather—clear, cold days, and frosty nights—the air snell and biting, to be sure, and keen of edge, as might be expected on the uplands; but in places sheltered from the east and north it is delightfully bright and sunny, the incessant song of birds, the hum of wild bees, and the gay fluttering of early butterflies, making one think of Whitsuntide rather than All Fools' Day; the twittering of swallows and the cheery notes of the cuckoo alone are wanting to make the illusion perfect, and these, unless the weather should undergo some extraordinary and un-expected change, must certainly soon be heard, much earlier this year, we should think, than usual. We are particularly favoured in this respect along the northern shores of Loch Leven. Here, to quote Burns—

"Simmer first unfaulds her robe, and here the langest tarry;"

and as we wander afield we often apply the words of Horace to our own little spot, as from some neighbouring height we view it cozily nestling in the sunlight—

Ille terrarum mihi præter omnes
Angulus ridet ;

which may be rendered—

Whate'er the beauties others boast,
This spot of ground delights me most.

Or, as we prefer putting it in our own case—

Of brighter skies and sunnier climes let others boast and jabber,
Give me the sunny, southern shores of mountain-girt Lochaber !

Or yet again, if you will have it still more literally in Gaelic—

'S anns' leam na spot eil' fo 'a ghréin,
M' oisinneag bheag, ghrianach féin.

During the present clear, cold spring nights the starry heavens are very beautiful. Jupiter, just below Castor and Pollux, is at his brightest, and very favourably situated for observation, his cloudy belts and bright diamond-point-like satellites being visible in an instrument of very moderate powers. If between nine and ten o'clock the reader will turn to the north-east, he will find a constellation pretty high up in the heavens, and consisting of five or six principal stars, none of them, however, of the first magnitude, opening towards the pole star in the form of a widely spread-out W. This constellation will be an object of more than usual interest during the present year. It is *Cassiopeia*, or *The Lady in her Chair*, the scene of a very startling and strange phenomenon in 1572, which, it has been asserted with some confidence, is not at all unlikely to be repeated in 1872. In 1572 a new star of great splendour appeared in Cassiopeia, occupying a place that had hitherto been blank. It was first observed on the 6th August, by Schuler, of Wittemburg, shortly after which it arrested the attention of the celebrated Danish astronomer Tycho Brahe, who watched its rapid increase of brilliancy night after night with the liveliest interest.   Its magnitude at last rivalled, if it did not even exceed, that of Jupiter, with an effulgence equally bright and vivid. After shining with great splendour some time, and attracting the earnest gaze of the most distinguished astromomers of the period, its brilliancy began steadily to decline, changing its colour in a very remarkable manner as it became fainter and fainter, until finally it became invisible in March 1574, and has never been seen since. Sir John Herschel and other astronomers have suggested that its reappearance in 1872 is by no means an improbable event; and towards no constellation in the northern heavens, in consequence, will the observer's eye be so constantly turned throughout the present year as to Cassiopeia.   The reappearance of such a star would be certain to give rise to the most startling theories.   With the spectroscope in our possession, however, and the marvellous telescopic power at our command now-a-days, we could not fail to arrive at more intimate terms with such a stranger than was possible in the days of Tycho Brahe.   The interest and excitement in the astronomical world in connection with the sudden burst of splendour in the star in *Corona* a year or two ago was very great, but would be still greater in the event of the reappearance of the long absent stranger in Cassiopeia.   In the one case it was only a remarkable increase of light and lustre in the star already existent and visible; but the reappearance of a new orb in a spot blank and starless in the most powerful telescopes for three hundred years, would be almost equal to the sudden creation of a new sun.   Here, by the way, good reader, if you are ambitious, is a chance for fame. Be but the first to detect the reappearance of this remarkable star-stranger, and your immortality into all time shall be more secure than if you wrote an epic to rival the *Iliad*, or a tragedy equal to *Hamlet* or *Othello*.   The name and memory of George Palitch, the amateur peasant astronomer, who was so fortunate as to obtain the earliest glimpse of Halley's Comet on its first return to perihelion after its periodicity had been so boldly, and as some thought so rashly asserted, is more secure in that connection than if, either as king or conqueror, he had all the honours of the most imperishable brass or marble.

A hundred years ago or more, when Highlanders were more superstitious than they are now, or when, to be more correct, they took less pains to conceal their superstitious beliefs than at the present day, a certain hamlet in a remote part of the country was sadly troubled by an "evil eye," whose unhallowed powers wrought "mickle woe," to the manifest loss and discomfort of the good people around. The cows no longer yielded their lacteal treasures in the desired abundance, nor did the calves grow and thrive, as calves in good keeping should. Churns, however shaken and jolted, refused to turn out their hebdomadal pot of butter; or if, after much weary labour, they did reluctantly yield any, it was found to be pale and rancid as unsalted suet in the dog-days. Stirks and other young "beasts," though the rents depended on them, sickened and dwined and died, without apparent reason; and even children, hitherto in rude and ruddy health enough, were frequently prostrated by sudden and unaccountable illnesses. That an "evil eye" of more than ordinary virulence and power was at work was at last conceded even by the most sceptical as to such influences, and suspicion straightway fell upon a lone old woman, who lived in a hut on the outskirts of the township. Originally a stranger to the district, and of a taciturn and retiring disposition, she had long been looked upon with suspicion and dislike, and now a number of young men resolved to be revenged on her as the secret author of all that was amiss in the hamlet. At a late hour one dark night they proceeded to the poor old woman's hut, with the intention of setting fire to the roof and

burning it about her ears, not caring very much either even if the
" evil-eyed witch " herself, as they called her, should be buried under
the burning rafters of her cottage. As the young men noiselessly
surrounded the hut, they found that the old woman was just about
retiring for the night, and as some of them stood at her window,
and looked and listened, they could see her, by the light of a bog
pine fire, kneel at her bedside, and after a little they heard her
repeat the following prayer :—

> " Tha 'n la nis air falbh ùainn,
> Tha 'n oidhche 'tighinn orm dlùth ;
> 'S ni mise luidhe gu dion
> Fo dhubhar sgiath mo rùin.
> O gach cunnart 's o gach bàs,
> 'S o gach nàmhaid th'aig Mac Dhe,
> O nàdur dhaoine borba,
> 'S o choirbteachd mo nàduir fèin,
> Gabhaidh mis' a nis armachd Dhe,
> Gun bhi reubta no brisd',
> 'Sge b'oil leis an t'sàtan 's le phàirt
> Bi'dh mis' air mo gheàrd a nis."

Which, literally rendered into English, will read thus :—

> " The day has now departed from us ;
> Dark night gathers around,
> And I will lay me safely down (to sleep)
> Under shadow of my Beloved One's wing.
> Against all dangers, and death in every form,
> Against each enemy of God's good Son,
> Against the anger of the turbulent people,
> And against the corruption of my own nature,
> I will take unto me the armour of God—
> That shall protect me from all assaults :
> And in spite of Satan and all his following,
> I shall be well and surely guarded."

The old woman's confidence in the Divine protection was not mis-
placed ; the heart of youth is generous, and the beauty and
solemnity of the scene carried it captive. The young men felt
that one who could thus, on retiring to rest, commend herself to

God and God's Son, could not be the "evil" old woman they had thought her. Awed and impressed, silently and on tip-toe, they departed for their homes, leaving the old woman in peace. By-and-by things went well again with the cattle of the hamlet, sickness disappeared from the district, and the old woman continued to live the same quiet, unobtrusive life a few years longer, and was as much respected and loved latterly, the story says, as she was at one time hated and feared. Nor did she ever know of the young men's midnight visit to her hut on an errand so happily frustrated.

The following are a couple of very excellent "*toimhseachan*" that were sent us a few days ago. Finding the correct solutions will afford some amusement to our Gaelic readers during the first idle half-hour—

> Chi mi, chi mi thar an eas,
> Fear cruaidh, colgarra glas,
> Cirb do léine sios mu leis,
> 'S ceum an cirinnaich fo chois.
>
> A mhuc a mharbh mi 'n uiridh
> Bha uirceanan aice am bliadhna.

CHAPTER XXX.

ALONG the west coast the weather is now [May 1872] as mild and
May-like as you could wish; the swallow twitters gaily in the sunlight, and when he ceases his zig-zag flight for a moment to rest on
chimney-top or house-ridge, he sings a gladsome song, low and faint
indeed, and frequently lost on that account in the general chorus,
but exceedingly sweet and musical, as you will find if you give it
the attention it merits; while in the distance you hear the cheery
notes of the cuckoo, wild and startling as yet, as they burst
suddenly upon the ear from out the woodland glade or from the
old rowan tree that finds root room, you wonder how, in yonder
crevice in the rock above the foaming waterfall, but soon to
become familiar as the season advances, and pressed upon your
notice whether you will or no, and at all sorts of impossible times
and places, by the truant schoolboy's oft-repeated, though rarely
successful, attempts at imitation. For the first week in May the
temperature is unusually high, and we do not recollect ever before
having seen insect life so plentiful so early in the season. Midges,
gadflies, and other bloodsuckers are already astir in their thousands,
their taste for their favourite fluid keen and unabated, as they fail
not abundantly to manifest by an activity that one cannot help
admiring, even while wishing that it could possibly be directed to a
more legitimate and less personally annoying end. But "'tis their
nature to," as the hymn-book says, and we must grin and bear it,

protecting ourselves from their assaults as best we may, thankful the
while that the evil is no worse. Our winged pests are innocence
itself compared with their congeners in other lands. Our midge,
for instance, is to the mosquito as the dog-fish is to the shark,
as the domestic cat is to the tiger; while our gadflies and *Æstri*,
though sufficiently annoying to our cattle at certain seasons, are to
be regarded as absolutely harmless if we compare them with the
venomous *Zimb* of Abyssinia, or the still deadlier *Tsetse* of
Southern Africa. The Abyssinian insect, by the way—the
Zimb—is probably the *Zebub* of the Hebrew Scriptures, the estimation in which it was held from the earliest ages being clearly
enough indicated by its place in the word Beelzebub, "the prince
of devils." Livingstone's account of the *Tsetse* is one of the most
interesting chapters in his *Travels*. Shall the intrepid explorer
be restored to us? We are afraid not. It is only too probable that,
as Scott said of his *protegé* and friend, the author of the *Scenes of
Infancy*—

> " A distant and a deadly shore
> Has Leyden's cold remains ! "

The districts of Ardgour and Sunart have always had an
unenviable notoriety for the great numbers of adders and grass
snakes to be found in them, the reptiles frequently attaining to a
size unknown, we believe, anywhere else in the West Highlands.
Within the last two or three years we have noticed that they are
rapidly becoming numerous in Lochaber, much more so than they
used to be, though the general opinion, in which we heartily
concur, is that we were getting on very well without them.
During an ornithological ramble among the hills a few days
ago, we knelt to drink at a fountain that we fell in with, welling
up cool and sparkling beside a large moss-covered drift boulder
among the heather, when we were not a little startled by the
presence of no less than three adders that lay coiled together in

a sort of Gordian knot on a patch of green moss close by the fountain's brink. The day was hot and dry, and they had probably come there to drink and bathe ; but we were very thirsty, having just smoked a pipe on the top of the hill, and there being no appearance of water anywhere else for miles around, and knowing, besides, that there could be really no danger, even if the vipers had been ten times larger and more venomous than they were, we drank a long draught of the pure sweet water, and then proceeded with the stick in our hand to attack the enemy, and soon had the satisfaction of knocking them into wriggling, writhing bits, and crushing their heads under our heel. Our assault was so sudden and unexpected that they had no time to show fight ; otherwise an adder, when his blood is up and thoroughly on his guard, is an ugly customer to attack with no better weapon than a walking-stick, and nothing can be imagined more deadly, wicked-looking, and savage than such an animal, as with erected crest and flashing eye he steadies himself in act to strike. It is curious that the poison of these reptiles, though certain death if commingled in sufficient quantity with the blood through an abrasion or wound, is perfectly innocuous if taken into the stomach—a fact, by the way, that has been known from very early times. On taking our drink, for instance, from yonder viper-guarded fountain, we recollected that Lucan had something on a somewhat similar circumstance in his *Pharsalia.* Describing Cato and his soldiers coming to a fountain of water in the desert, and how horrified they were to find innumerable serpents of the deadliest kind—asps and dipsades—disporting themselves in and around the pool, he has the following fine passage, the finest indeed in the poem, which we took care to turn up when we reached home :—

" Jam spissior ignis,
Et plaga, quam nullam superi mortalibus ultra,
A medio fecere die calcatur, et unda

Rarior ; inventus mediis fons unus arenis
Largus aquæ ; sed quem serpentum turbat tenebat
Vix capiente loco ; stabant in margine siccæ
Aspides, in mediis sitiebant Dipsades undis.
Ductor, ut aspexit perituros fonte relicto
Alloquitur : Vana specie conterrite leti
Ne dubita miles tutos haurire liquores ;
Noxia serpentum est admisto sanguine pestis ;
Morsu virus habent et fatum dente minantur ;
Pocula morte carent.   Dixit dubuumque venenum
Hausit."

Which has been elegantly rendered into English as follows :—

" And now with fiercer heat the desert glows,
And mid-day sun-darts aggravate their woes ;
When, lo ! a spring amid the sandy plain
Shows its clear mouth to cheer the fainting train ;
But round the guarded brink in thick array,
Dire aspics roll'd their congregated way,
And thirsting in the midst the deadly dipsas lay.
Black horror seized their veins, and at the view
Back from the fount the troops recoiling flew ;
When, wise above the crowd, by cares unquell'd,
Their trusted leader thus their dread dispell'd—
' Let not vain terrors thus your minds enslave,
Nor dream the serpent brood can taint the wave ;
Urged by the fatal fang their poison kills,
But mixes harmless with the bubbling rills.'
Dauntless he spoke, and, bending as he stood,
Drank with cool courage the suspected flood."

Celsus, an older writer still, and styled the " Roman Hippocrates,"
tells us in his great work, *De Medicinâ*, that the poison of serpents
may be safely enough sucked by the mouth from the wound,
warning the operator, however, to be careful that the lips and
palate are free from any cut or excoriation by which the venom
might find its way into the blood, in which case it might be just
as dangerous as if introduced into the circulation by the fang itself.
It should be stated that the grass or ringed snake spoken of above
is not in the least poisonous, though ugly enough to look at, and

ready enough to assume a threatening attitude if rudely disturbed.
Nor, by the way, is the date of the present writing inappropriate to
the discussion of such a subject, as we have at this moment discovered by the merest accident. The 6th of May you will find is
a Saint's day in the Calendar, being dedicated to St. John *ante
Portam Latinam,* the legend connected with which is as follows:
—The Beloved Disciple, after preaching the Gospel in various
parts of the world, was in his old age taken to Rome by the
Emperor Domitian, and because he refused to renounce the religion
of Christ, was put into a cauldron of boiling oil before the Latin
Gate—*Porta Latina*—which, however, did him no more harm than
did Nebuchadnezzar's fiery furnace to Shadrach, Meshach, and
Abednego ; on the contrary, John came out of the cauldron re-
juvenated, younger, fairer, and more beautiful than before.
Afterwards a cup of deadliest poison was given him to drink, but
as he was putting it to his lips, the poison, assuming the appropriate shape of a venomous serpent, glided from the cup, leaving
the draught harmless and pure. He was finally banished to Patmos,
where he wrote the Apocalypse.

Old Fingalian rhymes and proverbs having reference to dogs and
the hunting of the stag, as it was then pursued, are very common
in the Highlands, and show how devoted to the chase were our
Celtic ancestors. Our neighbour, the Rev. Mr. Clerk of Kilmallie,
in his splendid edition of *Ossian*, gives some of these old rhymes
in his very interesting and learned notes on *Fingal.* The following
was sent us a short time ago, and as it has never appeared in
print, we present it to the reader with a liberal translation. We
are always glad to be able to rescue from oblivion even the smallest
shred of the folk-lore of the olden time. The story goes that this
rhyme was first of all taught by a fairy to a gay young hunter "of the
period," under the following circumstances :—Once upon a time, a
sprightly, green-robed fairy, a sort of princess in her way, fell in

love with a young Fingalian hunter, who had frequent occasion, on his way to and from the chase, to pass the *shian* or green knoll in which the fairy band of the glen had taken up their abode. The fairy and her hunter lover had frequent opportunities of meeting in secret, until some evil-disposed sister fairy divulged Brianag's— for that was the fairy's name—imprudent and unfairy-like conduct to the powerful fairy prince Aërlunn, who was himself over head and ears in love with the beautiful Brianag, though she gave him no encouragement at all ; on the contrary, she flatly told him that, great and powerful as he was, she did not love him in the least, and would have nothing to do with him. On hearing how things were going on, Aërlunn was very jealous and very angry, just as a mortal might be under similar circumstances, and he issued an edict, as Prince of the Fairies of that glen, by which, after reflecting severely on the unfairy-like conduct of Brianag and others of the band, he prohibited Brianag from leaving the *shian* on any pretence whatever, except for the one hour before midnight on the night when the moon completed her first quarter—perfect liberty to do as they like during this one hour in the month is every fairy's birthright, and no power can deprive them of it. He would have done something very dreadful to Brianag's lover, only the latter was protected from any evil a fairy enemy could do to him by a talisman of extraordinary value, which his uncle, a priest of the Druids, had given him, and which he always carried on his person. Brianag and her lover were thus able to meet for one hour in every month, despite the opposition of the angry Aërlunn, whose jealousy became at last so insupportable, that he resolved to shift his court and people from that glen to another at a great distance. To this arrangement, much as she regretted it, as it separated herself and her lover, Brianag dare not object. It is a prerogative appertaining to the Princes of Fairyland that they can shift their court at will, when and whither they please. The fairy palace thus forsaken is still to be seen in Glen Etive, and has ever since been called *An Sithean Samhach*—the Quiet or Deserted Fairy Knoll. On parting with her lover at their last interview, Brianag presented him with a silver horn, whose blast could be heard, loud and clear, over the Seven Hills and across the Seven Glens; and knowing that it was his ambition to excel all others in the chase, she instructed him as to the best kind of dog to have and hunt withal as follows :—

> Cuilean bus-dubh, buidhe,
> Ceud mhac na saidhe,
> Air àrach air meog 's air bainne ghabhar,
> Cha deach' air sliabh air nach beireadh.

Which may stand in English thus :—

> Get a yellow brindled dog, '
> First-born of his dam's first litter,
> With a muzzle black as jet,
> Reared on whey and milk of goats ;
> No stag in forest can escape him.

Those who rear deer-hounds, *et juvenes qui gaudent canibus,* might do worse than experiment a little according to the fairy's receipt ; we shouldn't wonder at all if a splendid dog was the result, for these old rhymes are rarely devoid of reason. There is no reason at all events why such a dog might not turn out well.

CHAPTER XXXI.

WHILE mild and May-like enough in the valleys and along the coast line, the weather [May 1872] is reported as having more of March than May about it on the uplands, owing to the prevalence of north-easterly winds, that are at once exceedingly piercing and unseasonably *snell*. It is pleasant at the same time to have to report that, so far, crops of all kinds look extremely well, and have seldom been seen so forward in mid-May. Potatoes have been distinguishable from field's end to field's end in regular drills for ten days past, and in some instances are already undergoing their first weeding and hoeing. Oats show a strong, healthy braird, and nothing but a deficiency of moisture in its present stage can prevent ryegrass from being the best crop that has been known in the West Highlands for many years. Much, however, will depend on the nature of the weather for the next fortnight : those who should know best say that the country would be all the better of more or less rain on every day for the remainder of the month, and we daresay they are right. The lambing season has hitherto been a highly favourable one, though the drought and the keen-edged easterly winds are beginning to be complained of by shepherds in charge of upland hirsels. As we write, however, there is appearance of rain, which cannot fail to be attended by a change of wind to a more genial *airt*, and it is hoped it may fall abundantly. The summer, by the way, is likely to be a hot and dry one, if there be

any truth in the popular belief that when the oak takes precedence
of the ash in presenting its rich green foliage to the light, a
cloudless, rainless summer is sure to follow. We observe that
everywhere the oak is now in leaf, while the ash is yet budless and
bare to its topmost bough, manifesting an unwonted dulness and
drowsiness for mid-May, as if it was loth, even at the call of
summer, to be roused from its hybernal repose.

We are indebted to the monks of the middle ages for the introduction into our country, and successful cultivation, of some of our
choicest fruits and most beautiful flowers; nor is it any wonder
that in times when herbalism and the culling of simples was
universally practised and believed in, numberless shrubs and plants
of real or supposed efficacy in the cure of particular ailments should
also be imported and assiduously cultivated by the same benefactors.
In some cases, however, the supposed plants of virtue then introduced have in our day turned out to be no better than noisome
weeds, extremely difficult of eradication, and one of these—how it
found its way into this district it would be difficulty to say—is
becoming a perfect pest in some parts of Lochaber. We refer to
the plant commonly known as *Bishopweed, Goatweed,* or *Herb
Gerard,* which the botanists have honoured by the high-sounding
name *Ægropodium podagraria.* Gout, as its botanical name
implies, was the disease in which this rank and foul-smelling weed
was supposed to be of extraordinary virtue, and for anything we
know to the contrary, it may still possess all the virtues at one time
so confidently ascribed to it; but then you see gout is altogether
unknown in Lochaber—we are too poor, and perforce live too
soberly, to be visited by such aristocratic ailments—and what
business therefore this weed has to grow and spread amongst us,
and become unto us a nuisance and a plague, we cannot imagine:
not knowing the disease, we could get on very well without the
unsavoury antidote. Bishopweed, if allowed free growth in suitable

soil, will quickly cover the ground, to the destruction of everything else, its innumerable stalks, crowned with pinnated ash-like leaves, attaining to the height of a foot or more. When a single plant once gets root-hold in pasture land, it spreads with amazing rapidity, damaging and crowding out the grass in all directions, so that whenever and wherever it appears its utter and thorough extirpation, whatever the labour and cost, should be insisted upon with the least possible delay. When plucked by the hand the plant emits a fœtid, sickening smell, all trace of which is only effaced from the fingers by a very thorough washing indeed. We have observed that neither horse, nor ox, nor sheep will of choice touch it, though its being in many places called goatweed would seem to indicate that it is no more rejected by that animal than many other acrid and poisonous plants and herbs which our other ruminants will not touch even if starving. Of all the ground pests with which we are acquainted, bishopweed is the worst, and we warn our readers, if ever they meet with it in any neglected corner of garden or field, to show it no mercy at all, for it is of an unmerciful nature itself, killing every blade of grass it comes in contact with, and choking unto the death every other vegetable that it can surmount and master.

The finest stag's head and antlers that we have ever seen form a trophy in the possession of our neighbour, Mr. Bill, Kilmalieu, the magnificent " monarch of the waste " that bore them having fallen to that gentleman's own rifle in Glengour two or three years ago. The other day, however, we were shown a set of larger horns, though not quite so handsome perhaps, or so faultless in spread and curve, and unfortunately imperfect from the loss of one of the tines, which was picked up by a shepherd in the Black Mount Forest many years ago. The size of beam throughout was something extraordinary, and one could not help regretting that it had not the head and neck attached, that it might be set up in the style for which the good city of Inverness has of recent years become so famous. Such a trophy of the chase, complete in all its parts, would have deserved the place of honour amid a thousand such trophies in the noblest hall in the kingdom. As we handled these antlers, and poised them at arm's length with admiration, the thought suddenly struck us that Edmund Waller, the poet, must have had some such magnificent trophy before him when he burst into the following apostrophe, in which a well-known fact in the natural history of the animal is so happily interwoven with the old mythological legend :—

> " O fertile head ! which every year
>   Could such a crop of wonder bear !
>   The teeming earth did never bring
>   So soon so hard, so huge a thing :
>   Which, might it never have been cast,
>   Each year's growth added to the last,
>   These lofty branches had supplied,
>   The earth's bold sons' prodigious pride ;
>   Heaven with these engines had been scal'd
>   When mountains heaped on mountains failed."

Lines, by the way, that would form a most happy and appropriate inscription for any really fine trophy of this kind.

Calling upon the Misses Macdonald of Achtriachtan the other day at Fort-William, we were shown some very fine old silver-plate, having a history of its own, to the recital of which we listened with no small interest. After the battle of Culloden, a party of "red-coat" soldiers entered Lochaber, and employed themselves in pillaging and plundering in all directions. Hearing that visitors so unwelcome were in the neighbourhood, Mrs. Cameron of Glenevis, a lady of great spirit and decision of character, had all her silver-plate, china, and other valuables buried deep in the ground outside the garden wall, after which she removed, with her children and personal attendants, to a spacious cave called *Uaimh Shomhairle* (Samuel's Cave), far up the glen, in the south-western shoulder of

Ben Nevis. Meanwhile the soldiers visited Glenevis House, but, disappointed at not finding the valuables they looked for in such a residence, they burned and plundered the glen without mercy, the terrified inhabitants taking to the mountains, only too glad to escape with their lives, while their homesteads were in flames, and their cattle either driven away or slaughtered on the spot. Lady Glenevis was at last discovered in her cave by a party of soldiers, who had somehow heard of her place of retreat, and had to undergo much rude treatment at their hands, because, in defiance of all their threats, she refused to tell where the valuables of which they were in search had been hidden away. As they were about to leave the cave, one of the soldiers, observing that she had something bulky in her breast, of which she seemed very careful, and over which her plaid, fastened with a silver brooch, was carefully drawn, made a snatch at the trinket, and, when the lady resisted, drew his sword and made a thrust, which cut open the plaid at its point of fastening, wounding her infant son at the same moment in the neck; for the hidden treasure in her bosom, though the soldier doubtless thought it might turn out to be something of more marketable value, was a child only a few months old. The soldiers at last departed, carrying with them the brooch and plaid as the only trophies of their victory over the defenceless lady of the cave. The wounded child recovered, though he bore the mark of the sword-thrust to his dying day. He lived to be laird of Glenevis, was father of the late much-respected Mrs. Macdonald of Achtriachtan, and grandfather of the ladies above mentioned. We remember hearing our friend, the late Dr. Macintyre of Kilmonivaig, repeating some very fine Gaelic lines to a waterfall, something in the style of Southey's address to *Lodore*, which he said was by the Mrs. Cameron of Glenevis above mentioned, and composed by her while in hiding in the cave. When quieter times came round, the buried valuables were of course exhumed, and were found to be none the worse of their temporary interment.

Most birds are endowed with considerable powers of mimicry, the exercise of which, under favourable circumstances, seems, we have observed, to afford them great delight. The bird most cele- brated in this respect is, perhaps, the mocking-thrush of America, the singularly expressive and appropriate name of which, among the Mexican aborigines, is *Cencontlatlolli*, which means *four hundred tongues or languages*, conferred upon it in honour and acknowledg- ment of the fact that, with a rich and varied song of its own, it correctly imitates all other songs and sounds as well. Though we have nothing equal to the four-hundred-tongued wonder of America, many of our native British birds are in truth excellent mimics, particularly after they have been some time in confinement, the tedium and irksomeness of their imprisonment being probably alleviated by a constant exercise of their gifts in this way, until individuals sometimes attain to a mastery in the art that is perfectly astonishing. Amongst our pets at present is a goldfinch cock, a very fine bird, still perfect at all points, though he must be at least a dozen years old, during ten of which he has been in our possession as a favourite cage-bird. He is a magnificent singer, and the wisest little fellow in the world ; you only wonder, indeed, how such a rich flood of song, clear and long sustained, can issue from such a tiny throat, and how such a little scarlet-capped head can contain so much intelligence and sagacity. " Cowie "—for so he is called, after the bird-catcher from whom we purchased him—is above all things an extraordinary mimic. We have never, indeed, known any bird to equal him in this respect. The chirping of the sparrow in the hedge opposite the window at which usually hangs his cage ; the twittering of swallows, as they flit past on their zigzag insect cruise ; the *fink, fink* of the lively chaffinch ; the *chirr* of the ox-eye tit ; the bell-like jingle of the blackbird scolding a prowling cat ; the lugubrious notes of the corn bunting's evening plaint ; the love- cheep of the lesser white-throat ; and the quick rasping utterances of the excited wren, into whose proper territories a rival has dared to intrude ;—these are each and all imitated by our little pet with marvellous exactness of note, emphasis, and tone. The querulous cheeping of a chicken that has met with some little accident, or for the moment lost sight of its mother, he mimics to the life ; and he will on such occasions stand on tip-toe, stretch his neck to the utmost, or cling parrot-like to the topmost wire of his cage, in order to catch a glimpse of the victim of his ridicule. When tired of this, the commoner and coarser part of his art, he will burst suddenly into song, which he will continue sometimes for an hour on end, introducing voluntaries and variations without number, in which you can readily distinguish longer or shorter strophes from the songs of almost all the birds he has ever had a chance of hearing. Any one, indeed, thoroughly familiar with bird-music could easily name the principal songsters in the district immediately around us solely from the singing of our talented little polyglot, so faultless is his imitation of the songs as well as " conversational utterances," so to speak, of all such birds as he is in the habit of hearing and seeing from his cage at the frequently open window. You may be sure that " Cowie " is an immense favourite with us all, and that his weight in diamonds would hardly induce us to part with him.

CHAPTER XXXII.

Potato Culture—Sensibility of the Potato Shaw to Weather changes—The Carline Thistle—Burns—The true *Carduus Scotticus*—The old Dog-Rhyme.

OF no place in existence, perhaps, is the old adage, in its most literal sense, truer than of Lochaber, that "it never rains but it pours" [June 1872]. When we last wrote rain was much needed; no mid-March could be dustier or colder than was our mid-May; rain, rain was the cry on all hands; the birds, as they alighted on the branches or flew overhead, cheeped it querulously; the ducks quacked it energetically; the hens cackled and gaped for it; while the cattle afield lowed for it in a manner the meaning of which there was no mistaking; and at last the change of weather, so universally wished for, came—came first of all in the shape of hail, the *dira grando* of Horace, the downright pea-size genuine article, which left the hills around as white as if, in questionable taste, they had whitewashed themselves for the season. *Hail!* fellow, well met, was the natural and appropriate greeting. Then came sleet, a milder form of the same visitation, not very pleasant, perhaps, but we were grateful; then with the wind from the west, soft and pleasant as the breath of a child, came warm, genial summer rain; the tiniest blade of grass felt the benign influence, and, in the beautiful language of oriental imagery, "the mountains and the hills broke forth before us into singing, and the trees and fields clapped their hands." It is now mild and beautiful exceedingly, with just enough of rain from time to time to keep everything fresh and green, and at full stretch of growth, so that crops of all kinds are everywhere making the most satisfactory progress; and although the unseasonable hail and intense cold of ten days ago was very trying to the young potato plants in exposed situations, we are glad to say that no serious damage has resulted, the change from cold to milder weather having been very gradual. The damage in such cases always depends on the suddenness, or the contrary, of the transition from a low to a high temperature; a night of frost, followed by a hot sun next day, being most dangerous to vegetable life, while frost, followed by rain and cloud, and so on gradually to heat and sunshine again, rarely does any more harm than merely to give a slight check to what might otherwise prove an unhealthy rapidity of growth. In the same way it is found that in the case of animals generally, and in man particularly, it is not the actual and immediate amount of cold undergone at any time that kills or maims, but the too sudden transition from a very low temperature to a comparatively high one. It is probably well enough known to the reader that very many of our flowers and plants are hygrometric, some of them very sensitively so. By hygrometric we mean that they spread out or expand their parts when the sun is bright and the weather is dry, while they contract or close them on the approach of moisture and cloud. We would at present draw attention to the fact that the potato plant, in its earlier stages of growth, is very sensitive in this respect, more so in some years than in others perhaps, according as the plants have come up, strong and vigorous and healthy, or the reverse; for we think our observations during many years warrant us in saying that the more vigorous and healthier the plant, the more sensitive will it be found to weather changes—its very sensitiveness in this respect, observe, helping forward its growth and preserving its vitality, by enabling it to avail itself of every favourable influence, just as it enables it to protect itself against such influences as are unfavourable or adverse. We were particularly struck with this

N

hygrometric sensitiveness in the potato plant a day or two ago.
We have an early planted field, more forward, perhaps, than anything else of the kind in the West Highlands, over which we took
a friend who happened to call upon us.　It was about mid-day,
with a bright, hot sun overhead, and our friend agreed with us
that he had never seen potatoes that had come up more regularly,
or that looked more healthy and vigorous at the same stage of
growth, the fully expanded plants already showing leaves broad
and beautiful as those of a hazel tree in June.　In an hour or two
afterwards we had occasion to pass the same field, and the change
in the appearance of the plants was extraordinary.　They seemed
to have actually grown a couple of inches since mid-day, and our
friend exclaimed, "Well, your potatoes are wonderful! look at
them now."　And we did look, not so much, however, at the
potato field as our friend did; *we* looked upwards and saw that
clouds were rapidly forming in the west, one black, finger-like
stripe of which had already nearly mounted to the zenith, and
looking at *that* and at our potato field, we assured our friend that
a heavy fall of rain, with possibly a gale of wind, was at hand.
Our companion was astonished; the sun was yet shining brightly,
and the greater part of the heavens was clear and cloudless; but
within little more than an hour afterwards the rain fell in torrents,
and a smart gale from the south-west was blowing.　Our potatoes,
however, had foreseen it all; were sensible of its approach, while
our friend and ourselves thought ourselves in the midst of fine
weather that might, perhaps, last unbroken for days; and what
struck our companion as a sudden and mysterious addition to the
height of the plants was merely the effect of their having gathered
themselves together—contracted all their parts into the least possible
compass—thus assuming an upright pyramidal form, as best enabling
them to withstand the assaults of the approaching storm.　Plants
of less health and vigour would, according to our theory, have

shown the same sensitiveness in the circumstances, but in a manner not so immediate, and to a degree less marked and striking. Our companion of that day, who got a thorough *drouking,* as we say in Scotland, on his way home that afternoon, writes us with some humour that " as he has always had a great regard for potatoes on the table, both mashed and ' balled,' in their ' jackets,' so in future will he, in acknowledgment of their infallibility in the matter of weather changes, view them with respect even in the field." It should be stated, by the way, that this hygrometrical property in the potato plant rapidly diminishes in sensitiveness as the haulm increases in height and strength, as if it felt that when approaching its full growth it could afford very much to disregard such weather changes as are incident to the mid-summer season ; but the reader who has the opportunity may verify all we have said upon the subject for himself.

Another plant still more remarkable for hygrometric properties is the common carline, or carlen thistle, the *Carlina vulgaris* of botanists. It is common enough in some districts of Scotland, though those who do not know it already need not be in the least ambitious of the honour of its acquaintance, unless indeed from a purely scientific point of view, for the carline, wherever it appears, is almost always the infallible sign of a poor soil, miserably farmed. The species receives its name of *Carlina* from an old story that Charlemagne introduced it into Europe on account of some valuable medicinal qualities attributed to it ; its virtues in this respect having been revealed, it was said, to Carolus Magnus by an angel in a vision of the night during the prevalence of a deadly plague. Certain preparations of its roots and leaves were for centuries afterwards held of great virtue in such internal complaints as demanded violent purgatives for their removal ; and to this day it is, we believe, held in great repute by herbalists for the cure of vertigo, headache, and other cerebral diseases. As a weather prog-

nosticator, it is perhaps unequalled by any other British plant, the
sensitiveness of its involucral scales to the slightest weather changes
being so extraordinary as to have from very early times attracted
the attention and aroused the wonderment of those unacquainted
with the fact that similar properties, in a greater or less degree, are
common to all plants and flowers—to the whole vegetable kingdom
indeed. The carline has a stem of some eight or ten inches in
height, and bears many pretty purple flowerets set in the midst of
straw-coloured rays. The carline's sensitiveness to weather changes
continues long after it has been cut or pulled, provided the heads
have not been much hurt or bruised in the process; on the same
principle, we suppose, that some animals are known to manifest
unmistakeable signs of muscular irritability long after they are
otherwise, as we should say, to all intents and purposes dead. We
have generally met with the carline thistle among sickly-growing
oats, on poor, thin soil, and sometimes among other luxuriant weeds
in a neglected potato field. It is amusing, by the way, sometimes
to see bonnet-badges and pictorial representations of what you are
supposed to believe is the Scottish thistle, evidently copied to the
life from one of the carline family! which are but pigmies in
stature and absolutely harmless in the matter of prickliness compared with the grand stately fellow bristling with prickles strong
as darning needles, and sharp and venomous as the sting of a bee,
with "*Nemo me impune lacessit*" in the very look of him—the true
national emblem! You remember Burns' reference to it in a very
fine stanza that has been often quoted, that indeed everybody has
by heart—

> "Even then, a wish (I mind its power)—
> A wish that to my latest hour
>   Shall strongly heave my breast—
> That I for poor auld Scotland's sake
> Some usefu' plan or beuk could make,
>   Or sing a sang at least.

The rough burr-thistle, spreading wide
A mang the bearded bear,
I turn'd the weeder-clips aside,
And spared the symbol dear :
  No nation, no station,
    My envy e'er could raise ;
  A Scot still, but blot still,
    I knew nae higher praise.'
  —(*Epistle to the Guidwife of Wauchope House.*)

The true *Carduus Scotticus* is not fond of cultivated land, but is a tremendous fellow when he gets hold of a waste outlying corner to himself, sometimes attaining a height of four or five, or even six feet, with a stem as thick as your wrist, and prickles—no, *spikes* is the word—with spikes, then, as formidable as the bayonets of a kilted regiment going into action.

An anonymous lady correspondent in London sent us a manuscript sheet of paper of the last century, containing a very old dog-rhyme. "The paper has been in our family as long as I can remember, and I have heard my grandfather repeat the lines often before we left the Highlands fifty years ago. The Ronald Mac Ronald Vic John mentioned in the rhyme was, I believe, one of the Glencoe family, a celebrated hunter of deer in his day. He was killed, as I have heard my grandfather relate, at the battle of Philiphaugh. It was the fairy dog-rhyme in one of your recent letters that brought to my mind that such a thing was in my possession." Owing to the faded state of the writing, and a very peculiar orthography, we had some difficulty in deciphering the lines ; but, modernising the spelling a little, the following we believe to be an accurate transcript :—

An cù 'bh'aig Raonull-mac-Raonuil-'ic-Iain,
'Bheiradh e sithionn a beinn :
Ceann leathan eadar 'dha shuil, ach biorach 's bus dubh air gu shroin.
Uchd gearrain, seang-leasrach ; 's bha fhionnadh
Mar fhrioghan tuirc nimheil nan còs.

Donn mar àirneag bha shuil ; speir luthannach lùbta,
'S faobhar a chnamh mar ghein.
An cù sud 'bh'aig Raonull-mac-Raonuil-'ic-Iain,
'S tric thug e sithionn a beinn.

Which, rendered as literally as possible, many stand thus in English—

Ronald-son of Ronald-son of John's good dog,
He could bring venison from the mountain.
He was broad between the eyes ; otherwise sharp and black-muzzled to
    the tip of his nose.
With a horse-like chest, he was small flanked, and his pile
Was like the bristles of the den frequenting boar.
Brown as a sole was his eye ;
Supple-jointed (was he), with houghs bent as a bow ;
All his bones felt sharp and hard as the edge of a wedge.
Such was Ranald Mac Ranald vic John's good dog,
That often brought venison from the mountain.

CHAPTER XXXIII.

A non-"Laughing" Summer—Rheumatic Pains—Old Gaelic Incantation for Cattle Ailments.

THE best thing, perhaps, that can be said of our summer up to this date [July 1872], is that it has, upon the whole, been amiable and summer-like; has, after the manner of a love-lorn maiden, wept much and often smiled, although, until within the last day or two, it has never actually laughed. You loved it, and couldn't help yourself, but your love wanted warmth and fervour, just because of *its* want of jocundity and joyousness. Even in our climate, summer is not summer by the mere reading of the thermometer, however sensitive and delicate its mercurial indications; one wants brilliant sunshine, with cloudless, or almost cloudless skies, to make up a summer as a summer proper ought to be. The poets of the East and South always speak of summer and summer scenes as "laughing," while in more northern and less favoured lands your poet is content to describe otherwise exactly similar scenes and situations as simply "smiling," "gentle," "sweet," "quiet," and so forth, so that an acute critic, by attending to this alone, could tell, were other proofs entirely wanting, whether a poet was born under northern skies, or lived and loved, soared and sang, in sunnier and more southern climes. Horace has—

—"*mihi angulus ridet.*"

His "corner," observe, does not merely smile; it "*laughs*" under the bright blue Italian sky. Lucretius has—

—"*tibi rident æquora ponti;*"

which Creech and Dryden, bards of a colder clime, have rendered
" smiles," but which literally and truly is honest, open, joyous
" *laughter* " in the southern bard. Metactasio has—

> " A te fioriscono
> Gli erbosi prati ;
> E i flutti ridono
> Nel mar placati."

" *Ridono*," observe—laughter again—like his earlier countrymen,
Horace and Lucretius. Our British poets rarely venture to make
spring or summer do more than smile ; they are afraid of the
laughter of the south, as being *quoad hoc* an over-bold hyperbole.
We can only quote at this moment two instances in which the
laughter of more favoured lands is boldly introduced. John
Langhorne, a poet and miscellaneous writer of the last century,
author of the *Fables of Flora*, very beautifully says—

> " Where Tweed's soft banks in liberal beauty lie,
> And Flora *laughs* beneath an azure sky."

And Chaucer, the father of English poetry, has the following :—

> " The busy larkë, messager of daye,
> Salueth in hire song the morwe gray ;
> And fyry Phebus ryseth up so brighte,
> That al the orient *laugheth* of the light."—

Very finely modernised by Dryden thus :—

> " The morning lark, messenger of day,
> Saluted in her song the morning grey ;
> And soon the sun arose with beams so bright
> *That all the horizon laughed* to see the joyous sight."

Our summer, then, thus far, has not been a "laughing," but, at
the best, a merely smiling summer. There has been but little
actual sunshine, rarely such a thing as a blue, unclouded sky ; but,
if we do not err, if the wish be not altogether father to the
thought, a splendid autumn, glad and golden—summer and autumn

in one, like the companion scenes in a stereoscope, in close and
kindly combination—is in store for us. Even as it is, the country
is very beautiful, and the rains of the west, if superabundant, are
at least perfectly harmless to any one in ordinary health, no matter
how often you get drenched through and through, as the saying is,
provided always you do not idly saunter or sit down for any length
of time in wet clothes; neglect this precaution, however, and you
may look out for an attack of rheumatism, and the taste of pains
to which the tortures of the rack were but a joke—pains as fiery
and intense as those threatened against the foul-mouthed Caliban
in the *Tempest*. You recollect what Prospero says—

> " Hag-seed hence !
> Fetch us in fuel ; and be quick, thou wert best
> To answer other business.   Shrug'st thou, malice ?
> If thou neglect'st, or dost unwillingly
> What I command, *I'll rack thee with old cramps ;*
> *Fill all thy bones with aches ;* make thee roar
> That beasts shall tremble at thy din ! "

Get wet, then, as often and as much as you like, in the West
Highlands, but don't sit down or idle about in wet clothes, is a
friend's advice ; otherwise, you will soon have a pretty correct idea
of the nature of the cramps and aches of which even the brutal
Caliban had such a horror that he exclaims :—

> " No, 'pray thee !—
> I must obey : his art is of such power,
> It would control my dam's god, Setebos,
> And make a vassal of him."

Supplementary to our last paper on the spells and incantations
of the Highlands, the following has been sent to us by our kind
correspondent, Mr. Carmichael, of the Inland Revenue, Island of
Uist, a gentleman of whom highly honourable mention is made in
Mr. Campbell's *West Highland Tales,* and in some of the notes to
the Rev Dr. Clerk's *Ossian.* Mr. Carmichael is more conversant,

perhaps, than anybody else with the antiquities and folk-lore of the Outer Hebrides. The incantation that follows was taken down by Mr. Carmichael from the recitation of "an honest, unsophisticated old *Banarach*, or dairymaid, in North Uist, who is even yet occasionally consulted about sickly cows" :—

Rann Leigheas Galar Cruidh.

Crìosd' 'us Ostail 'us Eoin
An triuir sin is binne gloir
A dh-èirich a dheanada na h-òra,
Roimh dhorus na Cathrach,
No air glùn deas De Mhic.
Air na mnathan mùr-shuileach,
Air na feara geur shuileach,
'Sair na saighdean sitheadach ;
Dithis a lasachadh alt agus ga 'na adhachadh
Agus triuir a chuireas mi 'an urra rin sin,
An t-Athair, 'sar Mac 'san Sprorad Naomh,
Ceithir ghalara fichead 'an aoraibh duine 's beathaich,
Dia ga sgriobanh, Dia ga sguabadh,
As t-fhail, as t-fheoil, 'sad 'chnàimh 'sad 'smuais ;
'Smar a thog Crìosd' meas air bharra gach crann,
Gum b'ann a thogas Edhiotsa
Gach sùil, gach gnù 'sgach farmad,
On 'là u dingh gu latha deireannach do shaoghail.   Amen.

In English—

A Healing Incantation for Diseases in Cattle.

Christ and His Apostle and John,
These three of most excellent glory,
That ascended to make supplication
Through the gateway of the city,
Fast by the right knee of God's own Son.
As regards evil-eyed women ;
As regards blighting-eyed men ;
As regards swift-speeding elf-arrows ;
Two to strengthen and renovate the joints,
And three to back (these two) as sureties—
The Father, the Son, the Holy Ghost.
To four-and-twenty diseases are the reins of man and beast (subject) ;
God utterly extirpate, sweep away, and eradicate them

From out thy blood and flesh, thy bones and marrow,
And as Christ uplifted its proper foliage
To the extremities of the branches on each tree-top,
So may He uplift from off and out of thee
Each (evil) eye, each frowning look, malice and envy—
From this day forth to the world's last day.　Amen.

"It is not always an easy task," writes our correspondent, "to write from the dictation of partially deaf and toothless old women," and we perfectly agree with him. "Ostail," in the first line of the above spell, we take to be an insular form of *Abstol*, voc.— *Abstoil* or *Abstail*—*the* Apostle *par excellence*, namely, Paul.　Mr. Carmichael appends the following elucidatory note :—"This *òra* or spell can be used for either man or beast, and is guaranteed to effect a cure in any case!　In the case of a four-footed animal a worsted thread is tied round the tail, and the *òra* or incantation repeated.　The "snàthaile" (*snàthainn*, a thread), as this charm is called, undergoes much mysterious spitting, handling, and incantation by the woman from whom it is got.　The *rann* or spell is muttered over it at the time of "consecration."　Usually two threads (*dà shnathaile*) are given, and if the first is not quite successful, the second is sure to be effectual!"

CHAPTER XXXIV.

Early sowing recommended—Vitality of Superstitions—Capnomancy—Hazel Nuts : Frequent
References to in Gaelic Poetry—How best to get at the full flavour of a ripe Hazel Nut.

A FORTNIGHT's incessant rain [September 1872]—rain descending
at times in solid sheets—not only wets the ground and puddles the
roads, but makes one's very brains feel soft and sloppy and mashed-
turnip-wise. You take up a book only to lay it down again. You
fill your pipe and set it alight, but with less than half a dozen
whiffs you are more than satiated. The weed has lost its flavour.
You sit down to write "doggedly," as Johnson says, but with all
your doggedness the pen totters over the sheet with pace uncertain
and listless, as if even he felt disinclined for the task, and the
sentences, like a squad of raw recruits, refuse to fall gracefully into
their places, and stumble against each other in ludicrous confusion,
to the consternation and grief of the most patient of drill-sergeants.
You will not, perhaps, believe it, but it is true, nevertheless, that
so persistent, penetrating, and inter-penetrating has been the last
fortnight's rain, that in nineteen cases out of twenty a lucifer
match, "vesuvian," or fusee will obstinately refuse to ignite by
any other process than putting it into actual contact with fire, and
in that case, why, a slip of paper is just as easily dealt with, as well
as more efficacious for your purpose. Hay and corn luckily stand
a good deal of rain without being completely spoiled, but we are
afraid to estimate the amount of damage that another week's wet
weather will cause over the West Highlands. All our own hay
and corn has been snugly housed more than three weeks ago. Why

shouldn't everybody sow in February or early March as we do, and have their ingathering in August, generally our best and driest month? In a climate so treacherous and inconstant as ours is, it is the greatest folly in the world to run the smallest risk that you can possibly avoid. We have been preaching this particular doctrine for a dozen years past, and it has had some effect in our immediate neighbourhood; but it is sad to see the country at large at this moment—corn and hay rotting in the fields, that might, with ordinary prudence and a little effort, be long ere now snug and safe under "thack and rape."

The more one inquires the truer does he find the dictum of a philosopher of the last century to be, that "the superstitions, as well as the languages, of all lands and ages are linked together by mysterious bonds, which neither time nor distance seem able to destroy." In our immediate neighbourhood an instance of a very old superstition was brought under our notice a few days ago, such as, with all our knowledge of such matters, we had hitherto never dreamt of as existing in the Western Highlands. A man went to market at a considerable distance to sell a good strong two-year-old colt. He did not return on the day his wife expected him, and she became uneasy, not so much for the well-being of her laggard liege lord and master—*he* had often gone the same errand before, and had always returned safe and sound, even if a little later than his better half had a right to expect—but as to whether he had sold the colt, and if for anything like the price settled between the twain as being his fair price before he left home. She put on a large fire on her hearth, placing, when it had reached a certain stage of ignition, a bundle of green alder boughs atop. When the whole was fully ablaze, she went outside and watched the direction of the smoke issuing from her chimney. The smoke was carried in an easterly direction, a lucky quarter, and she returned to the house and told her daughter that, whatever had come over the father—

and she threatened to tell him a bit of her mind as to his doings on his return—the colt at least had been sold, and well sold, for the alder smoke had gone in the best and luckiest of all directions, towards the east, in the direction of the rising sun; and she had never known the omen fail. The curious thing is that within an hour or so on that very evening the man returned, and counted into his wife's lap two pounds and four shillings sterling over and above the expected price of the colt, as agreed upon at home. The only other curious thing that we could gather in connection with the superstition is that the alder branches must be cut specially for the occasion, and by a virgin. It was so in this case; and we are gravely assured that, if it had been otherwise, the ascending smoke would either have drifted hither and thither without a purpose, unsteadily, or have uselessly intermingled with that of the neighbouring cottages. The superstition, you must know, is a very old one; the Greeks and Romans practised it, and from them it spread widely over the European Continent. In books on magic and divination it is called *Capnomancy*, derived, as our friend Professor Blackie could tell you better than anybody else, from the Greek *Capnos*, smoke, and *manteia*, divination, witchcraft. The ancients paid attention principally to the smoke of sacrifices, as well as to the briskness with which the fire burned. If the smoke ascended in a straight columnar body zenithwards, it was a favourable omen; if it was violently blown aside, or fell back over the altar and the sacrificers, it was of evil augury. Our Highland dame's notion of its taking an easterly course, towards the direction of the breaking day, of the dawn, and the morning sun, seems to us full of a rough and rude poetry such as you frequently meet with in carefully examining into the details of even the grossest superstitions. Having had occasion to be of some little service to the priestess in this rare act of divination, we had the whole from her own lips, though she was averse at first, as is generally the case when a clergyman is the inquirer, to entering upon the subject at all. How these practices root themselves among a people, defying eradication, is very extraordinary.

Did you ever, reader, crack a nut? Not the aristocratic walnut or filbert over your wine, but the far superior, rich, ripe hazel nut in its season from off the hazel bough, when the bright autumnal sun was overhead, and the autumnal breeze stirred the leaves around you, their multitudinous murmur resembling the far-heard music of the restless sea. A ripe hazel nut is good anywhere, but best of all when gathered by your own hand in its native wild wood from the overhanging branch, whence the beautiful cluster nods at you as if soliciting your attention, now and again, as you approach to pull it, seeming to delight in playing a game of bo-peep with you among the leaves, like as you have seen the Pleiades at times when, though the night be clear, many blanket-like clouds are chasing each other in wild career athwart the starry blue. Throughout the whole range of poetry, the hazel nut, though often mentioned, has never perhaps had so much justice done to it as by the Gaelic bard Duncan Bàn Macintyre. In his *Coire-Cheathaich*, one of his finest poems, he says :—

> Bha cus ra' fhaotainn de chnothan caoine,
> 'S cha b' iad na cacohagan aotrom gann,
> Ach bagailt mhaola, bu taine plaoisge,
> 'Toirt brìgh á laoghan na' maoth-shlat fann :
> S rath nan caochan 'na dhosaibh caorainn,
> 'S na phreasaibh caola, làn chraobh a's mhearg ;
> Na gallain ùra, 's na faillein dhlùtha,
> 'S am barrach dùinte mu chùl nan crann.

Ewen Maclachlan, commonly styled " of Aberdeen," because he taught the Grammar School there, and there died, but who was, in truth, a Lochaber man—nay, a Nether Lochaber man, born and bred, and whose ashes rest in Killevaodain of Ardgour, without, we are ashamed to confess it, " One gray stone to mark his grave ;"

he, born at Tarrachalltuinn—the Height of Hazel Trees—in our parish, knew something of hazel nuts, and thus happily describes them in their season :—

> 'S glan fàile nan cno gaganach,
>   Air ard-Shlios nan cròc bad-dhuilleach ;
> 'S trom fàsor am por bagailteach,
>   Air bharr nam fad-gheug sòlasach ;
> Theid brìgh nam fiuran slat-mheurach,
>   'An cridhe nam ùr-chnap blasadach ;
> Gur brisg-gheal sùgh a chagannaich,
>   Do neach a chaguas dòrlach dhin.
>
> 'S clann bheag a ghnà le'm pocannan,
>   A streup ri h-ard nan dos-chrannabh,
> A bhuain nan cluaran mog-mheurach,
>   Gu lùgh'or, docoir, luath-lamhach ;
> 'Nuair dh'fhaoisgear as na mogail iad,
>   'S a bhristear plaoisg nan cochall diu,
> Gur caoin am maoth-bhlas fortanach
>   Bhios air an fhros neo-bhruaileanach.

Our nuts are unusually plentiful this year, and of a size and flavour that we do not recollect ever to have seen equalled. They are now at that stage of ripeness when they are most delicious to the taste, and one may indulge in any amount of them with perfect safety. Most people are fond of nuts, but if the reader wants to enjoy the full flavour, to get out of a nut all that is in it, let him take the following recipe :—" First of all, let the nut be cracked, if possible, between your own *molars*, for these are, after all, the first and most natural and best of all nut-crackers, better *quoad hoc* than an instrument of the purest silver or steel ; and there is besides, remember, something pleasant to the palate in the feel and flavour even of an uncracked nut. Having cracked your nut, then— and fairly placed between the grinders, a really good nut is not difficult to crack, the worst nuts being always the most difficult to deal with, for the more insignificant the kernel the thicker and *dourer* the shell—having cracked your nut and extracted the kernel, *whole* if possible, introduce it into your mouth, not *per se*, by itself, as is commonly done, but with a small fragment of the shell,—a bit of pin's head size will do.   Proceed now to masticate the delicious morsel, and confess that there is a delicacy and flavour about a hazel nut that you knew not how to extract in full, although in your day you had cracked your bushels of them, until you were taught it from Nether Lochaber.   The philosophy of the thing is that the particle of shell introduced with the kernel causes the act of mastication to be performed more thoroughly than it otherwise would be, setting free the full flavour and aroma—all, in short, that a nut has to give.

CHAPTER XXXV.

THE strength of insects, proportionably to their weight and size, was probably the first characteristic in the minor world to arrest the attention and call forth the admiration of entomologists; and soon afterwards, we may believe, the ingenuity, patience, and perseverance displayed by these pigmies in dealing with any self-imposed piece of labour, must have made the intelligent observer feel and acknowledge, even if he could not repeat and had never heard of the mad-wise Hamlet's *dictum*, that—

> " There are more things in heaven and earth, Horatio,
> Than are dreamt of in your philosophy."

Take an example of something wonderful in insect life, as it chanced to come under our notice a few days ago [September 1872]. We were raking hay—raking hay, too, after others had raked the same ground shortly before us, for we are most particular that, both for the look of the thing, as well as for the profit, not a wisp, not a strawlet shall be left upon the ground—when, as we raked, we came across a dead mole. No rare or wonderful thing, the reader may exclaim, but rare enough when you come to think of it, and wonderful enough, too, to attract the attention of any one even less observant of natural history than Nether Lochaber. Lying on its side was the mole, already half-hidden by the swiftly growing aftermath. Touching it with the corner of our rake, and moving it slightly, we got a glimpse of a yellow-banded beetle busy underneath; and

at once understanding what was going on, we called our *bairns*,
a couple of girls and a boy, who were raking and laughing *a la
Madame de Sévigné* in the field beside us, to give them a lesson
on entomology; and as our lesson was fresh and to the point,
and interesting, though we say it ourselves, and rather out of
the common track of entomological experience, we give it to the
reader, that he may know and believe, and reverently ponder, a
truth that has never been so well expressed as by St. Augustine,
the sturdy, old, bellicose Bishop of Hippo, who of all the Fathers
had the most sensitive nose for the out-ferreting of a heretic, and
who, when he got hold of one, treated him very much as a Scotch
terrier does a rat—but who could say and do good things notwithstanding. *Deus magnus in magnis, maximus in minimis.*
God is great, that is, in great things, but greatest of all in least
things. The mole, as we have said, was lying on his side on a
grassy patch of fast-growing aftermath, and our glimpse of the
beetle beneath showed us that it was the *Necrophorus vespillo*, or
burying-beetle, rare anywhere in Britain, and so rare in Lochaber
and the west coast, that this was only the third or fourth instance
in which we had met with it. It is a black beetle, rather more
than an inch in length, with two bright orange-coloured bands
across the back, and more active in all its movements than any
of its congeners. There were just two beetles, observe—a pair,
male and female—engaged upon the mole, and the "mole" of
Adrianus, when a-building, showed not more labour and not half
the mechanical skill or indomitable perseverance on the part of
its constructors exhibited by these tiny but thoroughly skilled
excavators in the case of *their* mole. "You see that mole," we
said to our attentive audience, leaning upon our rake for the
moment, as if it were a sceptre of prerogative and power, as in
truth it was. "It is almost as big as an ordinary sized rat—bigger,
you will confess, than three full-grown mice. It has only been

dead, say, a dozen of hours; his sleek and still glossy coat proves
it. This pair of beetles, then, a single pair remember, have discovered him by an instinct and sense of smell which must be
wonderfully delicate and keen. They are now, as you may see,
busy digging under and around him, and after breakfast to-morrow
morning we shall come and see the result. "Suppose, papa," said
one of the girls, with a demure look, though with a merry twinkle
in her eye the while, "Suppose, sir, that this afternoon a passing
kestrel or owl should pick up our mole and make a meal
of him, what then could we see in the morning?" "What you
suggest is, no doubt, possible enough," was our rejoinder, "but we
believe the mole will be here to-morrow morning all the same,
provided you take example from the animal's proverbial wake-
fulness, and are up and have breakfast ready for us all in good
time." Meantime, that they might know it again, should they
ever come across it, we took up the male beetle, distinguishing
the sex from his being somewhat smaller and rather more active
than his mate, on the palm of our left hand, and with the fingers
of the right turned him on his back to show him properly, the
delicate markings of his abdomen, his muscular thorax and
cas-chrom shaped antennæ. We soon wished we had not done it;
it was a thoughtless proceeding on our part, and we should have
known better. We nearly fainted, and our children started back
in horror and alarm at the foul and fœtid smell of the carrion-eating
Vespillo. It was horrible; never in all our experience were our
olfactory nerves so offended. A pot of stale assafœtida from a
druggist's shop, all the proverbial many dozen stinks of Cologne in
combination, would have been a joke to it, a bouquet of
roses compared with our *Vespillo*. It made us quite sick
and ill for the moment; but we had the presence of mind
to lay down our malodorous beetle beside his beloved mole
ere we followed our audience, who were by this time scamper-

ing in all directions across the field, with their fingers tightly compressing their nostrils, and vowing that they would have no more to do with dead moles or burying-beetles, be they ever so brightly banded or interesting from papa's point of view. A message now came forth that tea was ready; but no tea could we drink, nor bread could we handle, on account of the horrible smell that still adhered to our fingers and palm. Washing with soap and water had no effect upon it, for it seemed to have instantly and thoroughly penetrated and permeated skin, flesh, and muscle, and to have reached and lodged in the very bone itself, whence it refused to be extirpated. It was only late at night, sitting by a briny rock-pool, and using the viscous clay of the beach after the manner of soap, that we managed to get quit of the foul odour; and even after a final washing with hot water and scented soap, as we retired for the night, we still persuaded ourselves that the loathsome smell had not altogether departed. All the carrion beetles, without exception, and most of the ground beetles proper, have always more or less of a disagreeable, sickening smell about them, but in this respect the burying-beetle is worse than all the rest put together; seeming to have centered in his own person a combination of the essences of all possible stenches in their worst and foulest form. In the case of the *Vespillo*, it is to be noted that the fœtid smell, though always there, and easily perceptible, is bearable enough while the animal is quiescent and undisturbed, and you do not approach it too closely. Tease it, however, in any way; touch it with the point of a switch, or take it up, as we foolishly did, in your hand, and the stench, emitted probably in self-defence, as in the case of the *skunk* and polecat, is of all others the most abominable in itself, and the most difficult to get rid of. Next morning, then, on visiting the mole, as proposed, we found it completely buried, with at least half an inch depth of earth neatly shovelled over it, with a slight ridge in the centre, and sloping

sides, showing that the *Vespillones* are practised grave-diggers.
Averse to disturbing a work that had cost the tiny excavators so
much labour, we only removed the earth sufficiently to bring a
small patch of the mole's fur to view, in proof to those accompanying us that the animal had really been buried by the beetles, as we
had said it would be.   A full-grown elephant buried by a pair of
field mice would hardly be a more wonderful labour.   The *rationale*
and *raison d'être* of the whole labour thus carried out with so much
diligence and engineering skill is this : the carrion of the dead
mole, mouse, or bird thus operated upon, serves in the first instance
partly as food for the beetles themselves (and they richly deserve
a feast, such as it is, in reward for their arduous labours), after
which the female lays her eggs in the fast-rotting carcase, and it is
then left as the doubtless savoury banquet of the larvæ, while the
parent pair cruise about in search of another dead bird or quadruped
of the proper size, whereupon to bestow similar attentions.   It is
principally owing to the labours of these beetles that it happens
that although you may see a dead mole, mouse, or bird lying in
the corner of a field to-day, you shall look for it in vain next
morning elsewhere than in a beetle-dug grave, as in the above
instance.   That a single pair of these comparatively small insects
should be able to perform such a gigantic task in so short a time is,
in truth, very wonderful, and must seem incredible to any one unacquainted with the habits and economy of the order.

There are doubtless many odd and curious ways of earning even
an honest livelihood in this world, but the oddest, and to us, while
uninitiated, the most puzzling we have met with for a long time,
was the following :—On a fine day lately, we took our boat to the
mouth of the Coe, and were leisurely proceeding up the far-famed
glen, when we saw, a little before us, a diminutive but still active
old man, whom, from his peculiar style of dress, we had no
difficulty in recognising as a peripatetic vendor of ballads, letter-

paper, steel pens, and other knick-knacks, who frequently pays us
a visit in Lochaber, and with whom, in lieu of better company, we
have had many a far from uninteresting roadside crack. As, with
a longer and livelier stride than his, we were rapidly overtaking him,
we noticed that he frequently stopped and picked up something,
now from the middle of the road, now from the footpath at the
side, and occasionally from the grass beyond, which something he
instantly deposited in a sort of canvas side-pouch or wallet slung
at his side. "Well, Willie," we exclaimed, as we came up with
him, "what in the world are you doing in the glen to-day, and
where's your pack? I wish to have a look at your bundle of
ballads?" "Weel, sir," was Willie's response, "my pack is laid
by at Duror just now; my present wark"—here he made a dart at
something on the grass that looked to us uncommonly like a big
black beetle, and transferred it to his wallet,—"my present wark,"
he went on to say, "pays far better, and is mair pleasant, besides,
in this dreadfu' hot weather.'" "But what is your present work,
Willie?" we inquired, "what are you so industriously picking up
along the road and transferring to your wallet? Snails? beetles?
what?" "No mony snails, or beetles either, sir," said Willie,
with more entomological good sense than we gave him credit for,
"abroad in such hot and dry weather as this is. I'm no very fond
of telling what I am doing to everybody; and when I see anybody
coming, I generally sit down and let them pass; but I saw you
coming, sir, and I kent ye brawly, and didn't mind. And now I'll
show ye what I'm gathering." With this he put his hand in his
capacious pouch, and took out a handful of *cigar and cheroot
stumps*, of all shapes and sizes. Some had been "smoked out,"
that is, till only an inch or so remained; others were only half
smoked, and a few had only afforded the smoker a whiff or two,
when, from a disinclination to smoke any further, or, perhaps, from
some defect in the cigar itself, it was thrown away as of no further

use. Of these cigar stumps " Willie " had at that moment nearly
a pound weight in his wallet, the result of his forenoon's labours.
We daresay we looked, as we really were, very much puzzled,
which, Willie observing, he politely asked us for a light for his
pipe, and invited us to sit on a ledge of rock by the roadside, and
he would " tell us a' aboot it." Our pipes alight, we sat down
accordingly, and Willie proceeds as follows :—" Weel, sir, I doubt
if ever there was such a number of strangers—tourists, as they ca'
them—day after day in Glencoe as there are this year. And a'
the gentlemen that goes up the glen smoke, and I have seen some
of the ladies—forrenders, I suspect—smoking too, the mair shame to
them. They a' maistly smoke cigars, and they throw them from
them when they're done with them ; sometimes only a short stump,
and sometimes almost a hail ane, as I have shown ye ; and I pick
them up and sell them in Greenock or Glasgow for three ha'pence
or tuppence the ounce, and that's a' aboot it." " But what," we
inquired, " do they make of them in Glasgow ?" " Weel, sir," he
replied, " I believe some of them, the cleanest, langest, and best
bits, are unrolled, and made up anew into cigars, and the shorter
and dirtier stumps are dried and broken down to mix with other
tobacco, in making the mixtures called ' bird's eye,' ' shag,' *exetry,
exetry."* We ordered Willie a glass of beer at Clachaig, and went
on our way with a bit of curious information, till that particular
date undreamt of in all our philosophy.

CHAPTER XXXVI.

FROM a utilitarian point of view, at least, the ancients seem to
have looked upon the sea and all its products—exclusive, of course,
of its myriad inhabitants of finny tribes—as absolutely worthless.
Homer in the *Iliad* constantly speaks of the sea as "unfertile,"
ἅλòς atrugétoio,—literally, the ocean where no harvest can be
gathered; and Horace in one of his satires says that a man may be
possessed of all the virtues, and all the accomplishments, &c. to
boot, but if yet *sine ré*—without means, moneyless, or to use,
perhaps, the best equivalent that our language can afford, without
substance—he shall be accounted "*vilior algá,*" viler than seaweed,
or, as we should say, viler than the dust on which he treads. Even
Virgil in the *Georgics* has no good word for the sea as in any
sense, directly or indirectly, subservient to husbandry, or an ally to
the tiller of the ground. Had these master-poets of Greece and
Rome, gentle reader, lived with us here in Nether Lochaber, in the
seventh decade of the nineteenth century, they would have thought
and said differently. Homer would have probably selected a more
appropriate epithet than that constantly employed by him; Horace
would have cast about for some other fitting dissyllable as a sub-
stitute for "*algá;*" and Virgil would have written, as he alone
could write, a score or two of unexceptionable hexameters in praise
of seaweed as an excellent manure and fertiliser of the soil. "It is

an ill wind," quoth the proverb, "that blows nobody good;" and disastrous in many a place as was the dreadful storm of the first week of this month [November 1872], here along the western seaboard it only blew us good, in the very tangible and *tangly* shape of thousands of tons of drift-ware, that, laid on the soil in fair abundance just now, prepares it without any more trouble for the reception of seed, when, ushered in by the vernal equinox, the jocund, jolly spring comes round. For the last fortnight, wherever you wandered about the coast, you found the people in every direction—men, women, and children—busy as busy could be gathering and carting afield this really valuable product of the sea— Homer and Horace to the contrary notwithstanding. We draw attention to the subject at present by reason of its timeousness, and because within recent years we have had it made clear to us beyond all cavil, and in the most practical manner possible, that for potatoes at least there is no manure for a moment to be compared with a heavy blanketing of drift-ware laid on the ground in early winter. On our own land this year a field of potatoes thus treated was a third at least better than another of equal size manured from the farmyard "heap" in the usual orthodox manner. The soil, observe, was the same, the seed the same, the date of planting the same— the only difference being in the manure. In the experience of such of our neighbours, too, as have tried it, the result has been precisely the same. The salts and other essential ingredients of seaware seem to be really antagonistic to the spread of "blight" among the tubers; and we would strongly advise as many of our readers as have the opportunity to experiment for themselves in the direction indicated during the present winter and spring, and we are ready to wager our good porcupine-shafted "Pickwick" steel pen against the vilest crow-quill, that, on the ingathering of the crop this time twelve months, our advice, in nineteen cases out of twenty, will have been found to be a sound and good one.

Since the cessation of the terrible gales of the early part of the month, the weather has been bright, bracing, and breezy, with occasional snow showers along the uplands, that have already converted the many mountain ridges around each into a veritable *Sierra Nevada*. On the nights of the 13-14th and 14-15th we sat up till a late, or rather an early hour, keenly on the watch for a meteoric display, in railway nomenclature, then due, but which, up to the date of the present writing, has not yet put in an appearance. Meteors there were, but they were the mere phosphorescent streaks rarely looked for in vain by the student of the heavens on a fairly cloudless night at this season. The lunar eclipse of the early morning of the 15th was well seen, the beautiful orb, like a shield of burnished silver, riding serene in the unclouded blue ; but the obscuration was too partial to be in any way interesting or striking to any one who had gazed on the phenomenon in its grander phases as often as we have done.

To our good friend Mr. Carmichael of South Uist we are indebted for the following contributions to our stock of ancient Celtic folk-lore, a subject much neglected, but of very great interest notwithstanding :—

URNUIGH SMALAIDH TEINE.

A prayer to be said at covering up the fire at bedtime.

(Taken down from the recitation of a man living at *Iocar* of Uist.)

Smàlaidh mise an teine ;
Mar a smàlas Mac Moire.
Gu'm bu slàn an tigh 's an teine,
Gu'm bu slàn do 'n chuideachd uile.
Co sid air an làr ?
Peadair agus Pàl,
Co air a bhith's an aire 'nochd ?
Air Moire geal 's air a Mac.
Beul De a dh'innseas,
Aingeal geal a lann'ras,
Aingeal 'an dorus gach taighe
Gu solus gael a maireach.

Which may be rendered into English as follows :—

> I will cover up the fire aright,
> Even as directed by the Virgin's own Son.
> Safe be the house, and safe the fire,
> And safe from harm be all the indwellers.
> Who is that that I see on the floor?
> Even Peter himself and Paul.
> Upon whom shall this night's vigil rest?
> Upon the blameless Virgin Mother and her Son.
> God's mouth has spoken it.
> A white-robed angel shall gleam in the darkness,
> An angel (to keep watch and ward) at the door of each house
> Till the return of the morrow's blessed light.

Having thus duly covered up the fire, and committed the house and its inhabitants to the Divine protection during the watches of the night, the following "Bed Blessing" was repeated by each as the people retired to rest :—

ALTACHADH LEAPA'.

> Laidhidh mise 'nochd
> Le Moire 's le 'Mac,
> Le mathair mo Righ,
> 'Ni mo dhion 'o dhroch-bheairt,
> Cha laidh mise leis an olc,
> 'S cha laidh an t'olc leam;
> Ach laidhidh mi le Dia,
> 'S laidhidh Dia ma' rium.
> Lamh dheas Dhe fo'm cheann,
> Crois nan naoi aingeal leam.
> 'O mhullach mo chinn
> Gu craican mo bhonn.
> Guidheam Peadair, guidheam Pòl,
> Guidheam Moir-Oigh' 'sa Mac.
> Guidheam an da ostal deug,
> Gun mise 'dhol eug le'n cead.
> 'Dhia 'sa Mhoire na gloire.
> 'S a Mhic na oighe cubhraidh
> Cumabh mise o na piantan dorcha,
> 'S Micheal geal' an cò'ail m'anama.

Which, fairly translated into English, will stand thus :—

A Blessing to be said at Bedtime.

This night I will lay me down to sleep
In the companionship of the Virgin and her Son,
Even with the mother of my King,
Who protects me from all evil.
I will not lie down to sleep with evil,
Nor shall evil lie down to sleep with me ;
But I shall sleep with God.
And with me shall God lie down.
His good right arm be under my head ;
The cross of the Nine Angels be about me,
From the top of my head
Even to the soles of my feet.
I supplicate Peter, I supplicate Paul,
I supplicate Mary the Virgin and her Son,
And I supplicate the twelve Apostles,
That evil befall me not this night, with their consent.
Good and ever glorious Mary,
And Thou, Son of the sweet-savoured Virgin,
Protect me this night from all the pains of darkness !
And thou, Michael, ever beneficent, be about for the safe
    keeping of my soul !

Apart from the appropriateness and almost absolute faultlessness of the rhythm and language in which they are couched, nothing about these old Hebridean "Blessings" seems to us so beautiful and striking as the nearness with which they bring Heaven and its active, ceaseless beneficence, to the very firesides and commonest affairs of men. Nothing is too small or insignificant to be placed, not in a general way observe, but in the most literal particular sense, under the Divine guardianship. With these old people, in their ocean-girt and storm-swept islands, God was not merely the creator, but the ever present, ever near father, protector, and friend, while to them His angels were in very truth "*ministering* spirits, sent forth to *minister* for them who shall be heirs of salvation"— not merely in spiritual matters, we are to remark, but in all the affairs of common, every-day life. Since the days of the ancient Hebrews, nowhere shall we find so firm and fixed a belief in a direct and constant intercourse and communion for good between Heaven and Earth.

The following "Blessing," to be said over cattle when being led to pasture of a morning, is exceedingly interesting :—

RANN BUACHAILLEACHD.

Siubhal beinne, siubhal coille,
Siubhal gu rèidh fada, farsuinn,
Banachag Phadruig ma 'n casan,
'S gu faic mise slàn a rithisd sìth.
An seun a chuir Moire mu 'buar,
Moch 'us anmoch 'sa tigh'n bhuaidh',
Ga'n gleidheadh o pholl, o eabar.
O fheithe, o adh'rcean a cheile,
O liana' na Craige-Ruaidhe,
'S o Luaths na Féinne.
Banachag Phadruig ma'r casan,
Gu'm bu slàn a thig sibh dhachaidh.

In English thus—

A RHYME TO BE SAID IN DRIVING CATTLE TO PASTURE.

Wandering o'er uplands, wandering through woods,
Hither and far away wander ye still,
St. Patrick's own milkmaid attend your steps
Till safe I see you return to me again.
The charm that Mary made to her cattle,
Early and late, going and coming from pasture,
Still keep you safe from quagmire and marsh,
From pitfalls and from each other's horns,
From the sudden swelling (of the torrent about) the Red Rock
And from Luath of the Fingalians.
St. Patrick's milkmaid attend your feet,
Safe and scaithless come ye home again.

The reference to "Luath," Cuchullin's matchless dog, so celebrated in the Ossianic poems and old Fingalian tales, is curious. The ghosts of the Fingalian heroes, existing in a sort of middle state— not yet exactly saved nor wholly lost—with those of their famous dogs, were believed to visit at times the scenes of their former exploits for the sake of the hunting, in which they so much delighted, and a cow or other animal, running about excitedly and wildly, and, to all human investigation, causelessly, was supposed to be the work of a passing Fingalian hunting party, invisible to mortal eyes, Luath, unmatched in spirit-land as upon earth, still leading the chase as of old. On the lines about St. Patrick's dairy-maid or milkmaid Mr. Carmichael has the following note, which will be read with interest, and which we give in his own words :—

" ' Banachag Phadriug mu'r casan.'
(St. Patrick's dairymaid be around your feet.)

Banachag is the Hebridean form of the *Banarach* of the mainland, and *Banachogach* or *Banacach* is the Hebridean term for the smallpox. You will observe the close resemblance between the Gaelic word for a dairymaid and that for the smallpox. I think the explanation is obvious. Dairymaids were wont to get the cow-pox, and people confounded the cow-pox with the smallpox. Hence, in the Highlands old people will tell you that effects of the cow-pox were known long before Jenner's celebrated discovery. Hence, also, you will rarely meet with a woman in the Highlands disfigured from the effects of smallpox. Not so the men, however. In England, again, in the rural parishes, the case is reversed. There you will see women pox-marked, but seldom men. The reason I take it to be is this :—In the Highlands it is the woman who milk the cattle, and in doing so they get the cow-pox off the cows in milking them. A Highlander would consider it unmanly to milk a cow. I have never seen or heard of one who could or would do this, except a young man in Lismore. Three or four young men, brothers, had a small farm among them. Their mother died and their two sisters married, and probably remembering Calum-Cille's celebrated saying—

' Far am bi bò bith'dh bean,
S' far am bi bean bithidh buaireadh.'
(Where there is a cow there will be a woman,
And where there is a woman there will be mischief.)

They resolved to do without a woman in their house at all; and they succeeded for a time, but not for long, for—

> 'Man, the hermit, sighed, till woman smiled.'

One of them ultimately brought home a wife, who soon became a cause of discord and ill-will among the previously happy and affectionate brothers. But this is digressing. In England it is the men who milk the cows. Most men in rural parishes can milk, and but few women. Consequently in the agricultural districts of England you hardly ever see an elderly man disfigured by the small-pox, but you can see many women so disfigured. These suggestions are simply the results of my own observations in England and in the Highlands. They may be to the purpose or not, I don't know."

We think they are to the purpose, and we are very much obliged to our correspondent for his many interesting contributions from the Outer Hebrides to our stock of "auld-world" folk-lore.

CHAPTER XXXVII.

In the poetry and proverbs of our country you constantly meet
with references which go to prove that alternations of sunshine and
shower [April 1873] have for ages been held to be the meteorological
characteristics of an April day throughout the British Islands, and
most of all, perhaps, in Scotland. To go no further, you will
remember Scott's concluding lines in *Rokeby*—

> " Time and Tide had thus their sway,
> Yielding, *like an April day*,
> *Smiling noon for sullen morrow,*
> Years of joy for hours of sorrow."

This, however, has been the driest April known in the West
Highlands for at least a score of years past. Hardly any rain has
fallen during the month, and with a bright sun overhead, and
drying north-easterly winds, rivers and streams have seldom been
at a lower ebb even in midsummer, while in some places you hear
complaints of an absolute scarcity of water even for ordinary household purposes—a very rare thing, indeed, in the West Highlands at
this season of the year, or for that matter of it at any season. There
was, however, such a superabundance of moisture in the ground,
from the heavy rains of the past winter, that vegetation has as yet
suffered little or nothing from the drought, and the country is
beautiful exceedingly in all its greenery of leaf and gaiety of ex-

panding blossom and bursting bud. Our wild-birds never had a finer nesting season, and they are now literally as merry as the day is long, for with the first flush of dawn in the east they begin their rich and varied song, which, with a short interval of quiescence and repose about mid-day, is continued without interruption until long after the sun has set and the earlier stars are already twinkling through the twilight gloom. April will be succeeded by the "merry month of May," which, with the exception of two, or at most three, cold days, with frost at night, about the 10th, is pretty sure to be an unusually fine month even for May. It was an article of belief in the hygienic code of the old Highlanders, and which you come across occasionally even at the present day, that the invalid, suffering under no matter what form of internal ailment, upon whom the sun of May once fairly shed its light, was pretty sure of a renewed lease of life until at least the next autumnal equinox, and how fine, by the way, and lightsome and cheery withal, Bishop Gawin Douglas' apostrophe (*circa* 1512) :—

> " Welcum the lord of licht, and lamp of day,
> Welcum fosterare of tender herbis grene,
> Welcum quickener of flurest flouris schene,
> Welcum supporte of every rute and vane,
> Welcum comfort of all kind frute and grane,
> Welcum the birdis beild upon the brier,
> Welcum maister and ruler of the yeare,
> Welcum weilfare of husbands at the plewis,
> Welcum repairer of woddis, treis, and bewis,
> Welcum depainter of the blomyt medis,
> Welcum the lyf of every thing that spedis,
> Welcum storare of all kind bestial,
> Welcum be thy bricht beams gladand all ! "
> (Prologue to "*xii. Buke of Eneados of Virgill.*")

The *Æneid* has been often translated into English, both in prose and verse, since the days of Gawin Douglas, but we doubt if the Mantuan bard has ever been more happily rendered than by the good Bishop of Dunkeld. The following is his rendering of perhaps

the best known and perhaps the most frequently quoted passage
in Virgil :—

> " Facilis descensus Averni,
> Noctes atque dies patet atri janua Ditis ;
> Sed revocare gradum, superasque evadere ad auras
> Hoc opus, hic labor est," &c.

> " It is richt facill and sith gate, I thè tell,
> For to descend and pass on doun to hell :
> The black yettis of Pluto and that dirk way,
> Standis evir open and patent nycht and day :
> But therefra to return agane on hicht,
> And bere aboue recouir this airis light,
> That is difficill werk, there labour lyis ;
> Full fewe there bene quhom heich aboue the skyis,
> Thare ardent vertew has rasit and upheit,
> Or yet quhame squale Jupiter deifyit,
> Thay quhilkis bene gendrit of goddis may thidder attane.
> All the midway is wilderness vnplane,
> Or wilsum forrest ; and the laithly flude
> Cocytus with his dresy bosom vnrude
> Flowis enuiron rounde about that place."

Warton (*History of English Poetry*) says of Bishop Douglas'
Æneid, that "it is executed with equal spirit and fidelity, and is
a proof that the Lowland Scotch and English languages were then
nearly the same." We may state that Douglas' *Æneid*, irrespective
of its many and great intrinsic merits, is especially interesting, as
being the first translation of a Roman classic into the English
language either in verse or prose. We have quoted above an old
Highland belief in the exceeding efficacy, even in the most serious
ailments, of the kindly beams of a May-day sun. Another belief
of theirs was this—

> " Geir fèidh air a ghabhail 'n ad bhroinn, 's air a shuathadh
> ri d' dhruim 's ri d' thaobh—
> Am fear nach leighis sid, cha'n 'eil leagheas ann."

That is—the fat of deer applied internally and externally, the
invalid whose sickness *that* does not heal, why, then, there is no

healing for him. The old Highlanders, you see, knew the value of deer : they hadn't a good word to say of sheep.

A few days ago we went into a cottage where a woman was sitting spinning, and singing a song we had not heard for many years, though we recollect hearing it frequently sung in boyhood. The soft and plaintive air was an old favourite, and her style of singing pleasing. With a very sweet voice and much feeling, she sang it all on requesting her to do so ; and after tea in the evening we threw the verses into English, as follows. It is, however, rather an imitation than a translation. The original, which is probably known to many of our readers, beginning—

> " Tha'n oidhche dorcha, dubh, gun reult
> Tha aibh's na speur fo ghruaman," &c.

is old ; how old we know not. Nor have we any clue to the name of the author, or more probably authoress. Of the authors, indeed, of many of our very finest Gaelic songs may be said what was said of the old nameless border-bard, that they—

> " Nameless as the race from whence they sprung,
> Saved other names and left their own unsung."

The song in Gaelic has no particular title. It is known by the two first lines quoted above, just as we say, "Of a' the airts the wind can blaw," and " Ye banks and braes o' bonnie Doon." In default of anything better, our English version may perhaps appropriately enough be entitled—

LIGHT AND SHADE.

> Dark and dreary is the world to me,
>   No sun, no moon, no star ;
> Vainly I struggle on my midnight sea,
>   No beacon gleams afar ;
> A wilderness of winter, frost and snow,
> Sad and alone I hang my head in woe.

'Tis vain to strive against the will of fate
    (No sun, no moon, no star) ;
Where I had looked for love, I found but hate
    (No beacon gleams afar) ;
I gave my heart, my all, to one who cares
Now nought for me—no one my sorrow shares.

Cares not my love though I were dead and gone
    (No sun, no moon, no star !)
God help me, I am weak and all alone
    (No beacon shines afar) :
I dare not reveal my grief, I dare not tell ;
The fire that burns my heart no tears can quell.

Traveller that passest o'er hill
    (May *thy* night have its star !)
Acquaint my love that you have left me ill,
    And seen my bleeding scar ;
'Twere better to have killed than maimed me thus—
A bird with broken wing in the lone wilderness.

I once was happy, and how bright was then
    Sun, moon, and every star !
Spotless and pure I laughed along the glen ;
    When, swift to mar
This happiness and peace, the spoiler came
    And left me all bereft—the child of shame.

And yet I do not hate him, woe is me
    (No sun, no moon, no star!)
But shun him, O ye maidens frank and free !
    'Twere better far
That you were lifeless laid in the cold tomb,
In all your virgin pride and beauty's bloom.

But God is good, and He will mercy have ;
    (How bright the morning star !)
Even the weary-laden find a grave—
    (The beacon shines afar !)
Bless, Father of our Lord so meek and mild,
    An erring mother and a helpless child.

The moral of our song is obvious, though you will observe the story is told with all possible delicacy and good taste, a characteristic, by the way, of our best Gaelic poetry. The reader may easily understand that, sung in proper time and place, and with proper feeling, such a song is calculated to have a good effect, and convey a healthy lesson in its own indirect way, when a sermon or moral exhortation, however well meant, would be altogether out of the question. There is much sound sense in Mackworth Praed's *Chaunt of the Brazen Head,* the first verse of which is this—

> " I think, whatever mortals crave
> 　With impotent endeavour,
> A wreath—a rank—a throne—a grave—
> 　The world goes round for ever ;
> I think that life is not too long,
> 　And, therefore, I determine,
> *That many people read a song.*
> 　*Who will not read a sermon.*"

At a bridal, baptism, or other merry-making, such a song as the above is calculated to do more good than the most laboured, well-meant, and goody-goody sermon that ever was preached. As we rode away from yonder cottage door, the woman resuming her task, and chanting a gay and lively air in accompaniment, we were reminded of a verse quite *apropos* to the occasion :—

> " Verse sweetens toil, however rude the sound :
> 　All at her work the village maiden sings ;
> Nor while she turns the giddy wheel around,
> 　Revolves the sad vicissitude of things."

And we also thought of the simple and beautiful epitaph on the tomb of a nameless Roman matron :—

> " *Domum mansit, lanam fecit,*"

which old Robertson of Strowan has so admirably rendered into our Scottish Doric :—

> *She keepit weel the house, and birlt at the wheel!*

A discovery of considerable archæological interest has recently been made by some people employed in trenching the moss of

Ballachulish in our neighbourhood. At a depth of ten feet in the "drift" subsoil, underlying six or seven feet of moss, only removed within recent years in the ordinary course of peat-cutting, was found the remains of what, in the far past, must have been a flint instrument manufactory on a large scale. Within an area of twenty or thirty square yards was disclosed several cartloads of flint chippings, manifestly broken off in the manufacture of flint instruments, for we have been able to secure several arrow heads, two roughly finished chisels, and a hammer head of curious shape, with a hole in the centre, which must have cost the maker no small amount of time and trouble in the manipulation. What renders this "find" more interesting is the fact that the material must have been brought to the place of manufacture from a considerable distance, flint being of rare occurrence anywhere in Nether Lochaber. Underlying such a depth of solid moss and drift, such a discovery necessarily carries us back to a race of men who lived in a very remote period indeed; how remote, even geology is as yet unable absolutely to say. We were unfortunately from home at the time the discovery was made, and were thus prevented from examining the whole *in situ*. This much, however, is certain, that under a diluvial bed of drift, gravel, and sand of upwards of two feet in thickness, underlying a thickness of at least six feet of solid moss, a flint instrument manufactory is found, the work of a people who lived before the deposit of that drift and the growth of that moss. How many thousands and thousands of years ago lived that flint-working race, who, in view of the extreme slowness of geological changes, can say? We know that in the celebrated case of the discovery of flint weapons at Abbeville and elsewhere in France the remains of extinct species of elephant, rhinoceros, and other mammals were found at an immense depth in the drift alongside of flint instruments unquestionably fashioned by human hands. Whether our Ballachulish discovery is to be held as a connecting link with a people of an antiquity as remote as those of Abbeville, it would be rash positively to assert; but the flint workers, some remains of whose labours have, as we have stated, been recently brought to light in our neighbourhood, must have lived at a period when the face of the country was geologically very different from what it is now; and remembering how slowly as a rule geological changes are brought about, we shall probably be still within the mark, if approximately we fix the era of the earliest flint workers at something like ten thousand years ago, and in the case of Abbeville, Continental archæologists have had no hesitation in suggesting a still remoter antiquity.

CHAPTER XXXVIII.

Warm showery Summer, disagreeable for the Tourist, but pastorally and agriculturally favourable—*Xiphias Gladius*, or Sword-Fish, cast ashore during a Midsummer Gale—Garibaldi dining on Potatoes and Sword-Fish steaks at Caprera—The General's Drink—Medicinal virtues of an Onion—Nettle Broth—Translation of a New Zealand Maori Song.

"RATHER showery, sir," exclaims the pleasure-seeking butterfly tourist as he stands at his hotel window, or settles himself as comfortably as may be on the box-seat of the coach in the morning. "Not a bit of it, sir," responds the sturdy agriculturist or well-to-do drover; "not a bit of it, sir, the finest growing weather we could have: cattle and sheep getting into condition famously!" [July 1873]. In such a case it is best to avoid declaring positively for either party. *In medio tutissimus ibis.* Both are right from their individual standpoint; that of the agriculturist and drover being the utilitarian and anti-poetic, while the sentimental tourist, bent on sight-seeing and recreation, very pardonably grumbles that instead of clear skies and refreshing breezes he is as often as not enveloped in mist and small rain. In any case the country is at present most beautiful, and despite the grumblings of a few, who foolishly expect to have "a' the comforts of the Sautmarket" about them whithersoever they wander, such batches of tourists as we forgather with from time to time are in raptures with our glens, and bens, and lochs, and richly wooded shores, as well they may. And never before in the West Highlands were all the conveniences for "touristing" with ease and comfort, and all reasonable despatch, so perfect and so varied.

A tolerably perfect, though not very large specimen of the sword-fish, the *Xiphias gladius* of ichthyologists, was cast ashore in our neighbourhood during an unusually heavy midsummer gale from the south-west last week. The length of the elongated snout, commonly called the sword or dagger, was two feet seven inches, a really formidable weapon, with which it has been known, whether willingly or unwillingly it would be difficult to say, to perforate the bottom timbers of the stoutest ships, the sword in such cases luckily breaking off as a rule, and thus becoming an immediate as well as an efficient plug or stop-gap to the perforation. It is a more frequent visitor to our shores than our natural history books would lead one to believe, hardly a summer passing but you hear of one or more being caught or cast ashore somewhere. This is the fourth specimen that within twenty years has come under our personal inspection here on the west coast. The largest and finest we ever saw was captured by a well-known Fort-William fisherman, *Iack Cràbach*, or Lame Jack. If we well remember, we think he told us that somebody gave him a sovereign for it. Its flesh is said to be excellent eating, while its liver affords an oil equal to eel oil in transparency, and of marvellous virtue, it is said, as a medicament. The favourite habitats of the sword-fish are the Sicilian and the Italian shores of the Mediterranean, where, at certain seasons of the year, it is caught in great numbers, the average weight being quite a hundred, and sometimes two hundred pounds or more. We have it in our *Common-Place Book* that Major Healy, of the yacht "Wildbird," informed us in Fort-William (August 1869) that he had just returned from the Mediterranean; had called on Garibaldi at Caprera, and dined with him on potatoes and sword-fish steaks, which the gallant Major pronounced excellent. We may state, as something curious, that while the Major at said dinner had his choice of very good wines, with lots of capital bottled "Bass" from England, the General himself drank a funny decoction composed of Marsala and water—half-and-half—in which a large onion, sliced lemon-wise, had been steeping for the whole previous night—a drink which the Major tasted, and in very emphatic phrase declared to be "beastly," but which he shrewdly guessed had something to do with the General's rheumatism and gout. Any of our readers having a tendency thitherwards might do worse than take the hint. There may be something in it, for we recollect, when a little boy in Morven, that an onion was somehow considered a *panpharmacon*, a perfect *panacea*—good for any and every ailment. That the mediæval herbalist, like the mediæval alchemist, was often a quack is very likely. In many instances he could hardly be otherwise when his profession was in such repute; but it is a question if our revulsion has not gone too far; if our modern medicinists do not rather much overlook, too contemptuously ignore, the inherent virtues, as to human ailments, of roots and herbs and "flowers of the field." An old lady in our neighbourhood, shrewd and intelligent beyond most of her class, told us not long ago as she was cutting nettles by the roadside, as an evening *bonne bouche* for her cow, that Stewart of Invernahyle, Sir Walter Scott's friend, made it a point every spring to have nettle broth or soup on three consecutive days about the season of the vernal equinox, which he religiously believed acted as a safe and efficient diuretic for the remainder of the year. From *Mairi Bhàn*, Invernahyle's sister, the

> " *Mhairi Bhàn gur barrail thu* "

of Macintyre's well-known song, are descended at least two Presbyterian clergymen, though the Invernahyles themselves were strongly Episcopalian—ourselves, namely, and the Rev. Mr. Cameron, Free Church minister of Ardersier. And the writing of the word "Episcopalian" above reminds us of the fact that the titular dignity of the Bishopric of Argyll and the Isles is at present vacant. The late Bishop, Dr. Ewing, with whom we had the honour of being on most intimate and friendly terms, was an unostentatiously pious, thoroughly good, and really very able man, whom nine-tenths of the clergy of his own Church would not or could not understand. Thank God that in the enumeration of the good men whom we have known, the fingers of both hands do not suffice ; and of the really good men whom we have been privileged to know and honour with affectionate regard was the late Bishop Ewing.

Some months ago we wrote to an old college *chum*, now farming in New Zealand, advising him, as some occupation for his idle hours, to pick up and send us such scraps of songs and poems as he might find among the Maori race around him. No uncivilised people that we had read or heard of seemed to us, in many respects, so like our ancient Highlanders—the Fingalians, so called, of our older ballad poetry—and we thought that so much of their poetry and folk-lore as could be gathered could not fail to be interesting. Our correspondent says :—"The Maoris, as you so shrewdly guessed, have a good deal of poetry among them ; short songs, however, for the most part, and rhymed proverbs, and "wisdom words," as they call them, very much like the Welsh "*Triads*," for they generally teach some *three* particular doctrines, or state historically some *three* particular facts. A few weeks ago I got an old man who came this way to sing me some aboriginal songs, and the one that most struck my fancy I now send to you. It is perfectly literal, for I know the native language well, and as you are fond of rhyming, you may put it into verse if you like. I can only send a true translation, line for line.

MAORI SONG.—(*Translation.*)

Fish in the pool ? No fish in the pool ;
And the women are sad because of it.
The men, too, are sad ; but to-morrow
The fish will be big, and fat, and many.

I heard the bird singing a pleasant song.
He sang of food ; he also sang of love.
The name of this bird is known to me,
But I will not tell it till we meet under the moon.

The stranger, with his face so ugly and pale,
Has come from far over the sea.
He loves us, he says ; but a Maori maid
Will not listen to his love.

The mountains and vales of our own land
Are pleasant to see and live among.
And the sun at his setting is very red—
Red with love to the Maori ; angry at the stranger.

My father lived here long ago ;
He lived here, and here also lived the *paraipa* (a kind of bird).
The *paraipa* is not here, and my father is dead :
Woe is me, I wander among strangers.

CHAPTER XXXIX.

Mountains—The Lochaber Axe, Ancient and Modern.

WITH occasional gales, by no means out of place or untimeous at this date [October 1873], with the sun already in its retrogression, almost half-way back through *Scorpio*, the weather is upon the whole mild and more autumn-like than was any portion of autumn proper itself. Winter, as yet, has hardly descended lower than the highest summits of our mountain ranges, and how beautiful in the golden after-glow, even at this season, are these same mountain peaks, impending over us like so many living presences! Tutelary divinities we sometimes fancy them, interested in all that belongs to the dwellers at their feet, with living hearts under their rocky ribs, loving us even as we love them, if we only knew it, and speaking to us in their own solemn and mysterious language, as at midnight, in our communings with the stars, we are startled now and again by the weird, inexplicable sighs and sounds, and deep-toned murmurings that seem to rise from glen and corry and frowning gorge—sounds of much meaning, doubtless, if one only knew the language, and could respond, as the sea seems to do, in the palpitation of its heaving waves, and the boom of its billows upon the beach. Pantheism and atheism are the very antithesis and antipodes of each other—errors both, just as blind credulity is the antithesis of stubborn unbelief—but, if forced to decide in favour of either, give us pantheism for choice, as the more poetical, at least, and pardonable error of the two ; for the recognition of a Divine intelligence pervading and dwelling lovingly in all things is surely preferable to the cold and bloodless anti-creed that professes to have searched the universe for a God, but failed to find Him. For our own part, we have dwelt so long among the mountains, and within sight and sound of the sea, that we have learned to love them with a strange, undefinable affection, such as one bestows only on what is at once weird and mysterious, as well as intelligent and potent, and, upon the whole, beneficent and friendly. So impressed are we with this feeling at times, that we fear that, however weighty the advantages otherwise, a city life for us would now be irksome and unenjoyable, and anything like a lengthened sojourn in a mountainless land, far from the sight of ocean waves, well-nigh unendurable. There is some meaning, however wild and improbable it may seem at first sight, in the theory that accounts for the Egyptian pyramids as erected by a nomade people, who finally settled along the valley of the Nile, in remembrance of the mountains of their native land, and to serve instead of these mountains in making the astronomical observations for which the ancient Assyrians and Chaldeans were so famous. Be these things as they may, we dearly love the mountains by which our humble home is surrounded, whether basking in jubilant sunshine or wrapt in sorrowing cloud, whether robed in midsummer green, in autumnal purple, in brown and gold, or snow-covered and ice-bound to their base ; what time the day is shortest, and the sun, almost shorn of his beams, shines but faint and far down at its farthest point of southern declination. It is recorded of Queen Mary, of sanguinary, or rather *igneous* memory, that so affected was she by the loss of Calais, that had been in the possession of England since the victory at Cressy under the gallant Edward III., upwards of two hundred years previously, that she declared in her last moments that, if her body was opened after death, the name of the lost city would be found written upon her heart ; probably the nearest approach to anything like poetry to be found in any word or act of her dark and bigoted and wholly unhappy life. If such things were possible—and the ancients, at least, believed they were—we should be apt to say the same in our own case of the mountain ranges and sea views around us, with which we have held such intimate fellowship for upwards of twenty years.

If one asked us where he could get coals, we should without hesitation be disposed, were it but to keep the well-known proverb in countenance, to direct him to Newcastle-on-Tyne. If he consulted us as to where he could best procure a serviceable and trustworthy sword-blade of finest workmanship and highest value, we should probably direct him to Damascus or Toledo. If slings and slingers, we should send him to the Balearic Isles; if bows and arrows, and how to use them with perfectest dexterity, to the Parthians; and in so advising the anxious inquirer for coals, or the warlike weapons in question, we should probably be disposed to feel that we had advised him wisely and well. And suppose one wanted a " Lochaber axe," where would he most naturally look for it but in Lochaber? And yet, in all Lochaber there is probably at this moment not a single specimen of a weapon at one time so common and so peculiar to the district as to have been called after it. The Secretary of the Royal Institution of a seaport city of England wrote us lately, begging us to procure for them a Lochaber axe, to be placed in a collection of shafted weapons in their museum. He wrote as if he thought there need be no difficulty about the matter; living as we do in Lochaber, he seemed to think that we could lay our hands upon such a weapon as easily as upon a tuft of heather or a twig of birch. We were, of course, obliged to write him in reply that neither in Lochaber proper, nor, so far as we knew, in any of the neighbouring districts, was there to be found a single specimen of the formidable weapon in question. There should be a good many Lochaber axes in the country however, though not in Lochaber. We wonder if such a thing as a

"Jeddart staff" could be had to-day in its proper locality? We recollect that during Her Majesty's first visit to Scotland in 1842, when she was received by such a splendid gathering of the Clans at Dunkeld, there was a company of a hundred men, commanded by the Honourable Captain James Murray, brother of Lord Glenlyon, the biggest men that could be got in Athole and the surrounding districts, all armed with Lochaber axes, and a very fine sight they were as they poised and swung about their ponderous and terrible weapons. We were then but a boy at school, just entering upon our teens, but the appearance of these kilted giants, with their dreadful battle-axes, is as fresh and vivid as if, since that bright and beautiful September noon, hardly thirty days had elapsed, instead of upwards of thirty years. We doubt, however, if the Lochaber axe, so called, as seen at Dunkeld on the occasion referred to, and as usually shown in our collections of weapons, is at all a true representative of the ancient arm so formidable in many a dour conflict in the hands of the Camerons, Macmartins, Macmillans, and Macphees of Lochielside, Glenarkaig, and Glenlochy, and of the Macdonalds of the Braes, and Mackenzies of Lochlevenside. The weapon as now shown is decidedly too big, too ponderous and unwieldy ever to have been used in actual fight. Only a Clan Samson or Clan Goliath, and all of them of ancestral stature and strength, could hope to wield such an arm in the heat and hurry of conflict with anything like dexterity and ease. Like the immense two-handed "Wallace" style of sword that is sometimes shown to you as having been the favourite weapon of some celebrated warrior of the middle ages and subsequent centuries, but which it is simply impossible that any mere man could ever have wielded with effect in actual fight, the modern Lochaber axe is too gigantic for use, and must have been manufactured, a big pattern of a lesser weapon, merely for parade and show. That a weapon of the kind, however, once existed, and was a favourite arm with the men of Lochaber, is unquestionable, and a truly formidable weapon it must have been. With a crescent axe face to cut with, it had a hook at the back by which horsemen could be caught hold of and dragged from their saddles, to be despatched at leisure as they lay helpless upon the ground. The shaft was necessarily of considerable length, about six feet, of ash or other tough wood, and of no greater girth than a common hay-fork handle. The shaft of the modern weapon, however, is between seven and eight feet long, and of a girth that an ordinary hand does not suffice to grasp. The axe proper, too, or head of the arm usually shown as a Lochaber axe, is nearly twice the weight of that of the older and more business-like weapon. An Indian tomahawk with a six-foot shaft, or a mediæval knight's battle-axe with a six-foot handle, such as that with which the Bruce cleft the skull of Henry de Boune at Bannockburn, would probably be nearer to the pattern of the original Lochaber axe than the ridiculously big and cumbrous modern article. You remember the scene in Scott's *Lord of the Isles*—

> " Of Hereford's high blood he came,
> A race renown'd for knightly fame.
> He burn'd before his Monarch's eye,
> To do some deed of chivalry.
> He spurr'd his steel, he couched his lance,
> And darted on the Bruce at once.

> " As motionless as rocks, that bide
> The wrath of the advancing tide,
> The Bruce stood fast. Each breast beat high,
> And dazzled was each gazing eye.
> The heart had hardly time to think,
> The eyelid scarce had time to wink,
> While on the King, like flash of flame,
> Spurr'd to full speed the warhorse came !
> The partridge may the falcon mock,
> If that slight palfrey stand the shock ;
> But, swerving from the knight's career,
> Just as they met, Bruce shunn'd the spear.

Onward the baffled warrior bore
His course—but soon his course was o'er !
High in his stirrups stood the King,
And gave his battle-axe the swing.
Right on De Boune, the whiles he pass'd,
Fell that stern dint—the first—the last !
Such strength upon the blow was put,
The helmet crush'd like hazel nut ;
The axe shaft, with its brazen clasp,
Was shiver'd to the gauntlet grasp.
Springs from the blow the startled horse,
Drops to the plain the lifeless corse.
First of that fatal field, how soon,
How sudden fell the fierce De Boune !"

A real Lochaber axe-head we have seen, never the complete weapon properly shafted, though surely real and genuine specimens of the old and famous war-arm must be found in some of our museums. At what period the Lochaber axe ceased to be carried as a battle-arm by the Highlanders it is impossible to say ; probably soon after the general introduction of fire-arms into the northern half of the kingdom, for it was certainly not used in the '45, nor, so far as we know, in the '15, nor even in the wars of Montrose ; so that for upwards of two hundred years at least it has not been used in actual combat.

CHAPTER XL.

WHEN a prophet's vaticinations are verified by the event, the world rarely fails to be reminded of it; when it is otherwise, however; when the vaticinations turn out to be the very reverse of true, people are rarely ever troubled with a note on the matter, least of all on the part of the disappointed vaticinator himself. The fact is that everything like vaticination had better, as a rule, be let alone; sooner or later, and in nine cases out of ten, or oftener, the prophet never fails to come to grief. So convinced, for our own part, are we of this, that while reserving our right to vaticinate and predict as much and as recklessly as anybody else, when it so pleased us, yet, as a matter of fact, we never do venture further into the treacherous territories of vaticination than the mere outskirts, so to speak, of what may well be called the debateable land of weather prognostics; and even there we tread as gingerly and cautiously as if at this moment we were on the banks of the Prah, in constant dread of a lurking ambuscade of fierce and fetish-valorous Ashantees. Our weather prophecies from time to time have often, as the courteous reader may remember, been fully justified by the event; but if the whole truth is to be told, we fear we must confess that they have almost as frequently turned out to be wrong, and it is not every weather prophet who will confess so much. It requires a larger share of magnanimity than the reader is perhaps aware of, to be able to confess one's errors with anything like complaisance, even in such a matter as weather prognostics, and we therefore trust that the following confession will be valued as it ought. Some time ago the number of Arctic sea-fowl in our creeks and bays, and the near approach of a rather early fall of snow to the sea line, justified us, as we thought, in predicting an early and severe winter, meaning by "severe"—for we scorn to be disingenuous in the matter—that it was likely to be excessively *cold* as well as unusually stormy. The experience of upwards of twenty years, during which we have been a keen and close student of meteorological phenomena and wild-bird life, seemed to us to warrant the conclusion at which we had arrived. But how at mid-winter stands the fact? Why, thus : that up to this date [January 1874], it has been, upon the whole, the "openest" and mildest season for at least a quarter of a century! How, then, about your Arctic sea-birds? the reader may exclaim, and we can only answer that their presence so early and in such numbers is to be accounted for by the almost incessant gales that have been sweeping over the Atlantic and northern seas, with such disastrous effects, for nearly two months past. Feeling the first blast of the approaching tempest, and assured of its prolonged continuance by a marvellous instinct, further and more correctly prescient of such matters than man, with all his boasted science, they fled to the shelter of our, to them in such cases, Friendly Islands ; for an Arctic web-foot dreads an unusual severity of hyperborean storms, long continued, quite as much as it dreads an excessive intensity of hyperborean cold, and for the same reason—both equally interfere with the allotted comforts of its economy and due supply of food. The winter, besides, is not yet past ; whistling before one is fairly out of the wood is proverbially foolish, and there is, after all, time enough yet betwixt this and the vernal equinox for the advent of any amount of cold, so that there is still a chance for our wild-bird friends and ourselves standing higher in the reader's estimation as weather prophets, ere

the winter is ended, than we do at present. Our web-foot visitors
from the far north, at all events, are still with us, and in large
numbers, and a very pretty sight a flock of them is as you quietly
approach them congregated in some sheltered bay, and with a good
binocular watch their graceful motions, now disporting themselves
and chasing each other in many a merry round over the surface of
the water; now, as if by common consent and in obedience to some,
to you inaudible, word of command, they seem to leap rather than
dive into the blue depths beneath them, until not one is to be seen,
then as suddenly reappearing, again to chase each other, and dis-
port and dive, as if they knew you were looking at them, and
admired and loved them, and would as soon cut off your finger as
think of levelling a murder-dealing weapon at creatures so beautiful
and harmless.

A bird generally rare in our inland waters is this year quite
common on all our shores. We refer to the goosander (*Mergus
merganser*, Linn.), one of the handsomest and most interesting of
sea-fowl. Of the *Merganser* family the goosander is the largest, and
the whole order is remarkable for their serrated mandibles, the
nearest approach to anything like *teeth* to be met with among birds,
and admirably adapted for retaining firm hold, when seized, of
their slippery prey, which mainly consists of eels, lampreys, &c.,
in dealing with which "kittle cattle" in deep water an ordinary
unarmed duck-bill would be a very inefficient weapon. Once in
the firm grip of the *Merganser's* serrated bill, however, the chance
of such comparatively small fish as it can alone feed upon must be
very small indeed. We saw a very fine male specimen a few days
ago, which a young man had shot, believing it to be a "wild duck,"
as he termed it, and necessarily good for eating. We told him
that he had been guilty of a piece of very unnecessary and inde-
fensible cruelty, for that the bird in his hand was in truth a
Merganser, and no more fit to be eaten than a ten-year-old herring

gull or an octogenarian guillemot. He looked at us with a smile, in which we thought we detected a considerable shade of incredulity, and we do believe that the thought passed through his mind at that moment that we only spoke so disparagingly of the bird because we wanted to get hold of it ourselves, either by its being given to us as a present, or for the smallest possible money payment, and then what a jolly feed we should have at the expense of his ornithological ignorance and juvenile simplicity ! Perhaps we do him injustice ; but, at all events, he carried the bird away with him, observing that he " would try it at any rate." We met his sister a day or two afterwards, and on inquiring if they had cooked the " wild duck," and how they liked it, we confess that it was with an inward chuckle of intense satisfaction that we listened as she told us that, after having duly boiled and cooked it *secundum artem*, until it *ought* to have been good and tender, it turned out to be so rank, and fishy, and tough, that no one could eat a morsel of it, and it had to be thrown into the dinner refuse basket as worthless ! These birds, though necessarily hardy, and able to outlive a vast amount of cold and storm, are exceedingly fond of still water, rarely resting or fishing when there is any surface disturbance beyond a slight ripple ; and hence it is that you so seldom meet with them elsewhere than in the most sheltered bays, creeks, and estuaries, where the water is least liable to the surface turmoil and commotion of a storm. The finest stuffed specimen of the *Merganser* we ever saw is at Achnacarry Castle, Lochiel's seat in Lochaber.

We have said above that the winter has thus far been almost unprecedentedly open and mild, by which we mean only that the temperature throughout has been unusually high, not, by any means, that it has been *calm*. The very contrary is the case. It has been one continued storm, with an occasional breathing time, so to speak, of a fine day at rare intervals, for upwards of eight consecutive weeks. But the storms have, *as to temperature,* been rather the storms of early summer or autumn, than the boisterously cold and burly shriekings of the lone winter " Storm King," as we used to know and fear him. The reader will best understand what we mean, when we say that, notwithstanding the storminess, *anemometrically,* of the season, not a single snowflake has fallen in the lowlands of Nether Lochaber this winter, except a little which fell last night, but of which there are no traces again this morning ; nor, except twice, and then only for an hour or so, has the thermometer touched the freezing-point. We much doubt if the thickness of a sixpenny piece of ice could be gathered at any one moment from pool or puddle in our district of Lochaber during the present winter. The consequence is, that in all our gardens flowers are at this moment in bloom that perhaps were never known to be in bloom at the same date before. Our privet and elder hedges bear quite a close green vesture of young leaves ; the columbine has already reached an April altitude of growth, and a woman who happened to walk from Fort-William early last week brought us a small bouquet of primroses that she had picked up while passing through the woods of Coirrechaorachan, as beautiful and perfect as if it were in truth the proper season of these favourite flowers, instead of the last days of the first month of the year. We shouldn't wonder, however, if we have to pay for it all yet, ere the truant schoolboy again begins to imitate the cuckoo's note, or " the voice of the turtle is heard in our land."

There is at this moment sitting in our kitchen a poor, half-witted natural, " LACHLAN GORACH," from Mull, whose conversation is always garnished with " Davie Gelletly "-like snatches of quaint song. Sometimes the rhyme is in English, and sometimes in Gaelic, and frequently has no connection whatever with what may be the immediate subject of conversation. On going up to have a crack with him a few moments ago—for poor Lachlan is, in a way, a great favourite of ours—he returned our friendly greeting of " Well, how are you, Lachlan?" with a hearty shake of the hand, and a bow that, for close proximity of forehead to the ground and duration, might have graced the court of Louis the Fourteenth, and immediately on regaining the erect position, struck, to an air that was probably original, into the following verse, which we took down on the spot :—

> " First the heel and then the toe,
> That's the way the polka goes ;
> First the toe and then the heel,
> That's the way to dance a reel ;
> Quick about and then away,
> Lightly dance the glad Strathspey.
> Jump a jump, and jump it big,
> That's the way to dance a jig ;
> Slowly, smiling as in France,
> Follow through the country dance.
> And we'll meet Johnny Cope in the morning."

It was very amusing. Where he picked up the uncouth rhyme we do not know, and it was bootless to inquire. Having ordered him some dinner, we bade him good-bye, when we caught hold of the following verse of Lachlan's favourite ditties as we disappeared :—

> " Kilt your coaties, bonnie lassie,
> As you wade the burnie through ;
> Or your mother will be angry
> If you wet your coaties now."

Poor Lachlan, always cheerful and perfectly harmless, is a welcome guest at every fireside throughout the many districts which he periodically peregrinates. We may have something more to say of himself and his quaint scraps of songs on a future occasion.

CHAPTER XLI.

It is true to a proverb that one may have too much even of a good
thing. It was the most natural thing in the world, for instance,
that our countrymen should have introduced the thistle, the
national emblem, into the fertile plains and straths of Australia
and New Zealand, to remind them of home, and to speak to them,
even at the Antipodes, of memories and traditions that patriotism
will in nowise " willingly let die." The inevitable result of such
introduction, however, was not foreseen, or rather was never
thought of. A correspondent in the province of Otago, in a very
pleasant letter by last mail [August 1874] informs us that the
" symbol dear " of Burns has so flourished and spread over large
tracts of land in New Zealand as to be already an intolerable
nuisance; so much so, that legislative enactments are being passed,
in view, if possible, to its total extirpation. " You may think I
exaggerate," says our friend, " but I positively do not, when I
tell you that in the course of a fifty miles ride the other day I saw
whole paddocks containing many hundred acres of splendid land
quite overrun with thistles, so close, and thick, and formidable,
that neither man nor horse could force a way through them. And
such thistles, too! I measured several that were quite eight feet
in height, and as thick in the stem as my wrist, with spikes on
them as large as horse-shoe nails, and as sharp-pointed as the
sharpest needle. The proprietor of one of the paddocks thus over-

grown with thistles swore at them awfully—and most unpatriotically, too, you will say, for he was a Scotchman—when I spoke to him on the subject. I assure you it is a very serious matter, for unless the obnoxious weed is somehow got rid of, many places will soon be uninhabitable, and, as you can easily understand, the evil is daily and rapidly becoming worse. The thistles are at present ripe, with large heads like cauliflowers, and when a smart breeze is blowing, where they are plentiful, the air is filled with thistle-down like a heavy snow-storm. If you, who know so many things, could only suggest some effectual way of ridding ourselves of this pest, you would be doing us a very real service." At home, too, thistles, if not more plentiful, are at least of larger growth than usual. In a corner of our own garden, for instance, there is still growing at the present moment a splendid fellow, nearly six feet in height, to which we pay a daily visit in admiration of its lusty growth, and the rich emerald green of its imbricated involucral leaves. We have purposely preserved it unhurt till now, as something of a curiosity, but in a day or two it must be cut down, for the seeds are fast ripening, and it were unwise, if not actually criminal, to allow them to escape on downy wings only to fall and germinate after their kind, a very nuisance, elsewhere. Most herbaceous plants will bleed to death if cut down two years running, just as they have about attained half their growth; and we can only suggest to our New Zealand friends that they should treat their thistle fields after a similar fashion. Let them be mowed down when about half, or rather more than half-grown, with the scythe for two consecutive seasons, and we believe the roots will infallibly die and disappear. We have known bracken, ragwort, and burr-dock, &c. very effectively disposed of in this way, and have some confidence that thistles, too, might be thoroughly eradicated by a similar process of vital wounding at the hastiest stage of growth. From our correspondent's description of them, we should say that the New Zealand thistles, so loudly complained of, are of the same species as that in our garden, the *Carduus marianus* of botanists, or Great Milk Thistle, a biennial common over all Europe, but nowhere so plentiful as in Scotland, whence it is probable that it is so frequently pointed to by poets, painters, and patriots as the Scotch Thistle, though its claims to the high honour of being the actual and real national emblem are somewhat questionable. The tradition in the south and south-west, where the true story, if ever there was a true story in the matter, is most likely to have rooted itself in its perfectest form, is to the effect that, during an invasion of the Norsemen, the Danes advancing against the Scots on a dark night, one of their barefooted scouts, when prowling about the Scottish encampment, chanced to tread on a thistle, the sharp prickles of which piercing his foot, caused him to utter a loud imprecation, which reaching the ears of the Scots, hitherto lying in fancied security, warned them that the enemy was at hand, and enabled them, instantly standing to their arms, to take their foes at such disadvantage that the fierce Norsemen were totally routed and driven to their ships with immense slaughter. The thistle that thus opportunely prevented the Scots being taken unawares is still pointed out, not, however, as being any of the large, formidable, long-stemmed varieties, but the *stemless* thistle that spreads out its leaves and spikes quite close to the ground, common enough in old pastures and waste grass lands. The stemless thistle is botanically known as the *Cnicus acaulis*, and lowly and unpretending as it may seem at first sight, there is, we make bold to assert, no species of thistle so well entitled to bear and boast the grand old legend, *Nemo me impune lacessit.* Its spines are as fine, and quite as tough and piercing withal, as the finest cambric needle ; impos-sible, too, of extraction, once it has fairly penetrated the flesh, except by a surgical operation ; and we have a shrewd suspicion that it is to some extent poisonous, for, from the moment one pierces the flesh till its expulsion by suppuration of the part, the pain is keen and excruciating beyond conception. Barefooted Dane, Saxon, or Celt, unexpectedly treading on a nearly ripe and full-formed *Cnicus*, might well be excused an oath, however lusty and loud, in acknowledgment and hearty execration of such an impediment. We can say something of a *Cnicus* spike wound from personal experience. Several years ago, when we were younger and lighter than we are to-day, we were vaulting over a wall that divided an infield of corn from an outfield of old pasture. Safely over, but alighting awkwardly, we slipped forward and fell, instinctively stretching out our hands to secure ourselves as we came almost headlong to the ground. The fall was nothing, but one of our hands had, as ill-luck would have it, alighted, with all our weight upon it, in the very bosom of a full-armed, irate *Cnicus*. The palm of the hand somehow escaped, but one of the prickles entered our wrist, and the pain was at once intense— stinging, sharp, and burning, as if the spike was the point of a red-hot needle from the fire. It could not be extracted, for it could not be seen; and there was nothing for it but patience and such local applications as might best aid the inevitable suppuration by which alone, after fourteen days' acute pain, relief was finally obtained. Upon the whole, then, and keeping the barefooted Danish scout tradition in view, we are disposed to consider the stemless *Cnicus* as the true national emblem. If there be any doubt, the honour, at all events, must be left between itself and the burly, big-stemmed *Marianus*. Of a certainty, in any case, the cotton thistle (*Onopordon acanthium*), though frequently spoken of by horticulturists and amateur gardeners as the Scotch thistle, cannot be the species indicated, for this last is not properly a Scotch plant at all, it being rarely, if ever, found growing wild anywhere north of the Tweed, though comparatively common in England. The first public and properly authenticated mention of the thistle as the national badge is, we believe, in an inventory of the jewels and wardrobe effects of James III., about the year 1467. Whether there was an "ancient" Order of the Thistle seems doubtful; what is commonly called the revival of the order dates from the reign of James the Seventh of Scotland, Second of England, in 1687.

A more natural and less apocryphal combat than the recent dwarf and bulldog business at Hanley is the following. Be not alarmed; ours is simply a brief account of a fight, fierce and and furious enough to be sure, but very natural—for of the *Phocidæ*, we suppose, as of the "bears and lions" in the well-known hymn, it may be predicted that "'tis their nature to"—a fight, then, between a pair of dog-seals in the bay under our house a few evenings ago. In nothing else are the results of the Gun Tax Act so pleasantly manifest as in the increased, and still increasing, confidence and friendly relations now so happily established between seals and sea-birds of every kind and the sea-side naturalist, as, throwing books and papers for the time aside, he takes his evening walk abroad within sight and sound of the setting sunlit sea, that gently murmers the while, as if for very gladness, in response to the rosy smile of the departing god. Ever since the beginning of summer, a large dog-seal, recognisable as such by his immense, square, bulldog-like head and fierce hirsute beard, has made our beautiful Onich Bay his favourite evening fishing-ground, until we have come to know him perfectly; no difficult matter either, for he has a curious grey patch, larger than one's hand, on his left cheek, and, unlike most seals, sinks, not log-like, when he disappears under water, but almost always with a lively "header," in which the whole back, arched and shining, is brought to view, as if for our special delectation, as we sit and watch his graceful motions with a glass powerful enough to detect the wary and intelligent glance of his beautiful dark-brown eye, and count, if need were, every separate bristle in his moustache. He is a big and powerful animal, and when in our bay doubtless accounts himself lord of all he surveys, for, of the hundreds of seals in Loch Leven, he alone constantly frequents this particular semi-oval, sandy-bottomed inlet, his size and strength probably ensuring it to him as a sort of reserve, in which woe unto the interloping poacher caught sight of *flagrante delicto* by the bright eye of " Lord Nelson," as we have long since called him, and all the people about call him, for he is now known to everybody in the hamlet, and frequently spoken about with all the interest attached to a wild animal, actually suspicious and shy, but perfectly harmless, when, with a confidence extremely rare in animals of its kind, it approaches human habitations. On the afternoon of Friday last, " Nelson " was fishing, as usual, in our bay, which at the time was mirror-smooth and calm as calm could be. We had watched him for some time through our glass, and seen him come to the surface more than once, and dispose of a flounder in his usual quiet and leisurely way, when, somewhat to our surprise, we caught sight of another seal, seemingly as large as " Nelson" himself, and about a hundred yards from him ; and at the same moment his " lordship " evidently saw him too ! There could be no mistake about it, for he, first raising himself half-way out of the water, and gazing excitedly around, with a splendid header and a very significant flourish of his hind flippers, instantly dived ; the stranger seal also, who probably knew what was coming, diving immediately afterwards. What happened below is only known to such subaqueous spectators as might be about at the moment ; we can only bear witness to what followed, and that was, that in about two minutes there was wild splashing and violent commotion of the waters near the spot at which the stranger seal had disappeared, from the centre of which turmoil the two seals soon emerged, fighting in fierce grip like a pair of enraged bulldogs. For several minutes this wild combat continued; Greek had met Greek; the belligerents hugging each other, bear-like, with their anterior flippers, and tearing at each other's heads and throats with their terrible fangs, for the canine teeth of seals are exceedingly formidable, and their strength of jaw enormous. All this time they wrestled and rolled over and over each other in deadly and desperate encounter, the sea for yards around them one sheet of boiling, hissing foam, here and there streaked with blood, as we could plainly discern by the aid of the glass, for we had, in the meantime, advanced to the very margin of the sea, and were standing within some thirty yards of them. In the wild hurly-burly of the conflict, it was impossible to see or say whether "Nelson" or "Villeneuve" was winning—for by the latter name had our son, who was along with us, already dubbed the stranger seal, as, with true boy-like interest and eagerness, he watched the fight. Had there been any betting on the event, we, knowing "Nelson," and believing in his prowess—for it was impossible to be impartial in such a case—would probably have laid two to one freely on our favourite; remembering, too, the pithy Gaelic adage, "*'S laidir cù air a dhùnan fein:*" Strong is the dog that has his own home knoll for a battle-field! As it was, the battle was fought out and finished under water, so that we were not privileged to see the last of it. After a final fierce worry, in which the combatants reared their bodies more than half-way out of the water, and much surface splashing and somersaulting, the belligerents, as if by common consent, disappeared, still fighting, however, as the hundreds of bursting bubbles that for a time kept coming to the surface clearly testified. In about a couple of minutes the stranger seal came to the surface, swimming rapidly seawards; *he* had evidently had enough of it; and shortly afterwards, "Nelson," known at once by the grey patch on his cheek, reappeared in the centre of the bay, quietly floating about, as if thoroughly tired of the tussle, and shaking his head dog-fashion now and again, from which we gathered that "Villeneuve," though beaten, had left his mark upon the victor, and the victor was in this wise very significantly acknowledging the fact. It is worthy of remark, that throughout the whole of this curious fight, though from first to last it was as fierce and furious as anything of the kind could be, not a sound was uttered by either combatant, except an occasional heavy, sigh-like breathing, which was probably involuntary, and merely the natural result of unwonted physical exertion. And yet seals are by no means dumb, for their curious bleatings— we can find no better word for it—in the breeding season, must be known to every sea-side naturalist. "Nelson," the reader will perhaps be glad to hear, is all right again, and, as yet, sole admiral of our bay, in which at this moment, as we write, he is busy fishing for supper.

CHAPTER XLII.

It is not generally known, we believe, that a wound from a stag's antlers, however slight—the merest scratch or abrasion of the skin, if only blood is drawn—is exceedingly dangerous. A short time ago [December 1874], on ascending from the cabin of a steamer, we went forward in order to enjoy an uninterrupted smoke in the fresh breeze that swept across the vessel, when we noticed a fine-looking young man, closely wrapped up in cape and plaid seated, in the shelter of the capstan, as if the breeze, to him at least, was, if anything, too brisk and keen. Glancing at him once and again, we observed that he was pale and sickly looking ; and concluding from his dress and caste of features that he must be a Highlander, we went over to him and addressed him in Gaelic. It turned out that although we did not know him, he knew something of us, and we were soon on friendly terms. He told us he was going to Glasgow to consult the doctors about a stag's horn wound in the thigh that was daily, in spite of all the salves, ointments, and healing applications that he and all the "wise" people of his glen could think of, getting worse instead of better. About two months ago he was helping to take a stag off a hill pony's back, when, by some accident, the sharp point of one of the tines penetrated the thigh for a short distance, and then, by the force of the falling weight of the head, rasped downwards for about an inch and a half, leaving an ugly, ragged gash, though of no great depth. He thought but little of it, he told us, having often had more serious wounds before, though not from a stag's horn, that gave hardly any trouble, and soon healed of themselves—of the first intention, as the surgeons have it. How it may fare with him among the Glasgow doctors we do not know : well, poor fellow, we sincerely hope, though we shouldn't wonder if the wound continued to trouble him all his life long. The subject of stag-horn wounds having thus been brought before us in a way that could not fail to interest us, we took the matter to avizandum, as the sheriffs say ; and, in dearth of anything better at this dull season, we present our readers with the result of our inquiries in every direction whence there was the least chance of enlightenment. Dogs wounded by stags' horns usually die from mortification or gangrene of the wound ; and even if the wound heals, and they recover, it is only in an unsatisfactory sort of way, for they are almost always afterwards paralytic in the wounded limb, or they are epileptic. An old forester, who knows more about deer and deerhounds than anybody else we ever met, tells us that in very few instances has he ever known a dog that has actually bled at the touch of a stag's horn, recover in such wise as to be fairly serviceable again. With the least drop of blood in such cases, they seem to lose all their courage. Another man, a shepherd near us, says that a very fine collie dog of his was once severely wounded by a stag in Glenarkaig, on Lochiel's estate, and that although the wound healed satisfactorily enough, and to the eye of an ordinary observer there was nothing the matter with the dog, it was, in fact, ever afterwards perfectly useless. "Chaidh e gòrach, le'r cead." A good dog before, "he became perfectly stupid, sir!" said the man. The above-mentioned forester says that the poisonous character of stag-horn wounds is well known to every one in the least acquainted with deer-stalking, as the sport was followed in the good old ante-breech-loading rifle days, when explosive bullets were yet unknown ;

and that rough contact with the tines of the animal, whether living or dead, was, in his younger days, avoided as one would avoid the tooth of a rabid dog or a viper's fang. A stag antler's wound, he avers, is dangerous at all times, but most so in the end of autumn—the rutting season—or, as he put it, "an àm dhaibh 'bhi dol 'san damhair," when they take to their " wallowing pools." Curiously enough, and by the merest accident, we have fallen in with the following proverbial distich from an old volume on *Venerie, or Hunting of the Buck,* published in London in 1622 :—

" If thou art hurt by boar's tooth, the leech thy life may save ;
If thou art hurt by buck's horn, 'twill bring thee to thy grave."

So that the venom of a stag's horn wound seems to have been quite as well known two hundred years ago as it is now ; better, indeed, for those who followed the chase in the olden time were more liable to such hurts than is possible in the case of the modern deer-stalker, when the aid of dogs and the " gillie's " knife to give the *coup de grace* to the " stag at bay," are matters of comparatively little moment. It was a much more serious and risky affair in the days of the old " flint "-bearing musket. There was a paragraph a short time ago about a serious attack by a stag on some men in the island of Raasay. It would be interesting to know whether blood was drawn on the occasion, and if so, how the wounds have healed.

Hardly anything in our old *Ossianic* ballads, of which we have such an interesting and ably edited collection in Mr. J. F. Campbell of Islay's *Leabhar-na-Feinne,* is so curious as the great number of dogs employed by the Fingalians in their huntings,—that is, if we are to read the ballads with anything like literalness. Fifty, a hundred, two hundred, and even five hundred dogs are spoken about as freely as a modern sportsman speaks of couples. In one ballad, for instance, recovered by ourselves, ten men, one of them the balladist himself, the last remnant of the Fingalian host, are represented as going to hunt in the "Glen of Mist," attended by fifty dogs a piece, or five hundred in all—surely an unnecessary, if not an impossible number. In these ballads, besides, you find frequent reference to scarcity of food, and the shifts the " heroes" were often put to, to provide for the barest wants of the passing day ; and yet, if such an army of dogs was necessary, it also had to be fed, which one conceives must have been a matter of some difficulty, when the heroes themselves were, as the ballads inform us, frequently reduced to the necessity of splitting " marrow bones," when all the flesh that covered them had already been used up. The whole question of the natural history of these old ballads is well worth more attention than has yet been bestowed on it. Some day or other we shall devote a special chapter to it. Meantime, let us merely say that we decided many years ago against the authenticity and genuineness of one at least of Dr. Smith's so-called *Ancient Lays*, because of the incorrectness of a reference to the natural history of a well-known bird, the common pigeon. Here are the lines in *Gaul* which first made us shake our head in dubiety over the genuineness of the composition—

> " Mar cholum an carraig na h-Ulacha,
> 'S i solar dhearca da h-àl beag,
> 'S a' pilltinn gu tric, gun am blasad i fein,
> Tra dh'eireas an t-seabhag 'na smuainte."

> As a dove on the rock of Ulla,
> That gathereth berries for her young ;
> Oft she returns, nor tastes herself the food,
> When rises the hawk within her thoughts.

On which passage we would first of all remark that pigeons are not berry eaters, and even if they were, they would not carry them to their young in such wise as the poet clearly implies. A pigeon itself eats the food meant for its young, and only after undergoing a certain process of maceration and digestion in the parent's crop,

is it again regurgitated in form suitable for the young.   In genuine
Gaelic poetry, the natural history is in a very remarkable manner
almost invariably correct.   Here it was not, and we recollect tossing
the volume aside, and remarking that while much of *Gaul* might
certainly be "ancient," quite as much was modern, and that,
wittingly or unwittingly, Dr. Smith had been dealing in patch-
work.   Dr. Smith cites a parallel passage to the above from
Thomson's *Spring*—

> "Away they fly,
> Affectionate, and, undesiring, bear
> The most delicious morsel to their young."

But the context shows that Thomson is not referring to doves, but
to *Turdi* and warblers that build

> "Among the roots
> Of hazel pendent o'er the plaintive stream."

And these do feed their callow young as represented in the poem,
though the *Columbidæ* certainly do not.

We observe that Mr. T. B. Snowie, of Inverness, has recently
been so fortunate as to secure a specimen of the *spotted crake* or
Crex porzana, a very rare bird indeed, of which we never saw a
living specimen.   It seems, however, to be a more regular visitor
to our shores than is imagined, specimens having from time to time
been met with in almost all parts of Scotland.   Our friend Mr.
Robert Gray, in his excellent volume on *The Birds of the West
of Scotland and the Outer Hebrides*, writes of the spotted crake as
follows :—"So far as I have observed, the spotted crake is a very
uncommon species in the western counties ; it is, however, more
numerously distributed throughout the eastern counties, extending
from Orkney to Berwickshire.   In Aberdeen and Forfar shires,
according to Macgillivray, it can scarcely be called very rare.   'In
Scotland,' says Mr. More in the *Ibis*, 'the nest has been found
only in Perth, Aberdeen, and at Loch Spynie, in Elgin ; but as

birds have been repeatedly taken in the breeding season in Banff-shire, Fife, East Lothian, and Berwick, it is not unreasonable to infer that the species nest in these counties also. In the west of Scotland, the spotted crake has been taken in Wigtonshire, Ren-frewshire, and Argyllshire ; but I have no authentic instance of its occurrence north of the last-named district. In its habits this bird closely resembles its congener the water-rail, and, like it, is not easily flushed from its haunts. Although a migratory species, the spotted crake appears to come early, specimens being occasionally taken about the beginning of April ; as a rule, it also lingers much later than other migratory birds, stray examples having been shot in November, December, and even January, so that it is absent not more than two or three months. It may, indeed, be yet found to be, in some of the southern districts, permanently resident. From its shy and unobtrusive habits, and its life of seclusion and silence in marshy places, from which it but rarely issues, it is much less frequently seen than birds which try to escape by flight when dis-turbed. Rather than take wing, it will thrust itself, when molested, into any hole or tuft of grass, and remain concealed until quiet is restored ; and on this account the comparative numbers of the species cannot readily be ascertained.' "

The bird is, however, unquestionably a *rara avis*, a *rarissima avis* even, in the north of Scotland, and to have seen the bird as Mr. Snowie was privileged to see and handle it, we should cheer-fully have walked ten miles, were it the coldest day in mid-winter.

CHAPTER XLIII.

It has been our habit for many years [January 1875] to take our morning walk along our beautiful sea-beach, one of the coziest and prettiest silver-sanded bays on the West Coast, descending now and again, when the tide is at ebb, to search for objects of interest in marine animal and vegetable life, in every likely spot along what *Ossian* calls " tràigh na faoch,"—the periwinkled shore. Our friend and neighbour Dr. Clerk, by the way, in his admirable edition of the great Celtic bard, renders it "the shore of *whelks*," and in a note gives us to understand that he thinks the expression so unpoetical, *infra dig.*, and every way inappropriate, as almost to warrant its rejection as a corruption of the text. As a conjectural emendation, he suggests " tràigh na *faobh*," the shore of *spoils*, as probably the true reading. *Faoch*, however, is not the whelk, but the periwinkle or *wilk*. The whelk is the *Buccinum undatum*, the *cnogag* or *cnocag* of the Gaels of the Western seaboard and Hebrides. The wilk or periwinkle is the *faoch* or *faochag;* and to it and not to the whelk the passage clearly refers. The whelk or *cnogag* rarely allows itself to be left behind on the beach by the receding waters, even in spring tides, when ebbs are at their lowest. The periwinkle, on the contrary, sticks, regardless of the receding waves, to its place or stone or algæ stem and frond, until the ebbing waters have returned, as return he knows full well they shall ; so that at any time after half ebb, a suitable shore, rich in algæ, presents a most interesting sight, every stone and smallest bit of sea-weed covered with millions of periwinkles at all stages of growth. It is to a scene of this kind that the poet refers, and very happily we think : "the periwinkled shore " is a thousand times better than the "barren, barren shore" of Tennyson. No one objects to "daisied mead " or "daisied lea," and "periwinkled shore," as we have seen it, and as hundreds, we make no doubt, of our readers have also seen it, is, to our thinking, every whit as poetical, and in no sense inconsistent even with epic dignity. Wilks having within recent years become an article of considerable marketable value, being carefully gathered on every beach, the "periwinkled shore " of Ossian is, of course, a rarer sight now-a-days than it used to be. Nearly as plentiful on our shores as the common periwinkle itself is its first cousin, the *Purpura lapillus* of conchologists, or yellow periwinkle, one of those creatures that furnished the famous purple dye of the ancients. It has a bitter, astringent taste, and is in consequence not eaten like its congener, the wilk. We have said that our favourite morning walk is invariably, if we can accomplish it, along the sea-beach ; and hardly a day passes but we can show something interesting and new, picked up in these our littoral perambulations. After a storm particularly, we endeavour, whatever our other engagements, to devote an hour at least to a ramble along the shore, and it is rarely we return empty-handed : some curious waif or other, cast up by the storm, seldom fails to be forthcoming as the reward of our matutinal diligence. After a severe gale one morning last week, we found a dead *kittiwake,* but perfectly plump and fresh, lying on the top of a mass of drift tangle. The bird itself was no great rarity, for the kittiwake (*Larus rissa,* Linn.), a very pretty little gull, is common on all our shores, even in winter. The curious thing was that, on taking up the bird in our hand, we found that one of its feet was firmly held in the vice-like grasp of a large mussel, the mussel in its turn being anchored by its *byssus* to a tangle root (*Laminaria digituta*) of immense size. The poor kittiwake had evidently been fairly trapped : the case was clear. Walking along the beach at low-water, in search of food, it must have stepped inadvertently and unwittingly into the jaws, so to speak, of the open, or rather half-open, mussel, which, in resentment of the intrusion, instantly closing with a steel trap-like snap, held the poor bird firm and fast. There was no chance or hope of escape, and the unfortunate little gull, thus anchored to the bottom, was miserably drowned by the advancing tide. Its body would, to a certain extent, act as a float or buoy to the mussel and tangle root, which, thus loosened, the storm would readily dislodge, and cast up on the beach, even as we found it. Web-feet of all kinds are, of course, as liable to death in all its forms, natural and accidental, as any other animals, but we dare to say that in any accurate return of the vital statistics of sea-birds, death by *drowning*, Ophelia-like, would be found about the rarest. In more ways than one, therefore, was our dead kitti-wake a curiosity of no every-day occurrence, though, in nineteen cases out of twenty, the passer-by would probably be content to kick it aside as a dead gull, and no more, if, indeed, he con-descended to notice it at all. We were lately told an amusing story about a Fort-William man who lived some fifty years ago, and was in his day a great shore-searcher after storms, incited thereto, not exactly in the interests of science, but by more mundane and prosaic considerations. Summer and winter, all the year round, he searched the shores (*Bhi'dh e g'iarraidh nan cladaichan*, was the phrase) of Achintore and Drumarbin after every gale of wind, wandering ghost-like in the grey dawn by the margin of the sea, and diligently picking up every conceivable article of *flotsam* and *jetsam* that came in his way. In all this there was perhaps nothing to object to ; but this mild specimen of a Cornish wrecker had the habit of appropriating, without compunction, such oars, thwarts, baling-dishes, and other articles of boat gearing as came in his way, even though he knew that they belonged to his neighbours, and had only been carried away from their proper places by an unusually high tide or a gale of wind. This was a breach of the etiquette and good-neighbourhood prevailing among boatmen that could not be tolerated. A Drumarbin man, therefore, who had lost some oars in a storm, and suspected that the Fort-William shore-searcher had found and kept them, determined on reprisal, and in hope of curing him of such shabby peculations, to give him a good fright, which could be done the more easily, as the shore-searcher was a nervous, timid creature, brimful of belief in apparitions, ghosts, and ghost stories of the wildest and most improbable character. Getting up one morning after a storm, the Drumarbin man put on a pair of new shoes, and slipping to the shore, unobserved by the wrecker, whom he could see wandering along the beach, as was his custom, in the grey day-break, he lay down at length on the shingle, and covered his head and body down to his ankles with the drift-ware that had been cast up by the storm. All he left exposed was his feet, on which we have said there was a pair of good substantial new shoes. Meanwhile the "wrecker" was advancing along the beach, carefully searching about, and stooping from time to time, oyster-catcher or curlew-wise, in order to pick up such waifs and strays as he fancied worth the while. At last he reached the recumbent and sea-ware-covered Drumarbin man. The shoes at once caught his eye, and as he gazed wistfully on what he considered the most fortunate and valuable *jetsam* that had fallen to his luck for a long time, he was heard to soliloquise,—"A drowned man! Poor fellow; but he has good shoes on, and as he can have no more use for them, I may as well take them now as anybody else later in the day." No sooner said than done. Throwing down his bundle of gatherings, he pulled the shoes evenly and steadily off the supposed "body's" feet, and was

moving away with them, when a smothered sepulchral voice from
under the sea-ware struck his ear—an ear painfully acute under
the circumstances,—" Gabh mo chomhairl' 's fàg na brògan sin ! "
" Take my advice, and leave these shoes alone ! "   At the same time
he saw the mass of drift-weed heaving and moving.   Dropping
the shoes as if they had suddenly become each a mass of red-hot
iron in his hand, he started off with a yell that frightened the sea-
birds all the way to *Camus-na-Gall,* and ran a terrible race without
once halting or looking over his shoulder, till, penitent and
breathless, he reached his own fireside.   He was completely cured
of shore-wandering, for, as our informant told us, he soon after
sickened and took to his bed, from which he never rose again.
Told in excellent Gaelic, and with a large admixture of the serio-
comic quiet humour so characteristic of an old Highlander, the
story made us laugh heartily ; and not the less so that it was told
in sly reference to our own frequent sea-shore perambulations.

It is many years since our wild birds have had to encounter a
winter of such unmitigated severity as the present.   Dead rooks,
blackbirds, chaffinches, and hedge sparrows are only too common
in copse, hedgerow, and open field, stiffened and starved all of
them, nothing but the bones, skin, and feathers remaining as you
take them up and handle them, so that one only wonders how it is
they did not drop and die long before reaching such a sad state of
utter fleshlessness and emaciation.   A whole month, however, of
intense frost, making every one exposed to its direct influence,
even for a moment, put their fingers to their mouths with a " poor
Tom's a-cold" attitude and grin—of intense frost, in which the
earth became hard and resonant as iron, clearly accounts for it all.
Some idea of the keenness of the frost at times may be gathered from
the following facts :—On Friday afternoon we had occasion to go
to look if our boat on the beach was all right, for the darkening
heavens threatened an immediate storm, a not uncommon end to

such rare meteorological phenomena as long continued frosts on
the West Coast. Sitting on the end of a log of wood that lay
on the beach, a little above high-water mark, was a rook or crow,
which, as we approached, attempted to fly away, but could not.
It stretched itself, and strained, and flapped its wings frantically as
we drew near, but there it was, tethered firm and fast, manifestly
unable to budge an inch, unless it carried the immense log bodily
along with it. We wondered for a moment what in the world
could be the matter, for we could not recollect ever seeing a
rook, of all our birds the most knowing, perhaps, and self-possessed,
act so absurdly. Running forward and laying hold of the bird, we
had a ready solution of the mystery in the fact that the poor,
struggling creature's feet were firmly frozen to the log—more
firmly than the best bird-lime or glue could have held them.
Thawing the frozen feet with some little trouble by the warmth of
our hand, we had the pleasure of setting the poor bird at liberty.
He—for it was a male—did not certainly weigh more, as we poised
him in our hand, than six or seven ounces, though the ordinary
weight of a rook in fair condition is nearly a couple of pounds.
Even within doors the frost was unusually intense. In a small
room off our own kitchen—and in the latter there is, of course, always
a fire, and generally a large fire, burning—the night's milk was frequently found frozen into a hard and solid mass in the morning;
so thoroughly frozen that the servant girl could, by tilting up the
vessel and smartly tapping its bottom get the solid contents of
frozen milk into her hand, and carry it, for the amusement of the
youngsters, about the house, from one room to another, as if it
were a Dunlop cheese. Such a frost we have not had on the West
Coast for at least a score of years. Our wild-bird levee of a
morning is a most interesting scene—the most pleasant episode,
perhaps, in the necessarily dull routine of a winter's day in the
country. On these occasions we can depend on the presence of

such birds as redbreasts, wrens, finches of all kinds, the lively and ubiquitous chaffinch, however, being most numerous; coral-billed blackbirds, shy at first, but easily made familiar and friendly enough; ox-eye tits, very pretty birds, but nervous and fidgety always; house and hedge sparrows, with a self-assertion and impudence that is most amusing, and a bold familiarity that would always place them in the front rank of bread-crumb recipients, if the redbreasts, seldom otherwise than quarrelsome and testy, did not drive them back. Most of those birds, when they found an open door or window, would boldly venture into the house, and eagerly pick up the bread crumbs from off the floor or table, undisturbed by anything one said or did, provided only you refrained from any attempt to lay hold of them; in that case they were off and out instantly, and in a manifest pet at your rudeness and inhospitality, shy to trust you again until the matter was forgotten, or perhaps only overlooked perforce of the inexorable logic of intense cold and gnawing hunger. All the birds that we have handled for more than a month past were but the merest skin and bone, emaciated to a degree altogether unknown in less severe winters. Curiously enough, however, we had a brace of woodcocks a few days ago which were as plump and fat as one could wish them; and some brace of snipe, shot in the neighbourhood of Inverness, kindly sent to us as a Christmas present, were in excellent condition, and good in every way. Why these long-billed, sucking birds should be fat, when all other birds are unnaturally lean, is to be accounted for by the fact that the intense frost drives the worms and minute animals which constitute their food into the open "eyes" and rivulets, which never freeze, like sheep in a fank; and thus the woodcock and snipe have their food with rather less trouble in frost than in more open weather. Some ten days ago, a very fine specimen of the jay (*Corvus glandarius*, Linn.; the *Scriachan-Coille* of the Gael) was sent us. This is one of our handsomest birds, and we are glad to say that it has within recent years becoming comparatively common in Lochaber. Like its congener the magpie, it is looked upon with considerable suspicion as an enemy to game ; eating up, it is alleged, grouse, and partridge, and pheasant eggs as a favourite *bonne bouche*, and even devouring the newly hatched young. It is a shy and solitary bird, even where it is common, and we do not know its habits and economy sufficiently to entitle us, much as we are inclined, to enter on its defence under such an indictment ; but, from all we have been enabled to gather on the subject, we should meantime be disposed to record the *tertium quid* verdict of " Not proven."

CHAPTER XLIV.

How intense was the recent frost [January 1875], and how hyperborean all our surroundings, may be judged of from the fact that
on coming out of church yesterday, one of our people, a greyheaded,
pious old man, spoke of the happy change to open weather and
" westlan' breezes " very solemnly as " the blessed thaw"—*an
t'aiteamh beannaichte.* Before any one else north or south of the
Tweed made any reference to the coming winter, our readers may
remember that we did, and that we inculcated on every one the
wisdom of keeping themselves warm and comfortable, by means of
good fires and otherwise, as the best way of being jolly in the best
and truest sense of that much misapprehended and frequently mis-
applied term. It was, in truth, a trying season ; but sensibly and
thickly clad in many a fold of honest home-spun *cùrain,* or plaiding,
our people for the most part got over it without any very serious
ailments. Influenzas, catarrhs, and colds in every form were of
course common, and, for a time, one was met on every side by an
uncomfortable and sometimes disagreeable amount of coughing,
expectoration, sniftering, sneezing, and nose-blowing ; but now all
this has almost or altogether passed away, and people are again
going about as usual, clad no otherwise than ordinarily, and as
becometh the inhabitants of a temperate zone : plaids, comforters,
double-ply mittens, and " bosom-friends," having been laid aside as
unnecessary incumbrances in weather that is now actually warm

and spring-like, as compared with that dreadful month or six weeks of Baffin's Bay-like temperature, that, when it got fairly at you, and off your guard, seemed capable of making the very blood freeze in one's veins, even as it froze the water in our subterranean and best guarded lead pipes. Nothing, perhaps, could more pointedly illustrate the healthy vigour and vitality of our people generally than the fact that, although we have amongst us many who have arrived at extreme old age, and some who have been more or less valetudinarian for years, there has not been a single death in the district—a district which, as we look around us, contains some two or three thousand inhabitants—since the beginning of last December; a fact which, considering the inclemency of the weather, and the high death-rate everywhere else, is something surely worthy chronicling. We are probably correct in believing that the worst at least of winter is already past, but much cold and stormy weather may be still in store for us, and as colds and coughs may return, we beg to make friendly offer of the following *probatum est* recipe, quite a popular cure in this part of the country for every form of winter influenza. Cure or no cure, the recipe has at all events the merit of being extremely simple, and to thousands of our readers very readily available at any time. Take a pint—say a tumblerful—of sea water that has been heated to the boiling-point, without having been allowed actually to boil. Sprinkle over it some pepper, rather more plentifully than you do in your soup; drink this as hot as you can bear it as you step into bed at night. Next day your cold and cough will have disappeared like an unpleasant dream. You may be weak, but you will, upon the whole, be well! We cannot personally vouch for the efficacy of this draught, but we find that many people here invariably resort to it as a ready and popular cure for their colds, and they speak highly of its virtues, and, contrary to what one would expect, of its comparative pleasantness and palata-

bility as well. A sensible old man whom we questioned on the
subject a few days ago, and a firm believer in the efficacy of this
"saline" draught, told us in confidence that the *rationale* of the
thing consisted in the fact that it immediately acted as a powerful
sudorific; and that to this, he thought, was to be attributed the
thoroughness as well as the rapidity of the cure. Probably he was
right. It is a simple, cheap, and readily available remedy at all
events, and dwellers by the sea-side might do worse than give it a
trial at a pinch, when more orthodox remedies have failed, or are
not ready to hand. One grand thing about it is the certainty that,
if it does no good, it cannot possibly do harm. Another old man
in our neighbourhood, still hale and active, though in his eighty-
fourth year, told us lately that he never took a dose, not a ha'penny's
worth, of medicine, druggist's or doctor's stuff in his life. "Whenever I felt out of sorts," he continued, "I just went down to the
sea and drank a good large draught of salt water; *that* was always
my medicine, and it never once failed to do me good." So that
there may be more virtue in sea water as a curative agent in
bronchial and stomachic ailments than the world generally wots.
And if so, how consoling the thought that *this* druggist's shop is
never shut; the supply is exhaustless, and no charge !

A curious bit of popular superstition is the following, which a
gentleman in a neighbouring district was good enough to bring
recently under our notice. After breakfast, at which, among other
good things, we had some excellent fresh eggs, he suggested that
we should go into the kitchen to smoke, "and watch," he said,
"what my housekeeper will do with the empty egg-shells as the
breakfast things are brought up from the parlour." We went and
stood and watched accordingly, and this is what we saw, chatting
with our host the while, that the housekeeper might not suspect
that we took any particular interest in her doings. We noticed
that when the girl came into the kitchen and laid the tray upon

the table, the housekeeper, a staid and respectable-looking woman, well advanced in years, walked over and took the egg-shells—there were four or five of them—and, placing them one after another into an egg-cup, she took a small knife, and passed it with a smart tap through the bottoms or hitherto unbroken ends of the lot, and then turned away to some other employment. This was all, for our host immediately suggested that we should visit the stables. We were a good deal puzzled, having seen so little, where we expected to have seen a great deal, and that little so seemingly without meaning and purposeless. When we got to the stables, our host asked if we understood the meaning of the old lady's manner of dealing with the egg-shells. We confessed our profound ignorance, having never seen—never, at least, seen so as seriously to notice—anything of this kind before. "My housekeeper, you must know," continued our friend, "is a most excellent woman, but much given to little superstitious observances and harmless *giosragan*. She will not allow a single egg-shell to go out of her sight without first making a hole through it, knocking out its bottom in short, in case, as she has more than once seriously told me, a witch should get hold of it and use it as a boat, in which to set to sea in order to raise violent storms, in which the ablest seamanship could not possibly save hundreds of vessels from being miserably wrecked!" "You may smile," he went on, "for it is supremely absurd, to be sure, that an otherwise sensible woman should give credence to such nonsense; but, after all, if you make inquiry, you will find that the superstition in question is quite a common one. Few middle-aged women, brought up in the Highlands, but will act as you saw my housekeeper act with the empty egg-shells, knocking a hole through their unbroken ends before throwing them aside, or frequently even more effectually providing against the possibility of their being used as witched life-boats, by crushing the whole shell into a crumpled mass bodily in the hand."

We haven't as yet had many opportunities of making inquiry into the matter, but from all we can gather from some old women in our neighbourhood, we believe empty egg-shells are, or perhaps we should say were, frequently treated after the fashion stated, and for the reason assigned. Some of our readers in the north-west Highlands and Hebrides may perhaps know something more about a very odd and curious superstition to be met with in the latter half of the nineteenth century. For obvious reasons, it is a superstition more likely to be prevalent among islanders and dwellers by the sea-shore than in the more inland parts of the country.

The following fragment of a curious old poem we picked up about ten days ago from the recitation of Alexander Maclachlan, shepherd, Dalness. It is unfortunately but a fragment, as we have said, but we give it here in the hope that some of our friends of the Gaelic Society, or of our many readers throughout the Hebrides, may be able to supply more or less of the remainder. Maclachlan heard the entire poem from a Glenetive forester, a very old man, some years ago, but this man is now unfortunately dead, and the reciter could not direct us to any one likely to be able to repeat the poem at length. Perhaps our friend Mr. J. F. Campbell of Islay, so indefatigable and marvellously successful in his search after Celtic song and story, "all of the olden time," may have met with it in a more or less complete form; if so, he would very much oblige us all in the north by giving us a version of it and its history, as far as he knows it. We may state that it does not appear in *Leabhar-na-Feinne*, which we have searched for it, though unquestionably a production of considerable antiquity. Maclachlan told us that the old forester, in reciting it, called it *Conaltradh nan Ian*, or *The Parliament of Birds*. The following were evidently the opening lines of the poem, and likeliest to be remembered by one who only heard it repeated once or twice :—

CONALTRADH NAN IAN—(Fragment).

" Nuair 'bha Gaelig aig na h'eoin,
  'Sa 'thuigeadh iad glòir nan dàn,
  Bu tric an comhradh anns a choill
  Air iomad pong, ma's fhior na Bàird.
  Thainig piàid luath na gleadhraich,
  'S shuidh i air grod mheur còsach fearna,
  Ma choinneamh cò'chaig a ghuib chruinn,
  'Sa caog-shuil dhonn na ceann mar àirnaig.
  'N so dh'èirich a phiaid gu grad,
  'S thubhairt i 's i 's tailceadh a bonn,
' An tusa sin a'd mheall air stop
  Nuair a bhi's do cheod-cheann trom ?
  Am bi do theanga 'ghnath fo ghlais
  'S tu gun luaidh air reach na ùi,
  'S tu cho duinte ri cloich bhric
  'Bhi's air meall a chnaip gun bhri.'

.   .   .   .

" Bu treis dhaibh mar so a còmhstri,
  Gearradh, 'bearradh glòir a cheile,
  Ach gus an d'leum a nois an glas-eun ;
  'S rinn esan gach cùis a rèiteach,
  'S crog a phiaid air a ceann
  'S dh-fhag e i gu fuar, fann,
  'N sin bh'èirich firèun nan gléus
  A shinbhlas an spèur ga luath."

[*Cætera desunt.*]

This curious poem seems to have been throughout of a dramatic
form. Maclachlan says that, as he heard it repeated, almost all
our better known wild-birds were introduced, and had appropriate
speeches and parts assigned to them. He particularly referred to a
very funny speech by the wren, who finally quarrels with the
wagtail, by whom he had been insulted, and gives him a good
licking. The end of it all is that the eagle is unanimously elected
king of birds, with the glas-eun or falcon-kite as his lieutenant.
The throstle cock is elected bard of birds, and the dipper admiral
and commander-in-chief of the wild-bird fleet. Any one recovering
the whole poem would be conferring no small boon on Gaelic
literature.

CHAPTER XLV.

In a recent number of *Land and Water*, Mr. Frank Buckland, in writing about the *Ophiophagus elaps*, a serpent-eating serpent lately introduced into the Zoological Gardens, London, with all the honours due to a visitor so choice and curious in its diet, remarks that " the saying that ' Dog will not eat dog ' is proverbial amongst us." North of the Tweed, neither in Gaelic nor in guid braid Scotch, is any such proverb known. The nearest approach to it that we can think of at this moment [April 1875] is the saying that " Hawks winna pick oot hawks' een," and this is applied in a sense very different from that suggested by Mr. Buckland's proverb, if such a proverb exists. At all events the saying that dog will not eat dog is not true ; dog will eat dog, ravenously and greedily enough, when he is hungry and gets the chance. Notwithstanding his domestication and long acquaintance with the usages of civilised life, the dog is, under certain circumstances, as thorough a cannibal and savage as ever was Fiji islander in the days when that worthy Polynesian would give the best finger of his right hand for a prime haunch of full-fed and fat " missionary." Out of many instances that had come under our own observation of cannibalism in dogs, take the following, all the circumstances connected with which, although it is somewhat of an old story now, are for many reasons as fresh in our recollection as if they had occurred but yesterday. When we came to Lochaber, upwards of twenty years ago (*Eheu! fugaces.labuntur anni*), we had a large Labrador dog, a present, when a three-months-old pup, from one of the best and kindliest men we have ever known, the late Rev. Dr. Macnair, of the Abbey Church, Paisley. He grew to be a magnificent animal, the largest and most powerful dog, perhaps, ever seen in the Highlands, and as sagacious and good-tempered as he was big and bold and strong. The late Mr. Campbell of Monzie, an excellent judge of dogs, used to say that he was the finest dog he ever saw, and made it a point every year to call once or twice during the shooting season purposely to have "a friendly talk," as he termed it, with "Albert," for such was our canny Goliath's name. As a water-dog, he was simply perfect, as amphibious almost as a seal. Any stone that you took in your hand and threw into twelve, fifteen, or even twenty feet of water, he instantly dashed after, and took from the bottom, and laid at your feet, seldom making a mistake, though how he was able to select from a stony bottom the very stone that had been handled and thrown in by you was then, and is still, a puzzle to us : not by scent, one would think, for all traces of contact with the hand must surely have been lost in passing through such a depth of salt water. He probably was able to recognise the proper stone partly from its colour and shape, and from its being in a less saturated state, and less in contact with the bottom than were those that always lay there. On one occasion we had left our boat on the beach, neglecting to tie the painter, as we intended returning immediately. Something came in the way, however, that occupied us longer than we expected, and on returning to the shore, our boat was off and away, drifting before a land breeze that had already carried it quite a quarter of a mile from the beach. There was no other boat at hand in which to overtake the runaway, and to go round by the ferry, to meet it on the opposite side of the loch, was a longer walk than one cared about just then, and the boat, besides, was likely to be considerably damaged if it reached the rocks on the other side, as the chances were it would, before we could arrive. While thus in a state of anxiety and indecision, our eye fell upon "Albert," then our constant companion, afloat and ashore. "Albert, old fellow," we remarked, "the boat, you see, is adrift; what's to be done?" With a grand, deep bass bark in response, he dashed into the water, and ere we could well understand it all, he was a hundred yards away, swimming hastily and rapidly in the direction of the truant yawl. We could only sit down on a rock to watch and wait the upshot of the adventure. Soon overtaking the runaway boat, "Albert" swam once or twice round it, and then observing that the painter was dragging in the water over the bow, he seized the rope in his mouth, and strongly and steadily towed the boat towards us, against a stiff breeze and a considerable ripple of a sea, until he reached the beach, and dropped the painter on the shingle at our feet, and with a jolly, self-approving bark, in response to our words of hearty welcome, that made the mountain echoes ring again, he shook a perfect shower-bath of brine from his shaggy coat, and scampered away along the sands to dry himself. He was manifestly proud, as he well ought to be, of an exploit so timeously and sagaciously performed, and so, be sure, were we. "Albert's" readiness to take to the water was, on one occasion at least, attended by rather awkward circumstances. One beautiful summer afternoon, a young Oxford friend and ourselves were in the same boat, with "Albert," as usual, for a companion. It was too calm for sailing, and we were too lazy to row, so we allowed the boat to drift about at "its own sweet will," while we lounged on the thwarts and read the papers, of special interest then on account of the Crimean war. We were half a mile from land, and our friend by-and-by suggested that a swim in the invitingly cool, clear sea would be a good thing before returning home to dinner. As he was an excellent swimmer, with whom, for a small wager, we had the day before done a considerable distance, we readily agreed. We had long known, however, how difficult it is to get into a buoyant, floating boat of such a comparatively small size as ours was, without any purchase to aid but such as is afforded by the unstable water, and it was arranged that he should have his dip first, and when he was tired of it, and we had helped him on board, that we should have a plunge in our turn. "Albert," who had not been consulted in our arrangement, was stretched the while at length, half or wholly asleep, along the bottom of the boat. When he had stripped, our young friend stood up in the bow, with one foot on the foremost thwart and the other on the gunwale, and with a loud shout took a splendid header into the cool, green depths, disappearing like an arrow, with a clean, clear cut, that hardly left a ripple on the surface. "Albert," who clearly thought it an accident, and that the young man's life was in danger, with one brave bound, and before we could prevent him, was instantly over the side, and, diving after the swimmer, met him as he was returning to the surface, and laid hold of him awkwardly, though with the best intention, by the fleshy part of the left arm near the shoulder. When they appeared on the surface, the swimmer, who had manifestly lost all his self-possession, struggled violently to free himself from the dog, and would certainly have been drowned by his own struggles and the very exertions intended by the noble animal to save his life, if we had not quickly rowed the boat along-side, and taking our friend very unceremoniously by his "Hyperion curls," dragged him on board, panting and sputtering as only the half-drowned and wholly frightened can pant and sputter in such circumstances. On examination, his arm was found to be less hurt by the dog's teeth than we expected it to be; a firm and friendly grip with such kindly intentions as actuated the honest would-be rescuer being a very different thing from a bite and worry in good earnest. His back and shoulders, however, were seriously scratched in livid lash-like weals by the dog's nails, while they were hugging each other and struggling in the water. "Albert" was of course very little if at all to blame in the adventure, and his only punishment—if what indeed was to him always a delight could be called a punishment—was that, refusing to take him back into the boat, he was obliged to swim a full half mile to the beach ; which, however, he easily reached before us. Our friend felt sore and uncomfortable for a day or two, but was soon all right again ; and both he and we had got a lesson which we were not likely to forget in a hurry, that a powerful dog, no matter how well meaning and kindly his intentions, is rather a dangerous companion to a swimmer *in puris naturalibus* in deep water.

But what has all this, it may be asked, to do with Mr. Frank Buckland and his proverb that "Dog will not eat dog"? A little patience, as is your wont, courteous reader, and we shall come to the point without much more ado. When "Albert" was about four years old, and as powerful, and perfect, and pleasant a dog as ever growled in anger or barked with glee, it began to be rumoured abroad that he was fast falling into bad habits—whether from following evil example, or instinctively and *proprio motû*, was never determined. He was accused, in fact, of sheep-worrying, and of course we couldn't and wouldn't believe a bit of it. Other dogs might be guilty of such vulgar misconduct ; in the case of our dog the thing was impossible. Wasn't he regularly and well fed ? Didn't he sleep every night at our own bedroom door ? All this, of course, we said, and urged, and argued, and furthermore we urged a fact which seemed to us to be conclusive of our dog's innocence of the great misdemeanour laid to his charge—we had sheep of our own, and there were sheep belonging to others in our immediate neighbourhood, and with none of these, we pointed out, had our dog ever been known to make or meddle in any way further than by an occasional deep *bow-wow !* which, though it sometimes made them scamper, was uttered more in rollicking fun and merry make-believe than in anything like anger or earnest. Precisely so, answered a host of crook-carrying shepherds from farms five, seven, ten miles away : "Your dog is too knowing to kill sheep at your own doors; he goes to a considerable distance on his raids, the better to escape detection, slipping away at night or early in the morning unknown to you, and returning as innocent-seeming as the last sheep he has worried, before you appear in your breakfast parlour!" It was not alleged that he had ever been caught in the act, or actually seen eating forbidden mutton or lamb, *minus* the "mint sauce ;" but more than one shepherd averred that he had more than once been seen wandering at improper hours on hill-sides, where he had no good right or reason to be, on which occasions, too, he exhibited the stealthy, prowling pace, and all the hang-dog looks and other signs of an evil-doer. Half afraid that it was too true, but irritated by their strenuousness of assertion, and defiant to the last, "Catch him, then!" we exclaimed, "shoot him, kill him, if he is harming you; but I am not going to put away or kill my dog—and such a dog, too! worth the best *hirsel* in your charge!—simply to please you." And thus the matter rested for a time, but not for long. Early one Monday morning, about a fortnight afterwards, our good neighbour Mr. Linton, of the farm of Coruanan, seven or eight miles away, drove up to our door in his gig, and asked to see us. After the usual civilities, "Your big dog is killing my sheep, Mr. S.!" was the charge, straightforward and unqualified. We argued, of course, that it couldn't be, &c., as above, but Mr. Linton soon brought the matter to a very practical issue. "What is the value of your dog?" We couldn't say; he was very valuable, a great favourite, and we declined to put a price upon him. "Well," continued Mr. Linton, "say that he is worth £5, or £10, or £20. I charge him with killing two of my sheep this very morning. I have my gun here in the gig : let me shoot him, and if I don't find and show you wool and mutton-flesh taken from his stomach, I will gladly pay over the dog's price ; if I show you what I am certain I can show, his still undigested morning meal of mutton-flesh and wool, we are quits. That's surely fair !" And there was no denying that it was perfectly fair, but we declined, nevertheless, bringing the matter to the arbitrament suggested. We parted good friends, however, for we promised that whether he was to be shot or drowned, or sent out of the country, the dog would never again be allowed a chance of killing another sheep in Lochaber, and our friend Mr. Linton is, we are glad to say, still in life to bear testimony to the fact that we were as good as our word. On due consideration of the case in all its aspects, we decided that it was best, in the interest of peace and good neighbourhood, to have the dog shot forthwith, and shot he was accordingly within an hour of the interview above described. We directed the executioner of the sad sentence to open him, that we might examine the contents of the stomach, and sure enough, intermixed with wool enough to stuff a small cushion, it was found to contain many pounds of recently killed and undigested mutton. It was clear that some at least of the many grave charges against him were true. Anxious to preserve the skin for stuffing, the eviscerated body was placed in the fork of an apple tree in the garden, until we could procure the services of some one expert in flaying to do the job handsomely. Next morning, on going into the garden to have a look at all that remained of poor "Albert," what was our astonishment and horror at finding the *corpus vile—vile*, indeed, at last !—dragged from the tree to the ground, and almost entirely devoured by some half-dozen jackal looking curs, that were having what was manifestly to them a jolly banquet on the remains of the gallant animal whose single bark when in lusty life was sufficient to scatter a whole score of such sorry mongrels, as if each had a firebrand at his tail. Except a few ragged shreds of skin and the larger bones, they had devoured every particle of him; and so much for Mr. Frank Buckland and his proverb that "Dog will not eat dog." Won't he just, when he has the chance! Nor is this by any means the only instance of canine cannibalism that might be adduced from our common-place book in disproof of any proverb or saying whatever to the contrary. Poor "Albert!" we are ashamed to confess how much grieved we were for his death, his ovicidal tendencies notwithstanding. His upper jaw, showing a development of dentition of which a Bengal tiger need not have been ashamed, is the only relic of our gallant dog now remaining to us; and on the *ex pede Herculem* principle, we point to that with a melancholy satisfaction in telling how big and brave, afloat and ashore, was our matchless Labrador.

CHAPTER XLVI.

THE hero of one of our most popular old Fingalian tales is described as very marvellously gifted. In order to secure the hand of a beautiful Scandinavian princess, whose locks are as the beams of the setting sun, about the time the summer sea is flecked and barred with gold, and with whom he has long been in love, he has to undertake the most strange and startling adventures; and not the least important of his qualifications for combating the frequent difficulties of his position is a preternatural acuteness of eye and ear, of sight and hearing. His keenness of sight, for instance, is indicated by his being able to count the beats of the swallow's wings in all the gyrations of its flight over the summer grove; and as for his acuteness of ear, enough is said when the veracious chronicler does not hesitate to assert that his hero could hear the grass grow? We, in our unheroic and degenerate day, cannot boast of anything like this. We are content to know that the swallow skims the pool with a swiftness due to a motion of wing too rapid to be detected in its separate beats by the acutest eye, and that the grass does grow, and at times with marvellous rapidity, albeit the stir and tumult of its upward rush is inaudible to human ears. But if we cannot *hear* the grass grow, we can safely aver that in such exceptionally splendid seasons as this [July 1875], and without fear of being charged with any very culpable exaggeration, we can *see* it grow, not only from day to day, but almost literally from hour to hour—so rapid, so marked, and visibly perceptible is the progress towards a large and lusty maturity of grass and grain and every green herb of the field. Anything, indeed, to equal the sturdy vigour and upward rush of vegetation during the month of June last past we never did see before, and had it not come immediately under our own observation, we could hardly have believed it possible anywhere outside the tropics. The harvest must necessarily be a late one, though not quite so late as it was at one time feared must be the case. If we say that the season of ingathering will be later than usual by ten days, or a fortnight at the most, we are probably not far from the mark. But, late or early, it is sure to be an exceedingly abundant harvest, there being at present all over the West Highlands every promise of very heavy returns, the heaviest, perhaps, that, under any circumstances whatever, the land could safely bear, with the hope of an eventually fully ripe and lusty maturity.

Readers of our *Nether Lochaber* papers will in nowise be surprised to hear that we have all our lifetime made it a point to cultivate the confidence and friendly goodwill of keepers, foresters, and their followers, wherever we chanced to meet with them ; nor would it be proper to suppress our grateful acknowledgment of the fact that to them we have been largely indebted in all our zoological studies for a long quarter of a century. We look upon foresters and game-keepers as at the head of their profession, what the French call " princes of the game," and we have ever found them exceedingly courteous and kind, highly intelligent almost without exception, and not merely willing but well pleased to be examined, and cross-examined when occasion calls, on anything and everything apper-taining to, or at all connected with, their office. With their humbler brethren of the craft, too, we have long been thoroughly *en rapport ;* these humbler brethren being the fox-hunters, mole-catchers, and vermin-killers generally, by whatever name or designa-

tion known from the Moray Firth to the Clyde. Most readers
of poetry will remember how Pope, in one of his finest poems
(*Prologue* to the *Satires*), apostrophises his friend Dr. Arbuthnot as

> " Friend to my life ! which did not you prolong,
> The world had wanted many an idle song."

And if one dared to parody any couplet from a poem so beautiful,
we should be disposed to address the first fox-hunter or mole-
catcher of our numerous acquaintances among them who are
deacons of their craft, we chanced to meet, in some such words as
these—

> " Friend to my mill ! which did not you supply
> With frequent *grist*, I'd wither, wane, and die."

A few days ago the Ardgour fox-hunter, Donald Macdonald by
name, a Moidart man, and an excellent specimen of his class,
called upon us with his quarterly budget of news from glen and
upland, from hill and scaur, and den and corrie ; and a wonderful
season in his particular line he vows it has been.   Since the middle
of April last he has killed and bagged no fewer than *fifty-one* foxes
all told, besides a number, both young and old, that were worried to
the death by his terriers in the deepest recesses of their *saobhies*
or dens, whence, when the turmoil of battle had ceased, and his
dogs had emerged bearing very visible marks of the deadly conflict
within, it was impossible to dig them out.   All these foxes were
got on the borders of three conterminous farms—Aryhuelan (Dr.
Simpson's), Conaglen and Inverscaddle (the Earl of Morton's), and
Glennahuirich (Mr. Milligan's).   Donald, who has been a fox-
hunter for upwards of thirty years, never before knew foxes so
numerous, and this not in one or more favourite haunts within
a given district, but generally over the country.   He couldn't
himself in any way satisfactorily account for the fox fecundity of
1874-75, and we could only regret that we were unable to enlighten
him in the least, for he avowedly came for enlightenment on a

subject that was very naturally exceedingly interesting to him. We were obliged to confess that the matter was as much a puzzle to us as to himself, but promised to think it over. Account for it as we may, it is in truth a fact that has attracted attention everywhere, that not for many years, if indeed ever before, have foxes been so numerous all over the Highlands. In the three adjoining districts of Badenoch, Lochaber, and Ardgour, the last including a part of Sunart, we are assured that no less a number than *two hundred and forty-three* foxes have been killed or captured since mid-April, besides, as already stated, a considerable number worried in the recesses of their big rock dens which could not be actually "bagged" or charged for after the fashion of the craft by brush or pad, though there was no doubt at all of their having succumbed after, in each case, a more or less desperate battle, to the assaults of their terrier assailants. And here, good reader, you must permit us, *en parenthese*, a slight disgression, not altogether, we hope, uninteresting. We wonder if in the great family of dogs anywhere throughout the world there is anything to equal in hardihood, pluck, and all endurance the Highland fox-hunter's canine following? They are invariably a rough and ragged lot enough, and seemingly at sixes and sevens as to anything like assortment; no two of them exactly alike in colour, size, or breed; and they are usually low in stature, though of considerable bone and well developed muscle what there is of it; but be what they may in these respects, when you fall in with one of our fox-hunter's packs, six, seven, eight, or a dozen in number, as the case may be, be sure you have before you the gamest, *varmintest* little beggars to tackle otter, fox, or badger that the whole world can show. Our visitor of the other day had only one little fellow of his pack along with him. "What's his name, Donald?" we asked, pointing to his wiry follower, that we could easily see was, from the ink-black tip of his nose to the extremity of his tail, a "varmint" of the first order. "What do you call him?" "Speach," he replied, and *speach*, our non-Gaelic readers must be told, means a wasp or hornet, and, even like a wasp, we knew that that little fellow with his dander up in the labyrinthine recesses of a fox's den or a badger's *garaidh*, would fight against any odds until he was torn into ribbons, and on each and every occasion would prove himself

> " Impiger, iracundus, inexorabilis, acer,"

which old Robertson of Struan admirably rendered into our native Doric, without the loss of a particle of meaning or force—

> " A fiery ettercap, a fractious chiel,
> As het as ginger, and as stieve as steel !

"And is 'Speach' good, then, Donald?" we inquired. "Yes, sir," was the reply, "a very good little dog. He is but small, you see, and light; the smallest, indeed, at present in my pack, but he will take hold of fox or badger or otter at the readiest spot that offers, and, having once got hold, will never let go again while his antagonist is in life; *at every dig only burying his muzzle deeper into his opponent.*" We quite agreed with him that a dog that did *that* must be good indeed; and we are perfectly satisfied that he did not in the least exaggerate the indomitable pluck and never-say-die tenacity of his tiny favourite. Two very good things remain· to be said in praise of our Highland fox-hunters' dogs. They are never known to bite, and very rarely even to bark at human beings; and no fox-hunter's dog was ever known to be affected with hydrophobia or canine madness. The exemption from canine madness may, perhaps, be largely due to their open air and natural mode of life, but it is difficult to understand why they should be so entirely free from any propensity to bite or otherwise annoy a human being, a vice common enough to dogs of unexceptionable character and breeding otherwise, and from which even the highly intelligent and much-lauded *collie* is by no means so free as his many admirers seem to suppose. Even a collie is always prepared to bark, and oftentimes to bite on very little provocation, or no provocation at all. The fox-hunter's terrier, whether he is pure or a nondescript cross, very rarely indeed barks at a stranger, and never under any circumstances offers to bite. We question if there is a human being to-day in life who can honestly assert that he has ever been bitten by a fox-hunter's dog. With Macdonald we had a long and interesting crack, in the course of which we touched on some matters of sufficient importance to be introduced to the reader on a future occasion.

We had also a visit some little time ago from Sandy Macarthur, a well-known mole-catcher in Lochaber and the neighbouring districts; a very intelligent and civil man, whose only fault is that when you have collared him there is no spontaneity in his crack. Even when you have got firm hold enough of him, you have to extract his frequently very valuable information from him by a process akin to that which an ingenious and learned counsel employs in the case of a recalcitrant and unwilling witness at an important jury trial. Sandy, however, is a good fellow all the same, slow but sure ; and his quiet unobtrusiveness and reticence is perhaps to be attributed to the exigencies of his profession; a " rattling, roaring Willie " of a mole-catcher, with, to use a Gaelic phrase, his tongue constantly on his shoulder, would probably prove but an unsuccessful hunter of the velvet-coated quick-eared, and timid subterranean family of the Mac *Talpa*. Sandy, on the contrary, goes to work in dead silence and a-tiptoe, and bags his mole as quietly as an angler baskets his trout from out the glassy pool, over which, if but his shadow moved, he would angle long in vain. Sandy assures us that moles are to be found this season where they were never seen before, and where he was at first a good deal puzzled to account for their appearance. On a full consideration of the case Macarthur's theory is briefly to this effect: Moles are mainly underground dwellers, and even their travelling and migrating from place to place are done subterraneously. If, however, they find themselves, as in the Highlands they must frequently do, in a district or part of district separated from other parts in which they have never been by rocky spurs and ridges, they will not venture over these latter unless they carry sufficient earth to hide their tunnelling, which, it is needless to say, they frequently do not. The mole in such a case remains insulated, a prisoner, so to speak, within his present domain. Last winter and spring, however, according to Sandy's theory, the snow lay so deep and lay so long, that the moles took advantage of the fact, and making their tunnels under the snow, where it lay on spur and ridge, just as if it had been so much superincumbent soil, they easily got into fresh fields and pastures new. In this way alone can Sandy account for the appearance of moles this summer in places into which hitherto they had no means of ready access; and he may be right, though it is a point in the natural history of the *Talpa* well deserving further investigation. Sandy further avers that moles sometimes swim across rivers, fresh-water lakes, and even arms of the sea in their migrations; and this is just possible, though we took the liberty of expressing ourselves slightly incredulous. Sandy, however, ought to know; he has spent the best part of a life already approaching its grand climacteric in the careful and close and constant study of, as one may say, a single animal—to wit, the mole—and it is always hazardous gravely to doubt or contradict the deliberately expressed opinion of such a man on a matter strictly within his proper province. All the same we still venture to question the assertion that the mole ever voluntarily enters water deep enough to swim in, or ever dims the velvety sheen of its glossy pile even by such a luxury as a voluntary bath in the shallows, till we have some stronger proof for it than has yet been adduced.

CHAPTER XLVII.

Autumnal Night—Meteors—The Spanish Mackerel—Professor Blackie's Translations from the Gaelic—The "Translations" of the Gaelic Society of Inverness.

> " On the Rialto, every night at twelve,
> I take my evening's walk of meditation."

So says the love-sick knight in *Venice Preserved.* We have never, much as we should like it, had an opportunity of enjoying a Rialto midnight meditation ramble. There is poetry and romance in the very thought of it ; but we know something more poetical and in every way better still, namely, a midnight meditative stroll along our own beautiful silvery sanded beach, what time the sea is so calm that its breathings are low and soft as the respirations of a child whose sleep is undisturbed save by angel-whispered dreams ; the cloudless sky above, with its waning moon and thousands of sparkling stars, each star a living intelligence ; its sparkling speech, and no sound to disturb the solemn silence, except now and again the wakeful sea-bird's eerie scream, and the voice of many waters, as the mountain torrents leap adown their channels to the sea, a voice so mellowed by the distance that it becomes solemn and musical as the fast-falling concluding notes of a grand organ hymn—the Pentecostal " *Veni, Creator Spiritus,* for example. During the fine weather of this exceptionally fine season [August 1875] we have rarely gone to bed before midnight, more frequently, indeed, long after, and our last thing at night has been a sea-shore stroll, a half or quarter hour so thoroughly enjoyable that we have come to miss it sadly, if by adverse

weather, absence from home, or any other cause, we are obliged to forego it. In addition to all the other attractions of a midnight sea-side stroll in such weather as the tropics themselves might be proud of, the reader must remember that August is one of our meteor months—the second week particularly being remarkable for the number and brilliancy of the *Perseides*, so called from their seeming mainly to radiate from the direction of the constellation *Perseus*. Never was there a finer season to observe them than this; and although they have, perhaps, been less numerous than usual, the brilliancy of many of them was so remarkable, and their paths throughout so easily followed, that their very infrequency only added to the eagerness and interest with which one watched and waited for them. The finest display of the season was from midnight on to nearly two A.M. on the night of the 11th and 12th, in which time we counted thirty-three *noticeable* meteors—of which seven were what might be called first-class meteors of a nucleus brilliancy equal to or exceeding that of first magnitude stars, with broad, bright, well-defined trains, that wholly or in part, in three or four instances, remained in sight, mapping out the meteor's trajectory for several seconds after the disappearance or extinction of the parent orb or meteor proper itself. Mr. W. B. Symington, who was among the Hebrides at the time on a yachting cruise, writes on the subject as follows :—
"Notwithstanding your injunction to be on the *qui vive* as to the August meteors, I am sorry to say that I forgot all about it on the nights of the 9th and 10th, although the weather was beautifully clear. On the 11th, 12th, and 13th, however, the sailing-master and myself were sharply on the look-out, and our watchfulness was rewarded by the sight of some really very splendid examples. There were on each night scores and scores of the more common, lesser, and fainter meteors, but our attention was of course principally directed to the more brilliant ones.

Of these latter we had, during about an hour and a quarter's observation, four very fine ones, with long bright tails, on the 11th; nine on the 12th; and one magnificent fellow, that lighted up the deck, sails, and rigging of the yacht with a strange greenish glare, on the 13th. This last was at 11·5 P.M. One of the men said that before daybreak on the 12th there were some very large and bright meteors. As far as my observations went, the course of these meteors seemed to be mainly to the west and south-west, although two at least of the larger ones rushed in a directly opposite path, namely, to east and north-east. As I am likely to be at sea in November, though in a very different kind of craft, I will endeavour to give you a more careful and satisfactory account of the meteor display of that month. I may tell you that one of the men caught a *scad* of large size, the biggest, I believe, I ever saw. It weighed nearly four pounds. I thought it not bad eating, though the rest of them in the cabin said it was coarse and tasteless. It was caught by a long line and herring baited hook, that was allowed to drag after the ship in a breeze that gave us at the time a speed of at least eight knots an hour."

The fish referred to by our correspondent is also called the Spanish mackerel, it being very common on some parts of the Spanish coast. It belongs to the order *Scomberidæ*, and is a cousin of our own better known mackerel proper, though a considerably larger fish, and not nearly so good for the table as its beautiful congener. The Spanish differs from the mackerel proper in one very remarkable particular; it has an *air bladder* which the true mackerel of our shores has not, and yet the latter is one of the readiest and swiftest swimmers, and at all depths, of any fish in the sea. The fact is that the real use of the air bladder in the economy of fish still continues an unresolved and seemingly an unresolvable puzzle.

Lovers of living, healthy poetry—healthy as the mountain

breeze, and free and sparkling as the mountain stream, and more especially our Celtic friends who have been taught to honour and reverence the " kilted " muse—will be glad to know that Professor Blackie has in preparation the materials of what cannot fail to prove a very interesting volume, consisting of translations of some of the most admired compositions of our modern Gaelic bards. Macintyre's *Ben. Dorain*, Alasdair Macdonald's *Berliun*, with many of such lesser popular lyrics, as *Am Breacan Wallach, Failte na Mor-Thir, A Bhanarach Dhoun a Cruidh*, &c., will thus appear for the first time in a becoming Saxon garb ; not—to use the milliner's phrase—too tight a fit, observe, but natural and easy, though " made to measure," and we venture to predict that our English readers, who as yet know them not at all, and our Gaelic friends, who know them well and have long known them, will alike be pleased with the results of the learned Professor's gallant raid into bard-land. The Professor has been visiting us here lately, and we can honestly say that such specimens of his work as he was good enough to read to us—and there are few better readers than Professor Blackie—seemed to us admirably done. His version of *Ben. Dorain* particularly, which we had an opportunity of hearing twice, and of which we can thus speak most positively, is thoroughly well done ; so well, so faithfully, and with such spirit and *verve* as must delight not only the ordinary reader, but the very " ghost " of the original author—Macintyre himself—if, like the Ossianic departed heroes, he is permitted to know and appreciate sublunary affairs from out the bosom of " his cloud." The Professor translates these Gaelic poems into English verse just as, in our opinion, they should be translated ; not too literally, but with all necessary freedom and elbow roóm, and yet so literally that any one knowing the English version may rest assured that he knows also the original quite as intimately and correctly as it is possible in the circumstances for any mere outsider to know it. Johnson, in his *Life of Dryden*, referring to the latter's version of the *Æneid*, &c., has a paragraph which is worth quoting in this connection :—" When languages are formed upon different principles, it is impossible that the same modes of expression should always be elegant in both. While they run on together, the closest translation may be considered the best ; but when they divaricate, each must take its natural course. Where correspondence cannot be obtained, it is necessary to be content with something equivalent. ' Translation, therefore,' says Dryden, ' is not so loose as paraphrase, nor so close as metaphrase.' " With all this we entirely concur, more especially when such widely different languages as the English and Gaelic have to be dealt with. We do not know that Professor Blackie ever read the paragraph quoted, or, even if he did read it, that he now remembers it ; but to his translations from the Gaelic, to so much of them, at all events, as were submitted to our notice, Dryden's dictum is entirely applicable—they are not so loose as paraphrase, nor so close as metaphrase. They strike a golden mean very difficult of attainment in such efforts ; and on the appearance of the volume itself, we shall be disappointed if nine-tenths at least of the many readers it is sure to command do not entirely agree with us. But *nous verrons*, if we live we shall see.

The *Transactions* of the Gaelic Society of Inverness for 1873-4 and 1874-5, have reached us. The Secretary's paper on "Coinneach Odhar," the Brahan seer, is most interesting, containing as it does the best account that we have met with of that uncanny Ross-shire worthy. That he was an impostor, and a vulgar impostor too, there can be no doubt ; but the story of a man—clever, shrewd rascal as he was—in whom the people so thoroughly believed, is worth the telling, and Mr. Mackenzie tells it very well. He should, we think, give us, if possible, a second paper, containing the many other wonderful vaticinations attributed to his hero, who seems to have

latterly been too clever by half; for he who could foresee the misfortunes of others—the death even of a cow—couldn't evidently
foresee the well-merited fate that awaited himself; for he was
hanged, and we have no doubt at all that he richly deserved that
species of exaltation. What Thomas the Rhymer—him of Ercildoune—was in the south of Scotland at a much earlier period, this
Coinneach Odhar, comparing small things with great, seems to
have been in the North-West Highlands during the latter half of
the seventeenth century. "True Thomas," however, was a gentleman and a scholar; whereas *Coinneach* was, of course, utterly
illiterate, conducting his scheme of imposture solely by the aid of
natural talents, which must have been considerable, and a large
and ever-ready stock of impudence and cunning, nicely calculated
to impose upon the vulgar. He made his grand mistake when he
flew at such high game as Lady Seaforth and her domestic affairs.
She was too clever, too intelligent and well-educated to be imposed
upon. She ordered him to be hanged, a doom to which many were
led at that period who probably less richly deserved it than such a
prying, meddling, mischief-maker as was Kenneth the Seer.

CHAPTER XLVIII.

Crops—Potato Slug—Fern Slug—Brackens: How thoroughly to extirpate them—The Merlin—Falcon and Tringa.

WE have had a full fortnight of magnificent summer weather [August 1875], a bright sun over-head from morning till night, with brisk breezes, *a leanachd na gréine*, following the sun ; that is, beginning in the morning at east, and gradually wearing round *pari passû* with the solar march, till at sunset it is north-west, and so on round and round the compass day after day, a phenomenon usually attendant upon the very finest weather in our northern latitudes. Under these circumstances it will not surprise those who care for such matters to hear that our hay crop, about which we were in such anxiety, has been secured in splendid condition, in such condition, indeed, as we can rarely boast of in the West Highlands. Our meadow hay crop, too, is this year unusually heavy, and already, in obedience to the adage which teaches that it is well and wise to make one's hay while the sun shines, we are all busy getting it cut down and secured, although the old, orthodox season is not yet for a fortnight to come—about old Lammastide. Oats with us here are generally a light crop, but it will as such be easier to secure in good condition than a heavier crop would be, and, upon the whole, may thus turn out quite as profitable. Potatoes are not so heavy haulmed as usual, but in other respects they promise well, and there is no appearance of our old enemy the "blight." We hear, however, a good deal of complaint in some districts on account of the prevalence this year of yellow shaw, or *bar-buidhe* as our Highlanders term it, the work of a small grey slug that attacks the main-stem shaw just at its point of junction with the soil, and eating and tunnelling it through and through until the leaves first assume a yellow and withered appearance, and the whole shaw finally falls down paralysed, and practically useless and inoperative as to its proper functions, though not actually rotten or dead, as in the case of the "blight." Many such shaws in a field give it an unsightly appearance, but beyond this there is no great harm done after all, for as the slug seldom begins its work until the plant is large and well forward, the tubers underground, though they may be of smaller size than their neighbours that have escaped the slug's attentions, are yet sound and wholesome food enough either for man or beast. We have observed that this particular slug, or a closely allied species, is also much given to feeding on the stem of the common fern or bracken, dealing with it just as it does with the potato shaw, though, to be sure, it finds the fern a rather harder nut to crack; for the brave bracken, with its firmer contexture of stem, refuses to bend its head to the ground, no matter the number or direction of the slug's insidious tunnellings and perforations. If you glance at a fern clump as you ride along the road or climb the mountain steep, the yellow, withered fronds of an occasional plant, here and there painfully conspicuous amid the rich, dark, emerald green of its healthy companions, tell you where the grey slug—and a nasty, slimy little wretch it is—is busy at its evil work, drinking up, like consumption among the human race, the very heart's blood, so to speak, of the fairest and finest plants it can find. We have found in our own experience that the best protection of the potato from its ravages is to give the ground a sprinkling of lime just as the plants are appearing above ground, about the end of April or beginning of May. For the early varieties usually planted in our gardens, a sprinkling of soot is less unsightly and equally efficacious with lime.

And speaking of the bracken, let us observe that, while it is a
magnificent and beautiful plant, it is, like everything else of beauty,
most beautiful in its proper place. Meet it on mountain slope, in
copsewood covert, or greenwood glade, and you cannot admire it
sufficiently. In the end of autumn, particularly when its graceful
fronds have assumed a certain indescribable tinge of mingled brown
and ruby and gold, a bracken covert is beyond measure lovely. At
such a stage, and in the warm and mellow light of the setting
September sun, it is to ourselves all that an ocean of broom in
flower was to the great Linnæus. If, however, you live in the
near neighbourhood of brackens, you will find that it is apt to
creep down from its proper wild and upland habitat, and to
encroach unduly upon your old grass lands, wherever it can get an
undisturbed footing. If you consult books on the subject, they
will tell you that if you cut them down for a season or two running
before they ripen, they will die away and disappear. With our
large, soft-stemmed herbaceous plants, this method of eradication is
sometimes effectual enough ; with the bracken, as we know to our
cost, it avails nothing. The roots are so curiously ramified and
intertwined that they will live on and put forth a new growth year
after year, no matter how constantly and closely you cut and crop
them. We gave up trying a plan so futile, and only hit upon the
right way of dealing with them by the merest accident. Walking
along the edge of one of our old grass parks about mid-June some
few years ago, we wished to get hold of a switch or something
similar, wherewith to drive a fractious pony on before us to the
park gate. There was no switch just then at hand, and, without
thinking of it, we bent down, and with both hands pulled steadily
and straight upwards at one of the largest of a luxuriant bracken
patch that skirted the path beside us. To our surprise the plant
came up easily and from the very root, or we should rather say
with the very root attached, long, dark-brown, and something cigar-

like in shape and size. That particular plant, a slight examination satisfied us, was fairly or literally and for ever *eradicated, extirpated.* When you get hold of plant and root, you get all; no other plant can grow in its stead; no plant, at all events, can honestly call *it* progenitor. The thing now was clear; we knew what we had to do, and how simple it was! One afternoon soon afterwards we called all our people into that field along with us. In all such cases best lead yourself, if you would have the thing done right. We pulled a bracken or two straight up and steadily in their presence, and showed them how it was extracted, even as a practised dentist, "deacon of his craft," deals with an offending tooth—root and all complete. They then set to work along with us, and in an hour or so we had the whole field cleared of ferns—quite a large cart-load of them—each plant with its black root attached, all of which were afterwards found useful as bedding for the pony, and the largest and least broken for thatch. In that field no brackens have since shown themselves. So, if you are troubled with ferns, the proper way is not to cut them down, for they will grow again, but to deal with them as we did, and they will trouble you no more. There is some trouble about it, no doubt, though far less than you would suppose, and then, you see, we really know nothing at this moment worth the having to be had *without* trouble; so take the trouble and the good together, and be wise.

In your sea-shore wanderings, good reader, you must many a time and oft have witnessed the graceful flight of the tern or sea-swallow, the handsomest bird, perhaps, that ever saw its own image reflected in the glassy surface of a waveless sea; and you must have noticed its sudden dart and dip, now and again, after its prey into the bosom of the green, unbroken waves. This, of course, you have seen and admired a thousand times. But have you ever seen the merlin or merlin falcon (*Falco æsalon*), perform the same feat? No! Well, we did a few evenings ago; albeit the momentary immersion in the briny blue was probably, nay certainly, what the merlin would have avoided if it could. It happened in this wise : We were engaged on the beach painting our boat—there are few things but we can put our hand to with more or less success, always barring *shooting*, of our deficiency in which we recently made full and honest confession—when we suddenly heard that curious and indescribable half-scream, half-cheep, so well-known to the ornithologist, and which tells him so plainly that the utterer is a bird—usually a small bird—in dire distress, in constant fear and danger of its life. Looking round, we saw a merlin in hot chase of a sandpiper (*Tringa hypoleucus*), pursuer and pursued circling and wheeling in their arrow-like flight over the bent some hundred yards from the margin of the sea. Were it not for the manifest distress of the poor sandpiper, evidenced by its frequent scream, as if invoking all the kindly powers of heaven and earth to its aid, we should have considered it a most beautiful and interesting sight. The merlin was evidently hungry and in earnest, and we made no doubt at all, for there was no possible way that we could aid it, that the sandpiper was distined to be the fiery little falcon's evening meal. But *Diis aliter visum*—the gods had otherwise ordered it. All of a sudden it seemed to occur to the *Tringa* that if there was the slightest chance of escape for it, it must be in closer relationship with its favourite and familiar element, the sea ; and to the sea accordingly in one rapid dart the poor bird betook itself. The merlin, as if aware that there was now at least a possibility that its prey might after all escape its clutches, made a magnificent dash after, and just as the sandpiper was over the sea, reached it, and pounced to strike, but missed ; by the smallest fraction of a single second, a sharp zig-zag in the *Tringa's* flight kept it clear of the stroke, and the merlin, by the force and impetus of its flight, plunged head over ears into the sea, whence, with draggled plumage and brine-blinded eyes, it arose with difficulty, and betook itself to a rock ledge at hand to preen and dry itself, with no other consolation in its disappointment, probably, than a *sotto voce* merlin-wise muttering of the adage, "Better luck next time." The sandpiper, it is needless to say, was soon a mile away, winging its terrified flight to the opposite Appin shore. We were glad that the sandpiper had escaped, that the merlin was disappointed. It is always pleasant to see an evil-doer baulked in the accomplishment of his evil intentions. And yet we don't know either. We have called the merlin an evil-doer: are we entitled so to call him? Was he not as much entitled, could he have secured it, to have that *Tringa* for *his* evening meal, as we the delicious red rock cod that in an hour or two afterwards we enjoyed so heartily to our own supper? Let the reader think it over, and answer the question to himself at his leisure.

CHAPTER XLIX.

Audi alteram partem is a sensible maxim, so reasonable in itself, and mild and deprecatory of tone, that it rarely fails to commend itself to our sense of right and candour; for if we would arrive at a right conclusion on any matter in dispute, we must learn to listen without prejudice to both sides of a question. We can only hold our own convictions wisely and well, by knowing all that can be said in antagonism and *per contra*. The following letter from a correspondent in London, who writes under the pseudonym of "Observer," tells rather in favour of those who entertain grave suspicions as to the morality and harmlessness of our prickly friend the hedgehog, and, of course, against Mr. Frank Buckland and ourselves. We are honest enough, however, to give "Observer's" communication in full, meanwhile merely remarking that, obliged as we are to our correspondent for his attention, and really interesting note, we are by no means convinced that the hedgehog is either oviphagous or a bird-killer and bird-eater. At this date [February 1876], and with all our knowledge of the animal, we fear that nothing less than the catching of him in the very act would convince us, any number of uncompromising and hard-hearted gamekeepers, with "Observer" to back them, to the contrary notwithstanding.

᛫ While perusing your interesting article on the hedgehog, some slight personal experiences of this animal recurred to my mind, and I therefore thought it might be as well to communicate them to you, to show that, according to my limited experience, the hedgehog is not quite such a harmless and innocent creature as you endeavour to make him, and further, that your practical experiments with the hungry animals and the eggs are not sufficiently satisfactory to establish and set at rest once and for ever the hedgehog's innocency. To be brief : two or three summers ago, while living in the Highlands of Scotland, and within one hundred and fifty miles of the Highland capital, about ten o'clock on a beautiful Sunday evening in the month of June, and shortly after a most genial shower of rain had fallen to refreshen the young crops, my attention was attracted by the most alarming and violent cackling of a hen that had just begun to incubate on two or three addled eggs, or 'nest eggs' as they are called. Wondering what would be the cause of this noisy demonstration on the part of the hen, and thinking that probably a thief might be at hand, I at once repaired to where the hen was. I could see no one about, but there the hen was, as noisy as ever, looking towards her nest, advancing apparently to charge some unseen enemy, and then suddenly making a retrograde movement in the most frantic manner, without attacking her enemy. On stooping down and peeping into the corner where the nest was (for by this time it was almost dark), I observed a round dark object in comfortable possession of the nest ; this was a hedgehog. If I remember well, one of the eggs was broken, and there was very little of the contents left. This, I am almost sure, was the case, though I would hardly go so far as to swear to it at this distance of time. Probably in these circumstances you will say, 'Then, if you can't actually swear to it, your information deserves no attention.' However, bear with me a little longer. On another occasion, on a similar fine evening, about the same hour, and about four weeks after the above, I heard another hen, which, with a brood of some eight or ten fine young chickens, had taken up its night quarters quite near the scene of the first row, making a like noise. Thinking a cat might be about, and therefore must be the enemy now, I went up to see what was doing. There the hen was, standing a short distance from the nest, with only two chickens by her side; the others could not be seen. On going nearer the nest, there was another hedgehog in quiet possession. Below him in the nest were one or two dead chickens; their little heads were crushed quite flat and wet, as if some animal had been trying to chew the heads. Outside the nest were two more dead chickens, their heads being in the same flat and wet condition. The chickens were about a week old, and, so far as I can recollect, there was no other disfigurement. In the morning two more live chickens turned up, and the poor hen had to be content with a reduced brood of four or five instead of eight or ten. The hedgehog had been sentenced to a violent death, but, fortunately for himself, made his escape while search was being made for any of the surviving chickens. During the next summer a duck had laid a number of eggs—more than a dozen—in a quiet secluded spot at the root of a birch tree, and which were not discovered by human eye until they were rather far on in a state of incubation to be fit for use; so the duck was allowed to keep her eggs in order to hatch them. One night, about 11 or 11.30 P.M., some of the inmates of the house were disturbed by the duck coming to one of the doors, making a great noise, and would not leave. So, to save further annoyance, the servant rose and locked up poor duck with the other ducks. In the morning the prisoner was released, and allowed to go to resume possession of the nest, which, on examination, was found undisturbed, except that two or three of the eggs were amissing; but this was thought nothing of, and allowed to pass unnoticed. However, a few nights after this occurrence, the duck repeated her visit to the house, was in a greatly disturbed state, and would on no account whatever be pacified; so, as the night was dark, a light was procured, and the writer, along with a friend, went to the nest, and found a hedgehog sitting on the eggs. Some of them were broken, and the nest in a great mess. Outside there was an empty shell, and a large round hole in it. On this occasion the hedgehog had to pay the extreme penalty. Mentioning these things to the people about, the writer was informed that it was understood generally that hedgehogs destroyed eggs, but it had never been known to them that they attacked young chickens. However, they had never given the matter any attention. Perhaps these facts I have related may be of some use to you in making further inquiries about the hedgehog. At any rate, you may rely on the truth of my statements, as they are no hearsay stories, but facts that took place before my own eyes. *Query*—Granted that the hedgehog does not eat eggs, then what was he doing in possession of these three different nests? How were the eggs broken? What animal killed the chickens, if it was not the hedgehog? Perhaps a weasel would have done it, but in that case, would the weasel not have inflicted some serious wound about the throat, and which would have left some bloody marks?"

Of some half-dozen bird-catchers, or bird-fanciers, as they prefer calling themselves, that visit the West Highlands professionally from time to time, our favourite is Mackenzie, a north countryman, we believe, as one indeed might readily guess from his surname, and well enough known, we daresay, in and about Inverness, where during our last visit we noticed with pleasure—for it is a good sign of a people—that birds in cages were exceedingly common. "Old Cowie," another of the fraternity, is a respectable man, with more knowledge, perhaps, of things in general than any of his brethren that have chanced to come our way; but for a knowledge of our native wild-birds, their favourite haunts, food, song, and individual habits—idiosyncrasies—for a knowledge, we say, precise and accurate to the most astonishing degree on all those matters, you may trust Mackenzie, for he is far and away at the head of his class, positively unrivalled by any one else that we ever met with. Of the ornithology of books, of ornithology as a science, with its systems, classifications, genera, and species, he knows nothing, of course, but he knows every bird you can refer to under some favourite provincial cognomen, and he knows it so thoroughly that no one could possibly know it better. It is true that he knows little or nothing *but* birds, but he knows *them* so well (the birds of Scotland), so intimately, from constant intercourse with them in their native haunts and homes, that a " crack " with him about them, when once you get him fairly started, is no ordinary treat to any one so interested in all that concerns our wild-birds as we are, and have been for well-nigh a quarter of a century. Remembering that bird-catching is a sort of profession or trade, by which a livelihood, however precarious, is encompassed, an affair of demand and supply, with the usual prosaic result of pounds, shillings, and pence—or rather of shillings and pence without the pounds, these last seldom tickling the palms or troubling the purses of the order—one would expect to find the bird-catcher a dull, mechanical rogue, a mere bird-trapper and bird-seller in the dearest market, with no more of poetry or sentiment about him than about a white-aproned poulterer. This, however, is far from being the case, at least not always nor even frequently, for Mackenzie, " Old Cowie," and others that we could name, really and truly love birds for their own sakes, without a thought frequently of their market value, and you can gather as you converse with them from their frequent references to the delights as well as the *désagréments* of their profession, that they are by no means either unconscious of or indifferent to the poetry of birds and bird life in their native haunts, whether on moor or mountain side, by solitary tarn or stream, in copse and wildwood, amid the wildernesses of inland mountains or by the margin of the sea. We never knew any one

so correctly and minutely conversant with the language of birds as
Mackenzie is. By the language of birds, we do not mean their
song, for song is no more the ordinary speech of birds, though
most people think it is, than it is the ordinary speech of men.
Mackenzie, it is true, can imitate the songs of our different species
of warblers with great taste and exactness, but when we say that
he is conversant with the language of birds, we mean not their song,
but their little notes, abrupt chirpings, and faint whisperings, indica-
tive to the initiated of the particular thought or *motif* at the moment
predominant in the feathered breast, whether love or terror, or
mere apprehension of danger, or envy, or rivalry, or combativeness,
or notes of warning, or call of invitation to its kind—all these, and
for every separate species, Mackenzie imitates with such consum-
mate skill, exactness, and dexterity, that he not only deceives an
ordinary listener when off his guard—he has more than once
deceived *us*, though familiar with birds and bird-notes all our life
—but he deceives the very birds themselves, as we have often
witnessed with no little admiration and delight. That much of
this imitatory work is done ventriloquistically renders it all the
more effective, as well as more difficult of attainment by others of
the fraternity ambitious of catching and cultivating on their own
behalf so desirable a gift. This knowledge of bird language is,
of course, of great value to him as a bird-catcher, and accounts for
his success at seasons seemingly the most inopportune, and in
localities the most unlikely, that an ordinary bird-catcher would
probably search in vain for a single specimen of goldfinch or aber-
devine, linnet or redpole, or anything else in the shape of a valuable
song-bird. In passing and repassing our place, this wonderful
bird-man, as our servant girl styles him, always calls with such bird
news and rare specimens as he thinks most likely to interest us.
The other day he came in a state of great excitement to inform us
that just as he had got several siskins on his limed twigs, a bird—

not a hawk of any kind, he was certain—dashed out of a copse at hand, pounced upon one of the siskins, and bore it off and away before his very eyes, ere he could do anything—so sudden and unexpected was the attack—to prevent it! Momentary as was his glimpse of it, however, Mackenzie's quick and practised eye enabled him to take in the marauder's predominant colouring, its shape and size, and mode of flight; and on describing these to us, we at once exclaimed, a *butcher-bird*—a *shrike!* The description could apply to no other British bird-killer that we could think of; and that we were right we have no more doubt than if we had the culprit already in our cabinet. Mackenzie was in a rage. "You are right, sir; it must have been a butcher-bird, for now I recollect having once seen a specimen in Ayrshire. I'm bound, however, to lay salt on yon chap's tail before I am done with him; and you, sir, shall have him, dead or living. I swear it by all my illustrious ancestors, the Mackenzies of Kintail!" he exclaimed, with a melodramatic air that was very amusing; and shouldering his cages and other paraphernalia of his craft, he departed with a touch of his cap and a bow that showed that amongst birds he had learned good manners and politeness to an extent that as a navvy or hired labourer he would probably be all his lifetime very much a stranger. He has not returned to us as yet, so we suppose he is still in pursuit, detective-wise, of the shrike; and it had better look out, for Mackenzie is just the man to succeed sooner or later in laying salt upon its tail, as threatened. The butcher-bird, or shrike, is the *Lanius excubitor* of Linnæus, an exceeding rare bird in the West Highlands—in Scotland, indeed—so rare that we never saw a living bird of the order, only stuffed or otherwise preserved cabinet specimens. It preys on small birds, mice, insects, &c., which it does not tear up from under its feet like the hawk tribe, but fixes it on a thorn-prickle, or in the fork of a small branch, and then tears it to pieces with its bill, which is very strong, and toothed and hooked at the point. When Mackenzie catches the offender he is now in search of, we shall have something more to say about the butcher-bird, if butcher-bird it proves to be.

We have noticed, by the way, that all bird-catchers—all at least with whom we have had any acquaintance—are prodigious tea-drinkers, not sipping the grateful beverage from cups, observe, but literally drinking it in bowls'-full. They have assured us that they find it the best thing they can take, not merely as a refresher, but as a long sustaining element in their dietary throughout their many wanderings by flood and field. And like all large tea-drinkers, bird-catchers are a very sober class of men ; that they should be so is indeed a necessity of their craft, for a knock-kneed, shaky-handed, blear-eyed, nerveless bird-catcher would be as unfit for the successful prosecution of the labours incident to his profession, as would a similar physical wreck be for the successful manipulation of his tools in the more minute and delicate departments of mathematical instrument making.

CHAPTER L.

WE live in an age of intense literary and intellectual activity; the tendency of the highest culture of our time [March 1876], however, it is complained, being towards materialism and scepticism, the latter either in the form of indifferentism or absolute negation. The great mass of our people, however—the uneducated or only partially educated—stand at the other extreme; for whilst it is complained that those of the highest culture believe too little, or don't believe at all, the common people, it is averred, believe too much. And it is perfectly true that the latter are indeed superstitious to an extent of which the mere outsider can have no adequate conception; and yet, philosophically pondered, there can be no difficulty, we think, in arriving at the conclusion that of the two evils over-belief is better than its opposite; that it is better, upon the whole, to believe too much than too little. A man with any form of creed, even if it be false, may be led in time to believe aright, whereas the case of the utterly creedless man is well-nigh hopeless. For our own part, therefore, we do not look upon the superstitions of our people with such horror and alarm as many well-meaning persons, clerical or lay, feel or feign when brought in contact with an evil which, let the philosophers say what they will, has its good as well as its bad side. We greatly doubt if, under present circumstances, and in their present stage of civilisation, the inhabitants of Scotland generally, and of the Highlands, with which we are best acquainted, in particular, would be at all so religious and devout a people as they are confessedly allowed to be, were it not for the substratum of superstition that underlies their better founded beliefs and religious aspirations. Constantly *en rapport* with the supernatural and the unseen, they are more disposed than they might otherwise be to believe in and shape the conduct of their daily lives in accordance with the doctrine of a future world, with its rewards and punishments, feeling and acknowledging in a very remarkable manner, even through the medium of their superstitions—if erroneous, yet not always degrading—the full force and meaning of what the apostle speaks of in a general way as " the powers of the world to come." An interesting paper might be written in support of the theory here indicated, a theory that to some may seem a paradox, but meanwhile it must lie over for some more fitting occasion. Such a task requires time ; for of all the delicate tasks that the philosophic mind can concern itself with, the most delicate is the endeavour to discover and recognise the spirit of good things in things evil, and of reason in things un-reasonable. Meanwhile, it is the truth, account for it as we may, that notwithstanding the multiplication of ministers and churches, schoolmasters and school boards, " Increase of Episcopate " Bill, and all the rest of it, there is still a lively undercurrent of super-stition amongst our people, do what you can to stamp it out or otherwise ; and that those who believe in it most implicitly are by no means the worst people either. An example of a very common superstition is the following :—A few evenings ago, at an accidental gathering of some half-dozen families in a house in our neighbourhood, the subjoined conversation took place with regard to a recent death in the parish. Mrs. B.—" I suppose you have all heard of the death of X. L., poor fellow. It was reported he was better yesterday, but I knew last night that I should hear of a death some time to-day, and knowing of no one else at present unwell, I decided that it must be X. L.'s death that was foretold me." Mrs. C.—"Foretold you! how?" Mrs. B.—"Why, thus: long after dark last night, as I was busy getting the children's supper, the cock, that had gone to roost as usual, suddenly stood up on his perch, and crowed a long and loud crow that startled us all; and I made Katie say the Lord's Prayer, for I knew that a cock crowing at an hour so untimeous meant a death in our neighbourhood, and nothing else. On inquiry, I find that X. L. died just about that time." Mrs. D.—"I knew it too, that there was to be a death in our neighbourhood. My nose itched so much all last evening, and the itching was on the left nostril side, and I was certain that it was to be the death of a male that I should hear of. I had not, however, heard that X. L. was so very poorly." Mrs. F.—"While at breakfast this morning, I could hardly eat anything, so loud and persistent was the ringing in my ears. It was just like the tolling of the church bell." Now, the reader must remember that these were highly respectable women, of some education, and in every way of good repute; and yet they had no idea at all that there was anything silly or wrong about their superstition, of which they made no secret, and which was reported to us immediately afterwards by one who was present. Now, we ask, if one was present and heard it all, how could he best deal with the believer in this superstition, a superstition so wide-spread that it may be said to be universal. Any attempt at getting angry and driving it out of them by the mere force and weight of your superior enlightenment would be a false move, sure to be attended by no good results. Laughing at the whole affair might perhaps be a more successful way of dealing with the nonsense, but in neither way would you be likely to make them look at the matter from your particular light and point of view. Admitting that it was rank superstition and sheer nonsense, there was this one good thing attending it; it led to much moralising on the shortness and

uncertainty of human life, and the unabidingness generally of all
sublunary things; and the superstition was perhaps more effectual
in this direction than would be the most carefully composed sermon.
But the philosophic aspect of the case apart, let us inquire why the
facts mentioned should be held as premonitory of death. The crowing of the cock has probably some connection with the denial of St.
Peter, and in it, too, may perhaps be traced a faint remnant of the
bird divination of the ancients. As to the itching of the nose, we
confess our inability to say anything satisfactory, beyond the fact
that in old times anything unusual and difficult to be reasonably
accounted for in man's physical economy, as well as in his mental,
was at once attributed to a supernatural cause. Of this the ringing
in the ears, as well as the itching in the nose, must be held to be
an example. The well-known ringing in the ears does come with
extraordinary suddenness, as we have all experienced, and when it
comes makes the most staid philosopher look foolish and out of sorts
for the moment. Its connection with death is perhaps to be traced
to the passing bell of early and mediæval times, and to the tolling of
bells at funerals even in our own day. Sir Walter Scott, who
knew the peasantry of Scotland so well, and sympathised so much
even with their superstitions, has a happy reference to the death-
bell in a passage in *Marmion* :—

> " For soon Lord Marmion raised his head,
> And, smiling, to Fitz-Eustace said--
> ' Is it not strange, that, as ye sung,
> Seem'd in mine ear a death-peal rung,
> Such as in nunneries they toll
> For some departing sister's soul ?
> 　Say, what may this portend ?'
> Then first the Palmer silence broke
> (The livelong day he had not spoke),
> ' The death of a dear friend.' "

On this passage there is an interesting note very *apropos* to our
subject :—" Among other omens to which faithful credit is given

among the Scottish peasantry is what is called the 'dead-bell,' explained by my friend James Hogg to be that tinkling in the ears which the country people regard as the secret intelligence of some friend's decease." He tells a story to the purpose in the "Mountain Bard," p. 26—

> " O lady, 'tis dark, an' I heard the dead-bell,
>   An' I darena gae younder for gowd nor fee."

" By the dead-bell," says Hogg, " is meant a tinkling in the ears, which our peasantry in the country regard as a secret intelligence of some friend's decease. Thus this natural occurrence strikes many with superstitious awe. This reminds me of a trifling anecdote which I will relate as an instance. Our two servant girls agreed to go an errand of their own one night after supper, to a considerable distance, from which I strove to persuade them, but could not prevail. So, after going to the apartment in which I slept, I took a drinking-glass, and coming close to the back of the door, made two or three sweeps round the lips of the glass with my fingers, which caused a loud, shrill sound. I then overheard the following dialogue :—B.—" Ah, mercy ! the dead-bell went through my head just now with such a knell as I never heard." C.—" I heard it too." B.—" Did you indeed ? That is remarkable. I never knew of two hearing it at the same time before." C.—" We will not go to Midgehope to-night." B.—" No ! I wouldn't go for all the world ! I warrant it is my poor brother, Wat ; who knows what these wild Irishes may have done to him ?" Tinkling, however, which both Scott and Hogg use, is not the word. It is more of a ringing, so clear and loud at times, that we once heard a little girl say "there was a bell in her head." Our authorities above confess that it is called the " dead-*bell*" amongst the peasantry, and by bell they mean not a tinkling but a loud and very pronounced sound, as if of solid metal striking hollow metal, and causing the bell-sound with which we are all so familiar. Mickle, in his fine ballad *Cumnor Hall*, has a reference to the same superstition :—

> " The death-bell thrice was heard to ring,
>   An aerial voice was heard to call,
> And thrice the raven flapp'd its wing
>   Around the towers of Cumnor Hall."

To sneer at such beliefs, and pooh-pooh them superciliously and from a philosophical stand-point, is easy; it has been tried with but little satisfactory result. The true philosopher will be more and more disposed, the more he deals with such matters, and the closer he examines them, to fall back on Hamlet's dictum, "That there are more things in heaven and earth than are dreamt of in our philosophy." So ineradicable is superstition of this sort, that you may battle with it long enough—we have battled with it for years—and find it at last by no means the weaker of your assaults, no matter how cautiously and circuitously you select to deal with it.

After an unusually mild and open season, we have just had a taste of downright winter in the bitterly cold gales and drifting snow-storms of the last few days. Our weatherwise old folks are of course delighted that winter in proper dress and form has come at long last; better late than never, is the cry, and a bright and warm spring in due course is confidently predicted.

CHAPTER LI.

AFTER rather more than six consecutive weeks of weather so hot and dry and parching [May 1876], that we were all rapidly becoming hide-bound, brown-skinned, and sapless as so many Egyptian mummies, the rain came at last; came, too, not deluge-wise, and with a splash and a roar as is generally the case after such long-continued droughts, but calmly and softly as falls the dew of sleep on infant eyelids, and without a breath of accompanying wind. The earth, long agape with thirst, drank it in greedily, and vegetable and animal life alike rejoiced in the grateful quiet as well as in the copiousness of the blessed rainfall. You should have heard how, when the first drop began to fall, our wild-birds welcomed it. All at once, in wood, and copse, and hedgerow, they burst out into loud and gladsome song; nor did they cease when the rainfall was heaviest, as they usually do, but kept it up far into the night, the merle and song-thrush now and again breaking out afresh as if they couldn't sufficiently express their joy, even after we had retired to rest, and well pleased lay listening to the music of the raindrops as they fell plashing and pattering from the eaves. Even our least accomplished songsters took their share in this concert, and if they did not, simply because they could not, sing as well as their more gifted companions, they made at least, as the *Ancient Mariner* has it, a pleasant "jargoning," therein, dear reader, teaching us all this lesson, that if our gifts prevent us from playing any great or prominent part in the orchestra of life, we are yet all the same to perform the parts assigned us as best we may, and always cheerily and with a will. Next morning again was calm and mild and beautiful as a summer morning could be, while the country already looked so fresh and green and lovely that one could hardly believe that such a marvellous change had taken place in the course of a single night; so potent, in such circumstances, is the kindly touch of the Rain King's-magic wand.

The plague of mice in Upper Teviotdale is a very serious matter indeed, and the most energetic steps should at once be taken in order to check and, if possible, stamp out the evil. These little rodents multiply with incredible rapidity, and if they are to be fought *a l'outrance* and conquered, the sooner the campaign is opened, and the more vigorously it is conducted, the easier and speedier will be the victory. The short-tailed field-mouse is fortunately a rare animal in the Highlands, though we have occasionally met with it in the districts of Lorne, Lochaber, and Badenoch. We have also seen it on the lands of Drumfin, near Tobermory, in the island of Mull. Once seen, it is easily recognised again. Its colour, instead of being of the ordinary "mouse" shade of grey or brown, is red, or reddish; its head is more bullet-like and rounder, and its snout blunter than in any of its congeners; and its tail ends abruptly, giving that appendage a *docked* and stumpy look, as if by accident or design one-third of its proper length had been cut off in early life; and hence its common designation of short-tailed field-mouse. Every one who has tried to capture a common domestic mouse with the bare hand, knows to his cost how quickly and sharply it can bite; but the little field-mouse never once attempts to bite the hand that holds it. If pounced upon while running about in the rough bent grass in which it usually shelters, it no sooner feels itself fairly enclosed in

your hand than it seems to become paralysed through sheer excess
of terror, and you may handle it for a time and turn it about in
all directions as if it were a stuffed specimen, without its once
offering to escape or defend itself in any way. If, however, you
let it slip from your hand to the ground, it is at once off and away,
and, search for it as you may, you are never likely to see it again.
For its size the *Arvicola agrestis* is a very powerful little animal,
particularly strong in the neck, shoulder, and fore-arm, a provision whereby it is enabled to dig and burrow its way underground when necessary, with all the ease and rapidity almost of the
mole itself. It is very fond of water, which it drinks often
and greedily, and hence it is that it is never found at any great
distance from a plentiful supply of its favourite beverage. One
that a lady friend of ours kept for some months in a cage,
drank, more or less, she assures us, during every half-hour of the
day, and if its supply at any time happened to fail by any neglect
or oversight of its mistress, the thirsty little toper squeaked
querulously and nibbled angrily at the bars and wood-work of its
cage until its water-dish was replenished. When it had drank
enough, it frequently stepped into the dish, and frisked about in
such a manner as to wet its breast and lower parts of its body
thoroughly, when it would retire to a corner of its cage in which
was a little raised platform, and, sitting up on its quarters, squirrel-
wise, rub and cleanse its head and face with both paws in a
very comical manner. It was fed on succulent grasses and lettuce
leaves and endive from the garden, of which latter it was very
fond. It also ate bread steeped in milk, and apples, both raw and
boiled. It finally met the fate of most cage pets; the cat got at
it and killed it. We have only heard of one instance in which the
Arvicola became so numerous in the West Highlands as to become
a pest that was only got rid of with great trouble and no little
expense. This was on the estate of Ardgour, in our own parish.

x

About seventy years ago, the late Colonel Maclean, grandfather of the present proprietor, planted the greater part of the woods that now make the place so beautiful—at this moment one of the loveliest spots in all the Highlands. Shortly after the young trees were planted, the field-mouse made its appearance, and in a few months so rapidly increased its numbers, that they were on all hands declared a nuisance that must be got rid of at any cost. Their favourite food in this instance seemed to be the tender rootlets and bark of the smaller trees, thousands of which straightway shrivelled up and died away owing to the little rodent's unkindly attentions. Colonel Maclean, who was eminently a man of action, vowed that such a state of things was beyond all bearing, and must be put a stop to at all hazards. With a host of willing workers, he straightway set about what for a time appeared a hopeless task, employing every conceivable means that wit or ingenuity could devise in order to check, and if possible stamp out the mouse plague. Having heard of a plan adopted under similar circumstances in the Dean and New Forests in England, holes and trenches were dug in all directions, and pitfalls ingeniously constructed, in which very soon scores of the marauders were caught and killed every morning. The cats in every house in the hamlet, purposely kept for the time on short commons at home, were locked out at night and allowed to cater for themselves ; and they fell upon the rodents tooth and nail, doing such execution that they soon became sleek and fat as cats were never known in Ardgour before or since. At convenient spots large fires were kindled, on which cauldrons of water were boiled, kettles of which, as hot as hot could be, were poured into such burrows as showed signs of habitation, with a view to scalding the inmates to death. This was generally done in the early morning, to make sure of finding the enemy at home, for the field-mouse, like most of the rodents, is mainly a nocturnal feeder. The keepers had orders for

the time to cease annoying vermin—so-called—of any kind, the
result being that in a short time stoats, weasels, ravens, grey crows,
hawks, and owls abounded, and these, you may believe, did
yeoman service in the campaign ; they were the cavalry that swept
off the scattered fugitives. By such active measures the enemy was
exterminated in a single season, and never again, so far as we
know, showed face on Loch-Linnhe-side. It was Colonel Maclean's
opinion that the mice were imported ; that the first pair, or more,
perhaps, were brought from the south in the straw and moss and
matting in which the roots of the more valuable and delicate
plants and trees were packed. From the above our Teviotdale
friends may perhaps gather some wrinkles that may be of use to
them in their efforts to relieve themselves from their field-mouse
invasion.

And writing of the field-mouse reminds us that amongst our own
domestic mice there is at present what is generally, if somewhat
erroneously, called a "singing mouse." About a fortnight ago it
attracted the attention of a young lady, who heard it at midnight,
and thought at the time it was the twittering of some bird at her
bedroom window. It was afterwards heard by others, and finally
by ourselves, as we sat up late one night writing. That it was not
a bird we were certain, and guessing the truth—for years ago we
had become acquainted with the notes—we watched and waited
until the "jargoning" seemed to proceed from a closed press
immediately behind our chair, which we gently opened, and had a
glimpse of the performer, who vanished, of course, but soon again
began its voluntary, or involuntary rather, behind the wainscoting
in another corner of the room. It was, in short, a "singing
mouse ;" an involuntary music, however, with which the poor mouse
would gladly dispense if it could. Birds, as we know, are sometimes incited to song by sheer rivalry and rage ; sometimes by
poignant sorrow for the loss of a mate, or the despoliation of a nest

of its treasure of eggs or callow young; but as a rule a bird sings from pure joyousness of heart and exhilaration of spirits. When a mouse "sings" it is owing to a laryngeal disease, a sort of fungoid growth in the throat, which obstructs the breathing, causing the animal to emit the notes which have been foolishly called "singing," and which, the clearer and more bird-like they become, only in truth indicate the more advanced stages of a malady which invariably ends in death. Our attention was first directed to this matter by a distinguished comparative anatomist, the late Professor John Reid of St. Andrews, whose curiosity as a naturalist was unbounded, only equalled by the untiring patience and care and caution with which, step by step, he wrought out his conclusions. It is difficult to describe the "singing" of a mouse thus affected to those who have not heard it for themselves. It may be said to be in the main a half-whistle half-wheeze, now and again interrupted by some rapid clicking notes of a somewhat metallic ring, as if a small bit of stick was being smartly and rapidly, but very lightly, struck on the very extremity of the treble string of a guitar or violin. Our "singing mouse," in whom, poor thing, we were all much interested, has not been heard for a night or two; it has probably gone the way all mice, as well as men, must go when respiration becomes impossible.

An amusing paragraph is at present going the round of the papers about a farmer who, having ordered a hogshead of nitrate of soda for agricultural purposes, got hold somehow of a hogshead of sugar instead, which latter, in ignorance of its quality, he sowed broadcast over his land. Now, at length aware of the mistake, he is said to be waiting and watching with much curiosity as to how the saccharine crystals turn out as fertilisers. The story, which may be true enough, reminds us of an amusing mistake of a somewhat similar nature into which one of the crofters in our neighbourhood very innocently fell some years ago. He had attended the

Fort-William June market, and amongst other things brought home with him, on his return in the evening, two small parcels, one containing one pound of turnip seed, the other the same quantity red clover seed. Next morning he was up bright and early, and as an exercise that might perhaps help to drive away a headache, not uncommon on such occasions, he resolved, the day being favourable, to sow his turnip and clover seeds. He commenced, and, very unwittingly you may believe, sowed the turnip seed broadcast among the barley braird, and the red clover seed in the drills prepared for the turnips! The blunder was only discovered several days afterwards, when the seeds began to sprout after their kind, and matters were rectified as the case best allowed; but poor Donald never heard the last of the joke, which, when followed beyond certain limits, used to make him exceedingly angry.

Mackenzie the bird-catcher, *facile princeps* the king and head of his order, called upon us to-day, and made us a present of the bonniest little redpole we ever set eyes upon. Its colouring is exquisitely beautiful, differing from the usual plumage of the species in having several little snow-white spots irregularly sprinkled over the coverts of either wing, and its neck and breast of a mingled shade of pink and crimson of exceeding richness, that makes it far and away the handsomest bird of the order we ever saw. At first we took it for a foreign bird, or a bird that had been artificially painted in order to deceive us, and it was only on handling and thoroughly examining him that we became convinced that the bird was a genuine, though curiously coloured, specimen of its species, and that we had it before us just as it was captured some days ago in Glentarbet, near Strontian. Of all our cage-birds, the redpole (*Fringalla linaria*, Linn.) is perhaps the soonest reconciled to loss of liberty and prolonged captivity. Our little pet, whose cage hangs almost within arm's length of us as we write, seems perfectly happy, and is already singing with all his might, a goldfinch in another cage beside him busily scolding him all the time for having the impudence to sing so well, or sing at all, in interruption of his own louder and clearer notes. Cage-birds properly treated are a great amusement, and, if you pay them due attention, evince in a very short time a degree of intelligence so remarkable that you only wonder, philosophising craniologically, how so much of it can find lodging-room within their little heads.

Mackenzie is commissioned to go to Norway and Sweden this summer in search of a lot of crossbills, grossbeaks, and other birds, for a wealthy gentleman in the south, who is a great bird-fancier. Let him only once get to their habitat, and Mackenzie is just the man to lay salt on the tail of any bird that flies.

CHAPTER LII.

WITH a bright sun overhead, at noon as nearly vertical as it can
ever be in our latitudes, and a steady, kindly warmth, and no lack
now of genial showers, our West Highlands are now [June 1876]
beautiful exceedingly, almost at the height and heyday of their
summer loveliness, while crops of all kinds are at their present stage
all that we could wish them. Tourists in considerable numbers are
already on the move; and coaches and steamers alike are beginning
to carry daily increasing crowds of passengers, so delighted with
the attention paid them, and the elegance and comfort of their
surroundings whether afloat or ashore, that a crack with them, as
you chance to forgather of an evening, is always pleasant, for the
essentials of a pleasant conversation are there to begin with; they
are pleased, and you are glad that it is so; the rest is all smooth
sailing. You meet an occasional grumbler of course; a wretch,
miserable himself, and anxious to make every one else miserable
also. An extraordinary curiosity, in truth, is your thorough
grumbler. The faculty would probably explain it all away by a
reference to dyspepsia or some serious derangement of liver. From
frequent and close study, however, of a not uninteresting phenomenon, we are rather inclined to think otherwise. In the genuine
grumbler the disposition to look at things obliquely, and from a
false or foreshortened point of view, seems ingrained in and interwoven with his very nature. In everything he says and does you

detect a perverseness of disposition and a *thrawnness* of temper that you cannot believe to be temporary or accidental, but a veritable part and portion of the man's being from the first. The old dictum about the poet, which after all is only true in a sense, is true of the grumbler absolutely. *Grumblerus nascitur, non fit;* he was born a grumbler, and if you put his mother in the witness box, and she chose to entertain you with reminiscences of his infancy, her testimony, we venture to say, would go to show that he kicked and screamed at existence and all the surroundings of his nursery at the earliest moment possible for such an exhibition, and that this disposition to hit out right and left indiscriminately at every one and everything, grew with his growth and strengthened with his strength, till in fulness of time he became the thorough-bred grumbler who sat opposite you at the *table d'hôte* a week ago, or rode with you atop of the coach yesterday. With spur on heel, and once fairly in the stirrups, your grumbler is ready to tilt, in dearth of anything more substantial, at his own shadow. Any attempt to mollify him, however well-meant and carefully worded, only makes him worse. Do what you can, he remains a grumbler still—implacable, unappeasable. As we generally meet with him here, his grievances for the most part are as to the steamer or coach by which he has travelled, and the food that he has had to eat. Try to put him right according to your view of it, and you are sure to catch it hot and heavy for your interference in a matter which he declares concerns *him* alone, and yet with which he has been pestering everybody that would for a moment listen to him all the way from Oban to Staffa, or from Ballachulish to Tyndrum. Give a man of this kind the softest cushion in the coziest corner of Cleopatra's barge ; the box seat in the victor's own chariot in a triumphal procession ; a first and full supply of all the delicacies at the table of Apicius of *De rê Culinaria* fame, and he would still be the same fault-finder and grumbler. One way of shutting up the inveterate grumbler, very effectual in most cases, is to fool him to the top of his bent—to give him line, in the piscatorial sense. If he complains that his seat on the coach is hard and the rails behind hurt his spine, assure him at once, in a confidential sort of way, that you believe the axle is horribly twisted, and is as likely as not to snap in twain just about half-way down the next incline. If he complains of the dust, give it as your candid opinion that the Road Trustees should be heavily fined for not allaying the nuisance by a properly arranged water-cart service all over the Black Mount. If he complains that the steamer trembles in all her timbers, and the steam, as it escapes at the calling-places, makes a horrible noise, agree with him at once, hinting that an explosion of the boiler is by no means an unlikely event through the carelessness of the coal-begrimed stoker, who is just then cooling himself at an open air-hole, and wiping his brow with a wisp of tow. If at dinner he abuses the soup, ask him how it could possibly be good, seeing that the water whereof it is made was taken a week ago, by means of a tarry bucket, from the third lock of the Crinan Canal? Does he abuse his salmon? Shake your head sadly, and point with your fork towards the round of beef, hinting that at this season cattle sometimes die a natural death, and then their carcasses are to be had for a third of the market price of good beef. Go with him and beyond him in this sort of way for a little, and he will soon see that you are only poking your fun at him, and the chances are that he will cease troubling *you* at all events with his complaints for the rest of the day. After all, however, it is but justice to observe that even your inveterate grumbler is not infrequently a much more amiable person than he seems ; kind, too, after a fashion, and amazingly liberal when a proper occasion offers.

Fish are now becoming plentiful along our shores, and with a little trouble in selecting a very early or a very late hour, and watching the state of the tides, they may be caught in considerable numbers with rod and line ; and irrespective of their value as an article of food, the pastime is by no means contemptible even as a matter of sport, though, sooth to say, many people live within sight of the sea for years, and know little or nothing of the amusement that may be had so readily and cheaply in this way. Those caught at present are principally whitings, lythes, and seths, or coal-fish, with an occasional sea-bream. This last is reckoned a somewhat coarse fish, but it is by no means bad eating when properly cooked and served, and you recollect as you eat that the price of mutton is something like a shilling the pound, and frequently not to be had even at that.

More prone, perhaps, to superstition in every form than their more inland brethren, our maritime population have quite a number of *freits*, forms, fancies, and superstitious observances, most of them only silly and harmless enough, in connection with all their sea-fishing adventures, whether with rod, net, or line. A few evenings ago, as a party of four, douce and decent men enough, were preparing to launch their boat to go a-fishing, we chanced to pass along the beach, joining them, as has long been our habit in such circumstances, for a few minutes' conversation. Suddenly, as we were speaking, a large black-backed gull (*Larus marinus*) wheeled towards us out of a flock that were lazily circling about at a considerable distance seawards. Right towards us, as if on some express and special errand, came the gull, one of the largest and most beautiful of sea-birds, until he was within less than fifty yards of us, when by a change of poise, and a scarcely perceptible movement of wing, he slowly swept round our heads, screaming the while as only a black-backed gull can scream—a wild and eerie note that may be heard for a league. The gull's business, whatever it might be, was so manifestly connected with one or all of us, or with the boat, perhaps, round which we were standing on the beach, that it could not but attract attention and provoke comment from the most unobservant. After circling some half-dozen times round and round and right above our heads, the bird, with one loud parting scream—and yet scream is not the word either; the Gaelic *guileag* is nearer it—and with an upward oblique sweep, so beautifully easy and effortless that it seemed the result of a simple act of volition rather than a grand *pas* in volitation, flew away to join his companions, who were now heard clamouring over a coal-fish *goil* or boil, as the Highlanders call the ebullition of the surface play of a shoal of sea-fish. The men looked at each other and at us meaningly; and at last out it came. "Small chance," said one of them, "have we of anything like a good fishing this evening: better for us to stay at home." "Why so?" we quietly inquired. "Well, sir," was the response, "I never knew a gull act in that sort of way but it meant bad luck in fishing, and the non-accomplishment of one's errand afloat, whatever it might be." The rest agreed with the speaker, but we persuaded them, after some trouble, to proceed to their fishing-ground, to give it a trial at least; and when, at a much later hour, they returned, we were on the beach to meet them, and found that after all they had made an excellent fishing. There and then we sat down beside them as they were dividing their fish into equal shares, and told them the following story from Josephus, *Against Apion.* Quoting from Hecatæus, the great Jewish historian proceeds :—" As I was myself going to the Red Sea, there followed us a man, whose name was Mosollam ; he was one of the Jewish horsemen who conducted us. He was a person of great courage, of a strong body, and by all allowed to be the most skilful archer that was either among the Greeks or barbarians. Now, this man, as people were in great numbers passing along the road, and a certain augur was observing an augury by a bird, and requiring them all to stand still, inquired what they staid for. Hereupon the augur showed him the bird from whence he told his augury, and told him that if

the bird staid where he was, they ought all to stand still; but that
if he got up and flew onward, they must go forward; but that if
he flew backward, they must retire again. Mosollam made no
reply, but drew his bow and shot at the bird, and hit him and
killed him; and as the augur and some others were very angry,
and wished imprecations upon him, he answered them thus :—
' Why are you so mad as to take this most unhappy bird into your
hands? for how can this bird give us any true information con-
cerning our march, which could not foresee how to save himself?
For had he been able to foreknow what was future, he would not
have come to this place, but would have been afraid lest Mosollam
the Jew would shoot him as he has done, and kill him.' " The
men, who had listened most attentively, smiled as we concluded,
and agreed that Mosollam must have been a very sensible man;
and vowed that for the future they would attach no more meaning
or importance to a circling, screaming gull, than to the chirping of
a wren in the elder bushes at the cottage doors. And what after
all, the reader may ask, brought the black-backed gull circling and
screaming over your heads? Well, from its great and immense
spread of wing, it was probably the leader and guardian of its own
particular flock, and as such thought it his duty to reconnoitre in
person, in case the five men about the boat on the beach should
have sinister intentions as to him or his. His scream or *guileag*
was just his way of telegraphing the results of his observations to
his distant companions; or he may have been scolding us in his
own manner for our manifest intention of leaving the land, and
invading what he considered his own proper element and territory,
the sea. A more prosaic explanation, if it please you better,
is perhaps to be found in the fact that the boat was internally
largely incrusted with fish scales, and smelt strongly of fish, and
that that, to one of his sensitive olfactory nerves, was the only
or main attraction, the rest being mere idle curiosity, from which

birds are no more exempt than men. One thing only is certain, if difficult to be accounted for, and that is, that individual gulls frequently act as this gull acted when a boat is about to put off from the shore in the fishing season, which being occasionally connected, as must sometimes happen, however accidentally, with an unsuccessful fishing adventure, gave rise to the silly superstition which, by the aid of Flavius Josephus, we were able in this instance at least successfully to combat.

CHAPTER LIII.

THE unprecedented heat of mid-August lasted with us here precisely
a fortnight [September 1876]. Beginning on the 10th, it continued
with little intermission or mitigation till the 24th, when the wind
suddenly chopped round to the south-west, our rainy quarter; the
sky assumed the threatening aspect, an ugly interminglement of
black and dark grey, with which we are only too familiar, and rain
began to fall with that *dour*, persistent pattering, and aimless
horizontal drift, which sufficed to convince the most careless and
unobservant student of our West Highlands meteorology that it
was neither a thunder-plump nor a mere passing shower, but a
determined and regular "set-in" of probably some days, or, it
might be, of some weeks' duration. The last ten days have
accordingly been more or less wet, and as the corn over the
country generally is about ripe for scythe and sickle, many an
anxious eye is cast heavenwards with wistfullest glance, morning,
noon, and night, in hopes of a change of wind and a return to fair
weather. We are about tired of advocating the advantages of early
sowing to our friends of the West Highlands. We are content
with once again stating the fact that, having sown early, our own
corn was cut in ripe and good condition on the 17th August, and
safely housed without having once been touched by a single drop
of rain. A single armful of such well-preserved provender is
worth a whole back-burden of the washed-out and sapless stuff

that usually goes by the name of "wintering" and "winter keep" in this and the neighbouring districts. It is proper to say, however, that, though so difficult to move to an earlier date in corn-sowing, our people here have of recent years been more amenable to good advice in the matter of potato culture. This year a large breadth of potatoes was planted in March and early April, and the consequence is that these are now nearly ripe, and of the best quality, stronger too, and in every way better able to resist the attacks of blight—*absit omen!*—should it unfortunately come their way, as we hope it won't; while the still green and half-ripe tubers of later plantings would probably suffer largely under a similar visitation. Not even when it is quite ready for the sickle do people generally cut their corn timeously. Too often it is allowed to ripen overmuch, till the straw is over-dry and sapless, besides the inevitable loss of grain in the stooking and subsequent ingathering. It is very much the same with hay. As a rule, it is left too long uncut, by which its quality is sadly deteriorated. Nor is this mistake in haymaking peculiar to the west coast, but much too common over all the country. Even in Morayshire and about Inverness the hay crop is, as a rule, allowed to ripen over-much. If it were cut ten days or a fortnight earlier it would weigh more, smell sweeter, be more nutritious, and better every way than under the present system, which allows it not merely to ripen, but to more than ripen, to wither up and lose most of its sap and seed before it is cut and secured. It may, perhaps, be laid down as an axiom that root crops cannot be allowed to ripen over-much; cereals and grasses most certainly may.

Cavill's recent attempt to swim the Channel, in rivalry of Captain Webb's feat, was a failure, and had medical aid not been so opportunely at hand when the swimmer, comatose and unconscious, was lifted out of the water by his friends in the attendant lugger, the venture, noteworthy, though unsuccessful, for its pluck and

daring, would probably have resulted in something far more serious
than mere failure. In accounting for his non-success, and his state
of extreme exhaustion when taken out of the water, Cavill largely
blames the jelly-fish or sea-blubber, through perfect shoals of which
he had once and again to force his way ; and although he wore a
thin jersey, which must have been some protection, enough of the
bare skin was exposed to contact with the cold, clammy, slimy
Medusæ, to make him exceedingly nervous and generally uncomfortable throughout a full third of the distance covered. The number
of these Medusæ to be met with at certain seasons all along the
British shores is enormous ; and towards the close of summer and
early autumn they are more abundant, perhaps, in our western
lochs than anywhere else. Looking over the boat's side on a fine
day, we have seen them in our own Loch Leven in incalculable
numbers, thick as autumnal leaves in Vallambrosa, or the stars in
the Milky Way—of all shapes and sizes too, swimming about
aimlessly by a slow but constant contraction and expansion, regular
as the beat of a pendulum, of their umbrella-like bodies, fringed
like a lady's parasol, with a close edging of thread-like *cilia*, and
frequently having long, pendulous tentaculæ attached to their under
surface, giving the healthy animal, when busy in its proper element,
a very curious appearance. Though the jelly-fish is in constant
motion—in perpetual motion, so to speak, for it never rests, that
ever we could discover, either by night or day—its progress in the
sea is rather due to the set of the wind and the tide-drift than its
own exertions, its incessant labours of contraction and expansion
being performed not so much for the purpose of shifting its place in
the water, as for the purpose of grasping and sucking in at each contraction such microscopic organisms as form its food. It is true that
in a calm and tideless sea its motions cause it to be carried in the
direction of the contracting beat an inch or thereby at a time, but this
progress is clearly accidental and unintentional, so far as it is con-

cerned, the great object of the incessant contraction and expansion
being, as we have said, not so much change of place as the capture
and insuction of its ordinary food. The Medusæ swim at all depths
in the sea, but as a rule they seem to prefer feeding within a
fathom or two of the surface, particularly if the sun is bright and
the sea is perfectly calm. The mouth of the Medusa is in the centre
of the under concave surface, and the animal's *modus operandi* in
sweeping in its food towards this orifice is not difficult to understand.
Stretch out your right hand, with its back or knuckle surface upper-
most. First expand the hand and fingers to their full extent, then
contract so as almost, but not quite, to close the hand, not quickly,
but very firmly and decidedly. Continue in this way opening out
and closing the hand and fingers, not quite so fast as a second's
beating pendulum oscillates, and you have the perfect analogue, or
more properly the homologue, of the Medusa's action. If you can
fancy an orifice or mouth in the centre of your palm, and your
fingers to be the fringe surrounding the jelly-fish disc, and if you
perform the action indicated in a tub or pool of water, into which
a little flour or fine oatmeal has been thrown to represent the
animalculæ forming the Medusa's food, so much the better : you
will at once understand how the animalculæ and food particles are
swept and sucked in by the current created towards the animal's
mouth, or gastric cavity, as it might be more properly termed.
When one or more of these animals comes in contact with a swimmer's
skin, the sensation is anything but agreeable, a feeling of indescribable loathing and horror being engendered by the touch of the cold,
gelatinous mass, that you are yet conscious is not dead matter, but
an animated pulsating organism. But though contact with the
ordinary Medusa is bad enough, there is another species of jelly-fish
not uncommon in British waters at certain seasons, accidental contact with which is a very serious matter indeed. These are known to
naturalists as *Acalephæ*, from a Greek word signifying a nettle. They

are not so numerous on our shores as the true Medusa, but they grow to a much larger size, some of them measuring eighteen, twenty, or even twenty-four inches across the disc, and thick and heavy in proportion, large enough, when fresh from the sea, to fill a tub of considerable size. If one of these wretches comes in contact with the human skin, it is found to sting like a nettle, only much more severely, and hence its scientific name. A swimmer stung by contact with an acaleph feels not only the cruel smarting of the nettle-like and burning stinging, but he is in a few minutes frequently overcome by a feeling of languor and sickness, that lasts for a considerable time, and is sometimes only relieved by a violent fit of vomiting, just as if he was a sufferer for the moment under the influence of a powerful emetic. We have more than once been stung by an acaleph, and can speak *feelingly* on the subject. Only last season a boy on the opposite coast of Appin was, while bathing, so severely stung by one or more acalephs that he was for some days confined to bed, seriously ill, and under medical treatment. This power of stinging seems to be a wise provision in the economy of the animal, for the purpose of rendering helpless and numbing its prey, to make them easier of capture and subsequent deglutition, just as the *Mysotis*, or electric eel, with like purpose puts to a very important and practical use its electro-battery shocks. The true acaleph may generally be distinguished from the more harmless jelly-fish by having a good deal of colour in its tissues, being striated with red, pink, and pale green, which gives it a very beautiful appearance as under the bright sunlight it floats about, contracting and expanding with the regularity of a pendulum beat, near the surface of the calm, unruffled sea. The amount of solid matter in a jelly-fish of any kind, however large, is amazingly small. Within a thin, filmy skin, they are entirely made up of water, with a few threads spider-net-wise running through it to keep it in shape, like the ropes on which was stretched the immense *velarium* of an ancient amphitheatre. After

a summer storm we have seen the sea-beach covered with a considerable wall of jelly-fish that had been cast ashore, a yard in
breadth, perhaps, and a couple of feet in height; and before the
evening of the next day, during which the sun shone out hot and
clear, the whole had melted away like so much snow, leaving only a
thin film of gelatinous matter, which, if gathered together in a
single heap, wouldn't have filled our venerable but still useful
" *Clachnacuddin* " hat. There is a good story told of a farmer,
somewhere from the altitudes of *Druimuachdar*, who took some
land by the sea, not a hundred yards from our own neighbourhood.
One morning he saw the beach covered with a deep ring of jelly-
fish as above, and being an *eident* body, he got his horses and carts
in order, and commenced to cart them afield, in the belief that they
could not but prove excellent manure for the land. After working
at the job nearly half a day, a naturalist, who chanced to pass the
way, astonished the farmer not a little by assuring him that some
hogsheads of sea-water, *and a single pocket-handkerchief full of
manure* from the nearest dung-heap, would fitly and fully represent
all that he had on his land in the fifty odd carts of jelly-fish that
had cost him so much labour ! The story goes on to say that that
particular farmer looked askance at jelly-fish ever afterwards, and
didn't care much to have their natural history discussed in his presence
at kirk or market, at bridal or funeral, all his life long. The fact is,
that a mass of jelly-fish sufficient to load the " Great Eastern "
wouldn't probably yield a peat creelful of solid serviceable matter
for any purpose or purposes whatever. The jelly-fish is known to the
Gaels of the Hebrides and West Coast by a curious name—*Sgeith
an Róin* for the smaller ones, that is, the seal's vomit, and for the
larger ones, *Sgeith na Muicamara*, the whale's vomit, in the absurd
belief that they were the vomits respectively of the uncanny *Sealchs*,
of whom the Highlander had always a superstitious dread, and of
the largest of marine monsters, after they had gorged themselves

to repletion on a shoal of extra-oleaginous herring or mackerel. These names for the jelly-fish are doubtless absurd enough, and yet, in defence of the good old Gaelic name-givers, let us observe that they are not a whit more absurd than the *Caprimulgus* (goatsucker) of Linnæus as applied to the night-jar, or the *Frugilegus* (corn-gatherer) of the same high authority as applied to the common rook.

CHAPTER LIV.

THE meteorological vaticinations of our weather-wise octogenarian neighbours have met with abundant and speedy verification in the storms and heavy rains of the past ten days [October 1876]. For the month of October, however, the weather continues wonderfully mild; even with wind and rain the temperature is higher than it usually is at this date; an occasional fine day, besides, encouraging us in the hope that winter proper, winter with its thousand discomforts, its snow and sleet, its cold and cheerlessness and gloom, may be checked in his advance for some weeks to come, by the uncompromising attitude of an autumn so lusty of life and bright of eye, but, despite an occasional overclouding of countenance, it seems yet but only little past its prime. Agriculturally the season is being wound up satisfactorily enough; crops have, upon the whole, been secured in very fair condition, and although the herring fishing in our lochs as elsewhere has proved a failure, our people are prepared to meet the coming winter in comparative abundance, and with a cheerfulness calculated to disarm the gloomy season of more than half its terrors. The poet has philosophically observed that man

> " Wants but little here below,
> Nor wants that little long "—

where "wants," you will observe, has to be read in a restricted and peculiar sense : the plain prose of it being, that for all his essential needs man requires but little, that merely to live a little suffices, and that, on account of the shortness and certainty of human life, even that "little" is soon dispensed with—is no longer required. Granted, O Poet! but not the less true is it that during man's allotted time the "little," however small, is indispensable all the same, and any sensible diminution or curtailment of his "little" will make a man, however abstemious and sober of life, just as miserable as his fellow who has to bewail the diminution, not of his "little," but of his abundance. Nothing pleases us in our people here more than their constant cheerfulness in the enjoyment of their "little." They would doubtless take more if they could get it, and rejoice exceedingly if their "little" could be converted into an abundance; but meantime they have the good sense to be contented, and even happy with what they have, and that, too, to a degree that no one perhaps less intimate with them than we are could believe possible in the circumstances.

Our "Indian summer," that seems still to linger, as if loth to leave us to the tender mercies of a winter that is likely to prove unusually inclement, has been a season of unwonted jubilation to our wild-birds; for, guided by an instinct that is a monitor sufficiently to be depended upon in ordinary circumstances, they had already, each after his kind, prepared themselves, not for equinoctial warmth and sunshine, but for equinoctial storms. All the more, then, from its very unexpectedness, did they feel bound to rejoice in the incalculable blessing of twenty free days of midsummer warmth and calm at a time when, in the usual course of events, the tempest should have been howling through the woods and careering over moss and moorland, they the while glad to cower for shelter and safety in such crevices and corners as might be best suited to their purpose. At and after the autumnal equinox, in ordinary seasons, the only one of our native wild-birds that sings, or attempts to sing, a fairly finished song, is the redbreast; though,

to be sure, the wren also sometimes strikes up an occasional voluntary when we least expect it ; the lively Lilliputian in his song, as
in everything else, being a creature of unbridled impulse, guided
solely by the whim and caprice of the moment, as if in utter
contempt and disregard of the method and order by which other
birds are fain to regulate the conduct of their lives. Not the redbreast alone, however, backed by the intermittent melodies of the
wren, who, Sims Reeves-like, only sings when the humour seizes
him, obstinately silent when you would expect him to sing, and as
obstinately singing when you would expect him to be silent ; but
the blackbird also, and chaffinch, the corn bunting and goldfinch,
have been of late delighting us with their music, in volume and
compass and exquisite finish hardly inferior, though so out of
season, to their most successful performances in spring and early
summer, which, be it noted, is *the season* for wild-bird song at its
best. Our poets, as if by tacit arrangement and preconcert, do all
in their power to impress us with the notion that June is not only
the month of flower and leaf, but the great bird music month as
well, a mistake partly owing, no doubt, to their ignorance of bird
life, but mainly, we suspect, arising from the fact that " June " and
"tune" are such pat and perfect rhymes, that the poet dealing
with summer glories and summer joys never fails to pounce upon
them for instant use, without a thought of their inappropriateness,
so far at least as bird music is concerned. It is true that with
reference to bird song our poets are also liberal enough with their
" *May*" and " *lay*," which, as nearer to the mark, is somewhat
better. Better still, however, would be April, if our poets would
be correct, to which we might perhaps suggest " *trill* " as a rhyme ;
not a good rhyme to be sure, even if " April" could be decently
placed at the end of a line (as in the old " valentines ") without
being misaccented ; but we ornithologists could forgive the halting
rhyme and barbarous accent for the sake of the correctness of the

"colouring" otherwise. The truth is that our best wild-bird music time may be set down as properly belonging to the eight weeks between the 15th March and the 15th May. Let our poets, then, look out for and find appropriate rhymes for "March," "April," and "May." It is their business and not ours ; but for any sake, in dealing with wild-bird music and summer joys, let them beware of the fatal facility of the rhymes of "June" and "tune." Poets and poetry apart, however, it was extremely interesting to watch the conduct of our wild-birds during our late "Indian summer." For the first few days they fluttered about and chirped interrogatively amongst themselves, as if in a state of doubt and indecision, if not of actual bewilderment, evidently puzzled what to say to it, but, upon the whole, of opinion that it was too good to last. Last, however, it did, longer than either they or we thought at all likely, and before the end of the week the chirping had developed into actual song, and the fluttering into a business-like activity, as if they had fully thought it over, and had decided that it was best, proverb wise, to be making some hay while the sun shone. Our attention was first of all attracted by a pair of house sparrows passing and repassing our study window, now with a stray feather, now with a bit of straw in their bills, with which they disappeared in a clump of ivy high up on a corner of the garden wall. On climbing by the aid of a small ladder to inquire what they were about, we found that they were repairing a nest, in which they had already reared a brood this season, and which the youngsters, in their unfledged and awkward babyhood, had considerably damaged and generally knocked out of shape—"into a cocked hat," in fact, as they say across the Atlantic. With a care and painstaking, however, which our "featherless biped" architects, in executing *their* repairs on our stone and lime habitations would do well to imitate, the sparrows in a surprisingly short time got their house in order, and in a few days thereafter we found a couple of eggs in it.

These eggs we took away, for it would only be cruel to allow a
brood to be hatched at this season, only to starve and die before
they could possibly be strong enough of wing to shift for themselves.   And here, in connection with these same sparrow eggs, let
us record a fact that seems to have hitherto escaped the notice of
our oologists (egg-students), even the most lynx-eyed and observant
of them, and it is this : that in the case of such of our wild-birds
as breed more than once in a single season, the eggs of the second
laying, and of the third, if third laying there is—of all eggs, in
short, dropped after the *first* laying—are, as a rule, either entirely
free from spots, or, if they have the spots, they are so faint as to
be scarcely distinguishable.   In the case of the sparrow eggs, for
example, taken from the nest as just related, they were perfectly
spotless, pearl-white and clean as they could be.   Even under a
lens of considerable power they presented hardly a trace of spot or
colouring in any form.   And yet take an egg from a sparrow's
nest in early spring—from the *first* laying that is—and you will
invariably find it to be spotted or blotched with a perfect constellation, so to speak, round its larger end of greyish and dusky brown
dots and markings.   On due examination, we suspect it will be
found to be the same in the case of all our "spotted" egg layers ;
and to this fact, that has been so unaccountably overlooked hitherto,
is to be mainly attributed, we make no doubt, the many dissensions
and disagreements that so frequently have set our best, and otherwise good-natured, oologists by the ears.   In another particular,
too, the eggs of later laying differ from those of the first—in the
thickness, namely, of the shell; that of the later laying being
thinner and more fragile in the handling.   On account of their
fragility, indeed, it is extremely difficult to *blow* without damaging
an egg of this kind, taken from one of our smaller bird's nests
towards the close of the season.   All which, the faintness of colouring in or total absence of the spots, with the thinness, transparency,

and general fragility of the shell, is doubtless due to an impaired vitality, *quoad hoc*, consequent upon the prodigality of energy thrown into the loves and labours of rearing the first or spring brood.

On this occasion, too, a pair of blackbirds began a nest *de novo*, either despising the labours of mere repairing, or having no old nest, perhaps, to repair. The blackbirds, however, wiser than the sparrows, left off before a third—the lower flat, so to speak—of their building was finished; as if they had duly thought it all over again, and had wisely concluded that it was better to wait till spring, it being manifestly too late to finish a nest and attempt to rear a brood any more this season. We fully expected to see the redbreast, and wren perhaps, also attempt the rearing of an " Indian summer" brood; and had they tried, they might, perhaps, have succeeded, for both birds in such circumstances select cozy corners about open sheds and out-houses, where they are pretty safe from the assaults of the weather, and can always find suitable food in more or less abundance. So far as we could see, however, they never once thought of anything like love-making or nidification, contenting themselves with thoroughly enjoying the calm and sunshine while it lasted, as was abundantly, and, so far as we were concerned, very delightfully evidenced by the frequency of their loud and lightsome song.

A recent paragraph in the newspapers about Provost Robertson of Dingwall, whose daughter was Mr. Gladstone's mother, reminds us of an anecdote which was told us some years ago by the late Mrs. Morrison of Salachan, in Ardgour, an old lady whose reminiscences of the people of the Hebrides and mainland of Ross-shire, about the beginning of the present century, were extremely interesting. Provost Robertson of Dingwall—Mr. Gladstone's grandfather by the mother's side—on one occasion paid a visit to London, for the first, and, we believe, the only time in his life. His friends in the metropolis put him under the charge of a gentleman, a far-away cousin of his own, who undertook to show him all the wonders of the great city, and look after him generally. The worthy Provost was thoroughly Scotch, and dressed after a somewhat *outré* fashion, *à la* Dingwall of the period. Walking one day along one of the streets of London, a little in advance of his guide, the worshipful Provost's appearance and *tout ensemble* attracted the attention of some half-dozen street arab boys, who, always ready for a "lark," desired no better pastime for the present than to chaff and poke their fun at the Chief Magistrate of one of Scotland's most distinguished northern burghs. The Provost, indignant at the impudence and rudeness of the young rascals, at last turned round, and, shaking his silver-headed cane at the offending *gamins*, exclaimed, in tones loud enough to be heard by his guide, who was almost choked with laughter at the scene, "Ah, you young vagabonds; if I had you in Dingwall, wouldn't I make you pay for your *davayrshon!*" The term "diversion" was then used, both in English and Gaelic, all over the Highlands, as indeed it still is to some extent, in the sense of fun with a backbone of mischief to it; rough horse-play, in fact, accompanied by what is now-a-days commonly called *chaff*.

CHAPTER LV.

THIS is the 1st of May [1877], sacred in the ecclesiastical
calendar to St. Philip and St. James the Apostles. In ordinary
speech we may now call it summer, we suppose, and it is to be
hoped that it may prove summer indeed, not in name merely, or
astronomically, but veritably, that is, meteorologically as well;
such a summer as delighted our boyhood with its bright sun and
cloudless skies, or with such clouds only as served to modify
and temper a brilliancy and heat that might otherwise have
been excessive; the earth verdant and flower-bespangled under
foot and around, the very floods and trees of the forest, in the
grand hyperbole of Scripture, "clapping their hands for joy:"
the singing of birds the while, jubilant and joyous, in copse and
wild-wood, its fitting bass, the murmur of innumerable bees; while
the fluttering of splendidly coloured butterflies, as they danced
along in many a lawless zig-zag and merry-go-round, constantly
verified and bore witness to the beauty of the Roman poet's
famous line, which may be rendered—

" Lo ! fluttering past, *flowers* swimming in liquid air ! "

However the summer may turn out, of the spring at least but little
good—speaking of course meteorologically—can be said. It was,
quoad hoc, an imposture, and nothing else, and always reminding

us of Hood's wicked parody on the opening lines of Thomson's big
and bow-wow invocation to the season :—

> " ' Come, gentle Spring, ethereal mildness, come ! '
> O, Thomson, void of sense as well as reason ;
> Why in our ears such arrant nonsense drum ?
> There's no such season ! "

To housewives in rural districts we offer a " wrinkle " that may
be found of use at the present season, when most vegetable gardens
may be ransacked in vain for delicacies that shall be common
enough at a later period. While rambling through the district
a few days ago, we chanced to drop in upon a widow lady and
daughter, who occupy a nice little cottage. They were going to sit
down to an early dinner, and although we were not very hungry,
and could have fasted till a later hour, not merely without incon-
venience, but from choice, yet on their earnest invitation we
sat down along with them. The fare consisted of soup and a
boiled fowl, the latter fat, tender, and good as a fowl should always
be, and the soup was simply delicious. A green vegetable of some
kind floating thickly in it, gave it a relish and *gout* that was very
remarkable, and we asked what it was. " Nettle-tops, sir," was
the answer, and had we not been told, it is probable that we should
have guessed and blundered long ere we could hit upon it. But
not only can nettle-tops be thus utilised as an admirable condiment
in soup at this season, but they may also be served up asparagus-
wise, and, to our taste, are every whit as good. In this latter form
we have eaten them often, and, as Johnson said, after swallowing
several platefuls of Scotch broth, in reply to Boswell's observation—
" You never ate it before ? " " No, sir, but I don't care how soon I
eat it again." And so say we invariably when we have finished
a dish of nettle-top asparagus. After our nettle-top soup it occurred
to us that there might be more truth in Goldsmith's remark about
the French than he was perhaps aware of, for he meant it as

satire, that they can roast a sirloin if they only had beef, and prepare " ten different dishes from nettle-tops."

We had occasion to be up and about very early this morning, not, however, for the purpose of washing our face in May dew, although the morning was very beautiful, and the dew lay plentiful enough and pearl-like on grass and birchen bough, but in order to go on what some may think an even sillier errand, to wit, a birds'-nesting. For this sort of thing the earlier the hour the better at this season, and as we mounted the coppiced slopes which we proposed searching, the sun was beginning to gild the loftiest peaks of Glencoe with purple and amber and gold, and all the cocks in the hamlet, as if at a preconcerted signal, were cheerily greeting the rising god, or if their thoughts were more mundane and prosaic, as perhaps they were, you may interpret the crowing of each individual chanticleer as some one else did before you in some such lines as these—

> " The cock rose in the morning ;
> He called his favourite hen,
> With a cockle-do-doo, and a how-d'ye-do,
> And how-d'ye-do again."

In the economy of birds, the most important labours are those of nest-building and incubation ; and owing to the wintriness of the spring, we were quite prepared this morning to find matters in a decidedly backward state throughout the length and breadth of bird-land, wherever we might wander. We were not, however, prepared to find things in anything like the sad plight in which we actually found them ; for in no district of the remotest Highlands, we venture to say, are the agricultural labours proper to man at this season so backward as are their own proper labours this year amongst our native wild-birds. Usually at this date nine-tenths of our birds have already completed the labours of nidification, and with some species even incubation is far advanced, if not actually completed. The results of our morning's ornithological ramble may be very briefly stated. Of thirteen nests discovered, four only contained eggs, and even of these four only one had its proper complement, that of a song-thrush, namely, which contained five bonny blue eggs, spotted with black at the larger end, a number rarely, if ever, exceeded. In a merle or blackbird's nest there were only two eggs, instead of the usual complement of four or five. A chaffinch's nest had only one egg, whereas four is the proper number; while in the nest of a greenfinch, there was also only one egg instead of five, and that one, from certain signs known only to the initiated, we decided had only been laid yesterday, or even early this morning—perhaps shortly before our visit. Of the remaining nests, a few were fairly completed, and ready for their egg treasures at any time, but the greater number were only partially finished, and in their unfinished state had suffered so much from sleet and wind and rain, that we much doubt if their builders will have anything more to do with them, for it is a curious fact, that with such rare exceptions as only serve to accentuate and emphasise the rule, all birds prefer building a new nest from the very foundation to occupying an old one, or making the slightest repairs on one that has met with any serious injury. And this, too, you will please observe—a bird never improves in his architecture and never declines. He builds to-day neither better nor worse than did his ancestors a thousand or five thousand years ago. The sense or instinct that taught him to build of certain materials and of a certain form, long before Homer was born or Troy was besieged, is the same sense or instinct still. Nothing added; nothing subtracted. From all we have seen, we should say that the annual addition to bird life in our country will be considerably smaller than the average. Even first broods will be so late that second hatching is out of the question. Bird-song, however, will last longer into the summer, and begin again earlier in autumn than in ordinary seasons.

On a dull day last week we were routed out of our study by a visit from Professor Geikie, who, accompanied by some half-dozen others, was geologising in the districts of Appin and Lochaber. In such a place as this, it was impossible but that they should find much to interest them geologically and otherwise; and we were glad to hear them all say that they were much delighted with their wanderings. An occasional invasion of this kind, sometimes, too, when you least expect it, never fails to do one good. It makes you, *nolens volens*, shake yourself clear, as best you may, of the accumulated cobwebs of months, and you return to your ordinary work not a little invigorated and refreshed by having had an opportunity of comparing notes, rubbing shoulders, and even crossing blades—in all friendship of course—with foemen worthy of your steel.

A lady correspondent writes us from London as follows :—" I was much pleased with your reference to the old pipe tune. The music I have long known, but the origin and history of the piece was unknown to me, nor had I ever heard any of the words attached to it. I agree with you that all such scraps of information should be collected and preserved, adding so largely as they do to the interest with which we Highlanders must always regard our national melodies. I need not, of course, ask *you* if you know the very fine pipe tune ' Macrimmon's Lament,' *Cha till mi tuilleadh*. When I was a girl in the Hebrides—I am afraid to say how many years ago—I often heard the following story associated with this tune. In the island of Mull there is a large cave which in popular belief reaches right across the island from the east shore to the west. This cave, in the old times, was inhabited, so ran the tradition, by a colony of wolves and other wild animals. No man in conseqence had ever the courage to explore its dark labyrinthine windings. At a wedding party assembled in a hamlet in the neighbourhood of the cave, its vastness and many dangers became the subject of conversation. All agreed that no human being could possibly pass through it and live. The piper of the district was a very brave man as well as an admirable piper, and in an evil hour for himself, as it proved, he offered for some slight wager to traverse the cave from side to side of the island, with a pine torch stuck in the front of his bonnet to give him light, and playing the pipes all the time. The piper thereupon entered the cave, playing a lively march, while most of the wedding guests followed above, led in the proper course by the music, which could be heard faintly from below. More than half the cave was traversed, when suddenly the music changed from a brisk march to a doleful lament. This lament, duly interpreted, told the people above that things were becoming uncomfortable with the piper; first, that the pine torch was almost burnt out, and again that his breath was failing him, while the boldest of the wolves slowly retired before him, only kept at bay by the flickering of the torch and the sound of the pipes, but ready to spring upon and devour him the instant the torch should be extinguished and the music of the pipes should cease. It was then that the doomed piper played *Cha till mi tuilleadh'* so mournfully—'I will return no more!' And this too—

> ' Mo dhìth, mo dhìth, gun trì lamhan ;
> Dà làmh 's a phìob, a làmh 's a chlaidheamh.'
> (' Alas, and my great want, that I have not *three* hands,
> Two for (playing) the pipes, and one to wield my sword.')

If he had only a third hand he thought he could manage to kill the wolves that were every instant becoming bolder, as if they knew he must fall into their jaws at last. The last notes caught by the people above were known to mean—

> ' 'Si ghall' uaine 'shàraich mi,
> 'Si ghalla' uaine 'shàraich mi !'
> (' It is the green bitch wolf that most harasses me !')

And then·the music ceased, and they knew that the poor piper had been torn to pieces by the wolves. Such is something like the story I used to hear in connection with the big cave in Mull and the well-known lament, more than fifty years ago."

The cave referred to is on the estate of Lochbuy. So far as it has been explored, its length is over 500 feet, with a breadth of some 25 feet, and a height of 40. It is proper to say that the people of Skye claim the whole story as belonging to their island. The piper was a Macrimmon; the cave is pointed out near Dunvegan, and the story of the wolves and the piper's sad fate is just as likely to be true of the one island as of the other. Our own opinion is, that so far as there is any truth in the story, it must be located in Skye rather than in Mull, although our friends in the latter island will perhaps be angry with us for saying so.

"It never rains but it pours," and nowhere is the familiar adage in its utmost literalness truer than in Lochaber. During a long protracted drought of nearly a couple of months' duration [June 1877], we were constantly calling for rain; and no wonder, for the earth was hard and hide-bound as an Egyptian mummy; sheep and cattle finding little more to gather on the parched uplands than if they were nibbling at the bulge of an ironclad laid up in ordinary. For full five and twenty years—so far back, *eheu* and alas! do our own individual meteorological records extend—we have had no May month so persistently ungenial and cold; nor, when one comes to think of it, is it much matter of surprise, for we have just been reading that in the North Atlantic, within a few hundred leagues of the British shores, and up to the very margin of the Gulf Stream, a ship recently arrived in port had to fight her way through quite a continent of drift ice, with occasional icebergs "from two to three hundred feet in height." With such grim, hyperborean neighbours on the one hand, and a keen-edged east wind on the other, it was impossible that it should be otherwise than cold and uncomfortable all round. On the 26th, however, came the long-looked-for change, the wind came slowly round to S.S.W., rain began to fall, and the effect was magical. There was instantly a blanket-like kindliness and a balminess in the air that was delicious. The birds, that a little before could only chirp dolorously, burst out into loud and jubilant song, the cattle lowed in their pastures, wild-flowers seemed to laugh with quiet delight, and the very boom of the big waves as they broke on the beach had a pleasant music in it. It has continued to rain more or less ever since, so that with regard to mere personal comfort one is ready to cry "Hold, enough!" but so far as the interests of agriculture and pasturage are concerned, not a drop too much has fallen. The fact is that, frequent as is the complaint about what people are pleased to speak about as our superabundant rainfall, we require it all. We question if a diminution of our annual rainfall by a third, say, or even by a fifth of its amount, would, from a practical and utilitarian point of view, be any improvement, but the reverse. A shrewd south country shepherd, with whom we had a long crack on Saturday, was right when, speaking of the rain, he remarked that " it would be a puir country for sheep at ony rate, if we had much less o't frae year's end to year's end." How ill the drought of April and May agreed with us here may be understood from the fact that there was an unusual amount of sickness amongst the people ; while the leanness of sheep and kine bore sad and emphatic witness to the scarcity of succulent pasture, and the general backwardness of the season is to this moment noticeable from our window as we write, for neither the lilac nor the hawthorn is yet in bloom, nor are potatoes, even the earliest planted, any more than just becoming discernible in regular drills. We should say that vegetation is generally quite a fortnight later than usual, and only an exceptionally fine summer and early autumn can bring about a fairly seasonable harvest-time. *Dum spiro, spero*, however, is a good maxim, and we shall hope that, even if harvest is late, the ingathering may be all the more pleasant and abundant. The drought, however, and persistent east wind, it is but fair to confess, were rather favourable than otherwise to the fruit trees of all kinds in garden and orchard. Bud and blossom were, to use a military term, held in check until after the middle of May, thus escaping the night frosts usual in the early part of the month. All sorts of fruit trees and berry bushes are consequently only now in full bloom, and a large fruit crop may very confidently be looked for, though it may be a little later than usual in attaining to perfect ripeness. Did you ever, by the way, good reader, look at an apple tree in full blossom on a calm, dewy night by candle-light? Recently we had occasion to go into our garden towards midnight in search of a bird that had escaped from his cage during the day. Coming under a large apple tree in full bloom, we held up the open lantern in our hand and peered a-tip-toe among the branches in hopes of getting a sight of the foolish runaway. Him we did not find then, but the apple tree, bending under its weight of blossoms "dew besprent," was the most beautiful thing we ever saw, and we called everybody about the place to come and look at it, and they all agreed that the sight was as beautiful as it was new to them. If you have an opportunity try it for yourself, and you will thank us all your life long for calling your attention to a thing of beauty, which the poet is not wrong in assuring you "is a joy for ever."

We didn't get our bird in the apple tree, but we were in great good luck notwithstanding, for who chanced to come the way next morning but Mackenzie the bird-catcher, who soon discovered the runaway's whereabouts in a neighbouring copse, and whistled him back to hand as easily as a shepherd whistles back his truant collie. It is a goldfinch, a magnificent singer, whom we have long had as a cage-bird ; and being unaccustomed to liberty, it was all the easier enticing him back to his cage, although we much doubt if any man in the kingdom could have done it so immediately and with such unfaltering confidence in his own power to do it as Mackenzie, who knows wild-bird music better than any one else we ever met, and can imitate it in its every twist and turn, chirp or cheep or chant, so deftly and unmistakeably as to deceive the birds themselves, each after his kind, the severest test to which such an accomplishment could be put. If there be any truth in the old doctrine of metempsychosis, Mackenzie, having shaken off the "mortal coil" of his present form, is pretty sure to reappear as a rock-linnet, redpole, or goldfinch. Like an honest man, who knows and acknowledges the value and force of an Act of Parliament, he hadn't on this occasion much to show us, but what he had was in part at least interesting, and captured in early spring. One curiosity was a linnet with one wing pure white, which he would insist upon was a different species from the ordinary linnet, because he had caught so many with a sinister or dexter, one or other, wing white or variegated. We fought a hard battle in trying to convince him that it was a mere accidental bit of colouring, due probably to some hurt received in its downy days, or at all events before its first moult; and made it no more a different species than an accidental hurt, which causes a man to go lame, makes him anything else than a specimen of *homo sapiens* all the same. Arguing, however, with men of Mackenzie's stamp is rather uphill work. He listened, to be sure, with a politeness and attention which seems to us to be inseparable from the character of the true practical naturalist, and seemed to give acquiescence in all we asserted, but we shouldn't wonder a bit if he remained of his own opinion still. A rather rare bird was a specimen, in excellent condition and feather, of the grey crow, at one time quite a common bird along the shores of the West Highlands, but owing to the incessant war waged against them by shepherds, gamekeepers, and vermin-trappers, now become so rare that we stopped our pony to have a good look at a pair that we saw the other day near Strontian, at the head of Loch Sunart. If you want a specimen of any British bird, just commission Mackenzie to get it for you. He will only bring you a specimen that is perfect of its kind, and if you only give him time he will succeed in getting it, even if he walked a thousand miles in the pursuit.

With reference to our explanation of the term *study* applied to a small plateau, a well-known spot at the top of Glencoe, a correspondent writes as follows:—" You do not seem to be aware that *study* is the word in common use in Lowland Scotland for an anvil as well as amongst the unlisping Celts. I wonder you forgot Burns' well-known lines—

> ' Nae mercy, then, for airn or steel ;
> The brawnie, bainie, ploughman chiel,
> Brings hard owrehip, wi' sturdy wheel
> The strong forehammer,
> *Till block and studdie ring and reel*
> Wi' dinsome clamour.' "

We are much obliged to our friendly correspondent. The quotation proves that the Lowland Scotch as well as the Highlanders have a difficulty with the lisping sound of *th*, preferring the simpler and more natural sound of *d*.

A gentleman from Badenoch greatly amused us the other day by his account of a certain superstitious observance on the part of a " wise woman " in his neighbourhood. The gentleman's wife was sitting with her baby, only a few weeks old, in her lap. It was of course a marvel of a baby ; for bigness and beauty the finest baby, like *all* babies, that ever was seen, and of which its parents were naturally and very excusably as proud as proud could be. The " wise woman " of the place had called to see the child, and congratulated the parents on their good luck. The crone got a chair opposite to that occupied by the happy mother, while the father looked on and smiled with becoming dignity and pride. As the old woman was looking at the child, it chanced to yawn, bored probably by the amount of attention paid to it, and getting sleepy. As it yawned, the old woman got up from the chair, and walking over to the " infant phenomenon," coolly and deliberately spat in its face ! The mother was horrified ; the father in a rage asked what the deuce she meant by spitting in *his* son's face ? The old lady quietly answered that the yawn was owing to an evil influence at that moment at work with the child, and her spitting in its face was the readiest and most effectual way of saving it from one or more of the mischievous tricks which ill-natured fairies are so fond of playing off on babies that are " beautiful exceedingly," and more especially when they are overmuch petted and bepraised by their parents and friends. The " wise woman" was at once liberally supplied with the refreshments usual on such occasions, and as soon as possible dismissed, care being taken the while not to offend her, which might have been a serious matter for baby and all concerned. It is not a little curious that although in all countries to spit at one is expressive of the utmost detestation and contempt, yet in the superstitions of the Lowlands of Scotland, as well as in the High-lands, to spit on a person or thing, under certain conditions and circumstances, is supposed to be counteractive of evil influences, and therefore a highly commendable act. We have seen a woman spit on the nets in a boat as it left the shore, to ensure a successful fishing; and when hand-line fishing, a man who has had little luck and is getting impatient, as he baits his hook afresh, spits on it before dropping it again into the sea, in the belief that good luck attends the act. An old woman who has just bound up a bruised or broken limb, whether of man or beast, will sometimes finish the operation by spitting on the bandage. In the superstitions of most countries, such involuntary and apparently causeless acts as sneezing and yawning are attributed to supernatural agencies, and spitting at the sneezer or yawner is still sometimes practised as a counter-charm by the oldest and most learned professors of such lore, an older superstition probably than the more common practice of invoking the Divine blessing on the subjects in such cases. Questionable, therefore, and rude as at first sight seemed the act, we assured our Badenoch friend that the " wise woman," in acting as she did, meant his bairn no evil or disrespect at all, but the very contrary.

CHAPTER LVII.

THE reader may remember that we concluded our last with a hopeful and jubilant note, believing that really fine weather—a long track of it, perhaps—was just at hand. We much regret having to say that our meteorological vaticinations proved utterly incorrect. It still rains [July 1877], not constantly, indeed, but with sufficient persistence to make everybody miserable, and to reduce our hopes of a good harvest almost to zero. Yesterday, for example, we had occasion to cross the Loch in our boat. It was a nice bright day enough at starting, with a fresh breeze from N.W., which carried us along at racing pace. All of a sudden the heavens became black and threatening; a terrible squall almost capsized us ere we had time to sing out to our companion to let go "everything by the run." He did, fortunately, let go just in time, and grasping an oar ourselves, and calling on him to take another, we had her head turned to the wind and waves as quietly but as quickly as possible. Thus we held her, just like a horse by the reins, while the squall lasted, and cunningly took advantage of its drift to get to the Appin shore. We managed to reach it, but in very sorry plight, as you shall hear. With the squall had come rain, literally the *heaviest* we ever saw, which drenched us to the skin; every drop big enough to fill as it fell the largest of thimbles, and driven by the squall, remember, it fell with the force of a spent bullet. As "drookit" and drenched we landed, and crawled with all the miserable, and woebegone, and shambling gait of the really and thoroughtly through-and-through wet, you would have laughed in the teeth of all the rain had you only met us; and we much doubt if any one who did not know us would just then have been disposed to appraise ourselves and our whole belongings at the value of a much bigger coin of the realm than a shabby florin. And this is just the sort of weather it continues to be. You cannot depend upon it for an hour. It is sunshine and blue above just for five minutes; it is all of a sudden gloomy and black as Erebus, and raining so multitudinously that you are fain to draw the skirts of your coat anyhow over your head and run for the nearest shelter. When we are to have better weather let the meteorologists, who ought to know, say.

There is an old and frequent proverb, though rarely heard now-a-days, to the effect that "there goes reason to the roasting of eggs," the meaning of which, as we apprehend it, is that the smallest culinary operation is of importance, and should be gone about with judgment and care. If the proverb, however, in its actual words, as a mere popular saw, is very much forgotten, it is a good sign of our time that its spirit at least is in this our own day claiming no little attention, as the establishment of "cookery classes," and the praiseworthy attempts to disseminate culinary lore amongst the people, abundantly testify. It has been said that the man who makes two blades of grass to grow where only one blade grew before is a benefactor to his species, and equally so, would we venture to assert, is he a benefactor to the human race who shows how any single article of food, usually cooked and served in an unsatisfactory and tasteless fashion, may, with no extra expense and little extra trouble, be made palatable and savoury. The other day, landing from our boat, we went into a cottar's house close by the sea, in a neighbouring district, just as the gudewife was preparing the family dinner. A pot of new potatoes was boiling on the fire, and as she knew that it would take us still some time to get home, she very good-naturedly invited us to wait a little and take a share with herself and her husband of the dinner about to be served, a bit of hospitality as frankly accepted as it was kindly offered. Looking now and again into the boiling potato pot, and *listening* with inclined ear to the sound, actually *musical* in such a case, of its boil and bubbling, she was ready at the proper instant to snatch it off the fire, and, carrying it to a corner of the kitchen, she poured off the water, and immediately re-hung it over the fire again, shortening the chain by which it was suspended by a link or two, that the fire might not, now that it was waterless, have too much effect upon it. She then got some half-dozen fresh herrings, caught early that morning—herrings large, and beautiful, and silvery scaled as a salmon—and drying them nicely with a cloth, she placed them flat-wise side by side on the top of the potatoes in the pot, the lid of which she was careful to make fit tightly by means of a coarse kitchen towel, which served at once to cover the contents, and to cause the lid to fit so tightly that all the steam was effectually retained. For the time being, in short, the pot by this ready expedient may be said to have been hermetically sealed. During a quarter of an hour, perhaps, and while the gentleman and ourselves carried on a lively conversation, the wife kept an attentive eye on the pot, never once lifting the lid, however, but from time to time raising or lowering a link of the chain as in her judgment was necessary. All being ready at last, she took the pot off the fire, and set it on a low stool in the middle of the floor. She then lifted the lid and the cloth, and the room was instantly filled with a savoury steam that made one's mouth water merely to inhale it. Occupying each a low chair, we were invited to fall to, to eat without knife, or fork, or trencher, just with our fingers out of the pot as it stood. It was a little startling, but only for a moment. After a word of grace we dipped our hand into the pot, and took out a potato hot and mealy, and with the other we took a nip out of the silvery flank of the herring nearest us. It was a mouthful for a king, sir! We have in our day a thousand times dined well and heartily both at home and abroad, but we greatly question if we ever enjoyed a dinner half so much as *that*. The savouriness of that potato and herring feast will haunt us till our dying day. What struck us was simply this: A new potato and fresh herring as usually served is something terribly insipid; as we got it that day it was a meal for an emperor. We actually felt inclined to lick our fingers after every mouthful, than which surely there could be no higher praise of any food whatever. Let such of our readers as have the opportunity just try a potato and herring cooked in the manner stated, eating it digitally, with their own proper fingers, and they will thank us, if they are honest, for bringing so savoury and delicious a dish to their knowledge.

One of the finest glens in all the West Highlands is Glen Nevis, which, opening out in the direction of the old Castle of Inverlochy, extends eastwards and inland, the valley gradually narrowing into glen and gorge as you proceed, for nine or ten miles, presenting at every turn and standpoint throughout its many windings a succession of the most striking and beautiful pictures imaginable, so striking and startling at times, and *new* at least in some of their details, that a genuine lover of mountain scenery wishes that he could devote an entire day to every separate mile of its extent, rather than have to hurry through it all in something like half a dozen hours, which is the way the thing is usually done. It is like being dragged, as happened to us once, by a nervous and impatient lady friend of ours, at a sort of half trot through a picture gallery, where, if you had your own way, you would gladly lounge and linger till the custodier of the place, perhaps, came respectfully to hint that the afternoon was far advanced, and that shutting-up time was at hand. With the entrance to Glen Nevis, as far as the mansion-house, we had long been familiar, and once at least we had a bird's-eye glance into the glen proper itself, from the summit of *Dundearduil*, which we had approached from the south in order to examine its curious and still inexplicable vitrifications. It was not, however, till Friday last, that we had an opportunity of thoroughly exploring the glen through all its windings, and coming with little difficulty to the conclusion already expressed, that of all our West Highland glens, it is, perhaps, the most beautiful and (Glencoe always apart) the most deserving of a thorough and leisurely examination. We were fortunate in having hit upon a highly favourable day—not too bright, for glaring sunshine and unclouded brightness amongst mountain scenery is a great mistake—and no less fortunate in our companions, each one of them blessed with eyes that, open, could really see, and hearts that, duly appealed to, could truly feel ; who knew full well what they had come to do, and from first to last did it admirably. Rarely, we should say, has the noble glen exposed its stern grandeur and innumerable beauties under favourable skies, to the glad and earnest gaze of more intelligently appreciative spectators ; and more rarely still, perhaps, have the splendid falls of the Nevis borne burden to peals of honester or merrier laughter than we indulged in as over the well-plenished luncheon basket we fortified ourselves for the ascent of the upper gorges,—a somewhat "stiff" climb, but neither really difficult nor dangerous. When we say that at Glen Nevis House our party was joined by Mr. Macpherson —*fear a ghlinne e féin*, the goodman of the glen *himself*, as the Highlanders say—who kindly accompanied us throughout, and to whom every foot of the glen was as familiar as the floor of his own dining-room, many of our readers will understand how really pleasant and enjoyable, *cæteris paribus*, must have been our upland wanderings on that delightful day.

We have no intention of entering on anything like a minute or

photographic description of Glen Nevis, for which, indeed, half-a-
dozen Nether Lochaber columns would hardly suffice ; we can only
hurriedly glance at what most instantly and indelibly struck us in
the day's excursion.　First of all, we were all struck by the exceeding pellucidity and crystal clearness of the waters of the Nevis.
Nowhere else did we ever see a mountain stream so beautifully transparent.　Standing on the brink of any selected pool,
many feet in depth, you distinguished the smallest pea-sized pebble,
its veins, scratches, and striations, as distinctly as if you had it on
the palm of your hand, under a lens, and within less than a
foot focus of your eyeball !　And all this remarkable pellucidity,
observe, not in one particular pool, or in any one particular stretch
of the river, but throughout all its beautiful windings.　Another
remarkable feature of the glen is the manner in which its natural
birch woods grow.　They occupy a pretty broad belt almost half-
way up the mountains, leaving a still broader belt between themselves and the river banks comparatively bare and treeless.　In all
the other Highland glens with which we have any acquaintance,
whatever of wood there is always begins, as seems most natural,
at the river banks, where it is thickest and most luxuriant, growing
away and upwards on either side to a greater or less altitude,
according to the nature of the soil and the shelter to be had from
the prevailing winds.　And speaking of winds, this is the place to
observe that of all our glens Glen Nevis is perhaps the stormiest,
the wind in a gale not blowing steadily, but in fitful gusts and
whirlwind-wise, striking in from the corries right and left, and
meeting in the centre with a force and fury unimaginable by
non-residenters.　How do you know, the reader may ask, for it was
calm and quiet enough during *your* visit on Friday ?　True, and
yet we failed not to notice a very striking proof of the storminess
at times of Glen Nevis notwithstanding.　As you pass the forester's
house at Auchreoch, lift up your eyes, and please observe how

carefully, how thoroughly, closely, compactly, and painstakingly it is thatched; and observe further and over all a network of wire as thick and strong as that used in our overland telegraphy, and to the end of each wire as it almost reaches the ground in front and at the back of the house, please notice suspended a large stone, water-worn boulders from the river below, each of a hundredweight or more, and you will not fail, we think, to understand how we so confidently decided that Glen Nevis at times must be an exceedingly stormy place. If you assert that other Highland glens may be quite as stormy in the season of storms, we shall not contradict you; what we do say is this, that never did a house-roof speak to us so eloquently of furious and frequent storm and whirl-wind as did the roof of that house at Auchreoch, and a very good house it is, and a very pretty place to the bargain. A little beyond Auchreoch, and to the left of the path, there is a bit of wild and rugged rock scenery well worth attention. Here and there, over the face of what seems the hard impenetrable rock, many trees grow and flourish as if through the very heart of the granite. The explanation of course is, that the rock which seems so homogeneous and solid at a distance is in reality fissured and fractured in all directions, and that in these fissures the trees find soil and food enough to sustain a wonderfully luxuriant growth and opulence of foliage for such a situation. About a mile further up the glen, we separated from our companions for a while, we having determined to cross the Nevis at this point in order to visit *Uaimh Shomhairle,* or Samuel's Cave, the entrance to which was pointed out to us by Mr. Macpherson in the face of the opposite steep. To get across the river we had to strip until in a state of almost *puris naturalibus,* and even then it was somewhat dangerous, a single false step might have been attended by very serious conse-quences. With a little circumspection and care, however, we got safely over, and half-dressed and barefooted we climbed the rock like a chamois, and in less than ten minutes we were standing at the mouth of the celebrated cave. Samuel's Cave is in fact *two* caves, the outer and smaller one, with a broad portal that admits abundant light and air, forming a sort of vestibule or antechamber to the inner cave. Provided with one or two old newspapers and some wax vestas, we improvised a couple of rude torches which we carried with us as we crept through a narrow opening by which alone access is obtained into the inner *antrum*. Lighting one of these torches, which answered our purpose quite well enough, we explored the cave at leisure, closely scrutinising the walls and roof as high as we could reach, in the hope of perhaps finding some scratch or sculptures, however rude, to prove that the place had been inhabited in the times of the "cave-men." Nothing of the kind, however, was discernible. The cave in its every part is exceedingly damp and cold, with green, slimy roof and walls, where not even the hardiest wild beast of mountain or forest would think of taking up its abode, far less any human being with the faintest notion of the value of warmth and comfort. There are scores of lesser caves and fissures in the rocks around where one would elect to live by reason of their dryness, in preference to the big and pretentious Samuel's Cave, which, as a mere cave, is perhaps interesting enough, and not unworthy of a visit; otherwise it is a "sell," in exploring which no one can spend more than the shortest five minutes to any good purpose. In the times of civil wars and clan feuds it is conceivable that one or more outlawed and "broken" men might find the outer cave a secure and not altogether unpleasant place of shelter to pass a night in where no better might be. As a place also to hide one's more valuable goods and chattels in an emergency, the cave may at times have had its value and use. It never, depend upon it, was *inhabited* for any length of time by any human being. A week of it would kill the stoutest, robustest savage that ever trod the

Caledonian wilds. An additional proof, if additional proofs are wanting, that Samuel's Cave can never have been "inhabited" in any proper sense of that term, or even much frequented for any purpose whatever, is to be found in the fact that there is not a vestige of a path either from the river bank below or from the hill above leading towards it. Had it at any time been much in use for any purpose, there must have been a path leading to it either from above or from below, and some traces at least, however faint, of such a path, must still exist. We searched and searched, above and below, and round and round, and no trace or vestige at all of such a path could we find. Go, good reader, and see the cave by all means when you have the opportunity; it is a fair enough cave as caves go; but take our word for it that the attempt to invest the vast dark, damp, slimy *antrum* with any archæological interest is the greatest delusion in the world.

CHAPTER LVIII.

Showers in Harvest Time— Magnificent Sunset— Night sometimes seeming not to descend but to *ascend*—Death of M. Leverrier—The Discovery of Neptune—Pigeon cooing at Midnight—The Owl at Noon—Cage-Birds singing at Night.

THE weather continues wonderfully fine for the season [October 1877], and with the exception of the potato-lifting, all our harvest labours are at length concluded. The ingathering has upon the whole been highly satisfactory, far more so than any one could have had the courage to predict up to the very advent of this our autumnal summer, which has already lasted just thirty days, uninterruptedly sunny and dry, without any more serious break than a mere passing shower, which invariably did more good than harm. More good? the reader exclaims interrogatively, how can a shower do good, how can it be otherwise than harmful in harvest time? Patience, courteous reader, and we shall explain. It is a case of something of this kind. You are driving along the road; the horse in the shafts before you is upon the whole a steady-going and willing animal enough, but you have let him have it just his own way for the last half hour, and dreaming, perhaps, of fresh fields and pastures green, he has for the moment forgotten your existence, and begins to lag. His usual pace of a good eight miles an hour is now hardly over five, and what in such a case shall you do? You drop the lash gently across his flank, as light and gently as falls the angler's cast on the waveless pool; you are too much of a Christian and a gentleman—the terms are or ought to be synonymous—to do otherwise until it is absolutely necessary. Your horse forgets his dream; becomes instantly alive to the work

before him ; gathers himself together, and with a responsive toss
of his head and a lively play of ears, goes along at rather more
than his average speed until the next stage is reached ; knowing
full well that the hand that laid on that serpent-like lash so
tenderly, can lay it on in very different fashion, hot and heavy
enough when occasion calls. Or, dropping metaphor, let us state
the matter plainly, thus :—Here in Lochaber, and we suppose it is
just the same over all the Highlands, when really fine weather
comes, we are for the first few days up and doing, busy enough.
But as one fine day succeeds another, we are very ready to fall into
the error that after all it is best to take things leisurely. Where's
the need, we ask ourselves, for so much hurry and bustle ? The
fine weather has lasted a week ; it may last a month, is indeed
likely so to last ; it is no more like rain to-day than it was
yesterday ; and thus we lapse, often unconsciously, perhaps, into
a spirit of dilatoriness and procrastination, out of which only a
lowering sky, and a shower that for all we know may become a
flood, can fairly rouse us. You slept long, for instance, this
morning ; you dawdled over your porridge and milk at breakfast
time, and it is now noonday. But see ! the heavens yonder in the
north-west are suddenly overcast ; an ominous gloom creeps over
the Outer Hebrides ; a few drops of rain have already fallen, one
on the back of your left hand, on which placing the index finger of
your right, you can find that it is wet, that it is rain ; a second on
your cheek with a soft, tepid thud ; and a third right into your open,
uplifted eye, and you straightway start into activity and life. All
hands on deck ! is the cry. You rush into the field amongst the
stooks ; you bustle about cheerily, and calling all hands into your
service, for idlers are now out of place, you cart and carry away as
fast as you can into your barn or stack-yard, and by sunset, so
expeditiously have you worked, that the field from head-rig to
head-rig is but bare and stookless stubble. It was after all but a

passing shower; the gloom has given place to cloudless blue; you have been cheated, so to speak. But what matters it? Your crop is safely stacked or housed, and were it not for the passing shower and temporary mid-day gloom, your stooks were still afield, running a risk there was no reason they should run; and so, good reader, you will understand how a slight shower in the season of ingathering may not always be an evil, but a very good thing indeed; and only a few such passing, labour-inciting showers have we known here for a whole month, and *that* is much to say when the month is to be counted from mid-September to mid-October.

And, O gentle reader, we only wish you were with us here to see for yourself, *propriis oculis*, for no pen can describe it, one or more of the many magnificent sunsets we have had in the course of this same bypast month of fine weather. The sunsets of the equinoctial seasons, both vernal and autumnal, are almost always beautiful, more particularly those of the autumnal equinox; but never before, we think, have we seen them so startling, gloriously beautiful, so gorgeously magnificent, as on several occasions lately. A few evenings ago, as we were busy in our study, a young lady burst in upon us in a state of great excitement, begging us to throw aside our pen for a little, and come out to see the exceeding glory of the setting sun. We readily complied of course, and taking the young lady by the hand we made a race of it till we reached our "coigne of vantage," a grassy green knoll, a favourite standpoint when any celestial phenomenon of importance to the W. or S.W. of us is to be observed. The scene, in truth, was indescribably beautiful, and we stood in speechless admiration, not unmingled with awe, in sight of the most glorious sunset our eyes ever beheld. Before us lay the whole expanse of the Linnhe Loch, shimmering as if gently aboil in a flood of pale golden light. Beyond, rose what seemed the one vast unbroken range of the mountains of Ardgour, Kingerloch, and Morven, bathed in a rich dark purple

hue, that for the moment so thoroughly obliterated every trace of
their native ruggedness, that our companion prettily observed,
"Haven't you the idea, sir, as I have, that if one were only near
enough these beautiful mountains to pat them lovingly with the
hand, they would feel to the touch soft and warm as a roll of
velvet?" a thought, unconsciously perhaps, tinged with poetry,
though the woman pure and simple comes out very unmistakeably
in the reference to the "roll of velvet." In the far background,
thirty miles away, rose the glory and pride of Mull (Blackie's
favourite island of all the Hebrides), the huge mountains of Benmore
and Ben-na-Bairnich, their base and middle zones ink-black, their
shoulders dark orange, here and there curiously streaked with
threads of pearly light, their summits and sloping ridges fringed
with living fire. Above, the whole western heavens was full of
vast continents, peninsulas, isthmuses, and islands of cloud, all afire
at their edges, with firths, ferries, and Mediterraneans of liquid
gold between. As the full-orbed sun, fiery and red, slowly sank to
the horizon, the clouds were rent asunder as if by the very
excellency of the glory that beat upon them; some of them
assuming fantastic shapes, in which a lively imagination had no
difficulty in tracing striking resemblances to the hugest animals of
our own and past ages, a monster saurian in sharply defined
silhouette, being so marvellously outlined that our fair companion
sketched it on the spot, as a memento of a sunset that neither of us
is likely ever to forget. As the sun's lower limb seemed just to
touch and rest an instant on the highest peak of the Kingerloch
range, a large mass of cloud immediately above him rapidly assumed
a columnar shape, perpendicular to the plane of the horizon, and, as
the splendid orb dipped and disappeared, this huge "pillar of
cloud" became a perfect Ionic column, sharply outlined, and
admirably correct in all its proportions from base to entablature,
and all aglow with living fire; shaft and pediment with richest

crimson ; frieze and architrave and cornice with the glow of molten mettle at "white heat" as it issues from a blast furnace. There was, truth to say, something terrible about the scene, a wild and weird combination of the sublime and beautiful such as Edmund Burke never beheld even in his dreams. It was impossible, in the presence of the "terrible majesty" of that glory, to avoid thinking of the awfulness that must appertain to a scene of which all of us shall one day be spectators, when the "elements shall melt with fervent heat," and the "earth also, and the works that are therein," shall be consumed with fire. The succeeding afterglow of that same evening was singularly beautiful. The mountains of Appin and Glencoe were for a time bathed from their summits to their shoulders in the richest purple and gold, making them look so soft and warm, that for the moment their actual ruggedness was utterly forgotten, and one felt towards them a far stronger and tenderer sentiment than mere admiration. And very curiously, as we gazed, did the night immediately succeed the afterglow, for of twilight there was none—there rarely is indeed in autumn, as the old Highlanders were too observant not to notice, for what saith the old and well-known rhyme?—

> " Mar chlorich a ruith le gleann,
> Tha feasgar fann, fogharaidh."

The meaning of which is, that no longer lasts the autumnal twilight than it takes a stone to roll adown the mountain steep into the glen below. We generally speak of the night's *descending ;* we say the *falling* night, the darkness *fell*, &c., as if the darkness came down from above, and sometimes, doubtless, it does seem so to fall —to descend like a curtain. On this occasion, however, and frequently, we have noticed, in the autumnal season, the night did not seem so much to descend as to *ascend*, like an exhalation from out the entrails of the earth ; the blackness of gorge and corrie and glen slowly creeping upwards, banishing the gold and purple

as it ascended, just as you have seen the earth's shadow in an
eclipse of the moon obliterate the silvery radiance of the lunar
disc—finally reaching ridge and summit and loftiest peak, and lo,
it was night, the ruddy orb of Mars over the now ink-black top
of Buachaill-Etive putting the fact beyond all question ; and, while
our fair companion went for a stroll along the beach, gaily singing
a merry roundelay as became her innocence and her years, we
retired in a mood of mind that, while it was pleasant upon the
whole, had yet a tinge of sadness about it, to our study and
our books.

France has recently lost one of her greatest men by the death of
M. Leverrier, her distinguished astronomer, the most distinguished
astronomer, it is not too much to say, of the present century.
Many, indeed, achieved greater triumphs with the telescope, for
with the telescope Leverrier did comparatively little ; it was as a
mathematical astronomer that he was unrivalled. He came first
prominently into notice while still a young man, with his cometary
investigations, and his researches into the motions of the planet
Mercury, constructing tables by which transits of the latter can be
predicted with such absolute correctness that the mean error never
exceeds *sixteen seconds* of time. But it is with the discovery of
the planet *Neptune* that Leverrier's name is imperishably associated. The case briefly stated was this :—It was found, after a
time, that the planet *Uranus*, discovered by Sir William Herschel,
did not actually follow the orbit which theory had assigned to it.
It had a mysterious trick of leaving the computed track, and
describing a greater orbit, if the law of gravitation was to hold
good, than the tables founded on that law warranted. Astronomers were puzzled to account for the vagaries of an orbit that,
according to their theory, ought to be well-behaved, and staid and
steady-going as any other member of the solar system. What
could the perturbations of Uranus mean? was the question asked ;

and at the suggestion of his friend the distinguished Arago, Leverrier undertook to answer it, and in due time *did* answer it in such wise as filled the world with astonishment and admiration. Resolutely grasping with his task, Leverrier laboured long and laboured hard to resolve the mystery, and as a first step with this result, that the problem was utterly unresolvable on any other conceivable theory or conjecture than that another planet, albeit unknown to astronomers, and hitherto as unsuspected as it was unseen, existed *exterior* to Uranus, and that it was to the attraction or disturbing influence of this hitherto undreamt-of orb that the perturbations and mysterious vagaries of Uranus could alone be ascribed. A memoir stating the conclusion arrived at, and all the calculations leading towards it, was read before the Royal Academy of Sciences in June 1846, and the young and daring astronomer straightway resumed his labours, of which the aim was now to determine the elements of the orbit of the unknown planet, in the existence of which he now believed as firmly as in that of the visibly perturbed orb Uranus itself. The astronomical world shook its head dubiously, and waited. Did such a planet really exist, and if it did, could this daring Frenchman find it? M. Leverrier meantime laboured on, and finally mastering every difficulty, he gave the computed plans of orbit, the mass and natural position of his constructed world, if in truth, that is, such a world existed. This was in a second memoir to the Academy of Sciences on the last day of August 1846. Towards the end of the following month (September 1846), Leverrier wrote to M. Galle, of Berlin, requesting him to level the powerful telescope under his charge at a particular point of the heavens, and there, in effect, said the wonderful Frenchman, you will find the cause of the perturbations of Uranus, a new and distant world, hitherto undreamt of and unseen by mortal eye, but existing all the same. M. Galle, on the first favourable opportunity, directed his telescope as requested, and there, within less than a *single degree* of its computed place, and flinging back its light from the enormous distance of more than three *billions* of miles, was the planet of Leverrier's analysis, with a diameter, magnitude, and orbit all as calculated and predicted. It was a glorious triumph, the most wonderful achievement in the annals of a science where all is wonder.

Publicly and privately has this query been put to us—Is it unusual to hear a pigeon cooing at midnight, and the owl hooting in bright noonday? We answer very unhesitatingly that it *is* unusual, so unusual in the case of the owl at least, that in a quarter of a century's familiar and friendly intercourse with our wild-birds under all possible circumstances, we have never heard an owl hoot except " darkling," as Milton has it, that is, from out the darkness or sombre shade. Even at night, if the moon is shining bright, it never hoots from a spot on which the moonbeams fall in full flood ; it selects the deepest shadow even in faint moonlight when uttering its eerie notes. It will hoot in twilight, and it will hoot when the heavens are bright ablaze with the most brilliant coruscations of the aurora, but never, so far as our experience has extended, does it hoot in honest daylight or even in moonlight, except when, as we have said, it is itself in deep shade. We have kept pets of all our native species of owls, and most interesting pets they make, and though, when angry or in any way out of sorts, it will utter a ready hiss, ending in a curious rasping guttural, we have never known it to hoot except in the darkness of night, and, more rarely, in the dim, uncertain light of evening or morning twilight. The cooing of a pigeon at midnight, while it may be said to be unusual, is yet a thing that, under certain circumstances, may be heard at any time. Many birds, captives in cage or aviary, frequently sing short and incomplete strophes of their special song in the warm stillness of summer nights, evidently in their dreams. Others, in their natural state of freedom, about the time of the longest day, when there is hardly any night in our latitudes, may be heard singing, generally unconnectedly, and in a faint, uncertain key. The pigeon will coo at any time when brooding, if rudely disturbed in any way, just as a brooding hen will *purr* and scold if you annoy her or her nest at any hour of the day or night. The cooing of a pigeon, therefore, at midnight is nothing very wonderful. The hooting of an owl at noonday, however, is surprising, and a thing which, although we live in a district where owls are plentiful, is altogether unknown in our experience.

CHAPTER LIX.

THE storms of the latter days of October [November 1877] were
exceedingly severe along our western seaboard, and terribly so, as
more than one correspondent assures us, amongst the Hebrides.
It is worth noting with what marvellous punctuality these Trans-
atlantically telegraphed storms reach our shores. They are "up
to time," with all the precision almost of our best appointed mail
trains; quite as punctual, at all events, to their predicted time on
several occasions lately as our ocean mail-carrying steam ships to
their appointed dates of arrival. This last October storm, for
example, was telegraphed as being due on our British shores on
or about Saturday, the 27th, and so correct, considering all the
difficulties of such meteorological vaticinations, was the prediction, that the storm actually reached us here on the evening of
the 26th, increasing in intensity throughout the night and until
mid-day of the 27th, the very day fixed upon, when it blew
with all the force of a hurricane, and the rain fell in torrents,
accompanied, too—that none of the essentials of a great storm
might be wanting—by vivid lightning, and thunder peals loud
enough to make the deafest hear, or at all events *feel*, for it is
no exaggeration to say that the very ground seemed at times to
thrill responsive to the aërial concussion. The 26th had dawned
bright and clear, and so continued throughout the day; one of
those "pet days," in short, not uncommon at this season,—the sea,

too, calm and glassy as a mirror. In the afternoon, however, we were called out from the tea-table to look at a phenomenon which had already attracted the attention of some of our more observant neighbours, and about which they wanted our opinion, as they had some thoughts of going a herring fishing. The phenomenon in question was this : Not a breath of air was stirring, Loch Linnhe was unruffled by the slightest zephyr, and yet a heavy surge quite suddenly began to break along the beach with a sudden boom that was remarkable in such a calm. A somewhat similar pheno-menon, lasting but for a short time, however, is observed in our lochs when, on a calm summer evening, one of the Messrs. Hutche-son's paddle steamers—the "Chevalier," for instance—passes at full speed close in shore. What could this swell and surge, troubling a loch otherwise calm as a mill-pond, mean? You might have safely carried a lighted candle exposed and lanternless along the beach on which that heavy swell with hollow boom was breaking —breaking in great green waves that showed not a bell or fleck of foam on their crests until they thundered on the shingle. It was, in a word, a phenomenon for which there was no apparent adequate cause. The sea, had it been in keeping with all its visible surround-ings, should have been calm and still; on the contrary, it was restless and perturbed, and there lay the mystery. Even had we recollected nothing of the telegraphed storm, it was easy of solution, and our instant interlocutor, as the law courts have it, was this : " A storm in the Atlantic, my good friends. Calm as it is here, there is a storm, and a wild one, depend upon it, outside yonder island of Mull, for all it basks so peacefully in the golden sunset. Nothing else can adequately account for such a swell on our calm inland waters on an evening so summer-like and warm ; and when I tell you that a storm likely to reach our shores to-morrow has been telegraphed from America several days since, I conclude that it is that very storm fast approaching us that causes this swell upon our shore. It must be just at hand; so haul up your boats high and dry; take down your nets from the drying-poles, and put them in a place of safety. Stay thankfully at home, and let the herring fishing stand over till the predicted gales have come and gone. Many a gallant fellow at this moment afloat would be glad to have his foot like you on *terra firma : a chas air talamh tioram* were the words,—his foot on dry land." With some such remarks as these, we sent the men home, still wondering, however; and within a couple of hours the storm was upon us with a loud prolonged shriek, that showed how thoroughly in earnest it was. Timeously warned, no danger was done in our district, and we are now unanimous in speaking with the utmost respect of the Atlantic cable in connection with storm warnings from the Western Continent. These telegraphic warnings from America, by the way, of coming storms are of the utmost importance and value, more particularly to the western shores of the British Islands. We have no doubt at all that on the western seaboard of Scotland alone many valuable lives were saved, as well as much valuable property, by the submarine cable notice that put us all on our guard with reference to the gale that raged on the 27th of October, and for several days subsequently. We wonder if from Britain or the Continent any of the terrible easterly storms of last winter were telegraphed to America—timeously and purposely telegraphed, that is— so as to be of benefit to our Transatlantic cousins, as their recent telegrams have been to us. We fear not. But now at least it is surely a matter of the merest courtesy and cousinly goodwill that we be prepared and ready to send them betimes telegraphic messages of all our *easterly* storms, in return for similar favours on their part in respect to those that are *westerly.*

Reading over the foregoing paragraph, which the reader may see was written *currente calamo*—at a gallop, as it were, and without a check, as the foxhunter says—we find that we have used the

often-quoted Latin phrase *terra firma ;* words which rarely fail to
make us smile in their connection with an anecdote current in St.
Andrews in our early college days.   It was to this effect : The
driver of a two-horse coach that ran at that time between St.
Andrews and Newport was a George Braid, a respectable old man,
familiarly known to everybody, and notably to the University
students, as " Geordie," a liberty with his Christian name which
Mr. Braid in nowise resented, for he was intelligent and shrewd, and
knew that he was thus spoken of and addressed out of goodwill and
kindly regard rather than otherwise.   Frequently patronised on his
route by learned professors and lively students, Geordie had picked
up many big words and learned phrases, which he was fond of
using in his family, and, as the Catechism says, amongst his
" inferiors and equals."   In connection with frequent storm and
shipwreck on the wild east coast, it was the most natural thing in
the world that Geordie should often have heard from the lips of
some of his learned " fare " the words *terra firma*, with which he
associated a general idea of protection, comfort, and safety.   One
terrible night of snow and storm, having driven a large coachful
from Newport to the city, Geordie, when he had duly seen to his
cattle, and paid a short visit to the bar of the " Cross Keys " hostelry,
wended his way by the West Port to his home, which lay beyond the
old city walls.   His wife, a brisk and *eident* bit body, had a roaring
fire and a cheery welcome for her goodman on his entrance, while
his children gathered round him to help him off with caps, coats,
leggings, and all the other belongings of the outer man of a driver
in the good old coaching days.   Reduced at last to something like
his natural dimensions, Geordie, having sufficiently rubbed his
purple hands before the fire, looked benignantly around and exclaimed, " Ah ! Meg, my woman, you and the bairns hae muckle
cause to be thankful to your Maker that ye hae *terra firma abune
your heads* this night !   Its just awfu' out yonder by the Guard

Brig and Strathtyrum." We have met with not a few in our day with a strange craze for using words and phrases of which they evidently knew as little of the real meaning and proper application as honest Geordie Braid with his *terra firma.*

The new moon of the 5th, aided by a wind that at times almost amounted to a gale, gave us along the western seaboard three very high tides in succession ; that of the afternoon of the 6th, however, being the highest. The naturalist who is fairly diligent on such occasions is pretty sure to meet with more or less interesting matter for thoughtful study ; nor, so far as our own experience extends, need the entries in one's note-book, even for what is called the " dead " season of mid-winter, be fewer in number, or less interesting or instructive than those of the pages devoted to the summer season itself. We have known naturalists whose note-books presented little but a dreary succession of blank pages for the winter half-year, and who thought it odd that we should be surprised at it. It has been said that the laws of disease are as beautiful as those of health, and that peace has its victories as well as war, and we have no hesitation in saying that to the true naturalist the winter season, if fairly and diligently encountered, is in its way just as interesting as the summer, and that the observer who has all his wits about him, and who goes to work with a will, may have *his* " victories " even in the season of the winter solstice—victories as important in their way and gratifying as are those of midsummer itself, when the days are at their longest, when summer seas are calm and summer woods are green. In the course of half an hour's ramble on the beach the other day, we fell in with some curious waifs, each of which might be made the text of an interesting monograph. Three drowned hedgehogs, for example, was a somewhat startling " find " to turn up in a swathe of seaware that the advancing tide was slowly rolling up the shingle. One was full-grown, a female ; the other two, both males, were but half or three parts grown. What brought them there? was the natural question; for a hedgehog, dead or living, on the sea-shore under high-water mark, is as odd and out-of-place an object as would be a mackerel far up the hills amongst the heather. The following is probably a satisfactory enough explanation of the mystery :—Hedgehogs, which twenty years ago were quite unknown in Lochaber, are now plentiful. A pair, captured on Lord Abinger's lands at Torlundy, were sent to us some dozen or fifteen years ago as a great curiosity; and in this district then they were a curiosity, so much so, that we can recollect that during the time they remained in our possession as exceedingly tame and most interesting pets, people from all parts of the country used to come in order to have a close look at the black-snouted, spine-armoured hedge pigs, as Shakespeare calls them, the *graineag* or *repulsive* one of the midland High-landers of Athole and Strathspey, where the animal has always been plentiful. They have now become so common in this district that a hedgehog is no more accounted a rarity than is a stoat or a weasel. Hedgehogs are fond of making their cozy nests of moss, grass fibres, and fallen leaves, near the roots of trees and bushes growing on the banks of rivers and mountain streams. These last have of late been frequently swollen beyond their usual bounds by the heavy rains; and in a spate of this kind poor Mrs. Hedgehog and her youngsters were caught napping, and carried away by the torrent to the sea, and ultimately cast ashore by the wind and waves, where we found them in their winding-sheet of slimy sea-wrack, and for a moment wondered how it came to pass that they lay there, like poor Ophelia, " drown'd, drown'd." One remarkable circumstance connected with these drowned hedgehogs was this : we found to our surprise that we could handle them with impunity; their spines, so formidable in the living animal, being quite soft and gelatinous to their very tips. This is by no means the case with the spines of such hedgehogs as are killed by trap, or otherwise on land. In this latter case the spines retain their point and prickliness, as in the living animal, till in the process of decay they separate from their sockets in the skin, and drop in brittle, broken fragments to the ground. A question, then, for future investigation is this,—Do the spines of *all* drowned hedgehogs lose their prickliness and point, and become soft and gelatinous ? If so, has fresh water alone this effect, or is it necessary that the animal should be some time immersed in salt water ?

Within a short distance of the drowned hedgehogs, lay a large angler or fishing-frog, the *Lophius piscatorius* of ichthyologists, and a frequent waif on our shores after a gale. It had evidently been caught by the storm in shallow water, and been beaten to death by the weight and force of the waves, for it was in excellent condition, and there was nothing to indicate death in any other way. Why in this fish such a huge head, with its formidable array of recurved teeth, and such a cavernous, capacious gullet, should be joined to a body comparatively so diminutive, is a puzzle that has never yet been satisfactorily solved ; nor can we ourselves, up to this present moment, advance even a plausible conjecture in explanation of an anomaly that must have attracted the attention of thousands. The disproportion between the immense head and the small and slender body is as great as if you erected a porch lofty and wide enough to serve as the main entrance to a cathedral, and vestibule to correspond, in order to enter a dwelling consisting after all but of a single bedroom. Or, to put it in another way, it is as if you built a large mill, with the most powerful machinery possible, in order to grind sufficient meal for the daily consumption of a single dyspeptic customer. The-fishing frog, has, we believe, been of late successfully introduced into more than one of our many aquaria, but we are not aware that any satisfactory explanation of the difficulty which we are considering has as yet been arrived at. A full and sufficient explanation, however, you may be sure there must be, if we only knew enough of the animal's economy to get at it.

But we must stop ; for hark ! an itinerant fiddler has this moment struck up " Bob of Fettercairn " just in front of our study window. He plays admirably too, lovingly caressing the polished base of his instrument—his bread-winner, poor fellow—with his wan and withered cheek, and wielding a powerful, yet light and delicate, bow-hand ; and we must go and have a crack with him. Nor must you sneer at us for so doing, gracious reader. The arrival even of a peripatetic, out-at-elbows fiddler is an event of some importance in such a place as this on a cold, grey November afternoon. We shall order him a big bowl of tea, with something to eat, satisfied that if in so doing we are not entertaining an angel unawares (though there is no reason that we know of why an angel should *not* appear in peripatetic fiddler guise, as well as in any other form), we are at all events entertaining one who by his appearance manifestly needs something warm and comfortable, and a little rest by a cheerful fireside at this season, not forgetting the while that he is a capital fiddler—of some intelligence, too, and full of capital stories we warrant him. Depend upon it that Homer, who was after all but an inspired *gaberlunzie*, has many a time and oft appeared in quite as sorry a plight, and with as little externally to recommend him as this same itinerant fiddler ; and think how proud and glad you and we should be to have a chance of entertaining the blind old Chian, wandering ballad-singer as he was ! You must, therefore, let us have our way with this poor old man, who, by the way, is not blind, but, on the contrary, has a good large dark brown eye of his own, so common, we have noticed, in people musically inclined, that it may be called the musical eye ; and if he is all we take him for, and he and we get on well together, you may perhaps hear of him again.

CHAPTER LX.

FAVOURED by the most splendid Christmas weather [January 1878], piercingly cold, indeed, but beautifully bright and clear, a run from Lochaber to Clydesdale on an agreeable errand is exceedingly enjoyable. Our first day in Glasgow was devoted to the Kelvin Grove Museum, which we had now an opportunity, for the first time, of examining thoroughly and at leisure, and with which, as the reader may believe, we were very much delighted. On handing our card to Mr. Paton, the curator, we were received by himself and his assistant, Mr. Campbell—the latter, of course, a Highlander —in the friendliest manner; and a couple of hours were very pleasantly and profitably spent in examining a really curious and valuable collection, so admirably catalogued and arranged, that we believe we saw and minutely studied everything to be seen as leisurely and satisfactorily as was possible in the time at our disposal. Our friend Mr. Snowie, of Inverness, had written us before leaving home that he was sending some contributions to the museum, of which he begged us to undertake the formal delivery, and see properly placed; and this of course we had much pleasure in doing. These contributions are a valuable acquisition to the museum, and are as follows :—(1.) Hoopoe (*Upupa epops*, Linn.), a female, in fine plumage, and admirably set up. This bird was captured by the boys at the Inverness Reformatory School, and dying, notwithstanding it received all the attention and kindly care that could be bestowed upon it, it passed into Mr. Snowie's hands. (2.) Wild cat, stuffed, an excellent specimen, with very prominent markings, trapped at Fasnakyle, on The Chisholm's estate. (3.) A *white* blackbird, and an albino bunting, both shot by Mr. T. B. Snowie near Inverness. (4.) Snipe and other marsh-bird skins, shot by the same. (5.) Two small hares preserved in a bottle; taken out of an unusually large-sized female shot at Dochfour in September 1875 ; a very interesting preparation. (6.) Head of otter, trapped on the River Peffer in 1876. (7.) Owl (*Strix flammea*, Linn.), shot in October 1877 by Mr. T. B. Snowie. (8.) Egg of golden eagle; this last, perhaps, the most welcome gift of all, as eagles' eggs are now become so rare as readily to command prices ranging from £5 to £10 each. Attached to the museum proper there is a fresh-water aquarium. In one of the tanks, in which several fine pike are " interned," we noticed that one of the largest, who advanced to the front of the tank, in order to examine as closely as possible a slip of paper which we were trailing along the glass by way of bait, had his muzzle, more particularly the anterior part of the upper jaw, seriously disfigured by a fungoid growth of jelly-like appearance ; and calling the curator's attention to the fact, we made the remark that the poor pike seemed too seriously diseased to live long. We were sur-prised when told that the fish was none the worse for his fungoid moustache ; that it had been long in that way, and that all that was needed was an occasional cleansing of the muzzle, as you would wipe away a clot of jelly that had accidentally fallen on your knife-handle at dessert, and the fish then seemed all right enough until it grew again to such a size as to be an incon-venience.

Leaving the museum, we had but barely sufficient time for dress and dinner before proceeding to take the chair at the Gathering of the Clans in the City Hall, and a very splendid and enthusiastic gathering it was. From floor to ceiling the huge building was crammed, and as we took our seat and bowed in acknowledgment of the truly Highland welcome that greeted us in the shape of round upon round of loud and lusty cheers, we could not help feeling a little nervous and out of sorts in realising the fact that we were for the moment "the observed of all observers," and, by the kind partiality of the Highlanders of Glasgow, made to occupy a position of which any one might well be proud. We were soon at our ease, however, and found no difficulty in discharging our duties in connection with a meeting which was from first to last, and in all its belongings, a great success. The dancing was excellent; the singing could hardly have been better; while the pipe music was of itself well worth going a much longer distance to hear than that which separates Nether Lochaber from the City Hall of Glasgow. No other living man, perhaps, can play reels and strathspeys as Donald Macphee can play them; and we do not think we ever heard anything more admirably played than was Malcolm Macpherson's *port mòr* or *piobaireachd* proper, *Fhuair mi pòg's laimh mo righ*, composed at Holyrood in 1745 by *Ewen Macdhomhnuil Bhuidhe*, a Macmillan from Glendessary and piper to Lochiel, on seeing his chief kiss Charles Edward's hand at a levee held in the palace of his ancestors by that Prince a day or two after the victory at Gladsmuir. Macpherson played this *piobaireachd* so exquisitely that some of us felt our eyes grow moist, and were in no wise ashamed of it, long ere he had reached the difficult but beautifully managed fingering of the concluding *urlar*. We have always had a warm regard for James Boswell, Johnson's biographer, for this amongst other reasons, that, on his own confession, music frequently affected *him* as it affected many of us on this occasion. "Sir," growled Johnson, "I should never hear it if it made me such a fool." But then a man, however great, cannot be everything; and Johnson was not only not a Scotchman, but the very antipodes of a Scotchman—he was an Englishman, proud and prejudiced, and deaf and dead as a stone to the charms of music, whether vocal or instrumental. When at Sleat, in Skye, many years afterwards, he made the confession that "he knew a drum from a trumpet, and a bagpipe from a guitar, which was about the extent of his knowledge of music." We parted with our friends of the Highland Association on the best terms ; they were good-natured enough to say that they were pleased with us ; we certainly had every reason to be pleased with *them.*

We were astir betimes next morning, in order to fulfil an engagement undertaken at the request of some naturalist friends in London—a visit, namely, to the Aquarium at Rothesay, an admirably conducted institution, one of the best in the kingdom. We expected to see a great deal that could not well fail to interest us, and we *did* see a great deal that pleased us very much indeed ; the best proof of which is that after several hours' wandering from tank to tank, it was with a sigh of regret that our attention was called to the fact that it was already time for us to put up our note-book and find our way as quickly as possible to the pier, if we would overtake the *Mountaineer* for Greenock, in order to reach Glasgow again that evening. Of all the tanks, that which we lingered longest before, perhaps, was that set apart for sea anemones, of which the collection is exceedingly curious and interesting. All the specimens seemed perfectly healthy and well-to-do, though, owing to the fact that the afternoon had now become wet and dull, they were disinclined to display their beauties in full. In another of the tanks, of which the most distinguished inhabitant is a conger eel of a large size, we were much amused with the conduct of a seven or eight pound cod, that seemed as if he would willingly have spoken to us if he could. As soon as he became aware of our presence, he came sailing out of a dark recess behind a rocky promontory—a sort of Mull of Kintyre in

miniature—which is his usual *howf,* and advancing straight to
the front of the tank, put his nose to the glass, wagging his
tail, and staring at us with an expression of countenance so queer
and comical, that it made us laugh outright. " Well, Nether
Lochaber, my boy," he seemed inclined to say, " how are you ?
This is all very fine, but on the word of a cod, believe me that I'd
far rather be cruising about the shores and shallows of Loch
Linnhe, down yonder in your own neighbourhood, than be confined here from year's end to year's end, to be stared at by a lot of
people who may pretend some interest in me from a purely
scientific point of view, but who, between ourselves, if the truth
were known, never see me but they straightway think of how I
should be boiled and served with sauce. Only the other day, for
instance, a lady visitor from Glasgow asked one of the attendants
what he thought might be my weight, and if he was of opinion
that a cod out of an aquarium tank would be quite as good eating
as one direct from the sea ? When I hear talk of that kind, it
hurts my feelings, I can tell you." All this, and a great deal more,
we fancied the cod would have said if he could ; and as we tapped
the glass at his nose and bade him a friendly good-bye, we almost
persuaded ourselves that he responded with a knowing wink, as
with a single sweep of his tail he put about and joined the conger
in a brisk constitutional round and athwart the tank—a tank so
crystal clear, and clean and comfortable, as indeed are all the tanks,
that the inmates, abundantly and regularly fed, ought to be
happy enough, were it not that, like Sterne's starling, they
probably find the great drawback on their happiness in the fact
that after all they are prisoners, that they can't get out. We
were much delighted with the seal-house and its lively and
intelligent occupants. The shape of a seal's head is sufficient to
convince the most careless observer that it must contain a great
deal of brains ; while its full and lively eye bespeaks a high and

active order of intelligence. Those at present in the Rothesay Aquarium, three in number, are most interesting animals, and almost as tame as lapdogs. It so happened that we entered their house at a time when they were exceedingly active and lively, for they were well aware that a large basket, which had just been carried to the side of their tank, contained fresh fish of some kind or other for their dinner; and they raced and leaped about in eager expectation of the treat, for they were evidently hungry—always a good sign of an aquarium inmate. The fish consisted of small flounders; and the agility and graceful ease of the motions of these seals, as they dived and dashed after a fish, which, while they were begging dog-like before us at one end of the tank, we suddenly tossed to the other end, was so admirable that we continued a long time to play at a sort of pitch-and-toss game that was quite as agreeable to them as it could possibly be interesting to us. We only ceased our part of the performance when we thought that for the time they must have had enough, the seal being probably as liable to indigestion as the result of a surfeit as is any other animal. When, however, they found that they had nothing more to expect from us, they showed their intelligence and *nous* by at once commencing to climb out of their tank, at the very spot, too, where it was easiest of accomplishment, on the side on which they knew the fish-basket was placed. What could they now be after? was the question we asked ourselves. One after another they got out and waddled along the pavement, awkwardly indeed, but as quickly as they could, past us, keeping their big and beautiful eyes steadily fixed on ours, till they reached the basket, and in a moment each had seized a fish, with which he instantly tumbled heels-over-head into the tank again at the point nearest him, evidently afraid that we might try and intercept him, and deprive him of a *bonne bouche*, which all of them seemed perfectly well somehow to understand they had no right to take in such reiving fashion. We noticed that when we threw a fish into the tank, and one of them got hold of it, the other two endeavoured to snatch it from him, and for the moment there was a wild tumult and tumble, in which the water was lashed into foam. In this, however, as far as we could judge, there was no manifestation of anything like anger, or the slightest attempt to hurt or injure each other. It was more like the rough and tumble play of children after a ball, or something of that sort, which all may strongly desire to possess, but which only one can have for the moment.

CHAPTER LXI.

WITH all their tendency, in their every reference to the past, to become *laudatores temporis acti*, the sturdy upholders of the superiority of all that *was*, in comparison with anything and everything that *is*, our weather-wise octogenarian friends here are all agreed that so summer-like a February [1878] month they never knew before. It is true that in making this admission they shake their heads sapiently, and hint that no good can come of such an unnatural commingling of the times and seasons. It will be well, they add, if before cuckoo day (*mun d'thig latha na cuaig*) we haven't to pay for it all in the shape of storm and cold at a time when these are as unseasonable and out of place as is summer calm and summer sunshine *now*. It was amusing to see these honest old croakers selecting the coziest nooks *air chùl gaoithe's air aodain gréine*, as the Fingalian tale has it,—that is, at the back of the wind and in the face of the sun—and thoroughly enjoying the calm and sunshine at the very moment that they would impress upon us the unnaturalness and unseasonableness of it all. The first fortnight of February was, indeed, wonderfully fine ; from the beginning of the month up to the evening of St. Valentine's Day, more like the close of April or early May than anything usually looked for while the sun is still in *Aquarius*. Driving overland to Oban on the 11th, and, by the ferries of Ballachulish, Shian, and Connel, a very beautiful drive it is, hardly to be equalled elsewhere even in the West Highlands; the day was so bright, and calm, and clear, that while mavis and merle, and hedge-accenter and chaffinch greeted us from copse and hedgerow with their rich and mellow song, the driver, sitting beside us, couldn't help observing as we passed by Appin House, "Na 'n robh chuag again a nis, bha 'n samhradh fhein ann!" "If we had but the cuckoo now, it would be summer its very self!" On the beach, a little above high-water mark, just under Appin House, and within an easy stone's cast of the public road, there is an immense spherical boulder of granite, to which there is attached a curious old story, which invests with additional interest an object deserving enough of attention for its own sake—for the sake, that is, of its huge size and almost perfect spherical form, this latter peculiarity, in the huge solid mass, making it the most remarkable thing of the kind on the mainland, at least of the West Highlands. The story of the Appin House boulder, or *Clach Ruric* as it is called, is, dropping minor and unessential details, to the following effect:—Long, long ago a Prince of Lochlin or Scandinavia, with a formidable fleet of war galleys, made a descent upon the Hebrides, killing and plundering everywhere with a ruthlessness known only, even in those days of rude lawlessness, to the Vikings of the north. Having thoroughly devastated the islands, Ruric—for such was the Prince's name—steered for the mainland of Morven, and took up his residence in the castle of Mearnaig, in Glensanda. In this stronghold, the ruins of which still exist, he resolved to pass the winter, with the intention of over-running and plundering the adjoining districts in the spring, and afterwards sailing homewards in the calm of summer seas, for his galleys were so deeply laden with booty that he feared to encounter the turbulence of the North Sea at any other season. In the early spring the cruel Northman was betimes astir, killing and plundering with but little opposition throughout the districts of Kingerloch, Sunart, and Ardgour, to the head of

Lochiel. While of his numerous fleet a single galley showed more than a foot and a span (*troidh agus rèis* were the words of the narrator) of gunwale unsubmerged, Ruric was unsatisfied, and to complete his ill-gotten freight he resolved on the plunder of the opposite district of Appin, the smoke of whose dwellings could be seen, and the lowing of whose numerous herds could be heard (when the summer morning was still and the Linnhe Loch was calm) by the pirate prince from the battlements of the castle of Mearnaig. One morning Ruric anchored his galleys in the Sound of Shuna, and landing, erected his tents on the green knoll now occupied by Appin House. With this spot as his head-quarters, it was his intention to plunder the district north and south of him at his leisure, believing that he would meet with as little opposition here as he had already met with elsewhere. The inhabitants of Appin, however, were partly on their guard, and determined to resist, and if possible chastise, the invader. And first conveying their old men, women, and children, with their flocks and herds, into the fastnesses of the upland glens, they resolved to watch the movements of the Norsemen, ready to fall upon them whenever a favourable opportunity should offer. That same night, as some cattle herds, acting as scouts, were on the hill immediately above the tents of the invaders, one of them directed the attention of his companions to a huge granite boulder with so slight a hold of the hill crest, that, with some little labour, it might be let loose at any time—a terrible messenger of wrath—amongst the tents of the enemy below, whose shouts of laughter at that moment, and snatches of rude song, proved that they had feasted plentifully and had no apprehension of immediate death or danger in any form. After much labour, the herdsmen managed so to dig about and undermine and loosen the boulder in its bed on the hill-face, that, on a given signal, their united strength sufficed to tilt it headlong over the steep, leaping and thundering on its terrible path. The

largest trees in its course snapped before the boulder like reeds :
when it came into momentary contact with a rock, the sparks flew
heavenward as if from an exploded meteor ! In a dozen of bounds
it reached the tents of the Norsemen, crushing, mangling, grinding
into pulp or powder (*a pronnadh agus a bruanadh,* are the Gaelic
words) everything it touched, and finally stopping where it now
stands, to be long regarded by the people of the district with a
feeling akin to superstitious awe, and to be known by the name of
Clach Ruric. In the morning, the Norsemen could only know by
the mangled fragments of their bodies that their Prince, with his
two sons, and many of those next to him in power, had met with a
terrible death. Before the Appin men could gather in sufficient
force to attack them, the Norsemen unmoored their galleys, chanting the death-song of their chief as they unmoored, and set sail for
Lochlin, never more to trouble the mainland of the West Highlands
with their invasions. The venerable *seanachie* from whom we
picked up this tradition, added that Castle *Cœfin,* or Cyffin, in
Lismore, is so called after a Danish prince of that name, who also
was connected with Ruric's expedition, though in what manner he
was unable to say.

Not far from Clach Ruric, on an island rock in the entrance to
the Sound of Shuna, are the ruins of another castle, of a later date,
however, and more recent interest than can be attached to the
many strongholds of the Viking period perched on the rocks and
promontories of this part of the West Highlands. This is Castle
Stalker, or, in the language of the district itself, *Caisteal-an-Stalcaire,*
the Castle of the Falconer or Fowler. The small rock-island on
which it is built is *Sgeir-an-Sgairbh* (the sea-rock, or skerry of the
cormorant), from very early times the gathering cry at once and
rendevous of the Stewarts of Appin in all their maritime expeditions. Castle Stalker dates from about the beginning of the reign
of James IV., for whose convenience and accommodation, when,

as frequently happened, he extended his hunting expeditions to
this district, it was built.   Stewart of Appin, who was a great
favourite with the king, was appointed hereditary keeper, and the
castle continued in the possession of the family until, about the
year 1645, the Mac Ian Stewart of that date, in a moment of
drunken folly, made it over to his wily neighbour, Donald Campbell of the Airds, receiving in return the handsome and adequate
equivalent of an eight-oared *birlinn*, or small wherry !   Stewart,
when sober, would have gladly cancelled so manifestly one-sided a
barter-bargain at any sacrifice, but Campbell, having got possession,
kept it ; while the disgraceful transaction so stung the pride of the
Stewarts that they practically deposed the *Baothaire* (the silly one),
as they nicknamed the chief, from his chieftainship, by unanimously electing his cousins of Invernahyle and Ardsheal to be
their leaders in the subsequent wars of Montrose.   For a short
time during Montrose's ascendancy in the Highlands, and for a
longer period towards the close of the reign of Charles II., Castle
Stalker was again in the possession of the Stewarts ; but at the
Revolution the Campbells had it all their own way ; they re-
possessed themselves of the castle, and it has remained theirs ever
since.   About forty years ago a gentleman of the family of *Ailein*
'*Ic Rob* of Appin, who had amassed a considerable fortune in the
West Indies, offered the then proprietor a large sum for the bare
rock and ruins of Castle Stalker, but the offer was refused.

From the wooded knoll to the left, as we entered the village of
Portnacroish, we heard some notes that, harsh as they were,
delighted us, for we had not heard them for many years ; and
the reader will perhaps smile when we confess delight in association with what was neither more nor less than the chattering
of a pair of magpies !   Knowing that it must be magpie chattering
and nothing else, though the lively confabulators were for the
moment invisible, we got out of our conveyance, and on reaching

an open glade we got sight of a pair of these beautiful birds perched on the topmost bough of an old ash tree; and so busy were they in the discussion of what must have been a matter of grave and immediate importance, that the usually shy and wary birds did not notice our approach till we were quite close upon them, when, with a scream of alarm and an indignant flirt of their tails, they glided in graceful curve, rather than flew, over the tree tops and disappeared. So rare has the magpie become in Lochaber and the immediately surrounding districts, that a sight of a pair of these handsome and sagacious birds delighted us exceedingly. We had little difficulty in concluding that their lively chattering on that bright and beautiful morning was about no less important a matter than the propriety of at once putting their house in order and setting about the labours of incubation. If there were any truth in popular superstition, that particular day ought to have afterwards turned out a disagreeable one to us; for had we not seen *two* magpies together, and what is more, did we not go out of our way to see them, when we might have easily passed on unseen of them, as they were invisible to us? In the south of Scotland the old pyet rhyme is something like this—

> " One 's joy,
>   Two 's grief,
>   Three a wedding,
>   Four death.'

In the old *sgeulachd* the Gaelic rhyme is of similar import—

> " Chunnaic mi pioghaid a's dh-éirich leam ;
>   Chunnaic mi dhà 'sgum b'iargain iad ;
>   Chunnaic mi tri a's b'aighearach mi ;
>   Ach ceithir ri'm linn chan iarrainn iad."

In our own case, on that particular occasion, the superstition could not have been more completely falsified by the event, for, maugre the magpies, our trip to Oban was in its every circumstance as agreeable and pleasant as it could well be. What a pity it is that these beautiful birds, whose favourite residence, too, if they were only permitted to live in peace, is the immediate vicinity of human dwellings, should be of such evil repute that gamekeepers everywhere consider themselves justified in accomplishing their utter destruction by every means in their power. Their *utter* destruction we have said; and it is only as to their total extirpation that we would venture on a word of expostulation with gamekeepers and their employers. It is true that the magpie is an enemy to winged game, being a cunning and persistent nest-robber, an adroiter sucker of eggs than the proverbial "grandmother" herself. That the gamekeeper should therefore dislike them is the most natural thing in the world, and that, in gamekeeper's own phrase, they should "be kept down" is proper enough. But we cannot agree that it is necessary that the bird should be utterly destroyed. Here and there on a wide estate an occasional pair of magpies might surely be tolerated for the sake of their beauty and amusingly lively manners, and on the divine principle of "live and let live." For our own part, in approaching a gentleman's residence, the sight of a pair of these birds flitting about " the old ancestral elms " always intensifies our respect for the place and the owner.

Crossing Loch Creran, by the Ferry of Shian, we are in Benderloch—classic ground, and archæologically the most interesting spot, perhaps, in all the West Highlands. " Everything here is beautiful," says Dr. Macculloch. "The distance between the ferries of Shian and Connel is but five miles; but it is a day's journey for a wise man." About half-way is *Dùn-Mac-Uisneachain* (the Fort of the Son of *Uisneach*), one of the most interesting of our vitrified forts, *quâ* such, and supposed to be the Beregonium of Hector Boethius, and the site of the still older Selma, the " Hall of Swords " of Ossianic song. That it was a place of importance long before the time of the Dalriad Scots seems very certain; and, leaving Macpherson's " Ossian " altogether out of the question, there occur in the old Fingalian ballads, and tales of the Féinne, about the antiquity of which there has never been dispute; numberless local references which seem in a very remarkable manner to point to this spot as the principal stronghold in Scotland (for they were of Ireland also) of the Fingalians at one period, and that the most important, perhaps, in their history. Within a short distance of Dun-Mac-Uisneachain, and commanding it, is a steep, rocky eminence of considerable height, called Dunvallary or Dunvallanry, the etymology of which may be *Dùn-bhail'-n-righ*, the Fortified Place of the King's Town; or *Dùn-bhail' n 'fhrìth*, the Fort of the Town on the verge of the Hunting Forest. Stretching away towards Connel and Loch Etive is the wide moorland flat of Achnacree, which, with its numerous cairns, Druidical circles, monoliths, and other relics of the olden time, may very well be the ancient "plains of Lora;" Lora itself, frequently mentioned in Ossianic poetry, and meaning *Luath shruth*, the loud, swift current, *par excellence*, meeting us face to face, so to speak, in the turbulently impetuous rapids of Connel.

CHAPTER LXII.

A FINER February month from first to last was never known in the
West Highlands. With an amount of sunshine that April might be
glad of, it was mild and open throughout; the sort of weather, in
short, that Thomson must have been dreaming about, when he
invoked the season of bursting bud and wildflower as "Gentle
Spring, ethereal mildness." March [1878], too, has come in, not
lion-like, as the meteorological proverb would have it, but "like a
lamb," as it is hoped it may continue and end. Everybody is now
astir, and "speed the plough" is the order of the day, as well,
indeed, it may, for the bud has already opened into leaf, and primroses are plentiful—so plentiful that they may be gathered in
handfuls from the hazel copse and woodland glade. As for our
wild-bird friends, they are in ecstasies with it all, everywhere in
full and fluent song, and making love with an ardour and directness of purpose that rarely fails of its reward. Nest-building, the
most important and serious labour of their lives, but a labour
of love all the same, is being rapidly proceeded with, the God-
taught architects knowing not only to labour, but *how best* to
labour, frequently resting a space to refresh themselves with
song :—

> " *Song* sweetens toil, however rude the sound,
>   All at her work the village maiden sings ;
> Nor while she turns the giddy wheel around,
>   Revolves the sad vicissitudes of things."

And while speaking of birds, this is, perhaps, the proper place to refer to a paragraph that appeared recently :—

"THE LILAC TREE AND BIRDS.—Burns has a song, 'Oh, were my love yon lilac fair,' &c. Cunningham has remarked that Burns had made an unhappy selection of a tree for sheltering his little bird ; for the feathered songsters are found to avoid the lilac when in flower, owing to its peculiar smell. We confess we are not skilled enough in natural history to attest the accuracy of Cunningham's assertion."—Paterson's *Burns*, vol. iii.

Fully to appreciate Cunningham's objection, it is proper that we quote the song in full ; but before doing so, it may be observed that it is founded on an older version, of which the best lines are retained, as is the case with not a few of Burns' finest love-songs. Writing to George Thomson in the summer of 1793, the poet says—

"Do you know the following beautiful little fragment in Witherspoon's *Collection of Scots Songs ?*—

"'Oh, gin my love were yon red rose,
That grows upon the castle wa.''

"This thought is inexpressibly beautiful, and quite, so far as I know, original. It is too short for a song, else I would forswear you altogether, unless you give it a place. I have often tried to make a stanza to it, but in vain. After balancing myself for a musing five minutes on the hind legs of my elbow-chair, I produced the following. The verses are far inferior to the original, I frankly confess ; but if worthy of insertion at all, they might be first in place ; as every poet who knows anything of his trade will husband his last thought for a concluding stroke :—

"Oh, were my love yon lilac fair,
Wi' purple blossoms to the spring ;
And I a bird to shelter there,
When wearied on my little wing.

How I wad mourn when it was torn
By autumn wild, and winter rude !
But I wad sing on wanton wing
When youthfu' May its bloom renew'd.

Oh, gin my love were yon red rose,
That grows upon the castle wa',
And I mysel' a drap o' dew,
Into her bonnie breast to fa' !

Oh ! there, beyond expression blest,
I'd feast on beauty a' the night ;
Seal'd on her silk-saft faulds to rest,
Till fleyed awa' by Phœbus' light."

Cunningham's ornithological objection to the song we believe to be well founded ; and it is not a little to his credit, as proving what a close and clear observer of the habits of our song-birds he must have been, that he was the first, so far as we know, to notice how reluctant they are to have anything to do with the lilac while in flower, though at other seasons they perch upon it as freely as upon other shrubs. We are not as sure, however, that our song-birds object to the lilac because of anything disagreeable to them in the perfume of its flowers. Except in the case of some of the *Raptores*, birds as a rule are neither acute nor delicate of smell, our little song-birds least of all perhaps. We rather think the reason of their dislike to it is to be found, partly at least, if not wholly, in the fact that while it is in flower, its bark, particularly along the smaller branches and twigs, is covered with a slimy secretion or exudation at once viscid and acrid ; and if there is one thing more than another which our wild-birds unanimously and with all their hearts detest, it is to have their legs or toes come in contact with anything glutinous or " sticky." Every bird-fancier knows how uncomfortable and generally miserable is a bird just upon being taken off a limed twig ; not, observe, because he is a captive— thoughts of *that* may trouble him afterwards—but immediately and in the first instance because of the bird-lime about his toes.

The first thing, therefore, that the bird-catcher does is to cleanse
the captive's feet and toes by rubbing them gently between his
finger and thumb with fine sand, and afterwards washing them
with water; an operation no sooner performed and the bird restored
to its cage, than it evinces its satisfaction at being relieved from
its state of intolerable discomfort in many little ways that cannot
well escape the notice of even the most unobservant. We have
known a newly captured chaffinch, placed in a cage directly on
being taken off the limed twig, and inadvertently left uncared for
till the evening, peck its toes until red flesh appeared, in his
attempts to rid them of the bird-lime attached to them. But
whether the song-bird's dislike to the lilac when in flower be
owing to its perfume or to the disagreeably glutinous exudations
of its bark in early summer, or to both combined, it is simply the
fact that such an aversion exists; and Allan Cunningham's objection
to the lilac in this connection is perfectly well founded. And even
if this particular objection had *not* been well founded, it would
have been better, we think, if Burns had selected some one or other
of our native flowering shrubs, such as the hawthorn, for example,
rather than a comparatively rare exotic like the lilac—rare now,
and rarer still a hundred years ago. If those who give any heed
at all to these matters will only consider the question, they will be
ready, we think, to confess that they never yet knew an instance of
a bird's nest in a lilac tree. About our own place here, where the
lilac grows to a large size, and flowers splendidly, we ourselves have
never known or heard of such a thing. Within the shelter of
every other tree and shrub of any consequence about the place,
we have known our song-bird friends to build at some time
or other—never once in the lilac, nor, it may be added, in the
fuchsia, which in the warm shelter of this genial spot grows to
the dimensions of a tree, all the year round too, without the
slightest petting or special protection of any kind, as hardy and

self-reliantly as its companion hawthorns, hollies, and hazels. The fuchsia is probably avoided for the same reason as the lilac. It also exudes in spring and early summer a viscid secretion almost as "sticky" and disagreeable, if you run your hand along a twig, as that of the lilac itself; and, as we have already said, anything of this kind is an utter abomination to the *Insessores* or perchers, who are as particular about their feet and toes as ever was dainty and delicate *belle* about the state of her hands and fingers.

Such of our readers as care about these things, and have the opportunity, may very profitably and pleasantly give an occasional half-hour to the doings of our song-birds at this season. Their little love quarrels and rivalries are very amusing. All this fore-noon a pair of cock chaffinches have been bickering and quarrelling after their fashion along the hedgerows and amongst the trees immediately opposite our study window. The *casus belli* is of course a female, handsome and coy, and fully conscious, you may believe, of her own value, who keeps flitting about at a little distance, proud and pleased, doubtless, to be the object of rivalry between a pair of such gay and lively chaffinch beaux. *Varium et mutabile*, she has evidently great difficulty in making up her mind as to which of the suitors she shall select; her state of indecision being probably akin to that of the renowned Captain Macheath in the *Beggar's Opera* :—

> " How happy could I be with either,
>   Were t'other dear charmer away !
> But while you thus tease me together,
>   To neither a word will I say."

The rival birds are in their gayest spring plumage; and when tired of mere vulgar scolding and abuse, they try to sing each other down; and then it is that they are well worth not merely the listening to, but the looking at. Directly opposite the gean-tree near the top of which the lady chaffinch sits preening her feathers, and occasionally uttering a *twink-twink* of self-admiration, is an aged hawthorn, on which the rivals select to hold their tournament of song ; and the energy and heart with which a bird sings in such a case must be seen and quietly studied to be fully appreciated. Swaying lightly each on his own bough, the rivals begin to sing as if their very lives depended upon it ; their throats swollen almost to bursting ; the feathers on their polls erected into a crest, and their whole bodies tremulous to the very tips of the quill feathers of their wings, as they pour forth a torrent of song so rapid, clear, and loud, that all the other birds in the neighbourhood are for the moment silent, as if they had purposely ceased their own aimless melodies to listen to the impassioned strains of the competitors in the thorn. Of human eloquence, Quintilian says, " *Pectus, id est quod disertum facit* "—the heart (and not the brain) is that which makes a man eloquent ; and even more than of eloquence, with all the might of its " winged words," is the same thing true of song. To be all it ought to be, and be at its best, it must well up a living stream from the hot, impassioned heart; not from the marble fountain of mere intellect, which, if always clear, is not the less always cold. If ever song came, in Quintilian's phrase, direct *a pectore*—from the heart, it is the song at this moment of the rival competitors in yonder thorn. It is only when one has seen and studied a bird singing after this fashion that the full force and meaning of a line in Gray's *Ode to Spring* can be understood and appreciated. Under the lens of a cold, critical analysis, the line is sheer nonsense ; in sight of the bird itself, as at this moment, singing with all his might, heart and soul in every note, its truth and beauty are at once apparent. The line is this—

> " The Attic *warbler pours her throat,*
> Responsive to the cuckoo's note."

Had not the poet seen, and closely and intelligently observed, a bird in the act of loud and excited song, he would never have ventured on an assertion that at first sight seems so curiously extravagant, that a warbler "*pours her throat.*" It is to be observed, however, that the really beautiful and expressive phrase is not original, but second-hand as regards Gray. He borrows it from Pope, in whose *Essay on Man* (Ep. iii.), published ten or a dozen years before Grays ode, occurs this line—

> " Is it for thee the linnet *pours his throat ?* "

But it is a pity to separate the line from its context, and as the passage is not too well known, we may be pardoned for quoting it :—

> " Has God, thou fool ! worked solely for thy good,
> Thy joy, thy pastime, thy attire, thy food ?
> Who for thy table feeds the wanton fawn,
> For him as kindly spread the flowery lawn ;
> Is it for thee the lark ascends and sings?
> Joy tunes his voice, joy elevates his wings.
> *Is it for thee the linnet pours his throat ?*
> Loves of his own, and raptures swell the note.
> The bounding steed you pompously bestride
> Shares with his lord the pleasure and the pride.
> Is thine alone the seed that strews the plain ?
> The birds of heaven shall vindicate their grain.
> Thine the full harvest of the golden year ?
> Part pays, and justly, the deserving steer :
> The hog, that ploughs not, nor obeys thy call,
> Lives on the labours of this Lord of all."

It will be seen that Gray makes his nightingale—his " Attic warbler "—feminine, " pours *her* throat," while Pope, more correctly, makes his linnet songster a mate, "pours *his* throat;" and Pope who, indeed, from his habits of life, must have known more about birds than Gray, is right, for it is the males of song-birds that sing, and not the females. Milton makes the same mistake as Gray, and adds to the blunder by saying that the nightingale sings "the summer long," which it does not. It is curious that our English poets should so frequently err, as Gray did, in attributing the melodies of song-birds to the females instead of to the males. The explanation, we suppose, is that, as amongst ourselves women as a rule are more musically inclined, and usually have sweeter voices than men, even so the poets, knowing no better, rashly conclude that the rule must hold good amongst song-birds also. The very contrary, however, is the fact. It is the male bird that always sings ; the female attempts at song being extremely rare, and when attempted always a failure, never for a moment to be compared with the rich and long-sustained melodies of the male. Of all our song-birds, the most frequently mentioned by the poets is, of course, the nightingale, and almost invariably they make it a " she " instead of a " he." One of the finest passages in English poetry is a reference to the nightingale in *The Lover's Melancholy* of the dramatist John Ford (d. 1639). We are fond of reciting this passage when " i' the vein " for such things, but we always take the liberty of changing the " she," " hers," and " her " of Ford, into the " he," " his," and " him " of ornithological fact.

CHAPTER LXIII.

IF for the first few days March [1878] seemed inclined to emulate the peaceful calm and sunshine of its predecessor, it very suddenly assumed a more warlike aspect; a change came over the spirit of its dream; it became boisterous and rude; snow, and sleet, and rain, and storm battling in wild comminglement. It still continued what is called "open" weather, however; there was no frost, no razor-edged and biting winds, and vegetation was rather temporarily checked than seriously hurt or hindered. After this wild burst, in vindication, it is to be presumed, of the month's right to be called after the bellicose Mars, things slowly but steadily improved, and the weather is now such as permits us to get on with our spring work uninterruptedly and pleasantly enough. We have not yet, however, had a sufficiency of the "March dust," so proverbially invaluable at seed-time; and nowhere perhaps so invaluable, so absolutely essential indeed, in its proper season, as in the West Highlands. The day, however, is now lengthening apace, and with a bright warm sun overhead, and brisk north-easterly breezes, we shall doubtless soon have dust enough and to spare.

Our reference to Mars the war-god, reminds us that Mars the planet, with whose fiery effulgence every one is familiar, has recently had an accession of dignity such as the old-world star-gazers never dreamt of in connection with the ruddy orb. It is found to have at least two attendant moons, small, and so exceedingly difficult of detection even by the aid of the best instruments, that it is only under the most favourable circumstances that they can be observed. It is more than suspected that a third, and even a fourth satellite, exists, and the planet will in consequence be subjected to the closest possible scrutiny at all the observatories at home and abroad for some time to come, in order to determine with certainty the number of its attendant moons, and whether they be two or more, to decide their sidereal revolutions, their diameters, masses, and inclinations of orbits. By reason of his retinue of satellites, Mars is now exalted to equal dignity with Jupiter, Saturn, Uranus, and Neptune; and by the discovery another point is scored in favour of the nebular hypothesists. It was on the night of the 1st January 1801 that the first of the planetoids, *Ceres*, was discovered by Piazzi of Palermo. Next year Olbers of Bremen discovered the second planetoid, *Pallas*, and so constant and searching has been the scrutiny to which the planetoidal zone, situated between the orbits of Mars and Jupiter, has been subjected, that the number of these minor worlds is now no less than 182, the last three in the series, Nos. 180, 181, and 182, having been discovered since the beginning of February last. Of these three, two were discovered by French observers; the third by Professor Peters of Hamilton College, U.S., America. This last, however, is suspected to be only a rediscovery, so to speak; to be identical with *Antigone*, discovered five years ago by the same indefatigable observer. If this be so, the asteroidal series amounts at present date to 181. In favour of the ingenious hypothesis that accounted for the existence of these minor orbs by suggesting that they might be the fragments of a large disrupted world—of a large planet rent asunder by some terrible internal convulsion—a great deal could be said while the number of fragments was under half a dozen or even double that number, but when the fleet of orblets began to be counted by the score, the disrupted world theory was dropped as no longer tenable in the circumstances. The hypothesis of Olbers, however—for it originated with the discoverer of *Pallas* —led to a great deal of curious research that resulted in no little gain to astronomical science; and if it had to be given up as insufficient in the case of a planetoidal zone, it left us a legacy that may yet be turned to good account, that such a catastrophe, namely, as the disruption of a planetary world into fragments that in the shape of minor orbs would continue to revolve in orbits coincident with that of the parent globe, is not only possible, but, under certain easily enough conceivable circumstances, a probable enough occurrence.

Occultations by the moon of planets and first magnitude stars are always interesting phenomena, and for many years we have rarely missed observing such conjunctions as they became due, even if the hour was otherwise inconvenient, if only the weather chanced to be favourable. Last week there were two occultations, which for particular reasons we were very anxious to observe, and as the weather was clear and bright we had but little fear of disappointment. The stars to be occulted were *Alpha* and *Delta* Leonis, the one on the night of the 16th, the other on the night succeeding. *Alpha* Leonis is of the first magnitude, distinguished, like some others of its class, from the mere alphabetical order of stars by its proper name of *Regulus.* Up to within a quarter of an hour of the computed moment of occultation or disappearance of the star behind the moon's disc, the sky was clear; and as we stood at our post everything promised a highly satisfactory and successful observation; but alas, as the moon and star, in nautical phrase, were close aboard each other, a huge bank of cloud, driven by a north-westerly breeze, swept over the scene, effectually occulting moon and stars alike from the most penetrating gaze. It was provoking enough, but there was no help for it. An observer in our climate must make up his mind to frequent disappointments of this kind. We were still in hopes that although the immersion was thus hidden from us we might be more fortunate in the case of the emersion—the reappearance, that is—of the star on the moon's western limb. But it was no use. Two or three times, indeed, the moon shone forth for a minute or two together from through an old cathedral porch-like rent in the intervening wall of cloud, but only to be again obscured ; and thus it continued so tantalisingly promising, that we stood to our post until a glance at the clock showed that the moment of emersion was already past, and it was useless waiting or watching any longer. The great object in closely watching these occultations is to observe, with all possible certainty, if there is any distortion or momentary projection on the moon's disc of the planet or star occulted at the instant of immersion and emersion, in order to decide if the moon has an atmosphere or not. We have seen enough, we think, from our own observations during the last five and twenty years, to lead us to the conclusion that such distortion and projection is occasionally to be seen, and that therefore, contrary to the general belief of astronomers, a lunar atmosphere very probably exists, though it may be of greatly less weight and density than our own. Looking over our astonomical note-book, we find that the winter just past— let us hope that at this date we may so speak of it—was remarkable for two things—the almost total absence, namely, of auroral displays, and the exceeding brilliancy of the zodiacal light. We have only two recorded instances of the occurrence of the aurora borealis, both in December, and both but partial, faint, and ill-defined. The zodiacal light, on the contrary, was remarkably bright and noticeable on almost every evening in February and early March, its apex reaching up to and beyond the Pleiades, and with an outline clear and sharply defined as ever was sheaf of the brightest auroral light. So noticeable was it on several occasions, that all the people of the hamlet began to speak about it, and inquire what it could mean, for its perfect quiescence, its appearance night after night in the same quarter of the heavens, and the absence of anything like accompanying storms or aerial disturbance, satisfied even them that it was not the *fir-chlis* or " merry-dancers " as they used to know them.   Let us assure our Celtic readers that an attempt on our part to explain the nature of the zodiacal light in *Gaelic* was no easy task ; and if the truth were known, we fear onr prelection *quoad hoc* was a sad failure.

We have received the following note from " A Constant Reader :"—

" Nether Lochaber.

" Sir—Would you kindly let us know, through the columns of the *Inverness Courier*, the proper name of the accompanying little bird, and what part of this country it is properly a native of.   It is never seen in Ross-shire but during very heavy snow, and then they fly about in large flocks, and disappear again as soon as the snow is gone.—I am, yours respectfully,

" A Constant Reader."

Neatly packed in a couple of lucifer match-boxes ingeniously conjoined, the bird reached us, and the *locale* of its being shot or captured we can only approximately indicate by the fact that the package bore the post-mark " Garve."   There was no difficulty in at once recognising the bird as the snow-fleck or snow bunting, the *Emberiza nivalis* of Linnæus, a common enough bird in early winter over the whole of Scotland.   Although it has been known to breed in Scotland, a few being found all the year round along the summits of the Grampians, and other mountain ranges to the north and north-west, it is probably a bird of considerably higher latitudes than ours ; visiting our shores as a migrant in October or November, according as the winter is early and severe or otherwise, and leaving us again in March or April.   It is a hardy little bird, of plain and rather sombre plumage, prettiest in the act of flight, when the white on the edges and tips of the tail-feathers, and quills, and secondaries, comes out in pretty bars, contrasting pleasantly with the dark and chestnut brown, which may be said to be the prevailing colour. The snow-fleck has hardly any song beyond a tremulous twittering, and a few call-notes so loud and shrill that in the strange and solemn calm that sometimes precedes a snow-storm, they may be heard at a great distance. Our correspondent should have stated where, when, and how the bird was got, a knowledge of such matters vastly enhancing the interest and value of a specimen, especially if it has any claims to be accounted a *rara avis.*

We are indebted to our excellent Celtic friend, Mr. William Mackay, Inverness, for a copy of his exceedingly interesting monograph on *The Glen and Castle of Urquhart*, one of the most interesting spots in the Highlands. Mr. Mackay attempts to make Glen Urquhart classic ground by associating the story of Dearduil and Clann-Uisneachean, as related in the mediæval Gaelic ballads, with the locality, by pointing out that there is a Dun *Dearduil* in the neighbourhood—a place so called after the hapless heroine of the ballad story. But in the old and unquestionably authentic ballads her name is not Dearduil but *Deirdri ; Deirdir* and *Daordir.* Dearduil is a much later form of the name, not older, Mr. J. F. Campbell hints, than the Darthula of "Ossian" Macpherson. But there are other Dun Dearduils besides that referred to by Mr. Mackay ; one, for instance, near us in Glenevis ; and it is to be observed that all the places so called are vitrified forts. An old man in our neighbourhood, one of our best *seannachies*, always speaks of the Glenevis vitrified fort as Dun *Dearsail* or *Dearsuil*, and this is probably the correct form of the term, closely connecting it with *dears* and *dearsadh*, to shine, a shining ; to beam and be effulgently aglow like flame of *fire*. Remembering that *all* the places so called present more or less marked traces of vitrifaction, in the formation of which *fire* and *flame*, on a large scale, must have been the chief and most remarkable agents, the name comes to have a fitting and appropriate enough meeting, without the necessity of taking in the name of Deirdri or Dearduil at all. Mr. Mackay next gives a translation of a couple of quatrains from the oldest known version of the Clann-Uisneachan ballad; that, namely, of the vellum manuscript in the Advocates' Library, bearing the date 1238, and quoted in the Highland Society's Report on *Ossian* :—

> " Beloved land, that eastern land,
>   Alba, with its lakes ;
> Oh, that I might not depart from it ;
>   But I go with *Naois.*
> Glen Urchain, O Glen Urchain,
> It was the straight glen of smooth ridges :
> Not more joyful was a man of his age
>   Than Naois in Glen Urchain."

Mr. Mackay will have it, of course, that this " Glen-Urchain " is his Glen Urquhart. The Gaelic name of Urquhart, however, is invariably a trisyllable ; but this apart, the Glen-*Urchain* of Mr. Mackay has no existence in the ballad from which he professes to translate. The quatrain stands thus in the original :—

> " Mo chen Glen Urchaidh,
> Ba hedh in Glen direach dromchain ;
> Uallcha feara aoisi
> Ma Naise an Glend Urchaidh."

It is Glen *Urchaidh*, observe, not *Urchain ;* the Glenurchay of Argyllshire, in short, not the Glen Urquhart or Urchadan of Inverness-shire. This is further proved by the context, the immediately preceding and succeeding stanzas, which speak of Glen Mason and Glendaruel in Cowal ; of Duntroon ; of Innisstrynich on Loch Awe ; of Eite or Etive, &c. In so far, in short, as this story of Clann-Uisneachan of Ireland has to do with Scotland, we find it connected with Argyllshire, where indeed we should most naturally look for it; and chiefly with Glen Etive and Loch

Etive, where we have Dun-Mhac-Uisneachan; Grianan Dheirdir; Caoille Naois; Eilean Uisneachan, &c. &c. In Argyllshire, too, it was that the Clann-Uisneachan ballads were preserved till discovered and taken down from oral recitation by the collectors. And if Dun-Dearduil and "Glen-Urchain" must be given up as having no connection with the ballads in question, so would it seem to follow that some other etymology than any connection with the name of *Naois*, must be found for Loch *Ness*, Inverness, &c.